Human Trafficking

Sara Miller McCune founded SAGE Publishing in 1965 to support the dissemination of usable knowledge and educate a global community. SAGE publishes more than 1000 journals and over 800 new books each year, spanning a wide range of subject areas. Our growing selection of library products includes archives, data, case studies and video. SAGE remains majority owned by our founder and after her lifetime will become owned by a charitable trust that secures the company's continued independence.

Los Angeles | London | New Delhi | Singapore | Washington DC | Melbourne

Human Trafficking

Applying Research, Theory, and Case Studies

Noël Bridget Busch-Armendariz
The University of Texas at Austin

Maura Nsonwu
North Carolina A&T State University

Laurie Cook Heffron
St. Edward's University

With Case Writers:
Diane McDaniel Rhodes
Terry A. Wolfer
Elizabeth Goatley

Los Angeles | London | New Delhi
Singapore | Washington DC | Melbourne

FOR INFORMATION:

SAGE Publications, Inc.
2455 Teller Road
Thousand Oaks, California 91320
E-mail: order@sagepub.com

SAGE Publications Ltd.
1 Oliver's Yard
55 City Road
London EC1Y 1SP
United Kingdom

SAGE Publications India Pvt. Ltd.
B 1/I 1 Mohan Cooperative Industrial Area
Mathura Road, New Delhi 110 044
India

SAGE Publications Asia-Pacific Pte. Ltd.
3 Church Street
#10-04 Samsung Hub
Singapore 049483

ISBN 978-1-5063-0572-1

Acquisitions Editor: Nathan Davidson
Editorial Assistant: Alissa Nance
Production Editor: Andrew Olson
Copy Editor: Jocelyn Rau
Typesetter: C&M Digitals (P) Ltd.
Proofreader: Ellen Brink
Indexer: Terri Morrissey
Cover Designer: Scott Van Atta
Marketing Manager: Jenna Retana

17 18 19 20 21 10 9 8 7 6 5 4 3 2 1

Brief Contents

APPENDICES

Detailed Contents

Chapter 4   The Economics of Human Trafficking   111
Bruce Kellison and Matt Kammer-Kerwick

Appendices

Preface

The Primer: An Introduction and Understanding Context

National Human Trafficking Resource Center 1-888-373-7888

Introduction and Overview

This textbook is aimed to engage students about the complex and troubling practices of human trafficking in persons within the context of human rights and social justice perspectives. While human trafficking as a human atrocity is not a new phenomenon, recently discovered awareness of this problem has made it a focus of public concern. In the past five years, academic attention on the topic has increased apace. In the year before writing this textbook, we found that 98 out of 108 (91%) Research 1 universities in the United States held a seminar, workshop, or other educational forum addressing human trafficking; 48 of 108 (44%) have offered a course focused solely on trafficking in persons. Human trafficking was most frequently taught as a 14-week upper-division undergraduate and/or graduate-level course. With no academic prerequisites other than academic standing, the course was typically 50 to 100 students, taught once or twice per year. This has undoubtedly increased since we originally evaluated the learning environment.

Also, as of this writing, there are slightly more than a dozen books on human trafficking or modern slavery that might serve as a core or supplemental text at the university level. In addition, there are dozens of exposés, journalist reporting–style narratives, or books available as support materials. We have cited many of these scholars and writers in this textbook and have used many of these resources in our own classrooms and seminars when teaching on the topic. This text is set apart from these existing resources in several ways. First, for nearly a decade we have been heavily involved in the development of empirical knowledge about human trafficking through original data collection and peer-reviewed publications. Our research has included interviews and surveys with victims and survivors, law enforcement, prosecutors, social workers, victim advocates, and policy makers, among others. We have also presented extensively to professionals, taught college students, served as expert witnesses, and supervised research practica on this topic. All chapters include our learning thus far on human trafficking, although we continue to develop our knowledge on this complex and evolving topic.

Building on an understanding of the meaning and scope of human trafficking, the text addresses specific vulnerabilities of human trafficking victims, medical-psychosocial needs of victims, and issues related to direct service delivery. Specific attention focuses on the identification of human trafficking crimes, traffickers, and the impact of this crime on the global economy. Legal and criminal justice issues, types of human trafficking, and typologies of traffickers are provided. Finally, the text provides information on national and international antitrafficking policies and prevention and intervention strategies, including offering clarity on the laws in place to protect victims and promising practices to combat human trafficking. Throughout the text, detailed case examples of human trafficking will illuminate real situations, responses of law enforcement, service providers, organizational challenges, and the cost of trafficking to human well-being. In addition, the text offers discussion questions and interactive classroom exercises and projects designed to deepen student understanding and application. Factual cases worked by social workers and law enforcement as well as prosecuted cases are the focus of case studies.

The text provides students with an ecological and intersectionality perspective that ties poverty, gender, prostitution, undocumented workers, and unpaid immigrant labor to the issue of human trafficking. The fundamental framework is built on a contemporary human rights perspective.

Audience and Our Perspective as Authors

The topic of human trafficking is related to a variety of fields of study. For this reason, this textbook is structured to optimize its use for instructors and students in a variety of fields such as social work, education, anthropology, criminology, women's and gender studies, sociology, social psychology, nursing, communication and rhetoric, law, criminal justice, foreign policy, economics, public affairs, peace and conflict studies, cultural studies, and foreign policy. It is intended to serve as a core text for a human trafficking course for either undergraduate or graduate students but could be used as supplemental reading in any human rights, violence against women, or law school clinic course.

We are challenged in two primary ways to bring a variety of voices and perspectives to this text. While we have extensive teaching and research experience in multidisciplinary human trafficking and other teams and much of this has been in other countries, we are U.S.-trained social scientists, academics, and licensed social workers. We have included materials throughout the text about the important international antitrafficking efforts in the world, perspectives that are unique to law enforcement, prosecutors, and social services providers, for example, while acknowledging that our perspectives are as American social workers and applying the relevant theories and research of our discipline to our allied professions.

The Challenge of Teaching This Content

The major challenges in teaching about human trafficking arise because of the breadth of the topic—from forced labor to commercial sexual exploitation and from understanding supply-side economics to social service delivery. A full taxonomy of the modern slavery—the ways in which human beings exploit other human beings—is much more difficult than perhaps originally conceived. Another challenge is the wide range of individuals impacted by the crime—from runaway homeless youth in the United States to migrant workers and adults and children. The liabilities of teaching this content are also its strengths. We have found that the major challenges facing students include the explicit nature of the crime and the breadth of the topic across disciplines such as social services, health, economics, and criminal justice. Attention to these critical issues is important.

Terminology: Survivor—Victim? Trafficker—Exploiter? Modern Slavery—Human Trafficking?

This textbook uses the terms *victim* and *survivor* interchangeably to refer to trafficked individuals, although neither label is meant to be demeaning or judgmental, to weigh passivity or agency, or to give the perception that it is an accurate label for any particular individual. On the contrary, it is important to consider that people trafficked have endured a significant trauma, usually a combination of physical and emotional abuse through threats, power and control, and/or sexual violence and trauma. Likewise, trafficked persons often simultaneously utilize tremendous strength, resilience, and choice. The term *victim* is often used in the criminal justice system and may reflect the provision of services under legislation in some states or those services that are protected by state law. The term *survivor* is often used by social workers and other human service practitioners and trafficked individuals themselves. Most notably, this term took hold by practitioners in the field of domestic and sexual violence. As social workers, our profession guides us to acknowledge individuals and how they choose to talk about their experiences (Busch-Armendariz, Nsonwu, & Heffron, 2014; Busch, Fong, Heffron, Faulkner, & Mahapatra, 2007). It is important for instructors and students to consider the terms and labels that describe people (victims and their offenders) as they learn about this topic. Terms, values, and labels are further discussed in Chapter 3.

Understanding the Ecological Perspective: Macro, Mezzo, and Macro

The social work profession is most often described as firmly rooted in an ecological perspective that addresses social and economic (in)justices. According to Hutchison (2010), "Social workers have always thought about the environment as multidimensional. As early as 1901 [with] Mary Richmond . . ." (p. 13). The ecological perspective as first described by Bronfenbrenner (1979) suggests that human beings are "nestled in a set of influential structures" (p. 3), but previously Germain (1973) took it a bit further to describe the ecological perspective as a process that involves the "adaptive fit of organisms and their environments and with means by which they achieve dynamic equilibrium and mutuality" (p. 326). And so, a social worker's ecological perspective is best applied as strengths based (Saleebey, 2002) and "relies heavily on ingenuity and creativity, courage and common sense, of both client and their social workers" (Saleebey, 2002, p. 1). In an earlier piece on this topic, we mused:

> A social work perspective, this implies two things. First, our understanding is based on the notion that individuals and systems are in continuous interaction with each other and that this dynamic interaction is either overtly understood by clients and systems or may be more clandestine. Nevertheless, this implies that social workers must also focus the analysis of the impact of those dynamics and coordination of them as it relates to improving clients and systems. In our human trafficking in persons research, the social worker's ecological perspective aptly fits with survivors and the professionals that serve them as it seeks to analyze these structures and bring harmony through the increased understanding and coordination among coalition members and between survivors and professionals. (Busch-Armendariz, Nsonwu, & Heffron, 2014, p. 15)

This text is built on these social work perspectives, where the ecological perspective offers the scaffolding of the textbook's framework and strength-based narrative is predominant. Although Bronfenbrenner suggests four levels of systems in the ecological perspective, we have collapsed our understanding and presentation to three commonly used categories: micro, mezzo, and macro.

The micro system involves direct practice with individuals, families, and small groups. Mezzo-system practice includes work with institutions, organizations, and larger communities such as school systems, health departments, or professional groups. The macro system is typically described as practice that includes working toward change focused on the broad cultural perspective and on governmental policies and legislation. The eco-systems perspective is not as neatly outlined as we may have suggested. Mary (2008) opines, "Social structures shape human activity, but participants in any type of social encounter continually create and re-create these structures" (p. 48). Although we have presented the micro, mezzo, and macro systems as somewhat mutually exclusive, it is merely for efficiency. It is much more compelling and accurate to consider their interrelatedness and dynamic nature that Mary (2008) refers to as the "web-of-life" (p. 47).

Social workers are often considered "bleeding hearts" and presumed to lack empirical judgements. As social workers and scholars, our intent is quite the opposite. Our goal was to provide a framework that is deeply engaged, broadly encompassing, informed by evidence, and with the resolution of exigency that this issue requires. Our readers will determine if we met this goal.

Attention to the Issue and Practice of Marginalization

On a related note to exigency, it is also important to call attention to truths that intentionally or unintentionally cause institutional betrayal, bias, and oppression. There are many examples of this throughout the criminal justice and social service systems, and with individuals. This text will address these issues throughout the discussion.

Infusion of Conceptual Frameworks

One of the unique aspects of this textbook is the integration of one or more theories or frameworks at the beginning of each chapter. To expose students to new ways of examining human trafficking and new ways of understanding its complexities and controversies, theoretical considerations are infused throughout this textbook. Integrating chapter content with theoretical frameworks propels students to think critically about the descriptive nature of the scope of human trafficking and to evaluate the responses to this crime through the policies and services that have developed. Theory infusion generates curiosity, questions, and discussion, as well as perhaps offering inspiration for students to explore the use and application of theoretical perspectives in other parts of their studies.

A variety of broad and overarching theoretical considerations were selected to conceptualize the social and economic injustice of human trafficking, including human rights perspective, Critical Race Theory, feminism, and intersectionality. Applied, or practice-based, approaches are also incorporated, including the ecological approach, strengths-based approach, trauma-informed approach, and transnational theory. The selected theoretical framework(s) are briefly explained at the beginning of each chapter to serve as a catalyst for understanding the chapter content and to provide the opportunity to explore with some depth human trafficking from this standpoint.

This textbook targets a wide range of academic disciplines, so students' understanding of the individual theories that are presented and practice with theoretical application will vary. Instructors and students will undoubtedly determine that a different theory may have been more useful than the one presented in a particular chapter to better understand human trafficking. We encourage and would appreciate this critical examination and feedback.

Infusion of Case Studies

Six chapters include case studies. These are not the typical case studies used in textbooks because they are decision cases collected and written through a specific methodology between the textbook author, case writers, and case reporters or practitioners. Decision cases are factual situations encountered by practitioners. In this textbook, the protagonist may be a social worker, law enforcement officer, prosecutor, immigration attorney, or a member of a coalition, among others. In decision cases, students must, as Barnes (1989) reflects, "untangle situations that are complex and undefined and impose a coherence of their own making" (cited by Wolfer, 2006, p. 6).

Unlike descriptive cases, decision cases are specifically designed to engage students both horizontally (across disciplines, for examples) and vertically (critical decision making). Faculty use the cases to help students, as Lundeberg (1999) describes, "to identify, frame, or find a problem; consider problems from multiple perspectives; provide solutions for problems identified; and consider the consequences and ethical ramifications of these solutions" (p. 8). In this way, decision cases provide the faculty with class discussions, assignments, and other structures for more "sophisticated decision-making abilities" (Wolfer, 2006, p. 10). Widely used in schools of law, business—and growing in social work, social sciences, and other disciplines—decision cases are reported by a protagonist (called a case reporter) about their lived experiences and written by an author(s) using a specific methodological framework. We have incorporated decision cases in this textbook from a variety of case reporters (social workers, law enforcement, and a prosecutor). The case reporters recounted their professional experiences working with a particular human trafficking case and the challenges that they encountered in the United States.

All the information presented in every case is factual. That is, no details were changed or modified to fit a particular outcome or lesson, with the exception of the names and locations that were changed to protect our protagonists' and victims' identities.

The renewed attention to this global issue has created perhaps unintended consequences in this field. It is helpful to have critical conversations to examine hyperbole that misstates or overstates any issues. At the same time, we have seen that critical analysis sometimes lacks substantiation, which can become problematic. Empirical research on human trafficking is still relatively scarce. As we have said in the past, while these issues are important to the dialog, our focus as social workers, scholars, and educators has been to continue to call for additional research about the impact of victimization including risk factors and vulnerability; the impact of trauma and assault; and needed resources for restoration and prevention strategies, strategies that promote or hinder coalition building among those who primarily respond to survivors, and the considerations of root causes. Research continues to be challenging because this is a hidden, highly controlled, victimized group.

The case writers are the primary authors of the decision cases. The textbook authors were responsible for and involved in recruiting cases, collection, disguising case details, securing final approval from practitioners, and making final revisions.

How to Use the Decision Case Model

To help students develop practical experience in open-ended, problem-based learning and critical thinking skills, Wolfer and Scales (2006) propose general goals for the decision case method as follows:

- Pre-Read the Case. The first reading should be a quick run-through of the case and second or third should include understanding and gathering data and facts. The instructor and student move from a mere inventory to actual overview of the problem.
- Develop Awareness and Empathic Understanding. Examine the problem from multiple perspectives and try to understand other points of view.
- Define the Problem and Key Issues. Think of defining the problem as a starting point, identify key issues broadly, from multiple perspectives, and constantly reframe and revise to accommodate new insight.
- Take a Stand and Draw Conclusions. Brainstorm and make recommendations tempered by analysis of alternate viewpoints. Look to support your conclusion while remaining open minded.

- Behaviors to Encourage and Avoid. Best teaching and participation practices include active listening and sharing of ideas and discouraging disrespect for other ideas or bias, diversion, domination, or withdrawal from discussion.
- Trust the Decision Case Process and Experiential Learning. Mastery of problem-solving skills is cumulative and develops over time. As in real life, decision cases are complex and ambiguous. Focusing on "here and now" allows for openness and learning new skills.
- Maintain Perspective and Focus on Long-Term Outcomes. Often, decision cases are unsettling for participants due to diverse opinions and emotions. Keep as the goal gaining practical skills and the learning process.

Classroom Ideas for How to Teach Decision Cases

A full discussion of the decision case may take one or more class periods, depending on the class length. Our experience teaching decision cases is that the application may take a full 2 or 3 hours of class discussion. If this is a new learning format, students may be divided into small groups and assigned a specific case. The expectation is that small-group members fully understand the case details and may conduct additional research about its elements to add to the class discussion. To fully utilize these cases, all students should read and be prepared to fully discuss the case that is assigned.

During the discussion, it is helpful if the instructor divides the discussion by four areas (facts, analysis, action, and reflection). The facts of the case should be fully reviewed. If this is a new teaching format, instructors may be surprised that to achieve an agreement about the case, facts will take fully vetted conversation. Instructors may choose to start the discussion by asking a student to quickly summarize the case (as in the first read mentioned above). It is often helpful to write the "facts" on the board. Once all the important facts have emerged and been agreed upon, the instructor could move students into an analysis discussion. During the analysis, students may opine elements of relevance to the case and/or add research about those elements to the discussion. Before moving to action, the class should work toward a clear and concise problem statement (see below). The action discussion should lead students into a discussion about all the possible options for the protagonist and the strengths and limitations of each of these actions. The class may have to choose between "goods" or choose between the lesser of the challenges. After the case discussion, students should be given the opportunity to reflect on how they individually and collectively performed. This is often the most enlightening discussion and provides for intralearning reflection for students. The instructor may address conflicts, colluding, values, and/or collaborations that happened throughout the case discussion. In a class that has deepening trust for the learning process, instructors are able to bring controversial issues into the reflection discussion. The controversies may be about the application of materials on human trafficking or about the class dynamics (students who are underprepared and depend on others to carry the heavy load, how students handle tensions on controversial issues, students who do not participate in the discussion, when it is obvious that students have not done the reading, etc.).

Teaching notes on each case are available for instructors. Since cases do not have "right" or "wrong" resolutions, the teaching notes are developed to assist instructors in guiding the discussions. Teaching notes can be acquired through e-mailing SAGE Textbook Technical Support at textbookstechsupport@sagepub.com.

Encouraging Critical Thinking and Engaged Learners

It has been important for students to be critical thinkers and engaged learners about the topic of human trafficking. Hyperbole, embellishment, and exaggeration are well documented in the field of human trafficking, and, as such, students should learn to beware and skeptical of zealots, fundamentalists, and perhaps celebrities and professionals in the field. Discussions about the emancipator and emancipation, sexual violence as a tactic of war, prostitution versus human trafficking, and the portrayal of women and children as disempowered victims are complex and central in human trafficking scholarship. Students learn best when given the opportunity to be compassionate while at the same time censoring information without becoming paralyzed by its heaviness.

Text and Chapter Organization

This textbook has three major sections. Section I: A Holistic Approach to Understanding Human Trafficking; Section II: A Holistic Approach at Micro, Mezzo, and Macro Levels; and Section III: A Holistic Approach to Taking Actions.

The chapters include learning objectives, summary of the applied theoretical framework(s), active learning exercises and discussion questions, suggestions for further learning (books, policies, websites, and films), and ideas for homework/assignments/projects. This textbook also includes practical and relevant case examples (e.g., cases as reported in the news) and nonfictional decision cases told from professionals working in the field of human trafficking as discussed above. Decision cases were collected for inclusion in this textbook to highlight the learning objectives, theory, policy, and other key elements for students. Further discussion about decision cases is provided below.

Chapter Summaries

Section I includes four chapters; Chapter 1: A Primer to Human Trafficking: Understanding Scope and Dimensions; Chapter 2: Understanding the Context of History; Chapter 3: Understanding Terms, Definitions, and Intersectionality; and Chapter 4: The Economics of Human Trafficking.

Chapter 1 is a comprehensive overview of human trafficking. It introduces the scope and dimensions of human trafficking. Chapter 2 provides a historical context that is particularly focused on the United States. Chapter 3 defines terms and concepts in human trafficking and examines the value-laden terms and intersectionality with other issues. Chapter 4 considers the economic impact and analysis of human trafficking.

Section II includes three chapters; Chapter 5: Understanding, Disruption, and Interventions at the Micro Level; Chapter 6: Understanding, Disruption, and Interventions at the Mezzo Level; and Chapter 7: Understanding, Disruption, and Interventions at the Macro Level. Chapter 5 focuses on direct work with individuals, families, and groups. Chapter 6 examines human trafficking efforts from institutional and organizational perspectives. Chapter 7 looks at policy and sociopolitical efforts in this field. Micro, mezzo, and macro terms are further defined previously.

Section III includes Chapter 8: Understanding Collective Impact and Individual Action. It turns our attention to action and a discussion about the capacity of individuals and communities to address human trafficking.

As licensed social workers and social scientists, our aim is to be scientific, practical, and meaningful. Our hope is that students and instructors agree that this textbook reflects the depth of our knowledge, teaching, and perspectives rooted in empirically grounded scholarship and survivor-centered practices. Human trafficking is an emerging science and field of study that is burgeoning with new information. We appreciate any feedback that you might choose to provide.

Warm regards,

Noël Busch-Armendariz, Maura B. Nsonwu, and Laurie Cook Heffron
January 2017

References

Bronfenbrenner, U. (1979). *The ecology of human development: Experiments by design and nature.* Cambridge, MA: Harvard University Press.

Busch, N. B., Fong, R., Heffron, L. C., Faulkner, M., & Mahapatra, N. (2007). *Assessing the needs of human trafficking victims: An evaluation of the Central Texas Coalition Against Human Trafficking.* Retrieved from The Institute on Domestic Violence and Sexual Assault website https://socialwork.utexas.edu/dl/files/cswr/institutes/idvsa/publications/evaluation_of_trafficking-2007.pdf

Busch-Armendariz, N., Nsonwu, M. B., & Heffron, L. C. (2014). A kaleidoscope: The role of the social work practitioner and the strength of social work theories and practice in meeting the complex needs of people trafficked and the professionals that work with them. *International Social Work, 57*(1), 7–18. doi:10.1177/0020872813505630

Germain, C. B. (1973). An ecological perspective in casework practice. *Social Casework, 54*(6), 323–330.

Hutchison, E. D. (2010). *Dimensions of human behavior: Person and environment.* Thousand Oaks, CA: Sage.

Lundeberg, M. A. (1999). Discovering teaching and learning through cases. In M. A. Lundeberg, B. B. Levin, & H. L. Harrington (Eds.), *Who learns what from cases and how? The research base for teaching with cases: A guidebook.* Mahwah, NJ: Taylor & Francis Ltd.

Mary, N. L. (2008). *Social work in a sustainable world.* Chicago, IL: Lyceum Books.

Saleebey, D. (2002). *The strengths perspective in social work practice* (3rd ed.). Boston, MA: Allyn and Bacon.

Wolfer, T. A. (2006). An introduction to decision cases and case method learning. In T. A. Wolfer, & T. L. Scales (Eds.), *Decision cases for advanced social work practice: Thinking like a social worker* (1st ed., pp. 3-14). Belmont, CA: Thomson Brooks/Cole.

Wolfer, T. A., & Scales, T. L. (2006). Tips for learning from decision cases. In T. A. Wolfer, & T. L. Scales (Eds.), *Decision cases for advanced social work practice: Thinking like a social worker* (pp. 17–25). Belmont, CA: Thomson Brooks/Cole.

Acknowledgments

We are deeply grateful to the survivors of trafficking with whom we have worked over the past decade. You have helped us listen with deep understanding and intent about your lived experiences. It is a privilege for us to be able to inform others through our writings. Our greatest hope is that we have accurately portrayed these lessons.

We have learned equally from the professionals working in this field. Their resolve to bring attention to this issue and provide competent and holistic services and responses is inspiring and humbling. The field of anti-human trafficking is fortunate to have the commitment of these individuals and organizations.

We are also grateful to our students, who have been consistent catalysts for this work, demonstrating intellectual curiosity and commitment to social justice by demanding increased opportunities to learn about human trafficking in the classroom and through engagement with research.

We are indebted to our many feminist mentors who continue to shape our understanding, serve as valuable sounding boards, and challenge and expand our theoretical and conceptual horizons. Women leaders have been particularly influential to us. One such leader is Hillary Clinton, the first woman to be nominated for the United States presidency by a major political party, who has worked tirelessly for equity of women's rights around the world and in the United States. She once said, "human rights are women's rights, and women's rights are human rights."[1]

We want to express our deepest gratitude to Kathy Hill and Mariel Dempster for their superb editorial assistance. Kathy and Mariel came into this project during a time when we were in great need of their skills and commitment. You have been integral to this textbook's completion. Thank you for helping make this project a reality.

Our appreciation is extended to the team of decision case writers Dr. Terry Wolfer, Dr. Diane McDaniel Rhodes, and Dr. Elizabeth Goatley, and to the multiple professionals who shared their cases with our team. The cases enrich this textbook and provide insight to the application of the many topics and issues that we discuss. The labor of our case writers and protagonists represents tremendous commitment to the education of current and future professionals working against human trafficking.

Our heartfelt thanks goes to our dear colleagues, Dr. Bruce Kellison and Dr. Matthew Kammer-Kerwick, for their willingness to coauthor one of the important

---

[1]From her speech to the United Nations Fourth World Conference on Women in Beijing on September 5, 1995.

chapters of this textbook. Your continued collegiality and friendship and expertise have contributed greatly to this project.

We want to recognize the generous support and guidance that we received from John Teleha, Steven Bollinger, and Nina Exner, librarians at North Carolina A&T State University who assisted us with our research. Your expertise was instrumental to springboarding and organizing our writing.

A very special thanks to Nakia D. Parker, a doctoral student in history at the University of Texas at Austin and a national graduate student representative for the Association of Black Women Historians, for reviewing the history chapter. Your comments have been invaluable to helping us accurately convey an important and indelible era for the United States and across the globe.

Finally, let us express our appreciation and gratitude to our original editor, Kassie Graves, and our current editor, Nathan Davidson, and the supportive staff at SAGE Publications, who advocated endlessly to make this book a reality in effort to educate the next generation of students to this cause. We also thank the many reviewers who lent their expertise to the evaluation of this project: Cathryne L. Schimtz, University of North Carolina Greensboro; Ericka Kimball, Augsburg College; Manuel F. Zamora, Angelo State University; Nancy L. Bridier, University of West Florida; Kali Wright-Smith, Westminster College; Manuel F. Zamora, Angelo State University; Nadia Shapkina, Kansas State University; Roksana Alavi, University of Oklahoma; Sue E. Spivey, James Madison University; Tazreena Sajjad, American University; and Wendy P. Stickle, University of Maryland. Their insight contributed greatly to the quality of this textbook.

I am inspired by those who have shared their stories of suffering, strength, and resistance; the vows to break the silence of oppression; and the commitment to ensuring that their stories may create new avenues toward an end to violence and exploitation.

I am profoundly grateful for the many colleagues, advocates, and activists who have offered inspiration, guidance, and support to me during my career and who continue to share their wisdom, frustrations, laughter, and visions for social change. In particular, I greatly admire and continue to benefit from Noël's and Maura's flexible and gracious mentorship, respect for family, and generosity of spirit and ideas.

I want to recognize the tremendous support of my family and their patience with a general onslaught of discussion and information about the world's deeply painful injustices. Thank you for your interest and your compassion and for keeping me firmly rooted in mama mode and in hope.

—Laurie Cook Heffron

I recognize and value the position that I have been given to hear poignant, profound, and agonizing stories of human trafficking that detail injustice and oppression. My hope is that our book will serve to educate others to take action as "social justice warriors" and to honor survivors' courage and professionals' advocacy.

My collaboration with Noël and Laurie has spanned a decade; I have felt immense admiration for their wisdom, creative perspective, feminist philosophy, and incredible work ethic. I cherish our sisterhood.

I am forever grateful for the unconditional love of my parents, Drs. Chris and Mary Anne Busch, who have always served as my teachers, mentors, editors, and sounding board. Their commitment to social justice issues has instilled the core values and beliefs that have led and grounded me in my profession. Their unwavering faith has allowed me to thrive and has secured me during challenging times.

I appreciate the support of my entire family. I am especially thankful for the love, laughter, and encouragement of my husband, Victor, and our children, Amaka, Robert, Zik, and Adora. My family has loved and supported me from season to season. Rooted together, we have nourished each other and have weathered and celebrated these changes. They remind me to tend to the garden of life, appreciate the various blossoms, and beckon me to strive for balance. I am so fortunate to feel your immense love. A fulum gi na anya.

—Maura Nsonwu

I am privileged to be working with my two coauthors, who are incredibly dedicated and skilled social workers and scholars, in the journey of this textbook. Maura and Laurie, I am fortunate to have had you as influential teachers throughout my career and in my life.

I am eternally grateful to my friends, colleagues, sheroes and heroes, and mentors all over the world who work in the field of social work and to end interpersonal violence as a life journey. After two decades, I continue to be astonished and inspired by the thousands of survivors, practitioners, feminists scholars, and policy makers who tirelessly persist, despite the obstacles and skepticism. Your individual and collective pursuit of justice and enduring resolve that every individual has the right to live free of violence touches me deeply every day.

I will undoubtedly do an injustice to the immense gratitude I feel for my family in North Carolina. When I think about all my privileges, it is the family to which I was born and my extended family that is among my greatest privileges. My parents and all my siblings have taught me to be a community member, admit my mistakes, and speak up when something is wrong. It is my current family of my husband, Larry, and my son, Daniel, who have so profoundly and positively shifted my life and perspectives of this world. I seek to pause daily and breathe in deeply the gratitude I have for you. It's hard to believe that I am deserving of your love, commitment, and enduring support for me and my life's work.

—Noël Bridget Busch-Armendariz

About the Authors

Noël Bridget Busch-Armendariz, PhD, LMSW, MPA

Dr. Busch-Armendariz has more than 20 years of experience working to end inter-personal violence. She is the University Presidential Professor at the School of Social Work and Associate Vice President for Research at the University of Texas at Austin. Noël teaches graduate courses in domestic violence, research, and social policy and an undergraduate course on modern slavery. Noël is the founding and current direc-tor of the UT Austin Institute on Domestic Violence and Sexual Assault (IDVSA), a collaboration of the School of Social Work, the School of Nursing, the School of Law, and the Bureau for Business Research with more than 150 affiliate community organizations. Since joining UT, Noël has directed research totaling more than $8.3 million dollars in external funding for the National Institute of Justice, the Office for Victims of Crime, the Office on Violence Against Women, the Office of the Attorney General of Texas, the Texas Association Against Sexual Assault, and the Texas Health and Human Services, to name a few. Her areas of specialization are interpersonal violence, refugees, asylees, survivors of human trafficking, and international social work. She is regularly called as an expert witness in criminal, civil, and immigration cases and directs statewide and national trainings on the topic. She is well published and has been recognized by her colleagues and students with many awards. Noël is a returned Peace Corps volunteer and a licensed social worker. She is happily married to Larry Armendariz and takes the utmost joy in parenting her son, Daniel. She is a survivor of sexual assault.

Maura Nsonwu, PhD, MSW, LCSW

Dr. Nsonwu is an associate professor and interim bachelor of social work program director at North Carolina Agricultural & Technical State University in the Department of Sociology and Social Work. Over the last 2 decades, she has also held previous teach-ing and administrative positions at the University of North Carolina at Greensboro, the University of North Carolina at Charlotte, and High Point University. For over 25 years, Maura has practiced as a clinician, educator, and researcher in the areas of refugee reset-tlement, human trafficking, health care, child welfare, and social work education. Since 2004, Maura has been a research fellow with the Center for New North Carolinians at the University of North Carolina at Greensboro, where her research has focused on working with refugee and immigrant communities and issues of human trafficking. Her collaborative work, on a number of interdisciplinary projects, has been recognized as the recipient of awards. She was the 2010 recipient of the Sister Gretchen Reintjes award, which recognizes persons who have made outstanding contributions to refugee and immigrant communities. Maura has conducted multiple funded research projects with coauthors Noël Busch-Armendariz and Laurie Cook Heffron at the University of Texas at Austin in evaluating the delivery of social services to human trafficking victims and creating typologies of traffickers. Their research team has presented at conferences throughout the United States and has numerous publications. Maura lives in Greensboro, North Carolina, with her husband, a Nigerian immigrant. They have three adult children.

Laurie Cook Heffron, PhD, LMSW

Dr. Cook Heffron is an assistant professor of social work in the School of Behavioral and Social Sciences at St. Edward's University in Austin, Texas. She has interest and expertise in the areas of forced migration, domestic and sexual violence, and human trafficking. Laurie has both direct social work practice and research experience with a variety of communities, including refugees, asylum-seekers, trafficked persons, and other immigrants. Her recent research explores the experiences of, and relationships between, violence against women and migration, with a focus on migration from Central America to the United States. Laurie studied Linguistics at Georgetown University and earned a master of social work (MSW) and doctorate in social work from the University of Texas at Austin. Laurie is, above all, a mother of two energetic and creative children.

About the Case Writers

Elizabeth Goatley, PhD, MSW

Dr. Elizabeth Goatley joined the Baylor University's Diana R. Garland School of Social Work (GSSW) as a lecturer in 2012. Today, she is an assistant professor in the school, where her research focuses on emerging community responses to human trafficking. Entering as a lecturer and transitioning to tenure track position has afforded Dr. Goatley the opportunity to teach across the three degree programs within GSSW, even allowing her to create new courses in both the bachelors and doctoral programs. Dr. Goatley is advancing scholarship in the area of human trafficking, having published in several social work and community journals. Dr. Goatley is a 2015 recipient of the Big XII Faculty Fellowship award and has recently been awarded a grant by the Dallas Women's Foundation to continue her research. Prior to working at Baylor University, Dr. Goatley served as the program director and victims' advocate for the Human Trafficking Unit at the Sandy Springs Police Department in Sandy Springs, Georgia. Dr. Goatley has additional professional experience in community mental health. Dr. Goatley currently serves on the board for The Cove and The Heart of Texas Human Trafficking Coalition steering committee. She currently serves as Student Development chair in the GSSW and is active with Girl Scouts of America. She earned her PhD in social policy and administration in social work from Clark Atlanta University in 2012; an MSSW from the University of Louisville in 2006; and a BA in psychology from Spelman College in 2004.

Diane McDaniel Rhodes, PhD

Dr. McDaniel Rhodes is a lecturer at the University of Texas at Austin, where her areas of research include partner violence, family violence, and social constructions of intimate violence with a focus on the presentation of partner violence in young adult fiction. Her teaching history includes Voices Against Violence, Domestic Violence, Introduction to Social Work, the Foundations of Social Justice, Social Work Practice in Organizations and Communities, and Leadership in Human Services Organizations. She has 28 years of social work professional experience including senior management roles in domestic violence and sexual assault prevention agencies.

Terry A. Wolfer, PhD, MSW

Terry A. Wolfer, MSW (1984, Ohio State), PhD (1995, Chicago), is professor and PhD program coordinator at the University of South Carolina College of Social Work (CoSW). Dr. Wolfer developed a case-based MSW capstone course, which has been taught at the CoSW since 2000. For more than 15 years, Dr. Wolfer has been writing decision cases and teaching other educators how to use the case method of teaching. To date, Dr. Wolfer has coedited or coauthored six collections of decision cases, including most recently *Decision Cases for Advanced Social Work Practice: Confronting Complexity* (Columbia University Press, 2013). Currently, he is coauthoring a set of decision cases for educating social work field instructors. He has published several journal articles and book chapters about teaching with decision cases. He has also led faculty development workshops for the Council on Social Work Education and several universities. For his work on case method teaching and case writing, he was awarded the C. R. Christensen Award for the Outstanding Teaching Case by the North American Case Research Association, the Garnet Apple Award for innovative teaching by the University of South Carolina, and the Distinguished Recent Contributions in Social Work Education Award 2009 by the Council on Social Work Education.

About the Chapter Authors

Matt Kammer-Kerwick, PhD

Dr. Matt Kammer-Kerwick is a research scientist at the Bureau of Business Research, the University of Texas at Austin. His research interests focus on decision making under uncertainty, mathematical optimization, quantitative analysis, and applications in information, logistics, and manufacturing systems. He is currently using mixed-methods research for problems in the domains of sexual assault prevalence, the economic impact of human trafficking, and consumer preferences in mobile advertising. Together with coauthors Noël Busch-Armendariz and Bruce Kellison, he is leading an ambitious research initiative to assess case readiness and improve law enforcement capabilities and prosecutorial outcomes in domestic minor sex trafficking (DMST) cases by developing an algorithmic decision support system. He is a coauthor on "Responding to Domestic Minors Sex Trafficking (DMST): Developing Principle-Based Practices," with Karin Wachter, Laurie Cook Heffron, Noël Busch-Armendariz, and Bruce Kellison, forthcoming from the *Journal of Human Trafficking* in 2017. He has presented his research on modern slavery to a number of roundtables and working groups in the antitrafficking community, including a presentation on Texas statewide prevalence estimates to Allies Against Slavery's Slave-Free City Summit in 2016. Kerwick is coprincipal investigator of a multiyear grant from the Texas Office of the Governor to study the prevalence and impact of human trafficking in Texas. He is also founder and president of Visionary Research, Inc., a research and strategy consultancy. His consulting clients have included a wide range of start-ups and established corporations, including Dell, IBM, General Motors, and Johnson & Johnson.

Bruce Kellison, PhD

Dr. Bruce Kellison is associate director of the Bureau of Business Research (BBR) at the University of Texas at Austin. He is responsible for strategic planning and research for the bureau, an applied economic research center, and a member of the Texas State Data Center network. With coauthors Noël Busch-Armendariz and Laurie Cook Heffron, he codeveloped and taught the course "Women for Sale: The Economic, Social, and Political Proposition of Human Trafficking" at the University of Texas at Austin. His trafficking research focuses on estimating the economic impact of modern slavery on victims and society, especially at the state and local level. Together with coauthors Karin Wachter, Laurie Cook Heffron, Noël Busch-Armendariz, and Matt Kerwick, he is coauthor of "Responding to Domestic Minors Sex Trafficking (DMST): Developing Principle-Based Practices," forthcoming from the *Journal of Human Trafficking* in 2017. Kellison is coprincipal investigator of a multiyear grant from the Texas Office of the Governor to study the prevalence and impact of human trafficking in Texas. He currently is president-elect of the Association for University Business and Economic Research, a leading professional organization devoted to improving the quality and application of research in public policy and business economics. The BBR is a research partner of the Institute on Domestic Violence and Sexual Assault, School of Social Work, the University of Texas at Austin, and Kellison has contributed economic impact analyses on studies not only on human trafficking but also on sexually oriented businesses, the rape kit backlog crisis, and sexual assault.

A Holistic Approach to Understanding Human Trafficking

A Primer to Human Trafficking: Understanding Scope and Dimensions

Slavery is a fundamental abuse of human rights and a major obstacle to social justice. It is an affront to our humanity and it has no place in the twenty-first century. And yet [45.8] [1] *million women, men and children are still trapped in forced labor all over the world, generating USD 150 billion in illicit profits for those who exploit them. There should be no need for the International Day for the Abolition of Slavery to exist. However, each day, men, women and children are tricked or coerced into abhorrent situations including bonded labor, prostitution and exploitative domestic work. Global commitment to combating modern slavery has increased but current responses still fall far short of addressing the entirety of the challenge or its root causes. Ending modern slavery requires strong*

---

[1] In 2015, Mr. Ryder reported that 21 million people were enslaved. In 2016, the Global Slavery Index determined that the world estimate was updated based on a Gallup poll. The current estimate is that 45.8 million men, women, and children are enslaved in 167 countries worldwide (Walk Free Foundation, 2016).

legislation, strict implementation, joint commitment of countries and social partners, along with effective support systems for the victims.

—Guy Ryder[2]
Director-General of the International Labour Organization (ILO)
December 2, 2015

[Trafficking in Persons and Work Exploitation
Task Force Complaint Line 1.888.428.7581]
[Trafficking Information and Referral Hotline 1.888.373.7888]

I. Learning Objectives

1.1 Students will examine a broad scope of human trafficking as a human rights problem in the United States and globally.

1.2 Students will be introduced to the definition of human trafficking, including various forms of exploitation for profit and modern forms of slavery-like practices in the United States and around the globe.

1.3 Students will appreciate the historical underpinning of modern-day slavery.

2. Key Ideas

As you read this chapter, take note of these central ideas:

2.1 A human rights perspective has been widely used as a thoughtful framework for understanding and addressing human trafficking.

2.2 The lack of a holistic and agreed-upon definition of human trafficking has made estimating the scope of the problem challenging in the United States and globally.

2.3 Push-pull factors, rather than country culture, are better explanations for the modern exploitation of people.

Chapter Overview

Human trafficking involves many antisocial and criminal traits. Definitions vary across professional disciplines and contexts. At the most fundamental level, human trafficking is about *compelled service*. The exploitation of women, children, and men and the violation of their human rights are at the center of that compelled service. Trafficking in people directly or indirectly impacts every country, leaving no country

---

[2]International Labor Organization (Producer). (2015, December 2). *ILO Director-General calls on governments to take action to end modern slavery.* [Online Video] Available from http://www.ilo.org/global/about-the-ilo/multimedia/video/video-interviews/WCMS_431705/lang—en/index.htm.

or community fully inoculated from its negative impact. Human trafficking includes the victimization of adults and children in the commercial sex industry and forced labor. Although sex and labor may be presented as the two major archetypes, it will soon become apparent that people are being exploited in many demoralizing, intersecting, and complex ways. This introduction chapter provides a broad overview of the research to date; policies, programs, and services; and strategies for next steps, including what is known about survivors, the professionals and organizations serving survivors, and the traffickers exploiting survivors. Subsequent chapters provide more depth on these issues, including a community response to ending modern-day slavery. Some chapters may include a factual human trafficking decision case and a selected theory or framework to position the content.

3. Decision Case

The Tale of the Paleteros[3]

The state capital is home to a strong representation of federal agencies. In the center of the state, the large capital city is also home to the University of Texas, three other colleges, and a thriving technology industry.

The Austin, Texas, Division of the U.S. Department of Labor

Located in the complex of new and old buildings adjacent to the State Capitol building called the J.J. Pickle Federal Building, the offices of the division are split between the fifth and eighth floors. The building was built in 1965 to satisfy the housing needs of federal agencies in Austin's Central Business District. It is an 11-story concrete structure, which includes a partially below-grade ground level and a basement level comprising over 200,000 square feet. This building houses a suite of offices—the "LBJ Suite"—that were used by President Lyndon B. Johnson during his term in office.

The Pickle Federal Building is currently recognized as eligible for listing on the National Register Historic Places. The building was named for J.J. "Jake" Pickle, a United States Representative from the 10th Congressional District of Texas from 1963–1995. The building is part of a master facility that includes a large plaza and is connected by tunnel to the Homer Thornberry Building. The two-building complex makes a strong federal presence in downtown Austin and is near the State Capitol building. The Department of Labor shares the building with the U.S. Department of Transportation, Secret Service, Ted Cruz's office, and Lloyd Doggett's office. The

---

[3] This decision case was prepared solely to provide material for class discussion and not to suggest either effective or ineffective handling of the situation depicted. While based on field research regarding an actual situation, some names may have been disguised to protect confidentiality. The authors wish to thank the case reporter and the Department of Labor for cooperation in making this account available for the benefit of students and practitioners (Wolfer & Scales, 2006, p. 29).

11-story concrete building is a pale rectangle amidst the rosy granite Texas state buildings that surround it.

Through the early 2000s, the San Antonio Division of the U.S. Department of Labor handled the investigation of labor-related cases and complaints for cities as diverse as Austin, San Antonio, and San Angelo. In 2014, the Division was split and a new Division was established in Austin to handle Austin cases and the surrounding area.

Nicole

Nicole Sellers grew up in Waco, Texas, and moved to Austin as a senior in high school. She went to North Texas State University, where she was a cooperative education student from the beginning of her junior year working for the Department of Labor, which allowed her to learn about being an investigator. After she graduated, she began working full time for the department. She has been with the Department of Labor for 26 years in Texas. She is halfway through a master's degree in counseling and shifting to statistics. In 2014, she became the Director of the Austin Division.

During the year Nicole took on the leadership of the division, a case began developing that looked like a potential incident of labor trafficking. The agency had provided staff with extensive training around labor trafficking in concert with its trainings on common illegal labor practices. Nicole recalled, "In the recent past as an Area Office, we brought a few potential trafficking cases to the Assistant U.S. Attorney but were not able to meet the preponderance of evidence for a criminal case." After transitioning from an Area office to Division status, Nicole assumed responsibility for building and improving relationships with other law-enforcement entities that handle criminal concerns.

"We wanted to get to know our partners on the task force better and develop a better sense of who does what. We just started talking along those lines when we get this complaint. About this same time, we met with the APD officer to get to know APD, and he us."

One of her first official visitors to the new Division office was an Austin police officer from the unit working trafficking cases. The visit began in a predictable fashion with a brief tour and description of the Labor Department's work. Once in the conference room, the APD officer took the time to outline what the department looks for to start a criminal investigation in a labor trafficking case.

The Case:

As Nicole showed Officer Cleary around the offices, talking to him about how her staff worked, she was highly aware of how her context and role had changed within the Labor Department.

"We have technicians who do complaint screening and provide information to the public, as well as investigators in the office who go out and look into various aspects of employers," she explained. "We also do planning focused on industries with high violations and provide outreach and education to make investigations and corrective actions."

"I don't really understand what kind of complaints can be sent to y'all." Officer Cleary's Texan drawl was pronounced and easy going.

"The department focuses on preparing workers for better jobs, workplace safety and health, fair work environments, and helping workers secure job benefits. The department's Wage and Hour Division's mission is to promote and achieve compliance with labor standards to protect and enhance the welfare of the nation's workforce," Nicole began. "We ensure that workers receive a fair day's pay for a fair day's work."

Cleary nodded. "So investigating when someone should get time and a half for overtime and they don't?"

Nicole nodded. Overtime pay is something easy to understand in a labor environment where the law can be complicated and detailed. "Yes, depending on how their job is classified and compensated."

They arrived in her office and sat at the small conference table together. "I have an example of an investigation we are working on right now. A former employee was told through a friend that he would be coming from Mexico and working in a factory here in Austin. When he got here, he was actually pushing an ice cream cart. The employer confiscated his passport, which was never returned. No social security number was ever issued and he was only paid $20 a day, when he was selling up to $90 worth of ice cream each day."

"Really?" Cleary leaned in, obviously interested. "How'd he get into the United States?"

Nicole shook her head. "Well, it's a little complicated. You see, American companies are able to hire foreign workers legally through the H-2B laws that bring over low-skilled workers in non-agricultural jobs to do work that the employer says they cannot find U.S. workers to perform. But, there are proper procedures for that. In this case, our investigation found that the employer offered a legal job but then kept the person working here illegally in a pretty vulnerable position."

"So, what'd you do?" Cleary asked.

"We are investigating. It sounds as if there are 50 to 60 people still working there. We might be able to get back pay for this employee." Nicole stopped talking, because Cleary looked ready to ask a question. When no question came, she continued slowly. "The investigation also found that they housed thirteen or fourteen of them in an apartment. The situation sounded like serious exploitation, beyond just our labor laws."

"I was just sitting here picturing the guy wandering around with the ice cream cart in my sector. You know, I always kinda wondered if it was possible to make a living that way, but I never really gave it much thought." Cleary rubbed his upper lip absently. "Have y'all done any more investigating?"

"We have a lot of information," Nicole said. "They're also working from 9 a.m. to 9 p.m., and there seem to have been some threats to families in Mexico if the workers don't comply. We had information from a former employee that this happened almost three years ago, but the employee didn't report it then for fear of reprisals."

"Three years is a long time," Cleary said.

Nicole shrugged. "The company is still in business. There are still people selling ice cream for them from the bike carts. Others might be in the same situation.

This former employee really wants his passport back. But, we'd like to get some wage restitution for him and make sure the other workers are being protected."

Cleary rested his elbows on Nicole's table. "You know, we might be able to help out on this thing. Let me run this past my Commander and see if we can help y'all develop an investigation with some of the other agencies. No telling what might be going on out there. These guys might be laundering drug money and not even know it."

"During the dog days of summer in Texas and across the southwest, the 'paletero' – kind of like an ice cream man – is a staple in most Hispanic neighborhoods. Children and adults alike anxiously wait for the familiar tiny bells or bicycle ringer to signal a frozen piece of happiness is on its way. A *paletero* will walk for miles under the sun pushing around a heavy cart to sell tasty frozen *paletas* and ice cream treats. It's a hard job."

—Rodriguez, J. (2016, February 4). The Ice Cream (or "Paletero") Man Deserves Fair Pay, Too. Retrieved from https://blog.dol.gov/search/node/Paletero

While Officer Cleary vetted the idea of a criminal investigation, Nicole informed her regional management that the Wage and Hour Division is continuing to investigate the case. She assigned the case to an investigator, Tim Bugh. Tim was bilingual in English and Spanish and an experienced investigator. Together, they set up a phone call with the former employee's lawyer in California to learn as much as they could about the case specifics.

In a long conference call with the lawyer, Nicole and Tim were able to confirm the information from the e-mail about the employee and request the lawyer coordinate an interview with the employee. The lawyer explained her desire to get a line on the passport's location and any back wages.

As the lawyer wrapped up her concerns, Nicole asked, "What do you know about what happened? Has your client said anything about the current situation in Austin with others? Do we still have people trapped here in Austin?"

Nicole explained that the statute of limitations on back wages was two years. "With a trafficking component it may be longer. Even so, it's about to expire." She stressed the importance of having an interview with this employee soon. The lawyer agreed to facilitate that meeting for the next Saturday.

Nicole and Tim prepped for the interview on Saturday prior to the call. "We would normally want to interview a person face to face. It's hard to build rapport and garner trust over the phone." They talked about how important it would be to probe, use follow-up answers with more questions, and try to determine who was involved, who else was there. "You need to continue to probe until you get the specifics. Who else knows about this information? Can it be corroborated? When did it happen?" Also, to help support any criminal activity, they needed to ask questions around location, routes, living situations, and other aspects of the situation with which they might not normally be concerned.

After dialing into the call and introducing Tim and the lawyer, the conversation quickly switched to Spanish. The only person engaged who was not Spanish speaking, Nicole was left listening to the tone of the conversation, picking up random words, and waiting to get the story from Tim later. After seeing that the conversation was friendly and watching Tim taking copious notes, Nicole excused herself to her desk to distract herself with paperwork until the meeting closed.

Tim was on the call for nearly two hours. He came back into Nicole's office and sat down heavily in the side chair. Although the man was not familiar with Austin and had a hard time conveying specifics, Tim had gotten excellent information from the employee. The workers were recruited in Mexico by word of mouth, transported to the United States, and settled into crowded living conditions. They were promised factory work making $11.00 per hour and sponsorship for social security numbers. Instead, they were paid as little as $2.00 an hour for 12-hour days, biking and walking up streets through the city selling ice cream novelties. Their passports were taken and paperwork was completed for social security numbers, but the passports were not returned and no social security numbers were issued to workers. Trapped in a strange city without enough income to eat on, the workers were also subjected to threats toward their families in Mexico if they complained. Often, there were men stationed near the apartments to watch the employees.

It was not a lot of information to go on, but it was enough to secure the federal identification of the employer. Nicole asked the regional office to contact Employment Training Administration and provide all of the certifications they have on employees. Under the H-2B program, the employer must apply for certifications for workers. The Regional office was able to find the certifications for the employer from 2011 (the year this employee worked), 2012, 2013, and 2014. Each year, the employer got up to 60 certifications to hire workers. Tim also had information connecting the business to rent paid for apartments, along with addresses.

When Nicole and Officer Clearly compared notes at the end of the following week, they had some names and locations, and APD had some reports of ice cream vendors being assaulted.

Cleary was satisfied there was enough information with which to move forward. APD offered surveillance. "Give us all you have and we'll start watching them. We will put up some pole cameras at the business office. We may be able to isolate the workers and see what's going on." Cleary offered to coordinate a larger meeting with other agencies on the Austin Trafficking Task Force to help develop what the criminal angles of the case might be.

Police surveillance on pole cameras was not part of a routine investigation of labor law infractions. Nicole thought there must be some people to talk to, especially current workers. Yet, they were in a strange holding pattern waiting to gauge what other agencies might be part of an investigation. She kept her Regional Office informed in weekly phone calls. They counseled her to start talking to the Office of Inspector General (OIG) under the Department of Labor (DOL) to address the criminal needs of the case. On the federal side of the equation, the Department of Justice had to agree to take a criminal case to a judge. For a long week following her discussion with Cleary, the case was out of Nicole's hands, waiting on the local end and waiting on the federal end. Although she was waiting patiently, Nicole kept up a steady stream of e-mail reminders to ensure the interests of the employees were being taken into account.

A meeting was convened between APD, FBI, Homeland, Social Security, IRS, OIG, and DOL at an APD substation. One or two people were there from each agency. Different parties had different interests in the case. There was some posturing about which aspects of the case were most important. "Law enforcement was looking for an opportunity to catch, sentence, and punish someone. Legal is interested in making a good prosecution. The IRS and Homeland had concerns about possible fraud." Nicole felt frustrated that she had to keep reminding them that workers get restitution.

At the same time, the information about the case was already old—2011. Various statues and timelines were on the edge of expiration. Ongoing delays decreased the likelihood of restitution or accountability. As the conversation bounced around the room, Nicole paid close attention. If nothing else, she wanted to learn how to develop a good case. Yet, she felt impatient. She knew the regional office person was there to be the mouth of the agency in this investigation. She was frustrated with the process. "What are we doing, what are we not doing?" she thought. "Why aren't we doing something? Why aren't you more experienced people showing me how to proceed? Sounds like human trafficking, but we've actually got to do something one way or the other to figure it out." It felt like all talking and not taking any action.

After an hour of discussion, it seemed as if the agencies were backing away from the case, primarily because the report was about something that happened nearly three years ago.

Cleary paused the conversation to say, "Look, everybody hang on. We need to try many angles and hope something will stick. Because it has to be pretty good to go much beyond this point. The reason we wanted to bring y'all here is because these are hard cases to get past the U.S. Attorney and get some action." His frustrations were in his voice, but at the same time he was sincere in wanting everyone to stay at the table a bit longer. He showed the video surveillance tapes showing the long hours and the poor working conditions.

Nicole spoke up to mention that if the company did have current worker certifications on the books, there might be a current case here. "Because of the seasonal nature of the work, we won't have any employees here soon," she added. "We know those records are falsified because these employees aren't working in a factory."

The representatives from the Texas Workforce Commission and Homeland Security agreed that they could look into the fraud angle. Nicole wondered what the priorities were here—the civil issues or criminal interests? In fact, everyone felt like they could help, but for many it was too old. "Let us know if you find something more recent."

"Perhaps we could interview some current employees," Nicole suggested.

Epilogue

When current employees were interviewed by the police and by the Department of Labor, their stories confirmed fraud as well as foreign labor trafficking. Further investigation revealed a practice of foreign labor trafficking in Central Texas (from San Antonio to Austin). Back wages were estimated at $400,000. Nicole recalled, "The owner went to the bank and brought a check for $325,000 and gave us the check. The next day he was arrested for visa fraud and mail fraud. He bonded out and fled the country." They had learned how to build a trafficking case that would stick.

Later on, Nicole found out that everyone at the table with her that day was new to labor cases. This was the first labor case that was successful.

The Division subsequently added a Community Outreach and Resource Planning Specialist position to manage and deliver all the outreach to stakeholders including employee groups, nonprofits, federal and state agencies, local government, the Mexican consulate, and unions. With more than 100 outreach events per year, this specialist has been critical to building relationships, credibility, and trust with stakeholders.

4. Selected Theory/Framework

4.1 Human Trafficking Through a Human Rights Framework

Globally, the right to live in safety and free from exploitation are considered universal human rights. Therefore human trafficking efforts are most often considered from a human rights perspective. Human rights are concerned with the universal right to equal justice, opportunity, and dignity. Viewed as universally applicable, human rights are inherent in our nature as human beings and fundamental for a life of dignity, respect, and protection. The Universal Declaration of Human Rights (UDHR) is seen as a watershed development in the evolution of a human rights framework, even though elements existed prior to that in religious and political movements (Healy, 2008). Created in response to World War II, the UDHR was adopted by the United Nations (UN) in 1948. The Declaration provides a legal and conceptual framework for social justice and outlines civil and political rights, ensures freedom from curtailment of individual liberty, and affirms participation in social, economic, and cultural aspects of life (Healy, 2008).

While many, arguably all, of the rights listed in the UDHR apply to the complex nature of human trafficking, two stand out as overtly related to human trafficking—Articles 4 and 23. Article 4 states that "no one shall be held in slavery or servitude; slavery and the slave trade shall be prohibited in all their forms." Article 23 provides for the right to work and to have free choice of employment, favorable work conditions, and equal pay for equal work (United Nations, 1948, December 10).

Additional instruments developed by the UN provide structures under which member states of the UN can address human rights violations that are connected with human trafficking. Included among the important instruments that further develop a human rights framework relevant to human trafficking is the Convention on the Elimination of All Forms of Discrimination against Women (CEDAW), which was adopted December 18, 1979 (with date of entry September 1981), as an international bill of rights focused on women (United Nations, 1979). The Convention on the Rights of the Child was subsequently adopted on November 20, 1989, and includes protections against the economic exploitation of children (United Nations, 1989). Specifically addressing human trafficking, the United Nations adopted the Protocol to Prevent, Suppress and Punish Trafficking in Persons Especially Women and Children, commonly referred to as the Palermo Protocol, in 2000 (United Nations, 2000).

Ultimately, a human rights framework provides avenues to monitor the progress of nations in attempts to eradicate, prevent, and punish violations. Overall, the move to recognize human trafficking as a human rights violation gives attention to the root causes of human trafficking and brings exploitation and its underlying structural contributors into broader dialogue (Office of the High Commissioner for Human Rights [OHCHR], 2014). According to the OHCHR (2014),

> Such an approach requires analysis of the ways in which human rights violations arise throughout the trafficking cycle, as well as of States' obligations under international human rights law. It seeks to both identify and redress the discriminatory practices and unjust distribution of power that underlie trafficking, that maintain impunity for traffickers and that deny justice to their victims. (p. 8)

The OHCHR developed guidelines to further outline the primacy of human rights in antitrafficking efforts. One of these guidelines states: "Violations of human rights are both a cause and a consequence of trafficking in persons. Accordingly, it is essential to place the protection of all human rights at the center of any measures taken to prevent and end trafficking." Furthermore, guidelines assert that, "Antitrafficking measures should not adversely affect the human rights and dignity of persons and, in particular, the rights of those who have been trafficked, migrants, internally displaced persons, refugees and asylum-seekers" (OHCHR, May 20, 2002, p. 5).

4.2 Defining Social Justice

Social justice is a widely used term, although it has deep historic roots in religious context, particularly with Catholic teachings (Novak & Adams, 2015). Social work has given social justice practical meaning, referring to the value and rights of all people to have economic, political, and social access and opportunities (National Association of Social Workers, 2011).

**United Nations Human Rights Office of the
High Commissioner Appoints Special Rapporteur**

Urmila Bhoola is an international human rights lawyer and former Judge of the Labour Court of South Africa. Her judicial appointment followed 20 years of work as a labor and human rights lawyer in South Africa, and she has received many awards for her human rights and gender equality work. She has also been a technical advisor to the International Labour Organization (ILO) on labor rights in the Asia-Pacific region and was Chief Legal Drafter of South Africa's Employment Equity Act, designed to redress disadvantages caused by apartheid. She has also served as a part-time Member of the Competition Tribunal, appointed to regulate compliance with South Africa's Competition Act, and was a visiting Senior Lecturer at the Law School of the University of the Witwatersrand. She is the former Executive Director of International Women's Rights Action Watch (Asia Pacific), a women's rights advocacy organization that monitors compliance with the Convention on the Elimination of All Forms of Discrimination Against Women (CEDAW), based in Malaysia. In 2014, she was appointed UN Special Rapporteur on contemporary forms of slavery, including its causes and consequences. (http://bit.ly/28UnrrO)

5. Scientific Knowledge

5.1 Definitions by Policy Efforts

Although the abolition of slavery was passed by Congress through the 13th Amendment in 1885 and there is a persistent commitment by the United States and many other countries around the world to dismantle the institutional structures that supported slavery, trafficking in people for the purposes of commercial sex and cheap labor exists in civil society (Busch-Armendariz, Nsonwu, Cook Heffron, & Mahapatra, 2014; Polaris, 2015a; U.S. Department of State, 2015). In 2000, the United Nations led the world in describing human trafficking under the Protocol to Prevent, Suppress and Punish Trafficking in Persons, Especially Women and Children, defining human trafficking as

> (a) the recruitment, transportation, transfer, harboring or receipt of persons, by means of the threat or use of force or other forms of coercion, of abduction, of fraud, of deception, of the abuse of power or of a position of vulnerability or of the giving or receiving of payments or benefits to achieve the consent of a person having control over another person, for the purpose of exploitation. Exploitation shall include, at a minimum, the exploitation of the prostitution of others or other forms of sexual exploitation, forced labor or services, slavery or practices similar to slavery, servitude or the removal of organs; (b) The consent of a victim of trafficking in persons to the intended exploitation set forth in subparagraph (a) of this article shall be irrelevant where any of the means

set forth in subparagraph (a) have been used; (c) The recruitment, transportation, transfer, harboring or receipt of a child for the purpose of exploitation shall be considered "trafficking in persons" even if this does not involve any of the means set forth in subparagraph (a) of this article; (d) "Child" shall mean any person under eighteen years of age (p. 2).

Later in 2000, the United States followed suit, defining modern slavery with the passage of the Victims of Trafficking and Violence Protection Act. This legislation, known more simply as the Trafficking Victims Protection Act (TVPA), was reauthorized in 2003 (H.R. 2620), 2005 (H.R. 972), 2008 (S. 3061), and 2013 (as Public Law 113–4 under the Title XII of Reauthorization of the Violence Against Women Act). The TVPA defines human trafficking as "the recruitment, harboring, transporting, provision, or obtaining of a person for labor or services, through the use of force, fraud, or coercion for the purpose of subjection to involuntary servitude, peonage, debt bondage, slavery, or forced commercial sex acts" (TVPA, section 103[8]). The TVPA affords victims benefits and services to ensure re-establishment of victim well-being and to facilitate prosecution of the traffickers. The TVPA legislation also entitles foreign-born victims protection from removal or deportation actions in the United States (Kappelhoff, 2011). The TVPA 2013 reauthorization included specific provisions to combat child sex trafficking (Development Services Group, Inc., 2014). Force is the use of power or physical strength to control another person, including kidnapping, rape, and physical or sexual assault. Fraud is the use of deception as a method to recruit and entrap victims. Coercion is the use of intimidation, such as threats of serious harm, or persuasion to achieve compliance. All of these tactics are powerful methods of control that traffickers use over victims.

Prior to the passage of the Palermo Protocol and the TVPA, the United States passed the Mann Act, also known as The White Slavery Act (18 U.S. Code §2421 Public Law 114–38), in 1910 to address criminal activities and offenses, including prostitution and child pornography, that move across jurisdictions (Finklea, Fernandes-Alcantara, & Siskin, 2015).

Examples of Force, Fraud, and Coercion

Examples of Force

Physical abuse

Kidnapping

Physical restraint (such as restricting mobility, tying, or chaining a victim)

Examples of Fraud

Illegitimate contracts

False promises

Fake businesses

Fake visa documents

Examples of Coercion

Psychological manipulation

Spoken threats about the victim, the victim's family, or other victims

Implied threats such as "climate of fear" (electric fences, guns, and lies about law enforcement, immigration, and the outside world)

Control of children or threats to harm children

Traffickers' possession of documents

SOURCE: *Human trafficking: What the medical community should know*, August 6, 2010 (p. 8) by Central Texas Coalition Against Human Trafficking (CTCAHT) and Refugee Services of Texas, Inc. (RST), Copyright 2010 by RST. These materials were developed by CTCAHT social workers and the textbook authors based on their practice with survivors of human trafficking victims and a combination of other resources including what they were learning at trainings and in the literature. It has been adapted with permission.

5.2 Prevalence of Trafficking

Just over the last four years, our understanding about the scope and dimensions of enslaved people has increased. The most recent current estimates determined by the Global Slavery Index (2016) project that 45.8 million people are exploited worldwide (Walk Free Foundation, 2016). In 2012, the International Labour Organization (ILO) estimated that 21 million people were trafficked worldwide, and in 2013 the U.S. Department of State estimated in annual *Trafficking in Persons Report* (TIP) the number of victims to reach 27 million adults and children. Prevalence rates will likely continue to increase as countries and communities implement prevention, intervention, and awareness efforts. For example, efforts to apprehend and hold traffickers and facilitators, the continued improvement of concerned citizens in identifying victims and victims' own self-identification, the development of appropriate reporting portals and referral services, and implementation of corporate responsibility through policies and practices will all contribute to an increase in prevalence rates and the dimensions and circumstances of exploitation, including who is most at risk.

5.3 Explaining Elusive Underreporting and Underestimates

While there is still skepticism about the accuracy of human trafficking estimates, confidence is building about the recently released numbers. Our understanding of how to accurately measure this atrocity is challenging for a variety of reasons that negatively impact the identification and reporting of human trafficking crimes and help seeking among victims (Hepburn & Simon, 2010; Office of the Assistant Secretary for Planning and Evaluation, 2009). First, victims are most often liberated or leave their traffickers after months or years of enslavement possibly without having been physically restrained. Traffickers use a variety of tactics to hold victims captive including threatening them or their family members with physical violence, harm, retaliation, physical brutality, and sexual violence. Second, victims often are unaware of their rights as crime victims and the community-based organizations designated to assist them, or their traffickers have made them afraid to reach out to governmental authorities or law enforcement. Third, traffickers often select victims who are challenged by inadequate personal and familial economies and social context. That is, human trafficking is most often grounded in economic and gender inequality (e.g., girls and women living in poverty may be at the highest risk). Finally, traffickers and facilitators use nefarious trust-building tactics or develop intimate relationships with victims, making it difficult for them to leave the exploitative situation.

As it relates to understanding the scope of human trafficking, it should be clarified that victims are not responsible for estimates that remain elusive. Traffickers and facilitators (or middle-handlers) are controlling, cunning, and deceptive, and victims are often "hidden in plain sight" (Hepburn & Simon, 2010; Office of the Assistant Secretary for Planning and Evaluation, 2009). Victims are undetected by the general public and law enforcement, and, as such, estimates are difficult to accurately calculate because of weak data collection methodologies, gaps in research, and a lack of standardized definitions (Panigabutra-Roberts, 2012). Chapter 5 includes more descriptions of traffickers' tactics.

5.4 Efforts to Bolster the Numbers

Many efforts are under way to achieve better estimates. For example, in 2010, the United Nations Office on Drugs and Crime (UNODC) mandated a comprehensive overview of the scope and patterns of human trafficking worldwide, and as a result many nations are beginning to document the routes that traffickers use both transnationally and within their borders (United Nations Office on Drugs and Crime [UNODC], 2014). Understanding routes has improved our understanding of human trafficking. Also, in July 2015, led by the Walk Free Foundation, a small group of social scientists, practitioners, and policy makers gathered in Washington, DC, to discuss strategies to better estimate the number of human trafficking victims in the United States.

5.5 Economic Impact of Human Trafficking

The economic profits of these illegal activities are mind-boggling. The International Labour Organization (ILO) has estimated the profits from forced labor at USD 150 billion with industries including domestic work, child labor, sex work, and other forms of labor exploitation such as state-imposed forced labor (International Labour Organization [ILO], 2014). The ILO also estimates the economy by region, concluding that the Asia-Pacific region and developed economies including the European Union generate the highest illicit profitability (ILO, 2014). Most consumers have few warnings and limited access to information about what products and services rely on trafficked or forced labor, although this information is becoming more available. To understand that the goods they are purchasing may be produced by slave labor and/or that sex trafficking may be in close proximity to their regular lives can help to build the awareness necessary to address the drivers of human trafficking (Verité, 2015). Chapter 4 is devoted to a full discussion of the economics of human trafficking enterprises.

5.6 Increasing Identification Efforts and Next Steps

Over the last 15 years in particular, micro and macro efforts have emerged or been refined to identify and end trafficking in people. As the world has begun to take notice and action, dozens of additional industries have been identified in which human trafficking is occurring and the products are produced by victims. Awareness campaigns have gained momentum and consumers are able to purchase slave-free products. Global Businesses Coalition Against Human Trafficking (gBCAT) is one such effort. The mission of gBCAT is "to mobilize the power, resources and thought leadership of the business community in an effort to end human trafficking, including all forms of forced labor and sex trafficking (End Slavery Now, 2017, Mission, para. 1). Nonetheless, given its prevalence and insidiousness in our lives, ending modern-day slavery will require swift action. Governments and their citizenries need to act urgently with courageous micro and macro strategies that include dogged antitrafficking legislation (U.S. Department of State, 2015) as well as keen efforts that quickly identify victims and empower citizens and consumers. Perhaps most importantly is a collective commitment to end trafficking in people that begins with recognizing its root causes.

5.7 Explanations of Human Trafficking Definitions and Dimensions

5.7.1 Overview

Over the past decade, the exploitation of people (also referred to as human trafficking, modern-day slavery, contemporary slavery, and trafficking in people) has captured global and national attention as a major social issue and human atrocity (Busch-Armendariz, Nsonwu, Cook Heffron, & Mahapatra, 2014).

Human trafficking is about the dynamics of the relationship between the trafficker and victim. Therefore, moving or transporting victims across countries, regions, or state borders is not necessary for human trafficking to occur, although in the cases of foreign-born victims, involuntary migration may be an element (Jac-Kucharski, 2012).

5.7.2 Understanding the Trafficking Industries by Rate

Traffickers generally drive people into two broad industries for exploitation: sex and labor (Busch-Armendariz, Nsonwu, Cook Heffron, & Mahapatra, 2013; Busch-Armendariz, Nsonwu, Cook Heffron, & Mahapatra, 2014), although the *Global Report* by the United Nations Office on Drugs and Crime (2014) also reports organ removal as a circumstance vulnerable to trafficking and exploitation.

Labor trafficking involves service industries (e.g., restaurants, hotels, tourism, etc.), other markets that require labor (e.g., construction, agriculture, manufacturing, etc.), or may occur in private homes such as domestic servitude cases (Busch-Armendariz et al., 2013; International Labour Organization [ILO], 2012). The *Global Report on Trafficking in Persons* (GRTIP) by the United Nations Office on Drugs and Crime (2012b) concludes "the number of victims of forced labor as a result of trafficking in persons remains unknown" (p. 1).

Victims exploited in the sex industry are often forced into prostitution or pornography or may be forced to work in service establishments with other victims such as brothels, strip clubs/adult entertainment establishments, or bars (Busch-Armendariz et al., 2013; UNODC, 2014). According to Polaris, the "top venues" for sex trafficking in the United States are in commercial-front brothels and domestic work in labor trafficking cases (Polaris, 2015b). Children forced into prostitution are often referred to as domestic minors of sex trafficking (DMST) or commercially sexually exploited children (CSEC). In commercial sex industries, women and children are more often identified as the victims of male customers and, therefore, it is constructive to understand that sex trafficking often involves a theoretical gendered perspective (Banzon, 2005; Busch-Armendariz et al., 2013). However, a feminist framework also acknowledges that human trafficking affects both men and women and recognizes that all forms of forced labor are exploitive (Alvarez & Alessi, 2012). The term "victim" and its value-laden underpinnings are discussed in Chapters 3 and 5.

The UNODC GRTIP (2014) reported an increase in detection of trafficking for purposes other than sexual exploitation as well as an increase in detection of child trafficking victims. And, although women still constitute the largest percentage of sex trafficking victims, GRTIP reported that for the years 2010 to 2012, almost one third of forced labor victims were women and a growing number (28%) of convicted offenders of trafficking were women (UNODC, 2014). Although sex trafficking receives more media and public attention, human trafficking in labor industries may be greater (Clawson, Layne, & Small, 2006; Feingold, 2005), as the numbers of identified victims have increased every year.

The GRTIP (2014) reported that worldwide that in 2011, 53% of victims were exploited for commercial sex, 40% for forced labor, 0.3% for organ removal, and

Figure 1.1 *Sex trafficking routes in Southeastern Asia.*

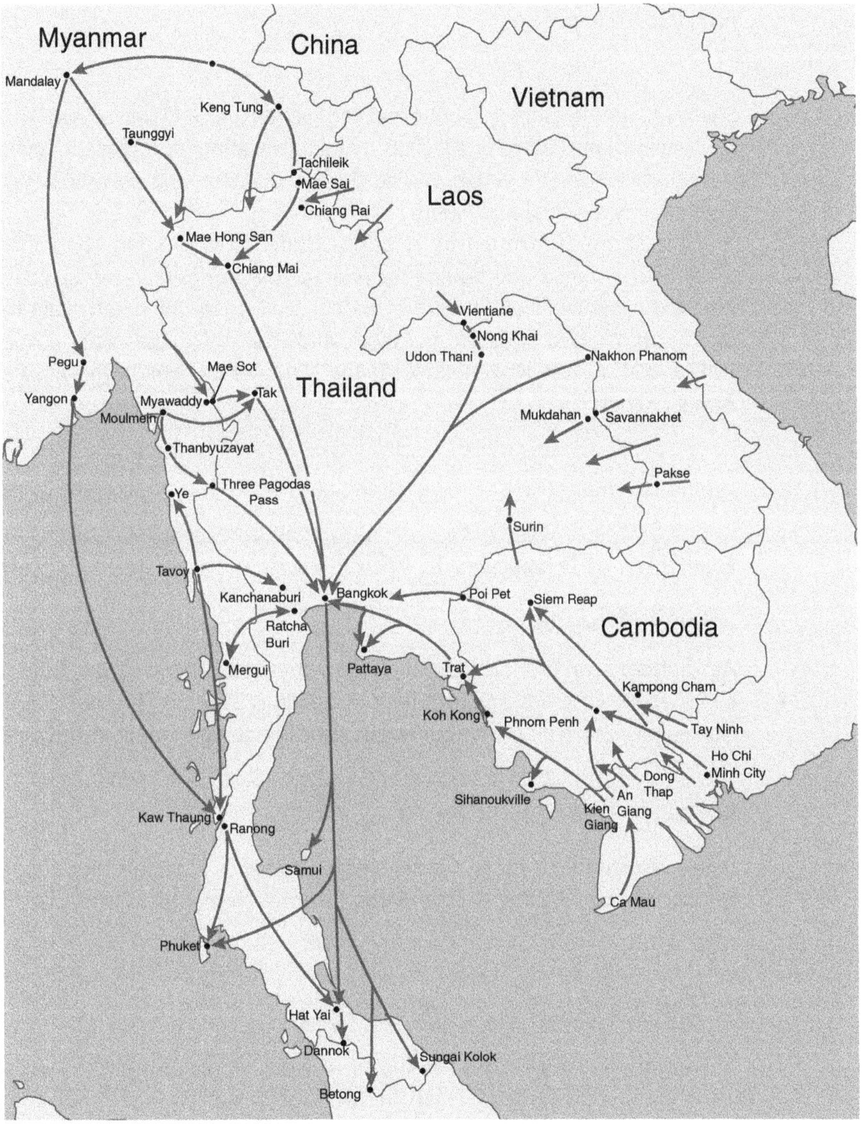

SOURCE: Reprinted from *Transnational organized crime in East Asia and the Pacific: A threat assessment* (p. 20) by United Nations Office on Drugs and Crime (UNODC), 2013. Retrieved from https://www.unodc .org/documents/data-and-analysis/Studies/TOCTA_EAP_web.pdf. Copyright 2013 UNODC. Reprinted with permission.

7% were categorized as "other." The GRTIP (2014) reports, "These [other] types are trafficking for mixed exploitation in forced labor and sexual exploitation, for committing crime, for begging, for pornography (including internet pornography), forced marriages, benefit fraud, baby selling, illegal adoption, armed combat and for rituals" (UNODC, 2014, p. 38).

> Shelly (2010) identifies the feminization of poverty (a term first coined by U.S. social work researcher Diana Pearce in 1978) as a major causation for trafficking. Women are disproportionately overrepresented among the world's poor, and poverty increases a person's vulnerability to social and health risks.
>
> The statistics reported by Polaris, a United States–based nonprofit that serves as a national resource and hotline for human trafficking, reported in 2015 that 75% of reported cases involved sexual trafficking, 13% were labor trafficking cases, 3% were cases that involved both sex and labor, and 9% of the cases were unspecified (Polaris, 2015a, 2015b). See Appendix A for the National Human Trafficking Resource Center Annual Report.

Examples of Industries in Which Victims Have Been Exploited

Labor Trafficking

Agriculture, Farm Work, Landscaping, Construction, Domestic Servitude, Restaurants & Food Service, Factories & Sweat Shops, Peddling & Begging, Hospitality & Tourist Industry, Nail Salons, Entertainment, Carnivals, Gas Stations, and Cleaning Services

Sex Trafficking

Street Prostitution Rings, Residential Brothels, Massage Parlors, Internet-based Commercial Sex, Hostess & Strip Clubs, Escort Services, Truck Stops, and Pornography

5.7.3 Push-Pull Factors and Trafficking Flows

One way to understand the forces at work in human trafficking enterprises is to identify push-pull factors. Push factors are circumstances that contribute to individuals' forced migration across borders, geographical areas, or districts and other vulnerabilities to being trafficked. Push factors include war, natural disasters, poverty, homelessness, overpopulation, unemployment, and social system collapse. On the other end of the tug-of-war rope, pull factors are those elements that draw people to cross borders or geographical locations and contribute to demand. Pull factors expand the demand for victims and include commercial sex industries, desire for cheap labor, and armed conflict in the case of child soldiers (Lusk & Lucas, 2009).

Push factors are also referred to the "supply side," while pull factors are also referred to as the "demand side" (Lusk & Lucas, 2009, p. 51). Absent one or both sides of this equation (either push or pull factors), the commodification of people would not be a sustainable industry. While some individuals or groups may be more vulnerable to push factors, traffickers and their middle-facilitators do not discriminate based on gender or age. That is, women and men and adults and children are exploited by compelled service across the world. Although push factors may contribute to the overrepresentation of vulnerable groups as victims, traffickers consider pull factors, or cost-benefit analyses, to determine volume and scope (Jac-Kucharski, 2012). Shelley (2010) offers that "demand has also increased as producers depend more on trafficker and exploited labor to stay competitive in a global economy in which consumers seek cheap goods and services, including easily available sexual services" (p. 2–3).

Another way to conceptualize human trafficking is to consider source, transit, and destination countries. Source countries are states where traffickers prey. Transit countries are the countries that traffickers use to route and transport victims, if victims are moved. Destination countries are locations considered by traffickers as high demand and where victims wind up. East Asia is considered one of the most active transnational "source" regions in the world because victims who originate from East Asia are moved across all regions of the world. Victims from other source countries are often centralized to specific geographies. For example, human trafficking victims from African countries are more likely to be moved "interregionally" or are often bound for Western Europe (UNODC, 2012b). It is important to understand that while the crime of human trafficking does not necessarily include the movement of people across borders or regions, individuals can be trafficked within their home countries, as can be the case with DMST and the commercial sexual exploitation of children in the United States. These trafficking dynamics are covered in more depth in Chapter 3.

5.7.4 Circumstances That Enslave

Lusk and Lucas (2009) outline four mechanisms of human trafficking that include debt bondage, slavery through false contracts, chattel slavery, and war slavery. Under these circumstances, victims find themselves trapped by a series of trafficker-controlled strategies.

Debt bondage involves traffickers charging astonishingly high, unfixed fees for expenses (e.g., travel expenses, housing, food, and clothes all related to their victimization) to victims that result in an accumulating and unending financial obligation. Victims of debt bondage are not able to negotiate fee rates or payment schedules; rather, they continue to work for the traffickers in the incongruous effort to reduce their often unending debt.

Slavery through false contracts involves "an apparent offer of legitimate work . . . supported by a fake contract . . . used to lure people into slavery. Once away from safety, the person is imprisoned and coerced to work" (Lusk & Lucas, 2009, p. 50).

Chattel slavery involves victims who are born or kidnapped and traffickers forcing them to work, including in the sex industry. Lusk and Lucas (2009) write, "It is the common form of slavery and the one most like institutional slavery" (p. 50). Bromfield (2016) refers to this dynamic as "white slavery" (p. 129). Chattel slavery is often thought of as being born into slavery, where generations of families and children are owned. Kevin Bales, a world leader, activist, and author, refers to this version of slavery as "old" slavery (Bales, 2012).

Most often, *war slavery* involves kidnapping children to serve in armed conflict, although there have been cases of parents exchanging their children for guaranteed safety. In 2008, the United Nations International Emergency Fund (UNICEF) reported that while our understanding of the scope of child recruitment and exploitation in armed conflict was limited, some research indicated that 300,000 children are being exploited in more than 30 armed battles around the world. Alarmingly, the number of armed conflicts has grown to 42 (International Institute for Strategic Studies [IISS], 2015). Children are exploited in these battles in a variety of ways, including as soldiers and for manual labor such as cooking, and are also highly likely to be sexually assaulted (Lusk & Lucas, 2009).

5.8 Understanding Victims of Human Trafficking

5.8.1 Identified Victims

The success of identifying victims is staggeringly low. According to the *Trafficking in Persons Report* (U.S Department of State, 2015), for the years 2012, 2013, and 2014, only 46,570, 44,758, and 44,462 victims were emancipated from their traffickers, respectively (U.S. Department of State, 2015). The report classified detected victims geographically, showing that for the year 2014, 21.4% were identified in African countries, 27% in Europe, 19% in the Western Hemisphere, 14% in East Asia and the Pacific, 11% in South and Central Asia, and 7.6% in the Near East (U.S. Department of State, 2015). Thus, every country is directly or indirectly impacted by trafficking in people, leaving no country fully inoculated from its negative impacts. Data on trafficking cases in the United States (including territories) can be gathered from the National Human Trafficking Resource Center (NHTRC). The NHTRC operates a national, antitrafficking hotline (toll-free, 24/7/365) and resource center for trafficking victims and survivors along with referral to community providers. Additionally, the NHTRC provides annual statistics on the number of contacts (i.e., phone calls, e-mails, or online tip reports) made about human trafficking in the United States. In 2015, 21,947 phone contacts were made to the hotline and 5,544 potential human trafficking cases were reported. Of these cases, the majority (75%) involved sex trafficking, followed by labor trafficking (13%), with a small number of overlap involving both sex and labor trafficking (3%). Nine percent did not specify the type of trafficking involved (Polaris, 2015b).

5.8.2 Terminology Is Important: Victim or Survivor?

This textbook uses *victim* and *survivor* interchangeably to refer to trafficked individuals, although neither label is meant to be demeaning or judgmental, to weigh passivity or agency, or to give the perception that it is an accurate label for any particular individual. On the contrary, it is important to consider that individuals who have been trafficked have experienced and likely overcome a significant combination of physical, emotional, and sexual abuse and trauma. Amid that trauma, trafficked persons often simultaneously utilize tremendous strength, resilience, and choice. Moreover, it is essential to recognize each individual and how they choose to talk about their experiences (Busch, Fong, Heffron, Faulkner, & Mahapatra, 2007; Busch-Armendariz et al., 2014). Lutnick (2016) disagrees with the label *victim*, particularly for domestic minors of sex trafficking, because, as she states, "labeling them victims oversimplifies their lived experience, is disempowering" (p. 2), and, as she cites from Zimmerman, "functions as an implicit character assessment of the . . . individual instead of an assessment of the social change" (Zimmerman, 2013, p. 12). A fuller discussion about the use and impact of labels is included in Chapter 3.

To fully understand victims, it is important to recognize the power dynamics at play in the trafficking relationship. In addition to the threats and use of physical and sexual violence, Kim (2011) identified situational coercion such as lack of legal immigration status, lack of knowledge about crime victims' rights, or income dependency as subtle, yet powerful, mechanisms used by traffickers to trap victims.

Many sociopolitical factors contribute to the existence of human trafficking including poverty, armed conflict and war, lack of work opportunities and family support (such as being orphaned, runaway, homeless, family collaborating with traffickers), and a lack of knowledge about traffickers' recruitment plans. The intersectionality of individual factors with these cultural and community circumstances heightens the risk of being exploited, particularly for children and women.

Homelessness is a risk factor particularly for youth and children (National Center for Homeless Education, 2014). Runaway and homeless youth involved with governmental protective services, particularly with histories of sexual abuse, have a heightened vulnerability to exploitation [Research Triangle Institute (RTI), Child Trends, & Pacific Institute for Research and Evaluation (PIRE), 2002]. Despite the implementation of widespread legislation to fight against child sex trafficking, the commercial sexual exploitation of children is rising (Leary, 2014).

Professional context also determines the use of labels. Law enforcement may use *complainant* and *suspect*, attorneys use *client* and *plaintiff*, and social workers may use *client* or *survivor* or *victim*, depending on the organization and its mission. Using a human rights framework, the underpinning value would be to consider the worth and dignity of the individuals and their preferred terms. It has often been the case to call people by name, when appropriate.

International Rescue Committee

Across 40 Countries

http://www.rescue.org/fighting-human-trafficking
    The International Rescue Committee's antitrafficking programs strive to provide timely, high-quality, comprehensive services to survivors of human trafficking.

Slavery No More

http://www.slaverynomore.org/
    The mission of Slavery No More is to resource a diversity of the most effective organizations working to combat and abolish modern-day slavery and human trafficking, and to create awareness and a diversity of opportunities for meaningful personal engagement.

JURIST:

http://www.jurist.org/
    JURIST is a 501(c)(3) nonprofit organization dedicated to bringing objective legal news and reasoned expert analysis to the public.

5.8.3 Efforts to Increase Identification of Victims

Several initiatives and resources to identify victims exist. Polaris (2015b) reported that since 2007, more than 25,000 cases have been reported in the United States through the national resource center either by phone, text, or web interactions. Another 252 cases of human trafficking occurring overseas have also been reported. In addition, Polaris reported more victims themselves are reaching out for help through the national resource. In 2015, 1,600 victims contacted Polaris, a 24% increase from the previous year (Polaris, 2016, January 28).

Macy and Graham (2012) argue for the use of service delivery systems to identify exploited victims. Identification of trafficking victims centers on screening and awareness. For example, human service providers across various disciplines of practice (mental health, child welfare, supplemental income, and health care, to name a few) are very likely to encounter victims of sex-trafficking, although they may not properly identity victims without training and protocols in screening and awareness. A number of screening questions that focus on victims' safety, employment, living environment, and immigration status/travel have been developed.

Red Flags for Human Trafficking

Common Work and Living Conditions

- Is not free to leave or come and go as he/she wishes
- Is under 18 and is providing commercial sex acts
- Is in the commercial sex industry and has a pimp/manager
- Is unpaid, paid very little, or paid only through tips
- Works excessively long and/or unusual hours
- Is not allowed breaks or suffers under unusual restrictions at work
- Owes a large debt and is unable to pay it off
- Was recruited through false promises concerning the nature and conditions of his/her work
- High security measures exist in the work and/or living locations (e.g., opaque windows, boarded-up windows, bars on windows, barbed wire, security cameras, etc.)

Poor Mental Health or Abnormal Behavior

- Is fearful, anxious, depressed, submissive, tense, or nervous/paranoid
- Exhibits unusually fearful or anxious behavior after bringing up law enforcement
- Avoids eye contact

Poor Physical Health

- Lacks health care
- Appears malnourished
- Shows signs of physical and/or sexual abuse, physical restraint, confinement, or torture

Lack of Control

- Has few or no personal possessions
- Is not in control of his/her own money, no financial records or bank account
- Is not in control of his/her own identification documents (ID or passport)
- Is not allowed or able to speak for themselves (a third party may insist on being present and/or translating)

Other Indicators

- Claims of just visiting and inability to clarify where he/she is staying/address
- Lack of knowledge of whereabouts and/or does not know what city he/she is in
- Loss of sense of time
- Has numerous inconsistencies in his/her story

SOURCE: Adapted from *Recognize the Signs* by Polaris, 2016 (http://polarisproject.org/recognize-signs). Copyright 2016 by Polaris. Adapted with permission.

NOTE: This list is not exhaustive and represents only a selection of possible indicators. Also, the red flags in this list may not be present in all trafficking cases and are not cumulative.

5.8.4 Understanding Victims' Needs

Victims of human trafficking require immediate, short-, and long-term services to rebuild their lives (Busch-Armendariz, Nsonwu, & Cook Heffron, 2011). Acute needs include immediate protection from traffickers, safe housing, medical care, food, and other basic human needs (Busch-Armendariz et al., 2011; Clawson & Dutch, 2008). Following the initial stabilization and securing of basic, short-term needs, victims also need trauma-informed mental health services. Over the long term, victims cite wanting help with long-term employment plans, legal services, permanent housing, and ongoing mental health care. Foreign-born victims may need language classes as well as assessment and planning for family reunification assessment, when possible through legal immigration remedies (Busch et al., 2007; Busch-Armendariz, Nsonwu, & Cook Heffron, 2009; Busch-Armendariz et al., 2011).

Identifying Fear and Process of Healing

In the beginning, I felt scared to move around on my own, and they would go everywhere with me. Little by little, I got to know places and started to lose the fear, and I began to want to explore a little bit on my own. I wanted to get on the buses and start learning new things. But when I did not feel that confidence yet, they were willing to take me everywhere, even if it was to go buy food.

—Human trafficking survivor and research participant
(Busch-Armendariz et al., 2009). Interviewed in Houston, Texas

---

Survivors have benefited from a single-point-of-contact model to address their needs (Busch-Armendariz et al., 2014). The single-point-of-contact model "[is] situate[ed] in a broader framework that encompasses casework, advocacy, interdisciplinary coordination of services, and cross-cultural competency" led by a social worker (Busch-Armendariz et al., 2014, p. 13). Social workers are trained to understand the importance of and build trust with traumatized people while considering a cultural context with the goal toward self-determination and healing (Busch-Armendariz et al., 2014). Chapter 5 includes more discussion about victims' needs.

Identifying Long-Term Needs

I need to learn how to manage my finances, because I know that in this country you need to work and save. I have worked until now, but the job I had earned me very little. With that job, I could not make ends meet. With roommates I paid $200, half the normal rent, and I still had barely enough for food and to send money to my son in Mexico and then I did not have anything left. I hope with this new job, which offers more money, that I can be referred to someone who can help me save. In the beginning, I know someone told me how, but it was not very helpful, because at that time I did not have anything to save. I would get my check and I would spend it that same day, because I needed to buy food, pay the bills, the rent, and the electricity.

—Human trafficking survivor (Busch-Armendariz et al., 2011).
Interviewed in Houston, Texas

5.8.5 Power and Control Strategies

Women and girls constitute the majority of victims who are either discovered by law enforcement, have escaped from their traffickers, or are seeking services from social service agencies. Traffickers maintain control over victims by using physical and sexual violence, isolation and entrapment, drug addiction, psychological and emotional abuse, and threats to other family members' well-being. The psychological coercion that victims face should not be understated (Busch-Armendariz et al., 2009).

For many domestic minor trafficking victims, the trafficker often uses coercive tactics such as buying necessities and gifts and promising to love and take care of her. In the latter, the trafficker becomes the victim's "boyfriend" and the exploitation begins after the "loving" relationship begins. The trafficker will then demand that the victim engage in sex acts or prostitution and give all her earnings to him (Smith, Healy Vardaman, & Snow, 2009). For foreign-born victims, traffickers may promise legitimate employment and wage-earning opportunities.

5.9 Understanding Traffickers, Facilitators, and johns

5.9.1 Identified Traffickers, Facilitators, and johns

The success in identifying and holding traffickers accountable is also limited to, and connected to, the bleak ability to identify victims. The United Nations examined the conviction rates of 128 countries and determined that between 2007 and 2010, 16% recorded no convictions of human trafficking. By 2012, convictions were up but still miserably low; 40% of the countries recorded less than 10 convictions per year and 15% did not record any convictions. The report also found that 64% of traffickers were citizens of the convicting country and the majority were men (72%) compared to (28%) women (UNODC, 2014).

However, unlike other crimes where the involvement of women is generally low, in human trafficking crimes women's involvement is not insignificant; 1 of 3 traffickers prosecuted worldwide were women (UNODC, 2014). Further, GRTIP indicated that women were more likely to be involved in trafficking girls. "Qualitative studies suggest that women involved in human trafficking are normally found in low-ranking positions of the trafficking networks and carry out duties that are more exposed to the risk of detection and prosecution than those of male traffickers" (UNODC, 2012b, p. 11).

A database of prosecuted traffickers in the United States maintained by the University of Michigan School of Law Human Trafficking Clinic provides some limited insight into this crime's scope. Since much of our understanding about the exploitation of people is based on prosecuted cases, experts agree that exploitation of human beings is likely underestimated and that our understanding is narrow. Typologies of traffickers have been developed by Busch-Armendariz et al. (2009) through an empirical examination of convicted cases. The research identified four typologies of traffickers under two broad classifications: *Shattering the American Dream* and *John's Demand*. Traffickers and typologies are discussed later in this chapter and in more depth in Chapter 5.

The United Nations Office of Drugs and Crime (April 2006) concluded in *Trafficking in Persons: Global Patterns* that the prostitution industry was responsible for the most sex trafficking exploitation. This correlation is well established. The illicit markets of prostitution and sex trafficking are, like any other market, driven by demand. Wherever demand occurs, supply and distribution emerge (Shively, Kliorys, Wheeler, & Hunt, 2012, p. vi). Shively et al. (2012) point out the limitations of focusing on efforts to curb supply and propose that demand-reduction strategies should be the primary prevention focus. Specifically, it is important to mention the reduction of demand for commercial sex by *johns*. The generic term "john" is used to describe men who purchase sex. In an earlier study for the National Institute of Justice, Shively et al. (2008) evaluated the First Offender Prostitution Program (FOPP), one of the longest-standing deferred adjudication programs for men arrested for soliciting commercial sex. In their final report, Shively et al. (2008) asserted that the "links between street prostitution and both domestic and international trafficking have been empirically confirmed, with the market forces of prostitution driving the demand for most human trafficking" (p. 12). Later, they opine, "with one out of every five or six men admitting to purchasing sex, it is clear that patronizing commercial sex is not the behavior of just a small minority of deviants" (p. 27). Shively et al. (2012) draw attention to the weaknesses of prevention strategies that in the past have focused on the supply side of this demand-driven market. Suppliers and facilitators are most often on the front end of the trafficking enterprise as the person who lures or originally connects potential victims with the trafficker. "Where demand is strong, interfering with supply chains usually results in shifting to other sources or other means of distribution. The 'service gap' is too great to close by addressing supply only" (Shively et al., 2012, p. iv).

It is important to note that prostitution and human trafficking are not transposable, particularly when using a legal framework. It may be useful to consider the nexus of human trafficking and prostitution as a Venn diagram. The intersectionality of these two issues (e.g., the degree to which they overlap) depends on one's viewpoint and values, particularly about prostitution. Nonetheless, not all prostitution is human trafficking and not all human trafficking is prostitution.

5.9.2 Organization of Trafficking Operations

The GRTIP (2014) organizes trafficking enterprises into three broad groups: small, local operations; medium, sub-regional operations; and large, transregional operations (UNODC, 2014). Shelley (2010) also considers typologies of traffickers, stating that "supply and demand have created a flourishing business for traffickers. Traffickers choose to trade in humans. There are low start-up costs, minimal risks, high profits, and large demands. For organized crime groups, human beings have one added advantage over drugs, they can be sold repeatedly. In drug trafficking organizations, profits flow to the top of the organization. With the small-scale entrepreneurship that characterizes much of human trafficking, however, more profits go to individual criminals—making this trade more attractive for all involved" (Shelley, 2010, p. 3).

In research that considered the characteristics of convicted cases, Busch-Armendariz et al. (2009) also categorized traffickers by operation, size, and dimensions. Archetype One, called *Shattering the American Dream*, includes organized labor exploitation for profit and family-based domestic servitude. These labor trafficking operations varied from large, income-generating enterprises to small organizations. Archetype Two, called *john's Demand*, included sex trafficking of U.S. citizens and sex trafficking of foreign-born victims. DMST and CSEC cases fall under john's demand, where the trafficking operations are generally, although not always, small, pimp-run operations that exploit chronic runaways or other vulnerable youth and children (Busch-Armendariz et al., 2009). Traffickers and facilitators will be discussed in more detail in later chapters.

These typologies are not exhaustive. In recent years, trafficking research, and law enforcement investigations in particular, have led to further understanding of trafficking exploitation including substance-abusing caregivers and parents sexually exploiting children in exchange for drugs, runaways involved in the sex industry who are not involved in the foster care system, the international marriage industry, and door-to-door peddling and begging industries.

5.9.3 Trafficker Conviction and Accountability Efforts

Micro and macro accountability mechanisms have had mixed success in the United States and worldwide; the prosecution of traffickers as a systemic effort has been unsuccessful. The GRTIP (2014) reports that only 4 in 10 countries reported 10 or more convictions in one year while 15% of countries reported no convictions (UNODC, 2014).

Low conviction rates are directly tied to the challenges that law enforcement face in identifying victims. One strategy that law enforcement may use to increase the identification of victims and traffickers is to understand the link between human trafficking and other criminal networks such as illegal drug trafficking and prostitution, or other issues such as natural disasters and war (Busch-Armendariz et al., 2014; UNODC, 2012a).

Several macro efforts to nudge policies and procedures have taken shape in the form of report cards. Polaris and Shared Hope International both provide report cards about progress in the United States. The focus of assessment criteria is slightly different. Polaris's assessment considers legislative efforts to end all types of human trafficking while Shared Hope International's assessment focuses on the criminalization efforts of DMST. Polaris's report card is based on 10 categories considered to be critical for structuring a legal framework to address human trafficking while Shared Hope International published *The Protected Innocence Challenge* (2015) to specifically assess states on efforts to address domestic minors of sex trafficking (Polaris, 2014; Shared Hope International, 2015).

5.9.4 Recruiting Victims as Facilitators

One of the most egregious acts of power and abuse by traffickers is their co-optation of victims as facilitators in the trafficking operation. Victims are sometimes compelled or coerced into recruiting other victims. The promotion within the trafficking organization is a strategy of power and control by the trafficker and accepted by victims to avoid further exploitation (Busch-Armendariz et al., 2009; Lloyd, 2011). An infamous trafficker, Pimpin' Ken refers to the co-opted victim as a "bottom bitch" (Pimpin Ken & Hunter, 2007, p. 178). In *Girls Like Us*, Rachel Lloyd, activist, author, and survivor, contextualizes the controlling and destructive dynamic for victims with which they cooperate for self-preservation and survival. This alignment with the trafficker serves as a shield from the trafficker's violence and from having to provide sex to customers (Lloyd, 2011).

5.10 A Brief Introduction to Important Terms and Policies

5.10.1 Smuggling and Trafficking

Smuggling human beings and human trafficking need further clarification because these concepts are generally thought of as similar or identical (Bruckert & Parent, 2002; Busch-Armendariz, Nsonwu, Cook Heffron, & Mahapatra, 2014). The two terms and their definitions are often confused due to the intricate ways in which they interconnect. Exploitation is the major difference between smuggling and human trafficking (Bruckert & Parent, 2002; Clawson et al., 2006). In the United States, the legal definition of human trafficking has three overarching elements: force, fraud, and coercion, while smuggling involves crossing a national border without proper documentation. More specifically, smuggling is defined as the illegal transport of an individual into a country (Albanese, Donnelly, & Kelegian, 2004) or "the facilitation, transportation, attempted transportation or illegal entry of a person(s) across an international border, in violation of one or more countries' laws, either clandestinely or through deception, such as the use of fraudulent documents" (U.S. Department of State, 2006, p. 2).

In the United States, the smuggler and the person being smuggled are considered to be committing a crime and may be subject to removal (e.g., deportation). Smuggling is also often a short-term venture while exploitation through trafficking continues once a victim is in another country. Individuals willingly smuggled into the United States may later become trafficked through forced labor or commercial sexual exploitation. Moreover, victims of human trafficking are considered victims of a federal crime, although individuals who are smuggled into the United States are considered criminals and are subject to deportation. Finally, in the United States, *certified* human trafficking victims are considered crime victims and are entitled to many protections and federal and state support services, including the application for immigration relief granted by the U.S. government.

It is well documented that people who are smuggled across borders are often vulnerable to many types of victimization since smugglers often use deceit, and they may later be exploited by forced labor or commercial sexual exploitation (Bruckert & Parent, 2002; Busch-Armendariz et al., 2013). The exploitation and danger often involved in smuggling should not be understated. These difficult circumstances lead to increased likelihood of physical violence including death, particularly for women. Research indicates a high percentage of victimization of sexual and physical exploitation prior to, during, and post transit (Cook Heffron, 2015).

Differences Between Human Trafficking and Smuggling

Human Trafficking	Smuggling
Must contain an element of force, fraud, or coercion (actual, implied, or perceived)	The person being smuggled is generally cooperating
Forced labor and/or exploitation	There is no actual or implied coercion
Persons are considered victims	Persons who are smuggled are complicit in the smuggling crime; they are not necessarily victims of the smuggling crime, although later become victimized
Enslaved, subjected to limited movement, isolation, or agency	Persons are free to leave, change jobs, etc.
No requirement to cross an international or regional border	Smuggling always involves crossing a border
Person must be involved in labor or services—that is, "working"	Person smuggled may only have crossed the border not necessarily working
The trafficker does not necessarily need to be involved in moving a victim	The smuggler facilitates the illegal entry of person(s) from one country into another

SOURCE: *Distinction Between Human Smuggling and Human Trafficking*, by U.S. Department of State 2006 (http://www.state.gov/m/ds/hstcenter/90434.htm). In the public domain.

NOTE: Chart does not provide a precise legal distinction of the differences between smuggling and trafficking. The chart is designed to illustrate general fact scenarios that are often seen in smuggling or trafficking incidents. Fact scenarios are often complex; in such cases expert legal advice should be sought.

5.11 Responding to Human Trafficking With Policy and Review Processes

In the last decade, worldwide organizations and individual countries have made major efforts to develop, ratify, and operationalize policies that outlaw human trafficking. By 2012, 134 countries and territories worldwide criminalized the exploitation of people congruent with the Trafficking in Persons Protocol (UNODC, 2014). Below, three of these efforts are described (the UN Protocol, the TVPA, and the TIP Report), although many countries and states across the globe have adopted country-specific antitrafficking legislation.

5.12 Palermo Protocol

The Palermo Protocol to Prevent, Suppress, and Punish Trafficking in Persons, Especially Women and Children, Supplementing the United Nations Convention Against Transnational Organized Crime (2000) directed global antitrafficking policy responses. To date, 166 countries have signed on to the United Nation's antitrafficking policy. Simply referred to as the Palermo Protocol, because it was signed in Palermo, Italy, its policy goal is to build a comprehensive international approach toward ending modern slavery. The Palermo Protocol defines human trafficking, recommends service provisions for victims, and focuses on prevention efforts in source, transit, and destination countries (United Nations, 2000).

Countries That Have Not Signed the Palermo Protocol

Bangladesh	Republic of Korea	Singapore
Bhutan	Maldives	Solomon Islands
Brunei	Marshall Islands	Somalia
Comoros	Nepal	South Sudan
Republic of Congo	Pakistan	Sri Lanka
Fiji	Palau	Tonga
Iran	Papua New Guinea	Uganda
Japan		Yemen
Korea (DPRK)		

SOURCE: U.S. Department of State 2015 TIP Report.

5.13 Trafficking Victim's Protection Act (TVPA)

In the United States, in addition to defining modern slavery, the Trafficking Victim's Protection Act (TVPA), signed in 2000 and reauthorized in 2003, 2005,

2008, and 2013, outlines benefits and services for trafficking victims and steps to exclude foreign-born victims from deportation. For child victims, the TVPA states that the standard of force, fraud, or coercion does not have to be met. In other words, children cannot consent to sexual contact, intercourse, or other sexual activities.

5.14 Trafficking in Persons Report (TIP)

The Trafficking in Persons Report (TIP) has been published by the Office to Monitor and Combat Trafficking in Persons of the U.S. Department of State annually since 2001. The TIP Report assesses and scores governmental and countries' efforts to address the crime of human trafficking (Busch-Armendariz et al., 2014) on one of four categories (Tier 1, Tier 2, Tier 2 Watch List, and Tier 3). The higher the tier ranking, the less compliant a country is with the TVPA benchmarks (e.g., Tier 3 countries are the least compliant in their antitrafficking efforts). Tier 1 countries are in full compliance with TVPA; Tier 2 countries are making significant efforts toward compliance; Tier 2 Watch List are making significant efforts toward compliance but have high numbers of victims or have failed to provide evidence of increased efforts; and Tier 3 are not in full compliance and have made no significant efforts to address human trafficking. Ten years after the TIP Report was first published, the U.S. Department of State began to rank the United States. The United States has remained a Tier 1 country since that time (U.S. Department of State, 2015).

6. Calling Attention to Complex Issues or Critical Discourse

6.1 Questioning the Credibility of the United States as the World's Judge: Implications of Delaying Self-Assessment

The United States, through the Department of State and the *Trafficking in Persons Report*, has advanced the global conversation about modern slavery and led efforts to confront countries and industries around the exploitation of human beings perhaps like no other country in the world. The TIP Report itself is an extremely valuable tool for understanding modern slavery. Yet there are issues that emerge about the United States in this position. First, the Department of State did not rank the United States in the *Trafficking in Persons Report* until its tenth publication. Does this delay of self-assessment carry implications for U.S. credibility? Also, it seems reasonable that rather than conduct a self-assessment, the Department of State may earn credibility by engaging other entities to examine the United States' efforts and assign an appropriate ranking. Also, it seems reasonable that neither the United States nor any other government, for that matter, should be the sole and only legitimate evaluator on this issue. Perhaps the field would be better prepared if the process of assigning ranks was shared.

7. Chapter Summary

Chapter 1 serves as a primer and introduction to human trafficking. Many relevant issues about modern-day slavery are covered such as the research on traffickers and needs of victims. This chapter also provides the best knowledge to date on the extent of the problem and a discussion of types of trafficking. The caveat of the chapter is that our full understanding of modern-day slavery is still evolving and, as such, additional research is needed.

8. Key Terms

8.1	Human rights perspective	8.7	Trafficking Victims Protection Act
8.2	Sex trafficking	8.8	Palermo Protocol
8.3	Labor trafficking	8.9	Traffickers
8.4	Modern slavery	8.10	Facilitators
8.5	National Trafficking Resource Center: Polaris	8.11	johns
8.6	Trafficking in Persons Report (TIP)	8.12	Victims/survivors
		8.13	Feminization of poverty

9. Active Learning Exercises or In-Class Discussions

9.1   Ask students to complete the Slavery Footprint before class, found at: http://www.slaveryfootprint.org. In class, have students work in small groups to put their Slavery Footprint scores along a continuum and answer the following questions: What was surprising to you about this educational tool? What are the benefits of the Footprint? Using the Footprint, how might you develop an awareness and educational campaign for your college? What factors may be missing from the Footprint?

9.2   Ask students to discuss the elements of a human rights framework as compared to what Shelley (2010) writes in *Human Trafficking: A Global Perspective*:

Everywhere in the world, the consequences of trafficking are devastating for its victims and the larger community. Those victimized in this open slave market were not only the young women destined for sexual slavery. All of society suffers from such victimization. Other causalities include the principles of a democratic society, the rule of law, and respect of human rights. The degradation of the women in full view of the public deals a direct blow to the rights of women and to gender equality (p. 3).

9.3   Ask students to watch Dr. Kevin Bales's lecture based on his new book *Blood and Earth: Modern Slavery, Ecocide, and the Secret to Saving the World* and consider the juxtaposition between modern-day slavery and environmental destruction. What are the similarities, push-pull factors, causes? What is different? What can be done?

https://www.youtube.com/watch?v=V3P1bDmIPd0

10. Suggestions for Further Learning (Books, Policies, Websites, and Films)

10.1 **Books**

10.1.1 Bales, K. (2012). *Disposal people: New slavery in the global economy.* Berkeley, CA: University of California Press.

10.1.2 Bales, K. (2016). *Blood and earth: Modern slavery, ecocide, and the secret to saving the world.* New York, NY: Spiegel & Grau.

10.1.3 Lloyd, R. (2010). *Girls like us: Fighting for a world where girls are not for sale, an activist finds her calling and heals herself.* New York, NY: HarperCollins.

10.1.4 Shelley, L. (2010). *Human trafficking*: A global perspective. New York, NY: Cambridge University Press.

10.2 **Policies**

10.2.1 Trafficking Victims Protection Act 2000, 2003, 2005, 2008, and 2013.

10.2.2 Also see the TVPA in Five Colors developed by the Protection Project at Johns Hopkins. Retrieved from: http://protectionproject.org/wp-content/uploads/2013/06/TVPA-in-5-Colors_2013_FINAL.pdf

10.2.3 U.S. Department of State. (2015). *Trafficking in persons report (TIP).* Retrieved from http://www.state.gov/g/tip/rls/tiprpt/2015/

10.2.4 United Nations. (1948). *Universal declaration of human rights.* Retrieved from http://www.un.org/en/universal-declaration-human-rights/

10.3 **Selected Websites**

10.3.1 U.S. Department of Health and Human Services, Administration for Children and Families campaign to rescue and restore victims of human trafficking: http://www.acf.hhs.gov/trafficking/index.html

10.3.2 Coalition Against Trafficking in Women: http://www.catwinternational.org

10.3.3 Free the Slaves: http://www.freetheslaves.net

10.3.4 Girls Educational and Mentoring Services: http://www.gems-girls.org/

10.3.5 Polaris: For a World Without Slavery: http://www.polarisproject.org

10.3.6   Shared Hope International http://www.sharedhope.org

10.3.7   Slavery Footprint: http://www.slaveryfootprint.org

10.3.8   UNICEF: http://www.unicef.org

10.3.9   United Nations Office on Drugs and Crime on Human Trafficking and Migrant Smuggling: http://www.unodc.org/unodc/en/human-trafficking/index.html

10.3.10 Human Trafficking Resource: http://humantrafficking.unc.edu/resources/

10.4   **Films**

10.4.1   Rescue and Restore: Look Beneath the Surface: Identifying Victims of Human Trafficking in the U.S. (training video available from the Office on Tracking in Persons URL link: https://www.acf.hhs.gov/otip/resource/look-beneath-the-surface-0)

10.4.2   Dying to Leave: The Dark Business of Human Trafficking (for purchase only, available from http://www.trainingabc.com/dying-to-leave-the-dark-business-of-human-trafficking/)

10.4.3   See website for resources: http://www.endslaverynow.org/blog/articles/lets-talk-about-sex-trafficking-documentaries

11. Suggestions for Further Research/Project/Homework/Exam Exercises

11.1 Slavery Footprint Exercise

Ask students to write to Slavery Footprint to offer suggestions for its improvement for accuracy with college students or inform Slavery Footprint how it is being utilized in class and at your institution of higher education as an educational awareness campaign.

11.2 Using Poetry and Film

Ask students to either read the poem "Minstrel Man" by Langston Hughes or watch the film *Whistleblower* (2010) directed by Bertram Verhaag. Write a reaction paper, reflecting on the following three questions: What is your initial response to this work? What components of human trafficking does this work portray well? Does this work represent something different from what you have learned about human trafficking? How is it effective (or ineffective) in telling its story? How might the current sociopolitical climate or events have played a role in the making of this work?

12. References

Albanese, J., Donnelly, J. S., & Kelegian, T. (2004). Causes of human trafficking in the United States: A content analysis of a calendar year in 18 cities. *International Journal of Comparative Criminology, 4*(1), 96–111.

Alvarez, M. B., & Alessi, E. J. (2012). Human trafficking is more than sex trafficking and prostitution: Implications for social work. *Affilia: Journal of Women & Social Work, 27*(2), 142–152. doi:10.1177/0886109912443763

Bales, K. (2012). *Disposable people: New slavery in the global economy* (3rd ed.). Berkeley, CA: University of California Press.

Banzon, M. Y. L. (2005). Combating trafficking in persons through gender-focused strategy. *UN Chronicle, 42*(1), 56–60.

Bromfield, N. F. (2016). Sex slavery and sex trafficking of women in the United States: Historical and contemporary parallels, policies, and perspectives in social work. *Affilia: Journal of Women & Social Work, 31*(1), 129–139. doi:10.1177/0886109915616437

Bruckert, C., & Parent, C. (2002). *Trafficking in human beings and organized crime: A literature review*. Research and Evaluation Branch Community, Contract and Aboriginal Policing Services Directorate. Royal Canadian Mounted Police. Canada. Retrieved from https://www.ncjrs.gov/App/Publications/abstract.aspx?ID=205725

Busch, N. B., Fong, R., Heffron, L. C., Faulkner, M., & Mahapatra, N. (2007). *Assessing the needs of human trafficking victims: An evaluation of the Central Texas Coalition Against Human Trafficking*. Retrieved from The Institute on Domestic Violence and Sexual Assault website: http://sites.utexas.edu/idvsa/publications/technical-reports/trafficking-2007.pdf

Busch-Armendariz, N., Nsonwu, M., & Cook Heffron, L. (2009). *Understanding human trafficking: Development of typologies of traffickers phase II*. Paper presented at the First Annual Interdisciplinary Conference on Human Trafficking, Lincoln, NE. Retrieved from The Institute on Domestic Violence and Sexual Assault website: http://sites.utexas.edu/idvsa/publications/technical-reports/

Busch-Armendariz, N. B., Nsonwu, M. B., & Cook Heffron, L. (2011). Human trafficking victims and their children: Assessing needs, vulnerabilities, strengths, and survivorship. *Journal of Applied Research on Children: Informing Policy for Children at Risk, 2*(1), 3.

Busch-Armendariz, N., Nsonwu, M., Cook Heffron, L., & Mahapatra, N. (2013). Trafficking in persons. In J. L. Postmus (Ed.), *Sexual violence and abuse: An encyclopedia of prevention, impacts, and recovery*. Santa Barbara, CA: ABC-CLIO.

Busch-Armendariz, N.B., Nsonwu, M., Cook Heffron, L. & Mahapatra, N. (2014). Human trafficking: exploiting labor. In C. Franklin (Ed.), *Encyclopedia of Social Work Online*. New York City, NY: Oxford University Press.

Busch-Armendariz, N.B., Nsonwu, M.B., & Cook Heffron, L. (2014). A Kaleidoscope: The role of the social work practitioner and the strength of social work theories and practice in meeting the complex needs of people trafficked and the professionals that work with them. *International Social Work, 57*(1), 7–18.

Central Texas Coalition Against Human Trafficking (CTCAHT) & Refugee Services of Texas, Inc. (2010). *Human trafficking: What the medical community should know*. August 6th 2010 (p.8). Retrieved June 30, 2016 from http://www.health.pa.gov/migra3on/Documents/vic3m_traf_08_2010_pdf

Clawson, H., & Dutch, N. (2008). *Identifying victims of human trafficking: Inherent challenges and promising strategies from the field*. Washington, DC: Office of the Assistant Secretary for Planning and Evaluation (ASPE). Retrieved from http://aspe.hhs.gov/hsp/07/HumanTrafficking/

Clawson, H., Layne, M., & Small, K. (2006). *Estimating human trafficking into the States: Development of a methodology*. Washington, DC: National Institute of Justice. Retrieved from https://www.ncjrs.gov/pdffiles1/nij/grants/215475.pdf

Cook Heffron, L. (2015). *"Salía de uno y me metí en otro:" A grounded theory approach to understanding the violence-migration nexus among Central American women in the United States* (Unpublished doctoral dissertation). University of Texas, Austin, TX.

Development Services Group, Inc. (2014). *Commercial sexual exploitation of children/sex trafficking*. Washington, DC: Office of Juvenile Justice and Delinquency Prevention. Retrieved from http://www.ojjdp.gov/mpg/litreviews/CSECSexTrafficking.pdf

End Slavery Now. (2017). Global Business Coalition Against Trafficking (gBCAT) Mission. Retrieved from http://www.endslaverynow.org/global-business-coalition-against-trafficking

Feingold, D. A. (2005). Human trafficking. *Foreign Policy, 150*, 26–30.

Finklea, K., Fernandes-Alcantara, A.L., & Siskin, A. (2015, January 28). *Sex Trafficking of children in the United States: Overview and issues for Congress* (CRS Report No. R41878) . Retrieved from Congressional Research Service. https://fas.org/sgp/crs/misc/R41878.pdf

Healy, L. M. (2008). Exploring the history of social work as a human rights profession. *International Social Work, 51*(6), 735–748.

Hepburn, S., & Simon, R. (2010). Hidden in plain sight: Human trafficking in the United States. *Gender Issues, 27*(1/2), 1–26. doi:10.1007/s12147–010–9087–7

International Institute for Strategic Studies (IISS). (2015). Armed Conflict Database. ACD Index Latest Figures. Retrieved from http://acd.iiss.org/

International Labour Organization (ILO). (2012). *ILO global estimate of forced labour: Results and methodology*. Retrieved from http://www.ilo.org/global/topics/forced-labour/publications/WCMS_182004/lang--en/index.htm

International Labour Organization. (2014). *Profits and poverty: The economics of forced labour*. Retrieved from Geneva, Switzerland: http://www.ilo.org/global/topics/forced-labour/publications/profits-of-forced-labour-2014/lang--en/index.htm

Jac-Kucharski, A. (2012). The determinants of human trafficking: A US case study. *International Migration, 50*(6), 150–165. doi:10.1111/j.1468–2435.2012.00777.x

Kappelhoff, M. J. (2011). Federal prosecutions of human trafficking cases: Striking a blow against modern day slavery. *University of St. Thomas Law Journal, 6*(1), 3.

Kim, K. (2011). The coercion of trafficked workers. *Iowa Law Review, 96*(2), 409–474.

Leary, M. (2014). Fighting fire with fire: Technology in child sex trafficking. *Duke Journal of Gender Law & Policy, 21*(2).

Lloyd, R. (2011). *Girls like us: Fighting for a world where girls are not for sale, an activist finds her calling and heals herself* (1st ed.). New York, NY: HarperCollins.

Lusk, M., & Lucas, F. (2009). The challenge of human trafficking and contemporary slavery. *Journal of Comparative Social Welfare, 25*(1), 49–57. doi:10.1080/17486830802514049

Lutnick, A. (2016). *Domestic minors sex trafficking: Beyond victims and villains*. New York, NY: Columbia University Press.

Macy, R. J., & Graham, L. M. (2012). Identifying domestic and international sex-trafficking victims during human service provision. *Trauma, Violence, & Abuse, 13*(2), 59–76. doi:10.1177/1524838012440340

National Association of Social Workers (NASW). (2017). Media Room. Social Justice. Retrieved from http://www.naswdc.org/pressroom/features/issue/peace.asp

National Center for Homeless Education. (2014). *Sex trafficking of minors: What schools need to know to recognize and respond to the trafficking of students.* Retrieved from http://center .serve.org/nche/downloads/briefs/trafficking.pdf

Novak, M., & Adams, P. (2015). *Social justice isn't what you think it is.* New York, NY: Encounter Books.

Office of the Assistant Secretary for Planning and Evaluation. (2009, August 30). *Human trafficking into and within the United States: A review of the literature.* Retrieved from https:// aspe.hhs.gov/pdf-report/human-trafficking-and-within-united-states-review-literature

Office of the High Commissioner for Human Rights. (2002, May 20). *Recommended principles and guidelines on human rights and human trafficking.* Retrieved from http://www.ohchr .org/Documents/Publications/Traffickingen.pdf

Office of the High Commissioner for Human Rights. (2014). *Human rights and human trafficking* [Fact sheet No. 36]. Retrieved from http://www.ohchr.org/EN/PublicationsResources/ Pages/FactSheets.aspx

Panigabutra-Roberts, A. (2012). Human trafficking in the United States. Part I. State of the knowledge. *Behavioral & Social Sciences Librarian, 31*(3–4), 138–151. doi:10.1080/01639 269.2012.736330

Pimpin Ken, & Hunter, K. (2007). *Pimpology: The 48 laws of the game.* New York, NY: Simon Spotlight Entertainment.

Polaris. (2014). *A look back: Building a human trafficking legal framework.* Retrieved from https:// polarisproject.org/sites/default/files/2014-Look-Back.pdf

Polaris. (2015a). *Sex trafficking in the U.S.: A closer look at U.S. citizen victims.* Retrieved from https://polarisproject.org/resources/sex-trafficking-us-closer-look-us-citizen-victims

Polaris. (2015b). *2015 statistics.* Retrieved from http://polarisproject.org/sites/default/files/2015- Statistics.pdf

Polaris. (2016). *Recognize the signs.* Retrieved from http://polarisproject.org/recognize-signs

Polaris. (2016, January 28). *2015 human trafficking hotlines data released* [Press release]. Retrieved from https://polarisproject.org/news/press-releases/2015-human-trafficking- hotlines-data-released

Research Triangle Institute (RTI), Child Trends, & Pacific Institute for Research and Evaluation (PIRE). (2002). *Sexual abuse among homeless adolescents: Prevalence, correlates, and sequelae.* Retrieved from http://www.acf.hhs.gov/sites/default/files/opre/sex_ abuse_hmless.pdf

Rodriguez, J. (2016, February 4). *The Ice Cream (or "Paletero") Man Deserves Fair Pay, Too.* [Blog Post]. Retrieved from https://blog.dol.gov/search/node/Paletero

Ryder, G. (2015, December 2). International day for abolition of slavery: A video statement by Guy Ryder ILO Director-General [Video file]. Retrieved from http://www.ilo.org/global/about- the-ilo/multimedia/video/video-interviews/WCMS_431705/lang--en/index.htm

Shared Hope International. (2015). *Protected innocence challenge: A legal framework of protection for the nation's children.* Retrieved from http://sharedhope.org/wp-content/uploads/ 2015/11/PIC2015REPORT2.pdf

Shelley, L. (2010). *Human trafficking: A global perspective.* New York, NY: Cambridge University Press.

Shively, M., Kliorys, K., Wheeler, K., & Hunt, D. (2012). *A national overview of prostitution and sex trafficking demand reduction efforts* (NCJ No. 238796). Washington, DC: The National Institute of Justice. Retrieved from https://www.ncjrs.gov/App/Publications/abstract .aspx?ID=260851

Shively, M., Kuck-Jalbert, S., Kling, R., Rhodes, W., Finn, P., Flyage, C., . . . Wheeler, K. (2008). *Final report on the evaluation of the First Offender Prostitution Program* (NCJ No. 222451).

Washington, DC: National Institute of Justice. Retrieved from https://www.ncjrs.gov/pdffiles1/nij/grants/222451.pdf

Smith, L., Healy Vardaman, S., & Snow, M. (2009). *The national report on domestic minor sex trafficking: America's prostituted children.* Retrieved from https://sharedhope.org/product/the-national-report-on-domestic-minor-sex-trafficking/

Trafficking Victims Protection Act of 2000, Pub. L. No. 106–386, 114 Stat. 1464 (2000).

Trafficking Victims Protection Reauthorization Act, Pub. L. No. 108–193 (2003).

Trafficking Victims Protection Reauthorization Act, 22 USC § 7104 (2005).

Trafficking Victims Protection Reauthorization Act, 22 USC § 7311 (2008).

Trafficking Victims Protection Reauthorization Act of 2013, 22 USC § 7109 (2013).

United Nations. (1948, December 10). *The universal declaration of human rights.* Retrieved from the United Nations website: http://www.un.org/en/universal-declaration-human-rights/

United Nations. (1979). *Convention on the elimination of all forms of discrimination against women.* (1249 U.N.T.S. 13). Retrieved from http://www.un.org/womenwatch/daw/cedaw/

United Nations. (1989). *Convention on the rights of the child* (1577 U.N.T.S. 3.). Retrieved from http://www.ohchr.org/en/professionalinterest/pages/crc.aspx

United Nations. (2000). *Protocol to prevent, suppress and punish trafficking in persons, especially women and children, supplementing the United Nations convention against transnational organized crime.* Retrieved from http://www.refworld.org/docid/4720706c0.html

United Nations Office of Drugs and Crime. (2006, April). *Trafficking in persons: Global patterns.* Retrieved from http://www.unodc.org/pdf/traffickinginpersons_report_2006-04.pdf

United Nations Office on Drugs and Crime. (2012a). *A comprehensive strategy to combat trafficking in persons and smuggling of migrants.* Retrieved from https://www.unodc.org/documents/human-trafficking/UNODC_Strategy_on_Human_Trafficking_and_Migrant_Smuggling.pdf

United Nations Office on Drugs and Crime. (2012b). *Global report on trafficking in persons* Retrieved from https://www.unodc.org/documents/data-and-analysis/glotip/Trafficking_in_Persons_2012_web.pdf

United Nations Office on Drugs and Crime. (2013). *Transnational organized crime in East Asia and the Pacific: A threat assessment.* Retrieved from https://www.unodc.org/documents/data-and-analysis/Studies/TOCTA_EAP_web.pdf

United Nations Office on Drugs and Crime. (2014). *Global report on trafficking in persons.* Retrieved from https://www.unodc.org/documents/data-and-analysis/glotip/GLOTIP_2014_full_report.pdf

U.S. Department of State. (2006). *Distinction between human smuggling and human trafficking* [Fact sheet]. Retrieved from http://www.state.gov/documents/organization/90541.pdf

U.S. Department of State. (2013). *Trafficking in persons report.* Retrieved from http://www.state.gov/documents/organization/210737.pdf

U.S. Department of State. (2015). *Trafficking in persons report.* Retrieved from http://www.state.gov/j/tip/rls/tiprpt/2015/

Verité. (2015, January). *Strengthening protections against trafficking in persons in federal and corporate supply chains.* Retrieved from http://www.verite.org/sites/default/files/images/Verite-Executive_Order_13627.pdf

Walk Free Foundation. (2016). *The global slavery index 2016 report.* Retrieved from http://www.globalslaveryindex.org/download/

Wolfer, T. A., & Scales, T. L. (2006). Decision cases for advanced social work practice: thinking like a social worker. Belmont, CA: Thomson Brooks/Cole.

Zimmerman, Y. C. (2013). *Other dreams of freedom: Religion, sex, and human trafficking.* New York, NY: Oxford University Press.

Understanding the Context of History

I. Learning Objectives

1.1 Students will be introduced to early historical accounts of slavery and indentured servitude to understand its connection with modern-day slavery.

1.2 Students will become familiar with the trans-Saharan slave trade and its relation to the Americas.

1.3 Students will understand the historical timeline of various enslaved peoples in the Americas.

1.4 Students will become knowledgeable about the resilience of enslaved peoples by learning about the Underground Railroad and maroon communities.

1.5 Students will be introduced to the concept of the African Colonization of enslaved peoples.

1.6 Students will become familiar with legislation that impacted slavery such as the Emancipation Proclamation, Black Codes, and the Reconstruction Amendments.

1.7 Students will be introduced to significant time periods that influenced human rights and social change such as the Jim Crow era and the civil rights era.

2. Key Ideas

These ideas are central to this chapter.

2.1 Understanding that human trafficking requires a historical analysis rooted in earlier contexts of slavery.

2.2 Historical advocacy and social justice efforts aimed to abolish slavery offer a blueprint for modern-day abolition efforts in combating modern-day slavery.

2.3 There are similarities and differences in history that contextualize modern-day slavery. The similarities stem from capitalist and inhuman perspectives about human beings.

3. Scientific Knowledge/Literature

Figure 2.1 *Exchanging citizens for horses.*

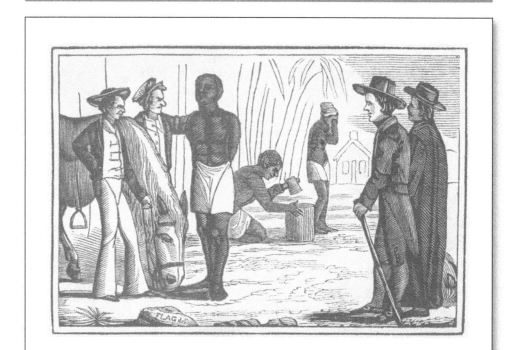

SOURCE: Schomburg Center for Research in Black Culture, Manuscripts, Archives and Rare Books Division, The New York Public Library. (1834). Retrieved from http://digitalcollections.nypl.org/items/510d47da-75b5-a3d9-e040-e00a18064a99. In the public domain.

3.1 Historical Slavery and Human Trafficking

This section describes the history of slavery and human trafficking in the United States and its cultural, political, and social backdrop. It illustrates the introduction of slave labor and indentured servitude to the Americas, struggles for freedom and emancipation, the experience of Reconstruction and Jim Crow, the struggle for civil and human rights, the role of recent labor organization, and constitutional and recent legislative history. Victim resistance and resilience emphasizing both individual and collective strengths of the victims in the face of the historical atrocities of slavery are addressed. Finally, an analysis of the implications of this history is discussed to more fully understand the contemporary problem of human trafficking. Although there are differences in history that contextualize modern-day slavery, an awareness of the similarities and an appreciation of historical advocacy and social justice efforts aimed to abolish slavery offer a blueprint for modern-day abolition efforts in combating modern-day slavery.

3.2 Early Historical Accounts

Slavery has existed within human societies whenever individuals, communities, and governments have violently controlled and exploited others. To better understand the nature of human trafficking, a contemporary social evil, one must examine its ties to historical slavery. Slavery has existed over time, milieu, and across multiple cultures, perpetuated by agents who have coerced and corrupted marginalized people. In fact, Genesis, the first book of the Old Testament, recounts the story of Joseph sold by his brothers to slave merchants and ultimately into servitude in Egypt; biblical scholars estimate Joseph's enslavement between 1800 and 2000 BCE. Later historical accounts of slavery in Africa date to the 7th century CE.

An historical overview of the trans-Saharan slave trade and indentured servitude in the Americas will be briefly introduced in this chapter to set a broader global context of slavery, however, this chapter will focus primarily on an analysis of human trafficking in the United States and will link historical slavery with current modern-day slavery.

3.3 Trans-Saharan Slave Trade and the Americas

Historical accounts of slavery in Africa date to the period between 610 CE and 733 CE, as developing trading routes facilitated the commerce of goods and people between the Moors and West Africans. Davis (2001) asserts, "black Africans never looked upon one another as a homogeneous African 'race'. Most tribes and kingdoms were accustomed to a variety of forms of servitude, and developed highly sophisticated methods for recruiting and bartering slaves for coveted commodities" (p. 64). Since there was not a pan-African identity at this point in history, people viewed themselves as Ashanti, Ibo, Yoruba, and so on. African societies used enslaved peoples as political and economic pawns. Slaves could also be war captives later adopted as kin to replace

Figure 2.2 *Slave traders branding an African woman at the Rio Pongo (in Guinea, West Africa).*

SOURCE: Schomburg Center for Research in Black Culture, Manuscripts, Archives and Rare Books Division, The New York Public Library. (1854). Retrieved from http://digitalcollections.nypl.org/items/4a47ac10–2658–0132–7bc8–58d385a7b928. In the public domain.

deceased relatives. As a result of this chattel slavery, many African slaves were transported to Portugal and Spain; these two countries became the primary agents in the lucrative trans-Saharan slave trade of the 900–1500 CE time period (Smallwood & Elliot, 1998). "As many as 4 million West African slaves were sold to North Africa, Morocco, Egypt, Southern Europe (Portugal, Spain), the Middle East (Persia), and Southwestern Asia (India)" (Smallwood & Elliot, 1998, p. 7). In 1482, the Portuguese established new trading settlements on "Africa's Gold Coast," where slaves were exchanged for ironware, firearms, and textiles.

Figure 2.3 *Slave traders marching their captives to the coast, butchering disabled ones along the way.*

SOURCE: Schomburg Center for Research in Black Culture, Jean Blackwell Hutson Research and Reference Division, The New York Public Library. (1903–1902). Retrieved from http://digitalcollections .nypl.org/items/510d47de-1c15-a3d9-e040-e00a18064a99. In the public domain.

In the late 1400s, as Columbus explored the Caribbean islands and the Americas, he was accompanied by African soldiers. These freed soldiers and seamen had previously been integrated into Portugal and Spain as a result of these two countries' immersion with the West African slave trade as well as their connection with North African Muslims (Smallwood & Elliot, 1998). In their exploration and colonization of the Caribbean and the Americas, the Spanish recognized that sugar, tobacco, and cotton plantations were a profitable commerce but necessitated an inexpensive labor force; therefore they turned to slave labor. Initially, the Spanish enslaved the native population but found that they quickly died from being overtaxed and exposed to foreign (European) diseases; the Spanish later focused on importing slaves from West Africa as this population was viewed as physically stronger and more resilient to contracting infections. Smallwood and Elliott (1998) report that "the Spanish were the first Europeans to practice African slavery in the Americas" (p. 13) but were followed by the Portuguese, Dutch, French, and English as these countries began to recognize how financially profitable the institution of slavery could be to their economies.

Africans were enslaved after being captured in warfare with other West African nations. Some slaves were captured as lawbreakers, but others were simply innocent

Figure 2.4 *Schematic drawing of an English slave ship, possibly the Brookes, showing the layout of the cargo hold areas for transporting African slaves.*

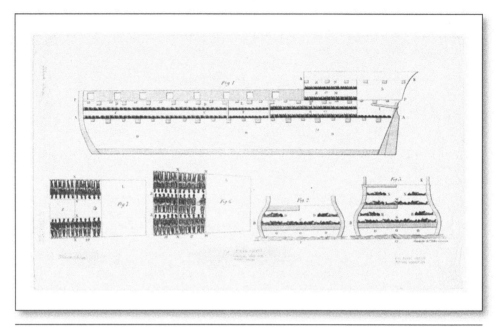

SOURCE: Schomburg Center for Research in Black Culture, Photographs and Prints Division, The New York Public Library. (1839). Retrieved from http://digitalcollections.nypl.org/items/ea7997f0–2657–0132–1964–58d385a7b928. In the public domain.

victims of kidnapping into chattel slavery. Irrespective of the basis of their captivity, all slaves were ultimately subjected to the harrowing transoceanic "middle passage" to the Western Hemisphere after forcibly being brought to the African coast and processed as an economic commodity through well-organized trading posts called "factories" (Howe, 2007). Davis (2001) reports that "West Africa offered a cheap and seemingly unlimited supply of slave labor, and the efforts of African kings to stop the ruinous sale of subjects were few and ineffective" (p. 64). The slave trade began to expand globalization, what Birnbaum and Taylor (2000) contend as "the integration of the far corners of the world into a single, expanding global capital system" (p. 7).

3.4 The Enslavement of People in the Americas

In 1619, 20 African indentured servants arrived in Jamestown, Virginia—America's first permanent English colony (Lee, 2012). These indentured servants from Africa were most likely captured by the Portuguese. Slaves would later replace indentured servants in providing labor to the Americas. Indentured servitude was a system

Figure 2.5 *The lash.*

SOURCE: Schomburg Center for Research in Black Culture, Manuscripts, Archives and Rare Books Division, The New York Public Library. (1864). Retrieved from http://digitalcollections.nypl.org/items/510d47da-75e7-a3d9-e040-e00a18064a99. In the public domain.

of labor that allowed a poor person to enter a work contract for a defined amount of time, typically years, in exchange for their passage to the New World. Between 1620 and 1775, a large number of people were ousted from Great Britain to the American colonies to become White slaves or indentured servants. In 1618, poor Irish and English children from London were either sent to the United States by their parents in the hope that they would be cared for or forcibly deported by government officials who wanted to rid the city of "troublesome urchins" (Jordan & Walsh, 2008, p. 12). These children and the family members whom they left behind were duped into thinking that they would learn a trade and become apprentices in Virginia. However, the real intention was to have these youngsters work the fields, being held as chattel; "half of them were dead within a year" (Jordan & Walsh, 2008, p. 13). Another 50,000 to 70,000 adult White slaves who were either convicts, panhandlers, prostitutes, or viewed as outcasts or nonconformists were expelled from England to America and Barbados where they would often face a life of enslavement (Jordan & Walsh, 2008). Others were forcibly deported and sold into servitude after being kidnapped by gangs who profited from this trade. The Irish were also forced abroad to live in slavery as England created an ethnic-cleansing policy in Ireland under Cromwell's rule. Another 300,000 people

Figure 2.6 *A slave auction in Virginia.*

SOURCE: Schomburg Center for Research in Black Culture, Photographs and Prints Division, The New York Public Library. (1861). Retrieved from http://digitalcollections.nypl.org/items/510d47db-c062-a3d9-e040-e00a18064a99. In the public domain.

willingly became indentured servants during this century, hoping to escape a life of poverty but often facing the same fate as slaves from Africa, as they were held in bondage (Jordan & Walsh, 2008).

From 1641 to 1750, slavery was legalized in 10 colonies—Massachusetts, Virginia, Maryland, New York, New Jersey, South Carolina, Rhode Island, Pennsylvania, North Carolina, and Georgia. The forced migration of large numbers of enslaved peoples changed the demographic landscape of the New World. It was widely assumed that slavery was crucial to the colony's economic development and "challenges to its moral legitimacy were rare" (Howe, 2007, p. 52). The mainstream culture during the colonial time period supported slavery and was maintained through legislation; this practice differs from modern-day slavery, where this practice is outlawed despite its pervasiveness around the world. During this time period, Virginia passed a law stating that slavery followed the condition of the mother (*partus sequitur ventrem*—a Latin phrase meaning "that which is brought forth follows the womb"). Other British American colonies later followed suit. This law was a change from English common law, which stated that the child's condition followed the father. This law perpetuated slavery in Virginia (and elsewhere); enslaved women could only produce enslaved progeny, no matter the father's status. Slavery, therefore, became a hereditary condition. Moreover, slave owners could increase their workforce by sexually assaulting and raping enslaved women without fear of punishment. Female slaves experienced brutal cruelty and domination from their slave owners as they were twice objectified; one as an agent to work for their master (synonymous to labor trafficking) and another to provide a sustained workforce by bearing future slaves (tantamount to sex trafficking).

However, some groups such as the Quakers of Germantown, Pennsylvania, did oppose this ideology, signing a petition in 1688 that declared that slavery was antithetical to Christian teachings and principles (Drescher & Engerman, 1998; Klein, 2002). Further advocacy to abolish slavery was continued by the Quakers into the 1700s as they took a moral stand against enslavement, voting in 1758 to exclude members of their Philadelphia Society of Friends who traded in slaves (Klein, 2002). The Quakers were the minority in enacting legislation that challenged social justice issues when many other jurisdictions and groups during that time period condoned slavery and its oppressive views. During the colonial times and the end of the Revolutionary War, independent colonies and states enacted laws to regulate and control slaves.

The 1740 South Carolina Negro Act is an example of legalization that excluded legal protection for slaves. With these restrictions on enslaved people, this act also solidified the idea that people of African descent were viewed as chattel, or property. This act also prohibited teaching slaves how to read or write. In 1787, there were proslavery compromises that sanctioned slavery in three places in the Constitutional Convention, and the Fugitive Slave Acts of 1793 and 1850 allowed slave owners the right to legally arrest, capture, and return people who attempted to flee enslavement; these laws also prosecuted individuals who aided runaways (Berry, 2000; Rodriguez, 2007). During this time period, enslaved African Americans fought on both sides of the Revolutionary War as both the American and English armies conscripted these bondsmen, promising them freedom for their allegiance when their side won (Howe, 2007).

Belief systems regarding slavery began to change during the Revolution as it "popularized Enlightenment ideas, synthesized them with elements of Christianity, and summed them up in the affirmation that 'all men are created equal,' in that all possess 'unalienable rights'" (Howe, 2007, p. 52). Despite this philosophical shift, except for a small number of abolitionists, "virtually no white Americans before 1860 believed in equality before the law irrespective of race. And on the eve of the Civil War no state accorded blacks the same rights as whites" (Froner, 2000, p. 103). Nevertheless, antislavery sentiments began to develop in northern states; New York implemented the Gradual Emancipation act for enslaved peoples born after July 4, 1799. Males could become free at age 28 and females at age 25; this act essentially indentured formally enslaved young people. In 1808, the U.S. Congress abolished the Transatlantic Slave Trade; however, approximately 1.2 million Africans continued to be enslaved in spite

Figure 2.7 *Selling females by the pound.*

SOURCE: Schomburg Center for Research in Black Culture, Manuscripts, Archives and Rare Books Division, The New York Public Library. (1834). Retrieved from http://digitalcollections.nypl.org/items/510d47da-75b1-a3d9-e040-e00a18064a99. In the public domain.

of this legislation. In 1815, 1.4 million captives were "held in hereditary slavery" (Howe, 2007, p. 52) out of a population of 8.4 million people in the United States. By 1820, more people had come to the Western Hemisphere as enslaved captives than the total of all other groups of "voluntary white immigrants and indentured white servants" (Davis, 2001, p. 64).

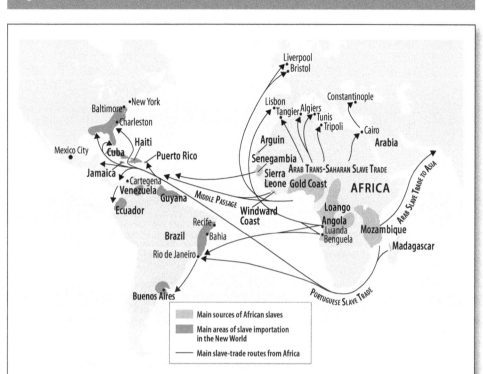

Figure 2.8 *Slave Trade Routes, 1518–1850.*

SOURCE: Introduction to sociology (p. 318), by George Ritzer, 2013, Thousand Oaks, CA: SAGE Publications. Copyright 2013 by SAGE Publications. Reprinted with permission.

3.5 Slave Resistance/Revolts, Underground Railroad, and Maroon Communities

For generations, groups of individuals held in bondage have been able to successfully resist enslavement, revolt against oppression, or escape captivity, demonstrating the ingenuity and resilience of victims. Most of the time, enslaved peoples attempted to risk fleeing confinement, hopeful that they would eventually gain freedom, rather than jeopardize fighting their captors as this was viewed as particularly dangerous due to the inequitable power differential inherent in slavery. The Underground Railroad is an example of resistance to forced labor as it demonstrates a collective effort to subvert the power and control exerted by institutional slavery. Maroon communities also exemplified resistance toward bondage and illustrated a shared or cooperative endeavor of enslaved peoples to work together to gain their autonomy; sometimes maroon communities participated in revolts toward their oppressor in order to gain their freedom. Whether enslaved individuals chose to flee or fight, it was their enduring struggle for freedom, pride, and self-possession that propelled them forward. Thompson (2006) asserts the significance of valuing the

Figure 2.9 *Hon. Frederick Douglass.*

SOURCE: Schomburg Center for Research in Black Culture, Jean Blackwell Hutson Research and Reference Division, The New York Public Library. (1903–1902). Retrieved from http://digitalcollections .nypl.org/items/510d47de-1c2d-a3d9-e040-e00a18064a99. In the public domain.

history of maroon communities in that it recognizes "the struggle of African peoples in the Americas to achieve human dignity in the face of great adversity" (p. 2).

The Underground Railroad was not a formal organization; it was "a loose network of people who attempted to move enslaved fugitives to and from safe places in a quick and largely secretive manner" (Johnson, 2012, p. 311). Various abolitionists, many of them former slaves, such as Frederick Douglass, Harriet Tubman, and William Still, took part in facilitating the successful escape of slaves (Bales, 2000; Gara, 1997). Slaves, or "cargo" (code word to keep their effort covert), who fled to the North via the Underground Railroad utilized the support of "conductors" who helped guide them to secure passage to "safe houses" or "stations" until they could find permanent safety in Northern cities, Canada, or Mexico. An estimated 100,000 enslaved peoples were able to make their freedom through the Underground Railroad (Johnson, 2012; Smallwood & Elliot, 1998). Additionally, there were many other enslaved African Americans during this time period who did not utilize the Underground Railroad system but were able to make their way to freedom on their own accord (Gara, 1997) as "self-liberated slaves" (Krauthamer, 2009). Both groups risked the threat of physical violence, severe punishment, and reenslavement as there were well-organized teams of slave catchers eager to receive payment for returning runaways to their slave owners (Foner, 2015; Johnson, 2012). Since the price of a slave was a considerable investment, "a person sold into slavery in 1850 in the United States cost more than $1000, roughly equivalent to $50,000 today"(Lusk & Lucas, 2009, p. 51), the slave owner viewed the slave and the potential labor that he/she could provide as a long-term asset (Bales, 2012). Therefore, the impetus to suppress slave resistance or revolts was high as it impacted the slave owners, "capital."

In the 1500s and 1600s, some enslaved peoples throughout the Caribbean, the Americas, and the United States resisted slavery and escaped from their plantations. These fugitives, referred to as maroons, hid away in the mountainous regions of South America and the Caribbean where survival was especially challenging due to the semitropical locations (Terborg-Penn, 2012). Groups of maroons were established in the Americas during the 1770s and 1780s as slaves living in the low country were able to flee into swamps and safely hide in heavily forested and fauna environments, many times assisted by Native American Indians. These runaway

Figure 2.10 *"Underground" routes to Canada.*

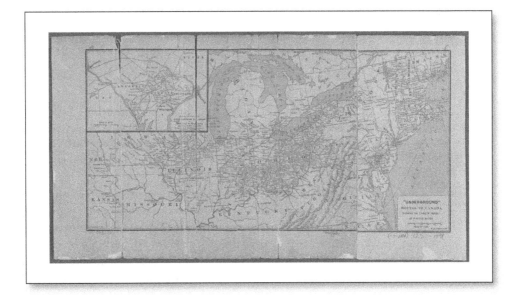

SOURCE: Lionel Pincus and Princess Firyal Map Division, The New York Public Library. (1898). Retrieved from http://digitalcollections.nypl.org/items/d64f0a80–4db6–0133–78eb-00505686d14e. In the public domain.

Figure 2.11 *Map showing the distribution of the slave population of the southern states of the United States.*

SOURCE: Schomburg Center for Research in Black Culture, Jean Blackwell Hutson Research and Reference Division, The New York Public Library. (1861). Retrieved from http://digitalcollections.nypl.org/items/43876320-faf6-0131-8025-58d385a7b928. In the public domain.

slaves created "maroon communities," self-contained societies composed of Indian, Black, or a combination of Indian and Black communities that provided shelter and protection from recapture. These communities created their own cultures, economies, and governments that were uniquely distinct depending on their location and time in history (Smallwood & Elliot, 1998). Most often, slaves fled rather than fought as the most successful form of resistance; however, some groups of maroons were fierce warriors, such as the Black Seminoles, who utilized guerilla warfare to defend their community and retain freedom (Klein, 2002; Terborg-Penn, 2012). In order to regain power and property, European armies in the 1500s and later slave owners intent on bringing escaped, enslaved peoples back to their plantations, would enlist Indians and other Blacks as "Rangers" or slave catchers to destroy maroon communities. The Rangers were skillful in understanding the methods of the maroons and their guerrilla tactics.

Enslaved individuals continued their resistance until 1888 as slavery was finally abolished in the Western Hemisphere when Brazil formally ceased this practice, passing what is commonly known as the "Golden Law" (Smallwood & Elliot, 1998; The New York Public Library & Schomburg Center for Research in Black Culture, 1999). At this point, existing maroon communities varied in size; some were small and composed of individuals or small groups of runaways who may have been forced back to enslavement or were able to remain independent; other maroon societies were larger self-contained communities (Klein, 2002). By then "more than one hundred maroon communities were established in the mountains, swamps and bayous of the United States" (Smallwood & Elliot, 1998, p. 47). Notable sites included the Great Dismal Swamp located at the northeastern border of North Carolina and Virginia, the Florida Everglades, and the Louisiana bayous; with the African state of Palmares housing significant numbers of maroon communities. Many of those communities continued to exist into the 20th century (Smallwood & Elliot, 1998).

Figure 2.12 *Emily runs away.*

SOURCE: Schomburg Center for Research in Black Culture, Jean Blackwell Hutson Research and Reference Division, The New York Public Library. (1940). Retrieved from http://digitalcollections.nypl.org/items/510d47dc-9f95-a3d9-e040-e00a18064a99. In the public domain.

Maroons or former slaves strategically positioned their communities in swamp-lands, jungles, or the mountain terrain to guard against intruders, fiercely defending their region with paramilitary tactics and organizing armies (Smallwood & Elliot, 1998). This secluded environment offered both dangerous and beneficial living conditions to the runaway slaves as it housed alligators, water moccasins, and rattlesnakes that posed physical risks but would also deter potential intruders (Diouf, 2014; Harris & Berry, 2014). The maroon communities were typically self-sufficient and relied on fishing, hunting, and farming for sustainment; however, some groups survived through "an illegal trade maintained with whites living on the borders of the swamps" (Terborg-Penn, 2012, p. 192). Many maroons or fugitive slaves were embraced by Native American communities who "accepted them as members of their nations; in some cases Africans and their descendants rose to become warriors, chiefs, and even great shamans" (Smallwood & Elliot, 1998, p. 19). Seminole tribes from Florida were a combination of a branch of Creek Indians and a Black maroon community and provided refuge for runaway slaves (Diouf, 2014; Franklin & Schweninger, 1999; Howe, 2007; Klein, 2002). Other maroon communities were led chiefly by women warriors. Accounts of warfare have been noted in Cabarrus County, North Carolina, in 1811 and in Princess Anne County, Virginia, in 1818 where women were the primary leaders of this resistance movement (Terborg-Penn, 2012).

The Southern African NGO Network (SANGONeT):

Southern Africa

http://www.ngopulse.org/about
SANGONeT was founded in 1987. Over the past 28 years, SANGONeT has developed into a dynamic civil society organization (CSO) with a history closely linked to the social and political changes experienced by South Africa during its transition to democracy. SANGONeT is still one of very few nongovernmental organizations (NGOs) in Africa involved in the field of information communication technologies (ICTs) and continues to serve civil society with a wide range of ICT products and services.

African Commission on Human and Peoples' Rights

Africa

http://www.achpr.org/about/
The African Charter established the African Commission on Human and Peoples' Rights. The Commission was inaugurated on November 2, 1987, in Addis Ababa, Ethiopia. The Commission's Secretariat has subsequently been located in Banjul, The Gambia. In addition to performing any other tasks which may be entrusted to it by the Assembly of Heads of State and Government, the Commission is officially charged with three major functions:

The protection of human and peoples' rights

The promotion of human and peoples' rights

The interpretation of the African Charter on Human and Peoples' Rights

3.6 African Colonization of Enslaved Peoples

In 1816, Paul Cuffe, the son of a West African father and Wampanoag Native Indian mother, and captain of the vessel *Traveller*, brought 38 free African Americans to Sierra Leone, Senegal, and the Congo to begin a new life in Africa. Cuff's intentions to travel to Africa differed from White emancipators and slaveholders who supported the repatriation of free African Americans during that time period. Cuff had a desire to connect freed Africans with their ancestral homeland; he also had benevolent feelings that were rooted in Christian beliefs. The forced removal or colonization (depending on one's viewpoint) of freed African Americans to Africa was viewed positively from opposing sides of the slavery debate. This was because the idea of free Blacks in America was seen as problematic. Slavery proponents regarded this option as desirable because it addressed their fear of revolts and reprisals from people whom they had formally enslaved; antislavery advocates had contradictory beliefs, hoping that the African colonization movement would curb slavery, but they also had concerns about the "Africanization" of America (Forbes, 1998).

Some free African Americans embraced a plan to begin a new life in Africa, but many "overwhelmingly rejected the option of exile, choosing instead to wage a battle against slavery and racism in their native land in the principles of liberty embodied in America's revolutionary heritage" (Forbes, 1998, p. 22) Liberia was founded in 1822 by the American Colonization Society as African Americans were repatriated to Africa. "Some of these individuals had been born free and educated in the United States; however, nearly half of these new settlers had been emancipated under the stipulation that they would leave the United States for Liberia" (Nsonwu, 2015, p. 305).

3.7 Emancipation Proclamation, Black Codes, and the Reconstruction Amendments

Following the American Revolution, Congress passed a series of increasingly stringent laws banning the international slave trade (while leaving the institution of slavery untouched), culminating in a law that made trafficking in slaves a hanging offense. Congress, however, did little to enforce these laws, and both slavery and the slave trade flourished until the Civil War and the passage of the Thirteenth Amendment (Bales & Soodalter, 2009, p. 8).

The Dred Scott decision of 1857 is an example of the continued perpetuation of injustice during that time period. Dred Scott, an enslaved man, sued his owner for his

Figure 2.13 *Reading the Emancipation Proclamation.*

SOURCE: Schomburg Center for Research in Black Culture, Photographs and Prints Division, The New York Public Library. (1864). Retrieved from http://digitalcollections.nypl.org/items/c5af6ce0-d32d-05f8-e040-e00a18065343. In the public domain.

freedom since his enslaver took him to a state not allowing slavery. The court ruled that Black people were never considered, nor could ever be considered, American citizens and therefore had no right to sue. President Lincoln signed the Emancipation Proclamation in 1863, declaring that all slaves in the Confederate states "shall be then, thenceforward, and forever free." This act changed the Civil War from a military plan whose purpose was to end the secession of the south to an antislavery agenda; the passing of the Emancipation Proclamation also allowed African Americans to be recruited into the military, and nearly 200,000 African Americans joined the Union army (Bales, 2000; Drescher & Engerman, 1998; Hum, 2005). Legislative provisions guaranteed the freedom of enlisted African Americans in the Union army as well as the freedom of their family members (Berlin, 2000). By joining the Union army, enslaved peoples contested their oppression and facilitated the disintegration of slavery (Froner, 2000).

Despite the intended loftiness of this legislation, the Emancipation Proclamation had little immediate impact and the end of slavery did not come until the passing of the Thirteenth Amendment two years later (Berlin, 2000; Berry, 2000; Klein, 2002). This law proclaimed that "neither slavery nor involuntary servitude, except as a punishment for a crime whereof the party shall have been duly convicted, shall exist within the United States, or in any place subject to their jurisdiction" (U.S. Const. amend. XIII, § 1). Even with the adoption of the Thirteenth Amendment and the end of the Civil War, Southern states resisted according the rights that were guaranteed to African Americans by constitutional law and created Black Codes; these policies served to further subjugate former slaves by preventing African Americans from exercising their constitutional rights. African Americans were denied the right to vote, bear arms, practice free speech, own property, and the protection against cruel and unusual punishment, thereby essentially relegating them to a life similar to slavery (Klein, 2002; Stussy, 1997). The passage of the Fourteenth and Fifteenth Amendments are often referred to as the "Reconstruction Amendments" (Berlin, 2000) and, with the Thirteenth Amendment, these formed "a new American constitution" as "there were revolutionary changes for a nation whose economy up to the 1860s rested in considerable measure on slave labor" (Froner, 2000, p. 103). The political, social, and legal infrastructure that reflected the Constitution sanctioned slavery up until this time period. The passing of the Fourteenth Amendment (U.S. Const. amend. XIV) prevented states from exercising Black Codes. The legislation was noteworthy in that it recognized "citizenship on the basis of birth or naturalization and required equal protection under the law for all citizens" (Guest, 2005, p. 231). The Fifteenth Amendment (U.S. Const. amend. XV) prohibited states from denying African Americans the right to vote (Klein, 2002). Despite this legislation, sharecropping and debt peonage were common in the South, leaving emancipated Blacks in economic conditions very similar to slavery.

3.8 Jim Crow Era

Although strides in civil liberties for African Americans began to gain momentum through the passing of the Thirteenth, Fourteenth, and Fifteenth Amendments, racism in the South worked to continue an oppressive culture. In 1877, the federal government withdrew troops from the South, marking the beginning of the Jim Crow system (Birnbaum & Taylor, 2000). The Jim Crow era significantly limited the constitutional freedom of African Americans by initiating policies that infringed upon or prevented African Americans from exercising their rights; this was done by force, fraud, coercion, and intimidation. Lynching, the illegal hanging of a person, was a common tactic that incited fear in African Americans who dared to challenge the cultural norms of the Jim Crow system; it also permitted the use/abuse of power and control by Whites. Long-time social justice activist Ida B. Wells lobbied for an antilynching law after witnessing the lynching of three of her friends. Her writing *Southern Horrors: Lynch Law in All Its Phases* highlighted how lynching instilled terror and fear to control and oppress African Americans during this time period (Wells-Barnett, 1997).

Although an international body, the League of Nations, passed the Convention to Suppress the Slave Trade and Slavery in 1926, outlining definitions of slave trade, there were no globally agreed-upon sanctions for violations during this time period (Bales, 2005). Almost 20 years later, the United Nations adopted the Universal Declaration of Human Rights in 1948, further condemning slavery and encouraging nations to "promote and protect human rights." However, these founding principles also did not carry any enforcement clauses (United Nations, 1948). Even the United Nations legislation of 1956, "The Supplementary Conventions on the Abolition of Slavery, the Slave Trade and Institutions and Practices Similar to Slavery" and "The International Covenant on Civil and Political Rights" that "helped to shape the legal framework for slavery in its more modern form" (Lusk & Lucas, 2009, p. 53), was void of enforcement clauses for nations that violated human rights through forced labor.

3.9 Civil Rights Era

Korstad and Lichtenstein (2000) assert that "the civil rights era began, dramatically and decisively, in the early 1940s when the social structure of black America took on an increasingly urban, proletarian character" (p. 363). As this change began, African Americans were living in large numbers in the North, having migrated from rural communities beginning in the early 20th century. Both labor union membership and registration in the National Association for the Advancement of Colored People (NAACP) increased (Korstad & Lichtenstein, 2000). The work of the NAACP began a decade earlier in the 1930s as a racially integrated committee committed "to advocate integration for black citizens" (Gardner, 2002, p. 97). The mission of the NAACP represented "the most sustained assault against the edifice of racial segregation" (Hine, 1991, p. 61) during this era. Other historians regard December 1, 1955, as the date when the civil rights movement began, marking the day that Rosa Parks refused to give up her seat on a bus, sparking national demonstrations. The next decade included considerable milestone events including civil rights protests in the United States from the Montgomery bus boycott to lunch counter sit-ins and marches throughout many southern states to ensure the right to vote and the ability to gain equal access to public facilities. Congress then passed the Civil Rights Act of 1964, seeking to end racial discrimination. The Civil Rights Act was followed by additional legislation including the 1965 Voting Rights Act that secured freedom and equal rights for all people.

3.10 Chapter Summary

Modern-day slavery, or human trafficking, has its roots in earlier instances of slavery. Similarities resound between these two forms of oppression as they both reflect how economic profits are gained from the illegal trafficking of bodies whether it is chattel slavery, debt bondage, or in the modern-day trafficking of individuals for sex and labor. During the African transatlantic slave trade, more men were enslaved. However, today women and children are vulnerable victims of modern-day slavery; domestically and internationally they are disproportionately targeted for exploitation in the sex trafficking industry.

Understanding models of how different human rights violations are intertwined is an important concept in addressing social justice abuses and issues. In 1926, the League of Nations formally defined slavery as "a status or condition of a person over whom any or all of the powers attached to the right of ownership are exercised" (Bales, 2012, p. 275). Prior to this definition, slavery had existed for generations in many nations as people sought to conscript others for their own benefit, often for economical purposes. Despite legislative reforms directed toward freeing enslaved African Americans in the United States, such as the Emancipation Proclamation and the Thirteen, Fourteenth, and Fifteenth Amendments, significant human rights violations continued in the form of Black Codes and Jim Crow laws. Civil rights advocacy and policy changes made significant strides in the 1950s and 1960s, and the Civil Rights Act of 1964 marked the most comprehensive legislation in American history that sought to end racial discrimination.

Unfortunately, racial discrimination and oppression exist today in the extensive trafficking of human beings. Slavery was abolished in the Western Hemisphere in 1888 after Brazil was the last nation in this region to formally cease this practice; however, the League of Nations Convention to Suppress the Slave Trade and Slavery was not approved until 1926 and did not include a clause that addressed "procedures for investigating slavery" (Lusk & Lucas, 2009, p. 53) or enforcement for nations that continued to participate in slavery practices. Today, despite federal legislative milestones such as the Trafficking Victims Protection Act of 2000 (TVPA) and Trafficking Victims Protection Reauthorization Acts of 2003 (H.R. 2620), 2005 (H.R. 972), 2008 (S. 3061), and 2013, slavery in various forms still exists globally and in the United States. It is clear that slavery is a pernicious evil despite repeated and organized efforts to ban it. So, the struggle must continue at all levels of human society, from the individual to those collective bodies responsible for keeping civil society safe.

History demonstrates the need to emulate the collective efforts of activists such as the early abolitionists and others of goodwill as they worked in the Underground Railroad or those in the maroon communities to resist and revolt against forced labor. We also appreciate from people of various faith and nonfaith traditions that peaceful demonstration and witness to their moral convictions about social justice and human dignity can turn the course of history. Finally, we learn from generations of survivors of Jim Crow and the Civil Rights era the courage and personal commitment needed to challenge structural and institutionalized oppression. We acknowledge that many of the current-day survivors of human trafficking possess the same resilience in resisting persecution, as they bear witness to their maltreatment and mobilize various efforts to advocate change and reform.

3.11 Historical Timeline

Date	Event	Explanation
1482	The Portuguese establish new trading settlements on "Africa's Gold Coast."	People are viewed as commodities in exchange for ironware, firearms, and textiles.
1619	Twenty African indentured servants arrive in Jamestown, Virginia—America's first permanent English colony. White slaves (consisting of children and the poor) and indentured servants were sent to America from England.	These indentured servants were most likely captured by the Portuguese. Slaves would later replace indentured servants in providing labor to the New World. The life of an indentured servant was often relegated to the same hardships and abuse as slaves.
1641 1662 1663 1664 1682 1700 1715 1750	Colonies legalize slavery: Massachusetts Virginia Maryland New York & New Jersey South Carolina Rhode Island & Pennsylvania North Carolina Georgia	Challenges to the morality of slavery were uncommon in early colonial times. Virginia passed a law stating that slavery followed the condition of the mother (*partus sequitur ventrem*—a Latin phrase meaning "that which is brought forth follows the womb." Other British American colonies later followed suit. This law was a change from English common law, which stated that the child's condition followed the father. This law perpetuated slavery in Virginia (and elsewhere) and made it easy to establish—enslaved women could only produce enslaved progeny, no matter the father's status. Slavery, therefore, became a hereditary condition. Moreover, enslavers could increase their workforce by having sexual relations with enslaved women without fear of punishment.
1740	South Carolina Negro Act	An example of legalization that excluded legal protection for slaves. With these restrictions on enslaved people, this act also solidified the idea that people of African descent were viewed as chattel, property. During the colonial times and the end of the Revolutionary War, independent colonies and states enacted laws to regulate and control slaves. The South Carolina Negro Act prohibited teaching slaves how to read or write.

Date	Event	Explanation
1754	Philadelphia Yearly Meeting of Quakers decides that slavery is a sin.	Abolition movement begins to take form.
1775–1783	Revolutionary War	Enslaved African Americans fought on both sides of the Revolutionary War as both the American and English armies conscripted these bondsmen, promising them freedom for their allegiance when their side won.
1787	Constitutional Convention of 1787	Slavery was expressly sanctioned in the Constitutional Convention of 1787.
1793	U.S. Congress passes the Fugitive Slave Law.	Slave owners are legally allowed to arrest, capture, and return people who have attempted to flee enslavement.
1799	New York implements the Gradual Emancipation Act for enslaved people born after July 4, 1799.	Males could become free at age 28 and females at age 25. This act essentially indentured formally enslaved young people.
1808	U.S. Congress abolishes the transatlantic slave trade.	Approximately 1.2 million Africans continued to be enslaved in spite of this legislation.
1809	New York legally recognizes marriage between slaves.	
1815	Isabella "Sojourner Truth," at 17 years old, marries Thomas, who was also enslaved by the Dumont family.	Sojourner Truth and Thomas have five children. It is speculated that the couple may have been forced to marry by their slave owner.
1815	In the United States, 1.4 million individuals are enslaved; the total population at that time is 8.4 million.	
February 1816	Paul Cuffe (a son of a West African father and Wampanoag Native Indian mother), captain of the *Traveller,* brings 38 free African Americans to Sierra Leone, Senegal, and the Congo to begin a new life and return to their ancestral homeland.	The migration of freed African Americans to Africa was viewed positively from opposing sides of the position of slavery. Proslavery proponents regarded this option as beneficial in addressing their fear of reprisals from people whom they had formally enslaved; antislavery advocates hoped that the African colonization movement would curb slavery.

(Continued)

(Continued)

Date	Event	Explanation
1817	New York accelerates the Gradual Emancipation Act.	Allows for the freedom of all enslaved peoples in New York born before 1799 but not until 1827.
1820	More enslaved peoples had traveled from Africa to the Western Hemisphere via the slave trade than had come from Europe.	
1850	The Fugitive Slave Act of 1850	The Fugitive Slave Act of 1850 played a crucial role before the Civil War because it exacerbated tensions between the Northern and Southern states, since it required runaway slaves to be returned to their enslavers and required citizens in the free states to aid an enslaver or agent of the enslaver in the recapture of an enslaved person.
1857	The Dred Scott decision of 1857	The Dred Scott decision: Dred Scott, an enslaved man, sued his owner for his freedom since his enslaver took him to a state not allowing slavery. The court ruled that Black people were never considered, nor could ever be considered, American citizens and therefore had no right to sue.
1860	There are approximately 4 million enslaved people.	
1861–1865	Civil War	
January 1, 1863	Emancipation Proclamation	President Abraham Lincoln declares that all slaves in the Confederate states "shall be then, thenceforward, and forever free." The signing of the Emancipation Proclamation changes the Civil War to an antislavery agenda. African Americans are recruited into the military as a result of this legislation.
May 10, 1865	Thirteenth Amendment to the U.S. Constitution	The passing of this amendment by Congress abolishes slavery in the United States except in slaveholding nations residing in Indian Territory: the Creek, Choctaw, Chickasaw, and Seminole, along with the Cherokee.
Ratified on July 9, 1868	Fourteenth Amendment	

Date	Event	Explanation
Ratified on February 3, 1870	Fifteenth Amendment	
1877	Federal government withdraws troops from the South; beginning of Jim Crow system.	
1888	Slavery was finally abolished in the Western Hemisphere when Brazil formally ceased this practice.	
1926	Through an international body, the League of Nations, the Convention to Suppress the Slave Trade and Slavery of 1926 is passed.	Definitions of slave trade are defined, however, no decisions on sanctions for violations are agreed upon.
1948	United Nations adopts the "Universal Declaration of Human Rights," condemning slavery and encouraging nations to "promote and protect human rights.	No enforcement clauses for violations are stipulated.
1954	*Brown v. Board of Education*	
December 1, 1955	Civil rights movement begins. Rosa Parks refuses to give up her seat on a bus.	
1955	Montgomery bus boycott	
1956	The United Nations passes "The Supplementary Conventions on the Abolition of Slavery, the Slave Trade and Institutions and Practices Similar to Slavery" and "The International Covenant on Civil and Political Rights."	These conventions are also void of enforcement clauses for nations that violate human rights through forced labor. This legislation helps to shape the legal framework for slavery in its more modern form.
February 1, 1960	A&T Four begin sit-in at Greensboro, North Carolina, lunch counter.	
1964	Congress passes the Civil Rights Act of 1964.	The most comprehensive legislation in American history that seeks to end racial discrimination.
1965	Selma to Montgomery March begins.	
1965	Voting Rights Act	

4. Key Terms

4.1	Trans-Saharan Slave Trade
4.2	Transatlantic Slave Trade
4.3	Indentured Servants
4.4	American Colonies
4.5	Quakers
4.6	Philadelphia Society of Friends
4.7	1740 South Carolina Negro Act
4.8	Fugitive Slave Acts of 1793 and 1850
4.9	Revolutionary War
4.10	Enlightenment, Slave Resistance/Revolts
4.11	Underground Railroad
4.12	Maroon Communities
4.13	Rangers, Colonization
4.14	American Colonization Society
4.15	Repatriation of African Americans
4.16	Emancipation Proclamation
4.17	Black Codes
4.18	The Civil War
4.19	The Reconstruction Amendments
4.20	Thirteenth Amendment
4.21	Fourteenth Amendment and Fifteenth Amendment
4.22	Jim Crow Era
4.23	Lynching
4.24	Civil Rights Era
4.25	National Association for the Advancement of Colored People (NAACP)
4.26	Civil Rights Act of 1964
4.27	The 1965 Voting Rights Act
4.28	The 1926 League of Nations Convention to Suppress the Slave Trade and Slavery

5. In-Class Discussion Questions/Exercises

5.1 How do the tactics of modern-day traffickers to conscript victims as recruiters in the trafficking industry both mirror and differ from strategies that governments and slave owners used in conscripting "Rangers" to fight against maroon communities who were revolting against enslavement?

5.2 How has resilience manifested in survivors of oppression both contemporary and historically?

5.3 List comparisons between the collective efforts to challenge oppression of historically enslaved peoples and survivors of modern-day human trafficking.

5.4 What are the similarities and differences between slavery and indentured servitude?

5.5 How has poverty increased the risk of individuals to become enslaved during historical and contemporary time periods?

6. Additional Reading

6.1   Walter Johnson, *River of dark dreams: Slavery and empire in the cotton kingdom* (2013)

6.2   Edward Baptist, *The half has never been told: Slavery and the making of American capitalism* (2014)

6.3   Calvin Schmerhorn, *The business of slavery and the rise of American capitalism, 1815–1860*

6.4   Sylvaiane Diouf, *Slavery's exiles: The story of the American maroons* (2014)

6.5   John Hope Franklin and Loren Schweninger, *Runaway slaves: Rebels on the plantation* (2000)

6.6   Douglas Blackmon, *Slavery by another name: The re-enslavement of Black Americans from the Civil War to World War II* (2009)

6.7   Talitha LeFlouria, *Chained in silence: Black women and convict labor in the New South* (2015)

6.8   Herbert Klein article "African women in the Atlantic slave trade," in *Women and slavery in Africa* (1983)

6.9   Joseph Miller, "Domiciled and dominated: Slaving as a history of women," in *Women and slavery: Vol. 2, The modern Atlantic*, edited by Gwyn Campbell and Suzanne Miers (2007)

6.10   Isabel Wilkerson, *The warmth of other suns: The epic story of America's great migration* (2010)

6.11   Ida B. Wells, *The light of truth: Writings of an anti-lynching crusader* (2014)

6.12   Ida B. Wells, *Southern horrors and other writings: The anti-lynching campaign of Ida B. Wells, 1892–1900* (1997)

6.13   Frederick Douglass, *Narrative of the life of Frederick Douglass, an American slave* (1845)

6.14   Frederick Douglass, *My bondage and my freedom* (1855)

7. Web Resources

7.1   www.abolitionseminar.org

7.2   www.historiansagainstslavery.org

7.3   www.gilderlehrman.org

7.4   http://people.duke.edu/~ldbaker/classes/aaih/caaih/ibwells/ibwbkgrd.html

7.5   Frederick Douglass Family Initiatives: http://www.fdfi.org/

8. Project Assignments and Homework Suggestions

8.1 Power and Control

Ask students to write a reflection or research paper on how power and control (i.e., coercion, force, fraud, and intimidation) were exercised in an historical perspective during slavery. How was it exerted during the Jim Crow era? How is it employed in the present day with human trafficking?

8.2 Compare Abolitionists

Ask students to write a paper that compares and contrasts historical abolitionists and modern-day abolitionists. What common and differing characteristics do you find among them? What common and differing strategies do they use? Why?

9. Films

9.1   *12 Years a Slave* (Regency Enterprises & River Road Entertainment)

9.2   *The Free State of Jones* (STX Entertainment)

10. References

Bales, K. (2000). *New slavery: A reference handbook.* Santa Barbara, CA: ABC-CLIO.

Bales, K. (2005). *Understanding global slavery: A reader.* Berkeley, CA: University of California Press.

Bales, K. (2012). *Disposable people: New slavery in the global economy, Update with a New Preface* (3rd ed.). Berkeley, CA: University of California Press.

Bales, K., & Soodalter, R. (2009). *The slave next door.* Berkeley, CA: University of California Press.

Berlin, I. (2000). Who freed the slaves? In J. Birnbaum & C. Taylor (Eds.), *Civil rights since 1787: A reader on the Black struggle* (pp. 90–97). New York, NY: New York University Press.

Berry, M. F. (2000). Slavery, the Constitution, and the founding fathers. In J. Birnbaum & C. Taylor (Eds.), *Civil rights since 1787: A reader on the Black struggle* (pp. 16–23). New York, NY: New York University Press.

Birnbaum, J., & Taylor, C. (2000). *Civil rights since 1787: A reader on the Black struggle.* New York, NY: New York University Press.

Civil Rights Act of 1964, Pub. L. No. 88–352, 78 Stat. 241 (1964).

Davis, D. (2001). *In the image of God: Religion, moral values and our heritage of slavery.* New Haven, CT: Yale University Press.

Diouf, S. A. (2014). *Slavery's exiles: The story of the American Maroons.* Retrieved from Ebook Library http://public.eblib.com/choice/publicfullrecord.aspx?p=1572868

Drescher, S., & Engerman, S. L. (Eds.). (1998). *A historical guide to world slavery.* New York, NY: Oxford University Press.

Emancipation Proclamation, January 1, 1863 (National Archives Identifier: 299998); Presidential Proclamations, 1791–1991; Record Group 11; General Records of the United States Government; National Archives. Retrieved from https://www.archives.gov/historical-docs/todays-doc/?dod-date=101

Foner, E. (2015). *Gateway to freedom: The hidden history of the underground railroad* (1st ed.). New York, NY: W.W. Norton & Company.

Forbes, R. (1998). United States. In S. Drescher & S. L. Engerman (Eds.), *A historical guide to world slavery* (pp. 21–27). New York, NY: Oxford University Press.

Franklin, J. H., & Schweninger, L. (1999). *Runaway slaves: Rebels on the plantation*. New York, NY: Oxford University Press.

Froner, E. (2000). The second American Revolution. In J. Birnbaum & C. Taylor (Eds.), *Civil rights since 1787: A reader on the Black struggle* (pp. 103–108). New York, NY: New York University Press.

Gara, L. (1997). Underground railroad. In J. P. Rodriguez (Ed.), *The historical encyclopedia of world slavery* (Vol. II, pp. 661–663). Santa Barbara, CA: ABC-CLIO.

Gardner, S. E. (2002). Coming of age in the movement: Teaching with personal narratives. In J. B. Armstrong, S. H. Edwards, H. B. Roberson, & R. Y. Williams (Eds.), *Teaching the American civil rights movement: Freedom's bittersweet song* (pp. 97–110). New York, NY: Routledge.

Guest, K. (2005). Fourteenth Amendment. In P. G. Min (Ed.), *Encyclopedia of racism in the United States*. Westport, CT: Greenwood Press.

Harris, L. M., & Berry, D. R. (Eds.). (2014). *Slavery and Freedom in Savannah*. Athens, GA: University of Georgia Press.

Hine, D. C. (1991). Fighting Back (1957–1962). In C. Carson, D. Garrow, G. Gill, V. Harding, & D. C. Hine (Eds.), *The eyes on the prize: Civil rights reader: Documents, speeches, and firsthand accounts from the Black freedom struggle, 1954–1990* (pp. 61–106). New York, NY: Penguin Books.

Howe, D. W. (2007). *What hath God wrought: The transformation of America, 1815–1848*. New York, NY: Oxford University Press.

Hum, T. (2005). Emancipation Proclamation. In P. G. Min (Ed.), *Encyclopedia of racism in the United States*. Westport, CT: Greenwood Press.

Johnson, K. M. (2012). Underground Railroad. In D. R. Berry & D. A. Alford (Eds.), *Enslaved women in America: An encyclopedia* (pp. 311–315). Santa Barbara, CA: Greenwood.

Jordan, D., & Walsh, M. (2008). *White cargo: The forgotten history of Britain's White slaves in America*. Retrieved from Ebook Library http://public.eblib.com/choice/publicfullrecord.aspx?p=3025612

Klein, M. A. (2002). *Historical dictionary of slavery and abolition*. Lanham, MD: Scarecrow Press.

Korstad, R., & Lichtenstein, N. (2000). Labor, radicals, and the Civil Rights Movement. In J. Birnbaum & C. Taylor (Eds.), *Civil rights since 1787: A reader on the Black Struggle* (pp. 363–382). New York, NY: New York University Press.

Krauthamer, B. (2009). The Seminole Freedmen: A history. *Journal of American Ethnic History, 28*(4), 136–137. Retrieved from http://ncat.idm.oclc.org/login?url=http://search.ebscohost.com/login.aspx?direct=true&db=a9h&AN=41522068&site=ehost-live

Lee, N. K. (2012). Chronology of enslaved women in America. In D. R. Berry & D. A. Alford (Eds.), *Enslaved women in America: An encyclopedia* (pp. xxv-xxix). Santa Barbara, CA: Greenwood.

Lionel Pincus and Princess Firyal Map Division, The New York Public Library. (1898). *"Underground" routes to Canada* Retrieved from http://digitalcollections.nypl.org/items/d64f0a80–4db6–0133–78eb-00505686d14e

Lusk, M., & Lucas, F. (2009). The challenge of human trafficking and contemporary slavery. *Journal of Comparative Social Welfare, 25*(1), 49–57. doi:10.1080/17486830802514049

The New York Public Library, & Schomburg Center for Research in Black Culture. (1999). *The New York Public Library African American desk reference*. New York, NY: John Wiley & Sons Inc.

Nsonwu, M. B. (2015). God-talk in the survival epistemology of Liberian refugee women. *Journal of Religion & Spirituality in Social Work: Social Thought, 34*(3), 304–327. doi: 10.1080/15426432.2015.1045680

Rodriguez, J. P. (2007). Fugitive Slave Act. In J. P. Rodriguez (Ed.), *Slavery in the United States: A social, political, and historical encyclopedia*. Santa Barbara, CA: ABC-CLIO.

Schomburg Center for Research in Black Culture, Jean Blackwell Hutson Research and Reference Division, The New York Public Library. (1861). *Map showing the distribution of the slave population of the southern states of the United States*. Retrieved from http://digitalcollections.nypl.org/items/43876320-faf6-0131-8025-58d385a7b928

Schomburg Center for Research in Black Culture, Jean Blackwell Hutson Research and Reference Division, The New York Public Library. (1903–1902). *Hon. Frederick Douglass*. Retrieved from http://digitalcollections.nypl.org/items/510d47de-1c2d-a3d9-e040-e00a18064a99

Schomburg Center for Research in Black Culture, Jean Blackwell Hutson Research and Reference Division, The New York Public Library. (1903–1902). *Slave traders marching their captives to the coast, butchering disabled ones along the way*. Retrieved from http://digitalcollections.nypl.org/items/510d47de-1c15-a3d9-e040-e00a18064a99

Schomburg Center for Research in Black Culture, Jean Blackwell Hutson Research and Reference Division, The New York Public Library. (1940). *Emily runs away*. Retrieved from http://digitalcollections.nypl.org/items/510d47dc-9f95-a3d9-e040-e00a18064a99

Schomburg Center for Research in Black Culture, Manuscripts, Archives and Rare Books Division, The New York Public Library. (1834). *Exchanging citizens for horses*. Retrieved from http://digitalcollections.nypl.org/items/510d47da-75b5-a3d9-e040-e00a18064a99

Schomburg Center for Research in Black Culture, Manuscripts, Archives and Rare Books Division, The New York Public Library. (1834). *Selling females by the pound*. Retrieved from http://digitalcollections.nypl.org/items/510d47da-75b1-a3d9-e040-e00a18064a99

Schomburg Center for Research in Black Culture, Manuscripts, Archives and Rare Books Division, The New York Public Library. (1864). *The lash (see page 203)*. Retrieved from http://digitalcollections.nypl.org/items/510d47da-75e7-a3d9-e040-e00a18064a99

Schomburg Center for Research in Black Culture, Photographs and Prints Division, The New York Public Library. (1839). *Schematic drawing of an English slave ship, possibly the Brookes, showing the layout of the cargo hold areas for transporting African slaves*. Retrieved from http://digitalcollections.nypl.org/items/ea7997f0-2657-0132-1964-58d385a7b928

Schomburg Center for Research in Black Culture, Photographs and Prints Division, The New York Public Library. (1854). *Slave traders branding an African woman at the Rio Pongo (in Guinea, West Africa). Taken from "Captain Canot, Twenty Years of an African Slaver," published 1854*. Retrieved from http://digitalcollections.nypl.org/items/4a47ac10-2658-0132-7bc8-58d385a7b928

Schomburg Center for Research in Black Culture, Photographs and Prints Division, The New York Public Library. (1861). *A slave auction in Virginia*. Retrieved from http://digitalcollections.nypl.org/items/510d47db-c062-a3d9-e040-e00a18064a99

Schomburg Center for Research in Black Culture, Photographs and Prints Division, The New York Public Library. (1864). *Reading the Emancipation Proclamation*. Retrieved from http://digitalcollections.nypl.org/items/c5af6ce0-d32d-05f8-e040-e00a18065343

Smallwood, A., & Elliot, J. M. (1998). *The atlas of African-American history and politics: From the slave trade to modern times*. Boston, MA: McGraw Hill.

Stussy, S. (1997). Thirteenth Amendment. In J. P. Rodriguez (Ed.), *The historical encyclopedia of world slavery*. Santa Barbara, CA: ABC-CLIO.

Terborg-Penn, R. (2012). Maroon communities. In D. R. Berry & D. A. Alford (Eds.), *Enslaved women in America: An encyclopedia* (pp. 191–192). Santa Barbara, CA: Greenwood.

Thompson, A. O. (2006). *Flight to freedom: African runaways and Maroons in the Americas*. Kingston, Jamaica: University of the West Indies Press.

Trafficking Victims Protection Act of 2000, Pub. L. No. 106–386, 114 Stat. 1464 (2000).

Trafficking Victims Protection Reauthorization Act, Pub. L. No. 108–193 (2003).

Trafficking Victims Protection Reauthorization Act, 22 USC § 7104 (2005).

Trafficking Victims Protection Reauthorization Act, 22 USC § 7311 (2008).

Trafficking Victims Protection Reauthorization Act of 2013, 22 USC § 7109 (2013).

U.S. Const. amend. XIII, § 1.

U.S. Const. amend. XIV.

U.S. Const. amend. XV.

United Nations. (1948). *Universal declaration of human rights.* New York, NY: United Nations.

Wells-Barnett, I. B. (1997). *Southern horrors and other writings: The anti-lynching campaign of Ida B. Wells, 1892–1900* (J. J. Royster Ed.). Boston, MA: Bedford Books.

Understanding Terms, Definitions, and Intersectionality

The concept of human trafficking is frequently seen as an issue largely separate from gender-based violence and child abuse when in fact it is part of the continuum of violence and trauma that children in the US, overwhelmingly children living in poverty, experience.[1]

—Rachel Lloyd, advocate and author of
Girls Like Us

I. Learning Objectives

1.1 Students will be introduced to definitions and terms used in the field of human trafficking response.

1.2 Students will be introduced to basic concepts of critical theoretical approaches.

1.3 Students will appreciate factors that may complicate the definitions and terms.

1.4 Students will be introduced to value-laden and contextual influences of definitions and terms.

---

[1] Lloyd, 2015, p. 1

2. Key Ideas

The central ideas of this chapter are:

2.1 Defining human trafficking is complicated. Human trafficking definitions are value laden, contextually situated, and culturally driven.

2.2 An intersectional lens involves the exploration of multiple, complex, and mutually reinforcing systems of oppression (such as racism, classism, ableism, sexism, nativism, homophobia, and heterosexism).

2.3 Terms and labels used to describe people are value laden and impactful.

2.4 An understanding of the ideological-laden influences in antitrafficking efforts is important. Consider the organizational missions of law enforcement, social services, legal services, or research, and the ways that these missions may align, be incongruent, and/or compete about how to think about a case and intervene.

2.5 Human trafficking definitions influence our involvement and responses with the issue.

2.6 Human trafficking intersects directly and indirectly with many other issues. Kidnapping, interpersonal violence, money laundering, and weapon or drug trafficking are examples of issues that may be directly related to human trafficking. Poverty, educational opportunity, homophobia, and ableism are examples of issues indirectly related to human trafficking.

3. Selected Theories/Frameworks

3.1 Critical Theories (Critical Race Theory and Intersectionality)

Critical theoretical approaches are useful in exploring the multiple factors that may play a role in the exploitation of people for labor or commercial sex. Primarily concerned with oppression and social justice, critical theories generally promote "a structural approach to addressing the problems of a diverse society, rather than merely expanding access to existing resources and opportunities" (Ortiz & Jani, 2010, p. 176).

Tenets of Critical Race Theory (CRT)

1. CRT recognizes that racism is endemic to American life, deeply ingrained legally, culturally, socially, and psychologically.

2. CRT challenges the dominant ideologies such as White privilege, race neutrality, objectivity, color blindness, and meritocracy.

3. CRT attends to Derrick Bell's theory of interest convergence, which contends that racial equality has been gained only when the interests of people of color promote those of Whites.

4. CRT insists on a contextual/historical analysis of race and racism not in order to dwell on the past but to move beyond it.

5. CRT appreciates the experiential knowledge of people of color as legitimate, valid, and critical to interrogate race and racism.

6. CRT relies on stories and counter-stories of the lived experiences of people of color as a way to communicate the realities of the oppressed.

7. CRT is inter/trans/cross-disciplinary, drawing upon other disciplines and epistemologies to provide a more complete analysis of racial inequalities.

8. CRT focuses on race and racism for a critical race analysis but includes their intersection with other forms of subordination such as gender and class discrimination.

SOURCE: *Understanding Narrative Inquiry: The Crafting and Analysis of Stories as Research* (p. 44), by J.H. Kim, 2015, Thousand Oaks, CA: SAGE Publications. Copyright 2015 by SAGE Publications. Reprinted with permission.

Critical Race Theory (CRT) is part of the broader umbrella of critical approaches that allow us to examine the ways in which socially constructed notions of race, class, and gender, for example, influence the ways in which trafficked persons are oppressed and experience oppression. In the case of foreign-born survivors of human trafficking, we may also entertain the added element of nativity, nationality, and/or citizenship status. Critical race theory has its origins in critical postmodern theory and is based on the assumptions that race is a social construction; race permeates all aspects of social life; and race-based ideology is threaded throughout society (Ortiz & Jani, 2010). Critical race theory focuses on social justice, liberation, and a transformative response to not only racial oppression but also to gender and class oppression.

Another useful aspect of a critical approach is the concept of intersectionality that recognizes that race, gender, religion, ethnicity, sexual orientation, and class coexist to shape social identity, behavior, opportunities, and access to rights. Introduced by Kimberle Crenshaw (1991), intersectionality refers to the ways in which multiple forms of oppression are interrelated. Social constructions of age, gender, and race, for example, do not act independently of one another in how they inform identity, discrimination, and social inequality. The concept of intersectionality offers a way to understand complex identities and the impact of social structures on the lived experience (Mattsson, 2014). Using an intersectional lens helps us explore multiple, complex, and mutually reinforcing systems of oppression (such as racism, classism, ableism, sexism, nativism, homophobia, and heterosexism).

Intersectionality

We'll need to move from a sensationalistic approach and an increasingly criminal justice approach to one that is grounded in the reality of the daily experiences of the children and youth we serve and that addresses the intersections of not only domestic violence and child abuse but how poverty, racism, gender inequity, and larger social issues ensure that some children are at much, much higher risk for recruitment into the commercial sex industry than others (Rachel Lloyd, 2015 p. 3).

With regard to human trafficking, gender, age, ethnicity, race, documentation status, and nativity may all combine to create unique experiences of oppression. In terms of domestic minor sex trafficking, for example, it is not gender alone that may impact a young person's experience of exploitation. Rather, many factors are at play in how minors may experience or respond to being trafficked. These include, but are not limited to, race and ethnicity, socioeconomic status, nativity, and immigration status (Crenshaw, 1991). Furthermore, it is important to recognize the layered complexities of race and intersectional identities of those who perpetrate human trafficking crimes as well.

Critical perspectives are influenced by Paolo Freire and his well-known contribution *Pedagogy of the Oppressed* (Freire, 1972). In it, Freire proposes that in order to transform these intersecting systems of oppression, we must engage in both action and in reflection, simultaneously. In reflecting on and taking action in the transformation of oppression, we develop critical consciousness. A critical consciousness approach promotes the notion that social change must be a collective endeavor that comes about through dialogue and interaction, not top-down intervention (Barak, 2015; Freire, 1972). Critical consciousness includes a "process of continuously reflecting upon and examining how our biases, assumptions, and cultural world views, affect the ways we perceive difference and power dynamics" (Sakamoto & Pitner, 2005, p. 441). This practice of critical self-reflection involves examining one's own multiple identities, locations, standpoints and how they impact our own narratives of our experiences and realities. Critical consciousness also entails examining our personal experiences through a political lens and considering the ways that the personal and political interrelate (Barak, 2015). Freire's work, critical consciousness, and anti-oppressive approaches reflect the idea that in order for social change to come about, we must go beyond individual self-reflection to understand and challenge inequality, oppression, and discrimination at structural levels (Mattsson, 2014; Sakamoto & Pitner, 2005).

Using context as a unit of context is also critical. Race, ethnicity, social class, sexual orientation, language, educational level, indigenous background, and other dimensions in which human beings may organize themselves in civil society take on different meanings in various cultural contexts.

4. Decision Case[2]

Anything but Ordinary

Connie knew the legalities of the moment were complex. The state law said when she took a child into custody she became the legal guardian. Yet laws often recognized a 17-year-old as an adult, too. It felt as if the entire county was involved in this case before it even became a case. No one wanted to screw up. What if Agustina was 17 and high? What if she was only 13 and terribly abused? What was the relationship between these three children?

Connie Blake

Connie Blake grew up as the middle child in a large Irish-Catholic family in a working-class section of Burlington, Vermont. One of nine children, four older and four younger, Connie was part of a big family, a close-knit neighborhood, and an organized faith community. She grew up with a lot of love, care, and compassion. Though families in her neighborhood lived marginally and worked hard, there was a deep sense of belonging and compassion in everyday life. Family members in Burlington and in Dublin, New Hampshire, worked in factories or in domestic roles. As soon as one was able, one worked, throwing papers, carrying groceries, babysitting, or cleaning house. Connie recalls her childhood as filled with family and very busy. Out of high school, Connie got her certification as a welder, along with steady work at a factory with two of her brothers. For 14 years she worked hard and made a decent living.

As she passed her 30th birthday, she decided she'd like to get a job more suited to her personality. She retired from welding and went to college. After earning a bachelor's and master's degree back-to-back, she was a therapist in a mental health clinic. Her first goal was to get her license. At the clinic she worked a lot with abused kids. Working with kids was a perfect match for her high energy, but she also learned quickly that she was not an office person.

When she learned of a job opening with the Department of Social Services (DSS) in foster care, Connie applied and was hired. From there, she transferred to the satellite office and got into investigations. There she found her niche. She loved it. The job was fast paced, mainly based in low-income housing projects, and required handling up to 500 investigations per month. The job fit her skills and temperament well, but she often felt as if the agency targeted poor families unfairly. She continued to look for a job, now knowing she wanted to work in investigations.

---

[2] This decision case was prepared solely to provide material for class discussion and not to suggest either effective or ineffective handling of the situation depicted. While based on field research regarding an actual situation, names and certain facts have been disguised to protect confidentiality. The authors wish to thank the case reporter for cooperation in making this account available for the benefit of students and practitioners (Wolfer & Scales, 2006, p. 29).

A job opening with DSS in Hall County, Georgia, attracted her attention, and she applied and got the job. Connie fell in love with the area, enjoyed the job, and generally felt as if she'd finally discovered the perfect fit. She was able to advocate for children and families and satisfy her drive to see what truly was happening in the home. The area was heavily Latino, so she made use of her fluent Spanish.

Connie lived in the county for 15 years, moving up through the ranks of investigations to the position of forensic investigator. In her role, Connie was often assigned the hardest cases. As she once explained to her sister, "When you love what you do, can you truly define it? It's more intrinsic to you. If you don't love it, you're not gonna make it."

Hall County

Hall County has a bit of a split personality. The affluent part of the county is very different from the rural chicken-farming area. There's class tension. Race relations involve people saying the right things, but the undercurrents are horrible. There is still some KKK in the county and there's a lot of discrimination, especially around the migrant families moving in and out of the county.

The Case:

Connie Blake had just turned the corner and started down Main Street when her phone began playing the ringtone she assigned to her job. She tapped the steering wheel button that opened the call as her office building came into view down the block. "Blake."

"North Side Elementary just called with an immediate response case. You close?" Wanda Getner, the intake supervisor spoke without preamble.

"Right around the corner," Connie answered. "Gimme ten to park and make a pit stop, then I'll be right up."

It was not unusual to have an assignment waiting for her to come in. But usually Wanda didn't call before she got into the office. *Must be a bad one*, Connie thought.

"I'm glad you're here." Jane Alexander greeted Connie as she entered the bullpen outside Jane's office.

Connie was always on time to work in the morning, so her boss's comment underscored the assumption that the case she was about to be assigned would be a hard one. Jane handed Connie a sheet of paper. Wanda stood behind Jane. *Two supervisors*, Connie thought. "What is it?" she asked.

"It's from North Side. Two boys. This is a preliminary write up. We need you to go to the school," Jane said.

"The police will meet you there," Wanda added. "Gina Davis called everyone. She's got two new students where a lot of things didn't make sense. It looks like the boys might be from out of state. They have the same birthdate, but they aren't twins. They've called the parents."

Connie looked back and forth between the two supervisors, gauging their expressions. The team had been together for a long time and Connie was used to their shorthand. She glanced at the preliminary report again. From what Gina reported on the call, the school staff was worried that these boys weren't where they are supposed to be. On the other hand, North Side served the county's wealthiest families, and the staff there could get excited about anything out of the ordinary. Connie suspended judgment. She would talk to the kids and find out what was happening. "If you're already thinking about removing the kids, you need to help me find a placement."

Jane nodded. "We've already got somebody looking."

Connie got another call from intake on her way to the car, this one from an intake worker. *What could possibly be happening at the school?* she wondered. While Connie climbed into the car, the intake worker reported on additional research about the boys. There was an earlier report on the same boys. A food stamp officer called in reporting conflicting information from the mom about the boys a couple of days ago. Connie talked with the intake worker briefly about finding a placement for the boys. When she ended that call, she put in a call to Melinda Beaudry, the child abuse specialist with the police victim service unit.

"Hey Meli, can you tell me what's going on? Can you give me a heads up?" Connie and Melinda had worked more cases together than Connie could count in the 15 years they had both been working in the county. "Why are you guys already involved?

Melinda explained the school social worker also called the police this morning. According to the school staff, a mom signed her two boys into school for the first time this morning and used the same birthdate for both boys, and when the school contacted her for clarification the mom seemed confused or conflicted about the information. The social worker also asked the boys things like where are you from, who's your dad, where is he? And the boys weren't giving consistent information in the answers. There is confusion about dads, men working in Gwinnett County, Mom and men. The school social worker had enough red flags to consult the school police officer. Melinda also expressed her own assessment that the reports weren't making sense. She was in the process of checking criminal histories on all the names the school had. Two detectives were dispatched to the school. Meanwhile, Melinda had the school secretary call the mom and say one of the kids was sick to bring Mom back to the school. As she listened to the details, Connie had a picture in her mind of people heading to the school like the incoming spokes of a wheel.

"Wait a minute," Connie interrupted. "One of the kids is sick?"

"No, no." Melinda's tone was matter of fact. "We're using the lie to get her back to the school."

"Okay," Connie said, although it wasn't okay. She confirmed the names of the incoming detectives before ending the call and disconnecting, her thoughts racing ahead. *Oh shit, what'm I gonna do? How am I gonna do what I need to do? The minute Mom sets foot on campus the police are gonna snatch her up. I won't find out how things got this way. And what will I tell these boys?* Connie vented some of her frustration on the steering wheel and some of it on the gas pedal.

Northwest Elementary School was situated on a sprawling campus composed of low brick buildings, lots of grass, and flowerbeds lining the walkways. Connie slowed at the lane and pulled around to the teachers' parking lot. She noted the two unmarked law enforcement vehicles tucked up near the cafeteria loading dock. She parked in a visitor's slot and walked up the sidewalk toward the school's front entrance. While she made her way into the building and signed in with the receptionist, she catalogued the information she had from the point of view of two little boys. It was the first day at a new school. There was not anyone in the building the boys knew. A lot of specific questions were being asked for which they did not have answers. She imagined the boys were frightened and confused by now.

The receptionist nodded her toward the principal's office. The door stood open and Connie stopped in the doorway. Principal Anna Harris sat behind her desk, the school social worker Sarah Conklin and school police officer Daryl Smith sat in the guest chairs, while Detective John Hough leaned against the bookshelves. At the sight of Connie, all four came to attention.

"Thanks for coming so quickly, Connie," Principal Harris said. "We were just talking about how to handle this."

Connie was about to ask what the "this" was when John leaned away from the wall. "Here's the plan. Mom should be here any minute. We've got an officer on both ends of the road."

Connie blinked. "Don't you think she'll see the cars?"

John smiled, a bit like a shark. Connie got the message. She hadn't seen cars at the end of the road, had she? His smile softened. "Nah, we've got it. We need you to go talk to the boys. We're arresting Mom. If you remove, we need you to take the boys back to the house to get their clothes."

Everything is moving too fast, Connie thought. She looked from Anna to Sarah, then back at John. As tempting as it was to begin asking questions and pointing out the pitfalls of entrapping Mom, Connie decided to meet the boys and sort out what was going on here after she had more information. "Any limitations on what to tell the kids?" she asked.

"Well, don't tell them we're arresting Mom. We've learned Mom is wanted in another state. We've already called the DA. Everybody is on call," John answered pointedly. Connie must have looked skeptical because he went on, "Those kids might have a mobile or something."

Connie nodded. "I need to see these boys then."

Sarah stood up and stepped over to the door. "They're in class. Come on, I'll get the room numbers. We can call the classrooms."

With the boy's names jotted in her notebook, Connie set off down the long hallway to social worker's office trying not to allow the reactions of the others color her first meetings with the boys. *I'm not walking in with the assumption of removing the kids. I have to make my own investigation. This is a nicer school where people may be overreacting to the kids, who are poorer and not clean.* Her thoughts also swirled with questions. *What will I hear from them that has started this fire? Whom will I interview first? How much am I gonna tell them? If they ask me to call their mom, how will I answer that question? Eventually I have to tell them about the police, but when do I tell them?*

Sarah's office was one of the more comfortable spots Connie had interviewed school children over the years. The room was tiny but somehow held a small desk, a love seat, and an armchair. There were children's books on the desk and several stuffed animals on the love seat. Connie settled in the armchair while Sarah went to get the 9-year-old out of class.

"Jeremy, this is my friend I was telling you about. Her name is Connie." Sarah introduced them before quietly ducking out of the room and closing the door.

The first thing Connie noticed was how cute he was. Small for his age, he had large dark eyes fringed with thick lashes. He wore jeans and a golf shirt, tennis shoes, and no socks. When he sat down, he made sure there was something between him and Connie. He picked up one of the stuffed animals, a bear, and put it on his lap. *Very unusual*, Connie thought.

"Hi, Jeremy." Connie took her cue from the bear in between them and scooted even farther back into the armchair. "I'm a social worker just like Miss Harris. Do you know what social workers do?"

"Yeah," Jeremy said slowly.

"This is a big school," Connie began. "When I was your age, my school was a lot smaller. Tell me something about you." She kept the conversation quite peripheral for a minute, touching on school subjects, sports, and television. When she asked where he was from, he balked. She circled back to talking about school. As time went on, he started to relax a little.

Eventually, he started talking about his other school, then paused. "I'm not supposed to tell you."

"Well all right, I don't need to know that," Connie said, thinking *I really need to know about that.*

The conversation kept running into topics Jeremy wasn't supposed to tell anyone at school about. Finally, Connie said, "You know what? This must be really hard for you. You don't know me. Is there anything you can tell me?"

"I can tell you I'm not supposed to tell you. My mom could get in trouble." Jeremy was trying to protect himself and his mom.

"Can you tell me one thing? Where did you come from?"

Jeremy considered Connie's request for a long moment and Connie thought she would hear the same words again. Instead Jeremy began listing. "We came from Mississippi—Louisiana—Oregon."

Uh oh, Connie thought, *this isn't going well*. The family moved around a lot, but he cannot tell her who was in his family. They were living in a trailer. He was supposed to protect his little brother. He was a little scared. All the time he clutched the bear to his lap with tight fingers. The interview had gone long enough, 30–40 minutes, when Connie changed the subject and began her "ups and outs." She asked some inconsequential questions, asked about a game he'd mentioned earlier in the conversation. She carefully lifted the conversation to a more cheerful interaction and began to say goodbye, assuring Jeremy she would see him again a little later.

His brother Lucas arrived in the office on a bounce. "Hey." Like Jeremy, Lucas was small for his age of 6, with delicate bones and fine features. Other than size and their identical clothes, there was nothing about the boys that would make you think they were related.

Connie started by asking, "Do you like school?"

"Yeah, when I'm here," Lucas nodded enthusiastically. Connie heard a trace of humor, maybe even sarcasm in his voice. His demeanor was entirely different from Jeremy's. He was eager to tell her things. "My mom says we're not supposed to tell people. Name, how old we are, where we live." But then he was perfectly willing to tell. He talked about school a bit then answered questions about home with lots of details. Those details were confusing and Connie began to understand why these boys were causing so much concern. Lucas alluded to things not feeling right and commented that he didn't like being around the men. Though he had earlier talked about several men living with them, Connie didn't quiz him down. Now was not the time to dig in.

"Is my mom gonna pick me up?" Lucas asked. "Is that why you wanted to talk to me?"

Connie answered carefully, "You know what? I don't have a good answer to that right this minute. I know that the school social worker wanted to talk to your mom about your birthdays and make sure that's right." Connie assured Lucas she'd talk to him later in the day and sent him back to class.

Connie went back to the office to call her supervisor. *What the hell have I gotten into?* As the forensic investigator, Connie usually got the broken bones and shaken babies. *What's going on?*

When Connie arrived back in the school front office, it was immediately clear that law enforcement got Mom and arrested her. Connie called her supervisor, Jane, and discovered that the arresting officers called DSS and requested that the kids be removed. Jane and one of the intake workers were vetting two possibilities for a foster placement. Connie's instructions now were to take the kids to their trailer and pick up personal effects then bring the kids in to the office. Although Jane didn't say, it became clear to Connie that the law enforcement plan was for Connie to get the boys to show her where they lived while law enforcement followed them.

Connie went with Sarah to get each of the boys from class. She explained, "The police just talked to me. They are taking your mom to the police station. She won't be able to take care of you. Until I can find someone to take care of you, you will be with me."

Lucas cried, while Jeremy became very still. Holding Lucas's hand, Connie led the boys out of the school building, where they said good-bye to Miss Harris and climbed into Connie's car. Connie clambered into the back seat with the boys and rolled down a window. She helped them with seat belts and asked if they knew anyone who can take care of them, grandparents, aunts and uncles, or family friends. They only knew of the nameless men with Mom. The boys settled into the car and looked at Connie expectantly.

"I hope you can help me find your house," she said. "I want you to have your clothes."

Although Lucas was still crying, he was also nodding. Jeremy was silent and clearly nervous. "Are you going to stay with us?" Jeremy finally asked.

"None of us will be able to stay at your house," Connie said, opting for honesty. "I will stay with you until we find a comfortable place for you to stay and someone else to stay with you."

Both boys knew where the trailer was located. Connie had no trouble finding the secluded piece of property. As she had suspected, they had a police escort for the short drive. The trailer was partially crushed and rotted out. The stairs were a mess. It didn't look as if anyone could live there. Connie parked near the door, feeling dismay and apprehension about the living situation.

Before Connie had turned off her car, the police officers piled out of four squad cars in an impressive hurry, causing Connie to wonder what on earth Mom could have said to them. She twisted around and glanced at the boys. Lucas's eyes were huge, staring at the men with weapons. Jeremy had retreated into himself, becoming even smaller. Connie spoke firmly, "Let me go inside with the police. Can you guys hang on here in the car?" She got eye contact and a nod from each boy before getting out of the car.

Connie stood by her car, arms crossed over her chest. If this group was storming the trailer she wanted no part of it.

John Hough came over. "You okay to knock on the door?"

Connie glared at him. There was a lot about this situation she wasn't okay with. She had been yanked around like a toy and wasn't able to do her job well. Someone was going to hear her thoughts about all of this. Later.

John caught Connie's mood. "We'll back you up."

Connie went to the trailer and looked up at the door. She wasn't risking the stairs. She reached up and knocked loudly. "Hello?"

There was no answer from inside the house. She heard some shuffling, maybe it was a pet. The smell coming from the gap between the door and the floor was nasty. She turned to John and shrugged. John stepped over and slowly opened the door.

In the middle of the tiny living area was a wood stove. The stove was not vented to the outside in any way and there was soot all over the house. There was newspaper on the floor and a trashcan near the door. Connie felt a chill, thinking about the boys living here. She followed John to the left where doors led to bedrooms, thinking she would grab what she could for the boys and get out. The first bedroom floor was covered with mattresses and men's clothing. The second room held one mattress and women's clothing.

The third bedroom floor was also covered with mattresses and in the corner there was a young woman. John froze at the door. The youngster was tiny, swallowed up in huge men's clothing, smiling up at them.

Connie brushed past him and got down on the floor with the girl. "Hi, I'm Connie. What's your name?" she said.

"Agustina."

"What are you doing in here?" Connie asked. Agustina looked back at her, confused. Connie tried again, this time in Spanish. "What are you doing?"

"Waiting," Agustina replied in Spanish, her expression clearing to the bright smile of before.

Vaguely aware of police officers continuing to check out the rest of the trailer, Connie began to interview Agustina. When all she could get in answer to questions was either one word or a headshake, Connie began to assess the girl. The girl looked very young, Connie guessed 13. When asked, Agustina said she was 17. She shook her head in answer to very basic questions. At the same time, the girl practically climbed into Connie's lap. Leaning very close, the girl touched Connie's hair and neck. Connie attempted to comfort the girl, but Agustina's touching was invasive and inappropriate. She pulled at Connie's clothing. With too little information to go on, Connie thought it was either infantile or sexual. Neither was good. Finally, Connie asked, "Will you come with me?"

"Yeah," Agustina answered. Connie led Agustina out of trailer and over to the car.

John bustled over with a hand up. "We need to interview her."

"You can't," Connie answered.

John squared his shoulders. "Can't?"

"John, she's a child."

"She said she's 17. Connie, this is a crime scene. I have to get her to interrogation. The DA wants to question her."

Connie was aware of Agustina climbing into the back seat of the car with the boys. Lucas and Jeremy were hugging her and patting her face; there were lots of smiles. Connie was also aware of the open police scanners and other officers watching.

"We're standing our ground on this," John asserted. "She's 17 and we've got probable cause on prostitution."

"But listen to me. She can't count, doesn't know her colors," Connie began.

John cut her off. "But when we get her downtown she'll come around."

"No, John, she's not high. She's a victim. She's a child." *A child in my custody.* The three children cuddling in the back seat of her car made Connie feel a ferocious sense of protectiveness. *Not even God at this point can take this child right now.* Connie realized feelings were running awfully high, things were continuing to ramp up, and things needed to ramp down to meet the needs of these kids.

5. Scientific Knowledge/Literature

5.1 Defining Human Trafficking

Chapter 1 provided a brief overview; this chapter provides a further investigation into the important definitions and concepts of human trafficking.

Social problems are value laden, in that their designations shape our understanding and responses, such as inclusion (or exclusion), significance, and resource allocation. The first chapter presented human trafficking in two broad categories—people exploited for labor or sex. Victims are found in all age groups and all genders; however, women and children are overrepresented in victim groups and more vulnerable to exploitation. Foreign-born victims are defined as victims who are not citizens of the country where they are being trafficked. Swepston (2014) argues, "The terms used are important, because different forms of the abuses of human rights that these represent have their own individual characteristics, and must be addressed differently in efforts to eliminate them. Using terms imprecisely may be useful for some purposes, but ultimately will be destructive" (p. 3). Human trafficking has been discovered in many countries around the world. It is considered a global problem that requires local, national, regional, and global responses, and swift and multifaceted interventions.

As discussed in Chapter 1, two early policies shaped human trafficking definitions and strategies to combat it. The Protocol to Prevent, Suppress and Punish Trafficking in Persons, Especially Women & Children: Supplementing the United Nations Convention Against Transnational Organized Crime (2000) defines human trafficking as

> the recruitment, transportation, transfer, harbor, receipt of persons, by means of the threat or use of force or other forms of coercion, of abduction, of fraud, of deception, of the abuse of power or of a position of vulnerability or of the giving or receiving of payments or benefits to achieve the consent of a person having control over another person, for the purpose of exploitation. (United Nations, 2000, p. 42)

The Trafficking Victims Protection Act (TVPA) of 2000 and Trafficking Victims Protection Reauthorization Acts (TVPRA) of 2003, 2005, 2008, and 2013 define human trafficking similarly as

> the recruitment, harboring, transporting, provision, or obtaining of a person for labor or services, through the use of force, fraud, or coercion for the purpose of subjection to involuntary servitude, peonage, debt bondage, slavery, or forced commercial sex acts. (TVPA, section 103[8])

These two early antitrafficking policies shaped prosecution efforts, the standards for the treatment or protection of victims, and prevention strategies (Busch-Armendariz, Nsonwu, Cook Heffron, & Mahapatra, 2013; Busch-Armendariz, Nsonwu, Cook Heffron, & Mahapatra, 2014; United Nations, 2000).

Not surprisingly, disagreements of and utility about the definition of human trafficking exist. While some experts have worked toward a broad definition to expand our understanding and scope, others point to the unintended consequences of the inclusivity. Chuang (2014) opines "Dramatic changes in the anti-trafficking field have led to a second generation of battles over definition and approach" (p. 610) and refers to this as "exploitation creep" (p. 611). Chuang (2014) argues for a narrower definition to increase legitimacy and application:

> By expanding the reach of anti-trafficking regimes to include forced labor, exploitation creep has also made labor policy and the concept of labor itself explicitly relevant to a field that had long been narrowly focused on sexual exploitation. From this labor perspective, trafficking needs to be understood as a product of weak labor and migration frameworks. A rising chorus of labor institutions and advocates is consequently seeking strengthened labor protections as a means of reducing vulnerability to trafficking. Exploitation creep has thus helped bring the anti-trafficking field to a crossroads: whether to stay the course of criminal justice—focused policy or to also pursue the structural changes that a labor approach prescribes. (p. 611)

Still, others think that the definition is incomplete, creating problems for the field:

> [Countries] need to be able to define exactly what conduct is prohibited and what is allowed in order to give certainty to the law enforcement and labor services . . . a definition of the violation to be attacked may indicate the terms of response. Debt bondage must be addressed differently from classic slavery, though both fall under the broader definition of forced or compulsory labor. (Sweptson, 2014, p. 23)

As this field continues to mature, our understanding of human trafficking and exploitation of human beings for profit will develop. The definition and our agreement will evolve, whether that entails the expansion or narrowing of the classification. Recently, discussions about the need for a nonlegal-based definition of human trafficking have emerged, giving way to continued critical thinking about how we assess criteria or qualifications of end users (professionals, victims, and offenders) and the programs, intervention, and prevention efforts, and laws and policies that are the result.

Catholic Relief Services

Brazil

www.crs.org

Catholic Relief Services (CRS) is an international nongovernmental organization engaged in a wide variety of humanitarian and development work across the globe. In Brazil, CRS works to strengthen the antitrafficking efforts of community organizations. Initiatives include raising awareness of slave labor in multiple industries (such as coffee plantations) and supporting policy and structural changes to eradicate slave labor.

5.2 Region and Migration as Influential Factors

Several factors have been considered that lead to an increased understanding of the definition of human trafficking. Region and scope are intertwined when examining the worldwide scope of the problem. For example, the International Labour Organization (ILO) reports, "When the prevalence of forced labor (number of victims per thousand inhabitants) is examined, the rate is highest in the Central and South-Eastern Europe and Commonwealth of Independent States (SEEE & CIS) and Africa region at 4.2 and 4.0 per 1,000 inhabitants respectively, and the lowest in the Developed Economies & European Union (DE & EU) at 1.5 per 1,000 inhabitants" (International Labour Organization [ILO], 2012, p. 16). However, as the ILO (2012) examines the distribution of forced labor, the regional differences shift, where the countries in the Asia-Pacific region account for 56% and Africa accounts for 18% of the global total of human trafficking (p. 16).

Migration has become another important factor to consider. For clarity, domestic victims of human trafficking are victims exploited in their countries of origin, and foreign-born victims are victims moved across borders or regions. More specifically, the ILO defines three migration classifications: cross-border (the forced labor takes place in a country to which a victim has moved or has been moved), internal (forced labor takes place in another location of the victim's country of origin), and no movement (forced labor takes place in the victim's country of origin) (ILO, 2012, p. 16).

Foundation Cristosal

El Salvador

www.cristosal.org

Foundation Cristosal uses a human rights–based approach to work against poverty and social exclusion and to defend the rights of those forcibly displaced by violence and inequality. While Cristosal's work is not specifically focused on human trafficking, the organization addresses forced internal displacement, which may increase vulnerability to exploitation and violence.

Figure 3.1 Global Estimate by Migration of the Victims of Forced Labor.

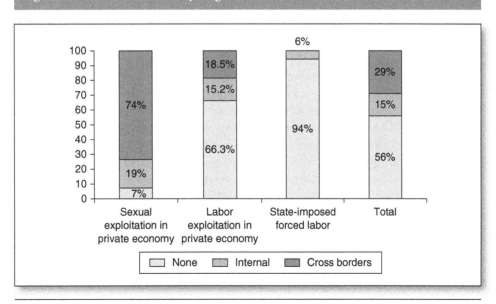

SOURCE: *ILO global estimate of forced labour: Results and methodology* (p. 16), by International Labour Office, Special Action Programme to Combat Forced Labour (SAP-FL), Geneva: ILO. Copyright 2012 by International Labour Organization. Reprinted with permission.

5.3 Understanding the Magnitude and Economies of Forced Labor

The dimensions of labor trafficking are not yet fully understood, and our understanding continues to evolve. Clawson, Layne, and Small (2006) suggest that the prevalence of exploitation for manual labor may be much higher than for sexual gratification. Similarly, Busch-Armendariz, Nsonwu, Cook Heffron et al. (2014) write, "Although there has been increased awareness to the crime of human trafficking, much less is understood specifically about labor trafficking and a full taxonomy of labor trafficking has not been developed" (p. 2). The *Global Report on Trafficking in Persons* (GRTIP) estimated that 40% of human trafficking victims worldwide were exploited for labor purposes using data collected over the period 2010 to 2012 (United Nations Office on Drugs and Crime [UNODC], 2014). Our understanding of forced labor has been shaped through examination of known cases, broad economics, specific industries where victims are exploited, and understanding the supply chain.

The United Nations Office on Drugs and Crime (UNODC), reported that the number of identified forced labor cases doubled to 36% over a 3-year period ending in 2010 (UNODC, 2012). In 2015, in the United States 13% of cases reported to Polaris (the nongovernmental agency that answers the national human trafficking resource and help line) were identified as labor trafficking, and 3% involved both sex and labor (Polaris, 2015a). The ILO (2012) estimates that more than half (56%) of labor victims are exploited in the country of birth or current residence and 26% are children or youth under the age of 18.

The International Labour Organization (ILO) (2012) estimated that 68% of human trafficking victims are exploited through traditional businesses including domestic work and 10% are exploited by state-run operations (the remaining 22% are sexually exploited). The ILO differentiates by the type of economy, suggesting that worldwide, 90% of exploitation takes place in private economies (that include industries owned by corporations or individuals) and 10% is state-affiliated forced labor such as government-run militaries, rebel armed forces, or prisons.

Labor trafficking classification has often been defined by the specific industries in which victims have been exploited (e.g., domestic service, agricultural, etc.). Busch-Armendariz, Nsonwu, Cook Heffron et al. (2014) explain, "Victims of labor trafficking may also be working in restaurants, hotels, agriculture, beauty salons, construction, manufacturing, or in tourism (such as on cruise ships) and may be psychologically or physically held through debt bondage, physical violence, or threats of physical violence against their family members. In some labor trafficking cases, victims might have also experienced sexual coercion or assault" (p. 2). More to the point, Swepston (2014) argues, "Changing social and political environments have spawned varieties of compelled labor that are adapted to changing realities" (p. 3).

Empirical evidence from San Diego County, California, suggests that about one third of unauthorized, Spanish-speaking migrant workers have experienced labor trafficking, and more than half of that population has experienced abusive labor violations or gross exploitation (Zhang, 2012). The highest rates of victimization were found in construction and janitorial services. While there is no national representative data on labor trafficking in the United States, Zhang (2012) uses San Diego data to estimate that among unauthorized Mexican immigrants, there could be almost 2.5 million victims of labor trafficking in the United States. Building off the San Diego study, Barrick, Lattimore, Pitts, and Zhang (2014) explored the prevalence of human trafficking among immigrant farmworkers in North Carolina and found that a quarter were potential human trafficking victims and 39% had experienced other abuses and exploitation.

Verité's *Strengthening Protections Against Trafficking in Persons in Federal and Corporate Supply Chains* (2015) report analyzes business sectors with high risk of human trafficking including agriculture, construction, electronics manufacturing, mining, fishing, forestry, health care, hospitality, housekeeping, textile and apparels, and transportation and warehousing. As a next step, Verité (2015) proposes to consider more than four dozen products including cotton, diamonds, flowers, tobacco, sunflowers, salt, and pineapple, to name a few. Verité (2015) also provides a summary of the six key risk factors for human trafficking in the global supply.

Key Risk Factors for Human Trafficking in Global Supply Chains

1. Hazardous/undesirable work

2. Vulnerable, low-skilled, easily replaced workforce

3. Migrant workforce

4. Presence of labor contractors, recruiters, agents, or other middlemen in labor supply chains

5. Long, complex, and/or nontransparent product supply chains

6. Substantial sourcing or subcontracting in high-risk countries

SOURCE: *Strengthening Protections Against Trafficking in Persons in Federal and Corporate Supply Chains* (p. 19), by Verité (2015). Copyright 2015 by Verité. Reprinted with permission.

5.4 Forced Labor: Understanding Domestic Servitude

Involuntary domestic servitude is a type of labor trafficking that occurs in private homes, making its detection particularly difficult for authorities, because victims of involuntary domestic servitude are often completely isolated or have limited abilities to leave the home. The servitude typically involves house cleaning, food preparation, laundry, child care, and tutoring, among other duties. Victims are often not paid or underpaid, kept from school or language courses, threatened with harm or retribution, and subjected to physical violence and sexual assault (U.S. Department of State, 2015). Similarly, child domestic labor is ripe for exploitation and human trafficking given the unbalanced power dynamics between employer and employee and the isolation that often accompanies domestic work. Often, recruiters deceive families and use coercion that is, in effect, the very definition of human trafficking (Blagbrough, 2008).

Domestic Servitude Case:
United States v. Supawan Veerapol, 1999

Defendant Veerapol, a Thai citizen and the common-law wife of a Thai ambassador to the United States, forced three Thai nationals to work as domestic servants and as workers at her Thai restaurant in Los Angeles. Beginning sometime prior to 1989, Veerapol recruited the victims from Thailand. Veerapol was able to obtain a passport and a 6-month visitor's visa for at least one of the victims, N. S., a non-English–speaking Thai citizen with a second-grade education, through her husband's contacts at the Thai embassy. Once in the United States, the defendant forced the victims to work long hours performing housework and child care. She opened bank and credit card accounts in the victims' names, which she used for her own benefit. Veerapol also used threats of legal action, verbal abuse, and physical violence to maintain control over the workers. At one point, the defendant threatened to kill one of the workers if she returned to Thailand. In addition to confiscating the victims' passports, she further isolated the women by prohibiting them from using the mail or telephone and by denying them access to Thai-language newspapers. The victims were not permitted to speak to the defendant's house guests. Veerapol permitted one victim to return to Thailand, after a Thai consular official intervened at the request of the victim's siblings. The two other workers eventually escaped from the defendant.

SOURCE: The University of Michigan Law School, 2016b, "Summary," para. 1–4. Retrieved from https://www.unodc.org/cld/case-law-doc/traffickingpersonscrimetype/usa/1999/united_states_v._supawan_veerapol.html?lng=en&tmpl=htms.

5.5 Traffickers in Domestic Servitude Cases

Busch-Armendariz, Nsonwu, and Cook Heffron (2009) reviewed 67 prosecuted cases, including 15 that were categorized as domestic servitude, and found that these cases most often involved single, foreign-born victims exploited by one or two traffickers, often a married couple from the same country of origin as the victim. Of the cases reviewed, the length of victimization varied, with the longest capacity of 19 years as discussed in *United States v. Elnora Calimlim* (see the shadow box Example of Domestic Servitude that follows). Victims are often from vulnerable social classes and economies and were promised better lives by their traffickers (Busch-Armendariz, et al., 2009).

Figure 3.2 *Domestic Servitude Awareness Poster.*

SOURCE: Reprinted from *Department of Homeland Security, Blue Campaign Resource Catalog, 2014*. Retrieved from https://www.dhs.gov/blue-campaign/materials/posters-general-awareness. In the public domain.

Example of Domestic Servitude:
***United States v. Elnora Calimlim* (2006)**

Irma Martinez worked as a servant for the Calimlim family in the Philippines from the age of 16. When the Calimlim family moved to the United States, they brought Martinez, at the time age 19, with them. Martinez entered the United States on a 2-year visa. After entering the United States, the Calimlim family took away all of Martinez's identification and travel documents and maintained control over her by refusing to teach her English and telling her that she had entered the country illegally and would be arrested if anyone found out she was there. The Calimlim family kept Martinez in the house as a servant, making her keep and maintain both their home and investment properties, telling her that she had to repay her debts for the plane ticket, food, shelter, and personal items. Martinez was kept in the basement when not working and was not allowed to contact anyone outside of the family for any purpose except for her family on four occasions. The Calimlim family kept Martinez in these conditions for 19 years until, acting on an anonymous tip, the FBI raided the Calimlims' home.

After their convictions, the defendants appealed their conviction and the government appealed the sentence. The appeals court upheld the conviction and remanded the case for resentencing.

SOURCE: The University of Michigan Law School, 2016a, "Summary," para. 1–2. Retrieved from https://www .unodc.org/cld/case-law-doc/traffickingpersonscrimetype/usa/1999/united_states_v._supawan_veerapol .html?lng=en&tmpl=htms.

5.6 Understanding Forced Child Labor and Child Soldiers

Children are included in labor trafficking estimates and are considered vulnerable to forced labor and other forms of exploitation. Even though children lawfully can work under certain conditions, the *Trafficking in Persons Report* (TIP) defines indicators of forced child labor as "situations in which the child appears to be in the custody of a non-family member who requires the child to perform work that financially benefits someone outside the child's family and does not offer the child the option of leaving" (U.S. Department of State, 2015, p. 10).

One of the most disturbing forms of human trafficking is the use of children as soldiers or other manual laborers in armed conflicts. Child soldiering is the unlawful abduction, recruitment, or use of children through force, fraud, or coercion by governmental or paramilitary armed forces. Children are used as combatants or for other work as cooks, servants, messengers, and spies. Male and female child soldiers are often sexually abused and/or exploited, and young girls may be forced to marry the commanders or other male combatants (U.S. Department of State, 2015).

5.7 Understanding Sex Trafficking

Although this textbook differentiates between sex and labor trafficking, human trafficking at its simplest definition is "compelled service," and many argue that

Figure 3.3 *The Facts on Child Soldiers and the Child Soldier Prevention Act* (CSPA, 2008). The CSPA requires the Secretary of State to identify countries that recruit and use child soldiers.

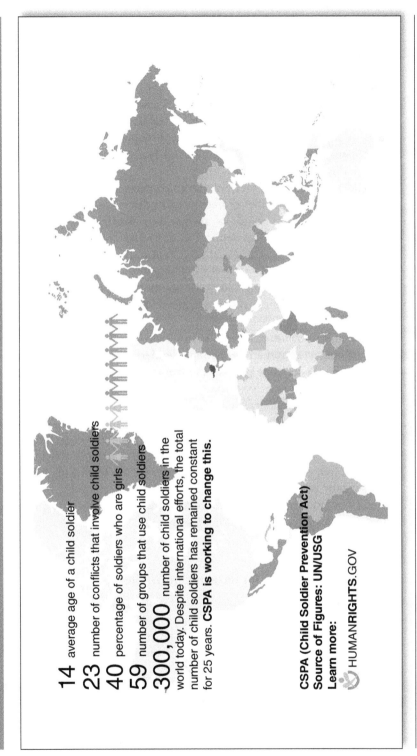

14 average age of a child soldier

23 number of conflicts that involve child soldiers

40 percentage of soldiers who are girls

59 number of groups that use child soldiers

300,000 number of child soldiers in the world today. Despite international efforts, the total number of child soldiers has remained constant for 25 years. **CSPA is working to change this.**

CSPA (Child Soldier Prevention Act)
Source of Figures: UN/USG
Learn more:
HUMAN**RIGHTS**.GOV

SOURCE: Reprinted from *The Facts on Child Soldiers and the CSPA* [online image], by HumanRights.gov, 2016, (http://www.humanrights.gov/dyn/the-facts-on-child-soldiers-and-the-cspa/). Copyright 2010 by U.S Department of State. In the public domain.

exploited sex is a form of labor (Busch-Armendariz, Nsonwu, Cook Heffron et al., 2014). Nevertheless, much of the literature in this field separates human trafficking that occurs in labor markets and human trafficking for the purpose of commercial sexual exploitation. The most common type of human trafficking identified in the UNODC *Global Report on Trafficking* (2014) based on data from 2011 was for sex exploitation (53%). In 2014, 75% of the U.S. cases reported to the Polaris hotline were for sex trafficking, and 3% involved sex and labor (Polaris, 2015a, 2015b). Thus far, our understanding of sex trafficking has been through a gendered analysis, by examining known cases, and considering the demand for commercial sex and the industries in which victims are exploited.

Gendered risk factors for human trafficking are important to consider. While traffickers exploit vulnerabilities of people, cases discovered among a diversity of victims underscore that traffickers do not always discriminate. That is, women and girls and men and boys of all socioeconomical, educational, and nationality backgrounds have been identified as victims of sexual exploitation. Nonetheless, gender is a critical variable to consider in commercial sex exploitation. Gender plays out in at least three important ways. First, women and girls are more frequently identified as human trafficking victims in commercial sex industries. Second, men are, by and large, the largest consumers of commercial sex. Third, traffickers benefiting from exploitation of human beings in commercial sex are more likely to be men, although a growing percentage of convicted human trafficking offenders in the sex industry are women (28%) (UNODC, 2014). In some parts of the world (including Europe), women encompass the largest percentage of convicted offenders, and the interplay of former victims becoming perpetrators needs to be further studied (UNODC, 2009).

Victims exploited in the sex industry are often forced into a wide variety of industry options including prostitution, pornography, brothels, strip clubs, and bars (Busch-Armendariz et al., 2013). Children forced into the sex industry in their countries of origin are often referred to as domestic minors of sex trafficking (DMST) or commercially sexually exploited children (CSEC). This terminology was developed in the Shared Hope International study funded by the Department of Justice in 2006 (Finklea, Fernandes-Alcantara, & Siskin, 2015).

International Center for Research on Women

http://www.icrw.org

Founded in 1976 as an applied research center focused on research dedicated to women and girls. The center was created in response to the recognition that international development efforts for women were being underfunded. One major area is violence against women

5.8 Understanding Domestic Minor Sex Trafficking (DMST)

Domestic minor sex trafficking (DMST) involves the commercial sexual abuse and exploitation of children and minors through the purchase, sale, or exchange of sexual services in their countries of origin. Children are trafficked into a broad range of commercial sex industries, from prostitution to pornography. A viable and accepted commercial sex market exacerbates the vulnerability of children already at high risk for human trafficking, including runaways and homeless youth and children in the child welfare system or foster care systems (Kotrla, 2010; Lloyd, 2011).

To date, there are no reliable global or U.S. estimates on the number of children being exploited in commercial sex industries. Several studies have worked toward increasing our understanding through prevalence. Richard Estes and Neil Weiner conducted one of the most notable studies funded by the National Institute of Justice on this topic. Citing the *First World Congress Against Commercial Sexual Exploitation of Children*, Estes and Weiner (2001) reported that between 100,000 and 300,000 minors are *at risk* for being sexually exploited in the United States (Estes & Weiner, 2001).

In a review of the literature on DMST, Fedina (2014) found that 78% of the publications included at least one flawed source. Lutnick (2016) states, "To rely on unsupported estimates is a disservice to knowledge building and shifts the attention away from the social factors that create vulnerabilities among youth" (pp. 6–7). Yet government actors, professionals working in the field, modern-day abolitionists and advocates, and concerned citizens are anxious to know the extent of the problem. Perhaps the most reliable and substantiated insights have been gained from qualitative studies and case studies about the lives of children that have been sexually commercially exploited.

Despite the passage of antitrafficking legislation designed to provide supportive services and protection, significant barriers to exiting the sex trade exist (Menaker, 2015). The public often misses that abuse and neglect by families of origin is often a gateway to child commercial sexual exploitation, with the average age of entry into the industry between 13 and 16 years. Moreover, stigma surrounding sexually exploited children exists particularly as they reach emancipation age, with the predominant response being criminalization (Menaker, 2015).

Survival Sex

Homelessness is an acknowledged risk factor for exploitation and known vulnerability to sex trafficking (National Center for Homeless Education, 2014). In addition, homeless youth report exchanging sex for shelter.

Survival sex is defined as involving individuals over the age of 18 who have traded sex acts (including prostitution, stripping, pornography, etc.) to meet the basic needs of survival (i.e., food, shelter, etc.) without the overt force, fraud, or coercion of a trafficker, but who felt that their circumstances left little or no other option (Covenant House, May 2013).

5.9 Traffickers, Facilitators, and the "Bottom Bitch"

Human traffickers are criminals who use and exploit other human beings by compelled service, either through forced labor or sexual exploitation, for personal and

Figure 3.4 *Sex trafficking awareness poster.*

SOURCE: Reprinted from *Department of Homeland Security, Blue Campaign Resource Catalog, 2014*. Blue campaign sex trafficking poster [Online image]. Retrieved from https://www.dhs.gov/blue-campaign/materials/posters-general-awareness. In the public domain.

financial gain. Facilitators are a part of the human trafficking enterprise and serve as a trafficker's recruiter or liaison. A facilitator may be known or unknown to the victim. Often, the facilitator is someone who develops a trusting relationship with the victim or is known to the victim. In some cases, family members are facilitators. Not all traffickers use facilitators in their operations. Convicted cases have established that no one typology of traffickers exists. Demographics of traffickers, size and scope of the human trafficking operations, and methods of control and coercion vary considerably, although it appears that consistencies within categories of human trafficking exist (Busch-Armendariz et al., 2009).

A "bottom bitch" is a victim who is co-opted by her pimp (trafficker) to recruit other victims. The role as a trafficker's "bottom bitch" may serve as a protective strategy against violence or abuse from the trafficker. However, often she may also serve as the trafficker's "functional girlfriend," such that he uses her for sex (Forth District, March 25, 2014).

5.10 johns

Insights may be gained by understanding the demand side of sex trafficking. Several studies in the last couple of years have focused on understanding *johns*, particularly those who purchase sex from young girls or suspected human trafficking victims. Specifically, researchers sought to examine attitudes and beliefs regarding prostitution. In a 2008 study in Chicago that involved 118 men who purchased sex, researchers found that 20% thought they were purchasing sex from a human trafficking victim and 75% involved a pimp. Significantly, more than half of the johns believed that most prostitutes experienced some type of childhood sexual abuse and almost a quarter (21%) felt that ending such abuse and creating better job opportunities would help eliminate prostitution. And yet it was also reported that the large majority of johns (87%) believed the misconception that most choose prostitution of their own free will (Durchslag & Goswami, 2008). In a similar study that took place in Georgia, researchers gathered data from 218 men that purchased sex from a minor female (The Schapiro Group, 2009). The research concluded that in any given month, 12,400 men pay for sex with a young woman, and 7,200 purchase sex from a minor. Chapters 4 and 6 discuss the demand side of human trafficking in further depth.

6. Factors Complicating Definitions

6.1 The Use of Labels and Terms in Context

Labels used to identify people are important. Different professionals use various labels to identify victims and offenders. Alter (2010) suggests, "Categorical labeling is a tool that humans use to resolve the impossible complexity of the environments we grapple to perceive. Like so many human faculties, it's adaptive and miraculous, but it also contributes to some of the deepest problems that face our species" (Alter, 2010, para. 2). In the human trafficking field, labor and sex trafficking may be referred to simply as human trafficking without any delineation about the circumstances of the exploitation. Sometimes the choice of one label over the other is to improve narrative efficiency, and other times, labels recognize experiences or context (Busch-Armendariz, Nsonwu, Cook Heffron, & Mahapatra, 2014). The terms *survivor* and *victim* may be used interchangeably, but in this and other fields, context is important. In the decades-old field of interpersonal violence (e.g., domestic violence, sexual assault), labels also imply political nuances. As an example, the term *victim* may more often be used in criminal justice settings or to acknowledge the criminality of the circumstances (Busch-Armendariz, Nsonwu, Cook Heffron, & Mahapatra, 2014); President's Interagency Task Force to Monitor and Combat Trafficking in Persons, January 2014) while *survivor* is often a term used in organizations whose mission is to provide support services such as emergency shelter and legal advocacy, for example. "'Survivor' is a term used by many in the services field to recognize the strength it takes to continue on a journey toward healing in the aftermath of a traumatic experience" (President's Interagency Task Force to Monitor and Combat Trafficking in Persons, January 2014). Still, in some settings, labels and terms may also be used without much forethought. Haltiwanger (October 7, 2014) suggests, "When it comes down to it, people have a right to be called whatever they want. However, as a society, we should consider the fact that labels often warp our perceptions of people. In essence, they promote both blatant and unconscious prejudice" (Haltiwanger, October 7, 2014, para. 4). Labels are particularly important in a field where people have been exploited and where trust has been eroded. The road to emotional and physical recovery may take months or years.

6.2 Values and Ideology

As with any social issue, human trafficking is shaped by a set of contextual and personal values reflective of the people and organizations that have decision-making authority (Karger & Stoesz, 2002). Karger and Stoesz (2002) argue, "Despite the best of intentions, social welfare policy is often not based on a rational set of assumptions and reliable research" (p. 5). Undoubtedly, this is true in human trafficking where there continues to be a dearth of reliable research.

In addition, the authors contend, "social values are organized through the lens of ideology. Simply put an ideology is the framework of commonly held beliefs through which we view the world. It is a set of assumptions about how the world works: what has value, what is worth living and dying for, what is good and true, and what is right" (Karger & Stoesz, 2002, p. 6). Additionally, it is important to highlight the dominance of a Western perspective in much of the published literature on human trafficking and smuggling (Schrover, 2015).

6.3 Individual Values

Engaging in advocacy/prevention efforts, providing direct practice, developing policies and programs, or conducting research in the area of human trafficking all confront the complex issue of addressing the value-laden aspect of this subject. The potential for continued harm may be great, beyond the initial trauma inflicted by the trafficker, particularly if the structure of response systems is not trauma informed, or worse, the system procedures and those who work in these systems criminalize or assign some level of culpability to victims for their victimization. Kotrla (2010) describes a demoralizing macro level example for sex trafficking victims as a "culture of tolerance, fueled by the glamorization of pimping (that) is embodied in multiple venues of daily life, including clothing, songs, television, video games, and other forms of entertainment" (p. 183). These distorted messages permeate society, conveying an acceptance of the objectification of women and the normalization of human trafficking. Vulnerable and impressionable youth who are abused and neglected are at particular risk. Child sexual abuse is oftentimes a precursor to the future exploitation of trafficking by creating emotional and physical susceptibility from being homeless and viewed as troubled or noncompliant. While perceptions are changing, youth and children have been considered "delinquent" by social service and criminal justice systems charged with their care (Mitchell, Finkelhor, & Wolak, 2010). For example, the language may incorrectly describe sex trafficking victims in ways that is demoralizing such as "child prostitute" (Mitchell et al., 2010). A systemic paradigm shift to reframe pejorative "blaming the victim" terms is needed. Victims of commercial sexual exploitation (CSE), or in cases of minors as the commercial sexual exploitation of children and youth (CSEC), domestic minor sex trafficking (DMST) or sex trafficking of minors are value-laden terms. It is important to acknowledge the victimization of this crime and provide needed services (Reid, 2010).

6.4 Secondary Trauma

Professionals working in the antitrafficking field must have a clear understanding of their professional and personal belief systems as well as continuously engaging in the self-reflective practice to examine their own values while working with victims or clients. The value-laden work of human trafficking is emotionally taxing, and many professionals experience compassion fatigue, secondary trauma, or vicarious trauma as a result of hearing victims' painful stories of exploitation through the counseling process, during a law enforcement investigation, or in witnessing the conditions in which a victim may have lived. Addressing issues of secondary trauma are discussed further in Chapters 5 and 6.

6.5 Principle-Based Organizations

Wachter et al. (2016) suggests that given "complex vulnerabilities and needs of [human trafficking] victims" (page number not available yet), services for survivors are enhanced when organizations incorporate principle-based practices. This research suggests that organizations ground their work in five principle-based practices. These include efforts to nurture the humanity and dignity of clients, contextualize survivor needs within a social justice framework, prioritize the immediate and practical needs of clients, support the dynamic nature of survivors' healing, and help identify and engage essential community and professional partners (Wachter et al., 2016).

6.6 Social Welfare Policies

Values and ideology are also expressed in the policies and human rights framework related to the prevention of human trafficking. Thus, it is important to understand the definitions that address critical social problems. Popple and Leighninger (2004) provide this working definition:

> Social welfare policy concerns those interrelated, but not necessarily logically consistent, principles, guidelines, and procedures designed to deal with the problem of dependency in our society. Policies may be law, public or private regulations, formal procedures, or simply normatively sanctioned patterns of behavior. (p. 33)

The approach of this textbook is designed to help guide a systematic understanding and framework of human trafficking. Chapter 1 previewed many policy efforts in the antitrafficking field and Chapter 7 provides an in-depth look at these policies. Policies are generally designed to provide assistance to human trafficking victims and guidance to professionals working in this field, all while expressing the values and ideology of those who developed them.

6.7 Competing Missions of Organizations

Competing missions of organizations involved in antitrafficking efforts influence and complicate the field. The TVPA was built on a framework often referred to as the three P's, or pillars, of antitrafficking work (protection, prosecution, and prevention). Partnership was included more recently as the fourth pillar to recognize the importance of collaboration among antitrafficking public and private organizations (U.S. Department of State, October 4, 2013). However, the missions of antitrafficking organizations and organizations engaged in the antitrafficking field may be perceived as competing because of the different perspectives on the best solutions to this problem. Much of the effort in the previous 15 years has added a criminal justice focus to the issue; however, as victim advocates may suggest, a criminal justice remedy is not always in the best interest of a traumatized victim. For example, compelling victims to testify in court or cooperate with law enforcement against the person or people who exploited them may increase the emotional and psychological costs to victims. In some cases, victims are concerned about financial implications for themselves or their family members when the human trafficking situation has provided for some modest means of livelihood or survival, despite immediate and long-term safety concerns.

Focused on a different argument, Chuang (2014) suggests that the field is languishing because of "exploitation creep," a widening perspective of the definition of human trafficking that now includes many other forms of exploitation, including all labor exploitation in a field that had once been mostly defined by sexual exploitation. While most may consider this development as positive because it embraces protecting more vulnerable individuals, the issue, as Chuang argues, is that it

> fend(s) off competing approaches calling for labor rights and migration policy reforms that are particularly contentious in the U.S. context . . . exploitation creep has thus helped bring the anti-trafficking field to a crossroads: whether to stay the course of criminal justice–focused policy or also pursue the structural changes that a labor approach prescribes. (p. 611)

7. Intersectionality of Human Trafficking and Other Issues and Crimes

7.1 Intersections With Other Criminal Activity

Human trafficking has been associated with many other issues such that women and girls face such concerns as female cutting or female genital mutilation, bride burning, and international marriage arranging as well as other illegal crimes such as extortion, bribery, money laundering, cash smuggling, and illicit gun and drugs sales. The full extent of these intersections is not known; however, the connection of human trafficking as an organized crime proposition is the most typically considered. A 2005 United States Department of Justice report considered the intersection of organized crime and terrorism, analyzing the relationship between international organized crime and terrorism. In doing so, the authors suggest, "There [are] striking similarities between terrorists and individuals engaged in organized crime. Both criminal types commit fraud, theft, forgery, and violent street crime. Both traffic in drugs and human beings. Both extort, intimidate, and bribe. Both do business in the legitimate economy, too. Both use subterfuge to conceal their real purpose" (Shelley et al., 2005, p. 10).

7.2 Migration

The movement and migration of people (both legal and illegal) can shed light on the economic drivers and enforcement pressures that impact human trafficking. Human trafficking often follows established migration patterns (both legal and illegal) or may veer from immigration enforcement patterns (adapting to routes with less scrutiny). Globalization has made it easier for transnational criminal networks to profit from the migration of individuals and export terrorism. Huge profits and unyielding demand for illegal drug and sex trade, cheap labor, and terrorism have fueled the growth of human trafficking. Globalization has also enabled these criminal networks to become more adaptive and less hierarchical, therefore harder to infiltrate and prosecute (Neumann, 2015). Shelley (2010) writes, "Migration flows are enormous, and this illicit trade is hidden within the massive movement of people" (p. 3).

Mapping criminal network vulnerabilities can be used to combat human trafficking in a manner similar to that used to counter terrorism, specifically involving multiple agencies (i.e., IRS, DEA, FBI, DOL, etc.). Sharing data, resources, and multiple agency involvement, coupled with a campaign to lessen consumer demand, is perhaps the best approach to countering human exploitation and the business of human trafficking (Neumann, 2015).

Although we looked at the differences and similarities of smuggling and human trafficking in Chapter 1, it is important to put context to the United States Immigration and Customs Enforcement's differences. Common misunderstandings include the idea that human trafficking involves transportation of the victim across borders and that victims are foreign born or undocumented (Kappelhoff, 2011). While this may be the case, it is not a criterion of human trafficking. And, although human trafficking and human smuggling may have similar push factors (e.g., poverty, unemployment, war, inequity, etc.) in terms of smuggling, the smuggled individual/customer and smuggler/facilitator are considered offenders, whereas victims of human trafficking are victims of crime. Of note, often customers of human smuggling may be exploited and become victims of human trafficking (Batsyukova, 2012). The United States Immigration and Customs Enforcement (ICE) agency especially delineates the definitions of human trafficking from smuggling. In the context of ICE, smuggling equates to transportation and human trafficking to exploitation. In terms of policy, smuggling is a crime against the state whereas human trafficking is a crime against the individual. However, the permeability and overlap of these two activities is noted, with smuggled persons often becoming victims of human trafficking (Busch-Armendariz, Nsonwu, Cook Heffron, & Mahapatra, 2014).

8. Complex Issues and Critical Discourse

8.1 Exploitation Creep, Definition Creep, and the Possibility of Self-Exploitation

This chapter highlights current rhetoric about the problematic issues and unintended consequences stemming from the definition of human trafficking that includes labor. Conversely, "exploitation creep," as an argument to narrow the definition of human trafficking, is relatively new in the antitrafficking field; over the last decade, much of the emphasis in the antitrafficking field has been to further clarify *and* expand the definition, not constrict it. Nonetheless, theoretical and practical concerns may be legitimate. For example, there are no universally agreed upon or clear differences between "acceptable labor practices and unacceptable exploitation (Chuang, 2014, p. 647). Chuang (2014) writes,

> Not all migrants who pay what might be considered excessive recruitment fees are harmed or cheated during the indenture. And for those who are not so lucky, some may have knowingly and willingly accepted the risk of harm as "temporal strategy"—accepting conditions of "unfreedom" and "self-exploitation" as presenting the opportunity to acquire and achieve a better future. While a

"situational coercion" analysis gives us greater insight into how coercion operates, it does not answer the question of what is acceptable 'self-exploitation.' (p. 647)

8.2 Intersection of Race, Class, and Gender

Pimps (human traffickers) are criminals and use nefarious tactics to break the spirit of their victims, including extreme physical violence. Glen Dukes is one such pimp. In two notorious trials, human trafficker Glen Dukes (pictured) was first convicted of human trafficking five women and later convicted of murder in San Antonio, Texas. In the human trafficking case, Dukes was given two life sentences. For killing one of his human trafficking victims, he was sentenced to life without parole. Not all human traffickers use physical abuse or kill their victims, however Dukes was notoriously violent. This raises complex issues of race, class, and gender, particularly for African American men. Dukes is perhaps the stereotypical epitome of a pimp, sharing characteristics of the protagonist in the movie *Hustle and Flow*. The movie's theme song, "It's Hard Out Here for a Pimp," written by Paul Beauregard, Jordan Houston, and Cedric Coleman and recorded by Three 6 Mafia, won the 2006 Oscar® for Best Original Song at the 78th Annual Academy Awards®, sparking outrage and conflicted opinions. In a *Washington Post* article, reporter Avis Thomas-Lester quotes a viewer of the award show:

Figure 3.5 *Photo of Glen Dukes in* San Antonio Current.

SOURCE: "San Antonio pimp convicted of murder sentenced to life, again" by Mark Reagan, 2015. Online image. Retrived November 15, 2016 from http://www.sacurrent.com/the-daily/archives/2015/09/23/san-antonio-pimp-convicted-of-murder-sentenced-to-life-again. Copyright 2015 by San Antonio Current. Reprinted with Permission.

> It was just like during the time when all the blaxploitation films were coming out with African Americans being portrayed as pimps and hos and gangsters. It [the Oscar win for the song] was another example of how they pick the worst aspects of black life and reward that. There are more important things in our culture that need focus more than the hardships of a pimp. (Thomas-Lester, March 7, 2006, para. 3)

Retha Hill, vice president of content for BET.com, commented:

> In the context of the movie, the song makes perfect sense. But if you have not seen the movie or are just watching the performance on the Academy Awards as members of Middle America and you hear someone talking about being a pimp, it is very difficult for you to understand. (Thomas-Lester, March 7, 2006, para. 13)

This case demonstrates the need to recognize that neither pimps nor victims represent a homogenous, monolithic group. That is, there exists great diversity of identity and background among traffickers and victims. Brown (2015) cites Lynch and Michalowski (2006), suggesting "that the potential of general criminological theory is substantially increased when they are linked to broader structural and contextual explanations of crime that incorporate race, class and gender relationships and power hierarchies" (p. 131). An intersectional framework is useful to more wholly understand the vulnerabilities of those who are victimized by human trafficking and as a useful lens for exploring traffickers and society's responses to them. The important dynamic to consider is the compounding and interrelated forms of oppression (e.g., racism, classism, sexism, ableism, homophobia, etc.) that shape the lives of those impacted by human trafficking either as victim or offender. Moreover, the key is to explore the structural injustices and inequalities that exist now and throughout history that set the contemporary stage for human trafficking including a historical context of slavery to the current and widespread incarceration of people of color. This critical analysis is not meant to minimize the responsibilities of offenders; rather, this discussion adds depth and discourse about power and oppression. Brown (2015) writes, "The aspects of gender and race have consistently correlated with criminal behavior in the majority of criminological literature. These characteristics have been identified as the strongest predictors of deviant behavior in a plethora of peer reviewed research" (p. 230).

9. Chapter Summary

Law enforcement, prosecutors, immigration lawyers, social workers and social service practitioners, other professionals, and the general citizenry are involved in eliminating human trafficking in their communities. Social scientists and economists are working to further clarify the extent of human trafficking nationally and worldwide. Human trafficking terms and definitions are complex and contextually derived and may reflect values and priorities of individuals and organizations. As a complex social problem, human trafficking intersects with many other societal problems. Lloyd (2015) proposes that vulnerability to human trafficking is often seeded in exposure to domestic violence and child abuse and also often overlaps with poverty, racism, and gender inequity. These connections place certain children at a higher risk for recruitment and exploitation into the commercial sex industry. According to Lloyd (2015), the susceptibility endures even after victims are no longer being exploited. Homelessness, poverty, and unemployment, for example, increase the vulnerability of survivors of sex trafficking to continued abuse in their intimate partnerships even after escaping or exiting the commercial sex industry.

10. Key Terms

This chapter focuses on terms and definitions. Thus, only unfamiliar terms that are not a subsection highlight are listed.

10.1 Critical analysis or theory

10.2 Intersectionality

10.3 Critical consciousness

10.4 Exploitation creep

11. Active Learning Exercises or In-Class Discussion Questions

11.1 Intersectionality

Consider the multiple and intersecting identities that may play a role in the various manifestations of human trafficking discussed in this chapter. How might racism contribute to or increase vulnerability to being exploited? How might the intersection of racism and sexism play a role in survivors' experiences of exploitation? Consider the ways that multiple and intersecting oppressions may play a role in someone's perpetration of human trafficking, including possible resulting criminal justice responses and consequences.

11.2 Critical Consciousness

How might we use a critical consciousness approach to examine our own experiences of oppression, of power, of powerlessness? And how might that impact our own role in the exploitation of others?

12. Suggestions for Further Learning

12.1 Books

12.1.1 *Caring for trafficked persons: Guidance for health providers.* (2009). Retrieved from http://publications.iom.int/bookstore/free/CT_Handbook.pdf

12.1.2 Crenshaw, K. (1991). Mapping the margins: Intersectionality, identity politics, and violence against women of color. *Stanford Law Review, 43*(6), 1241–1299. doi:10.2307/1229039

12.1.3 Freire, P. (1972). *Pedagogy of the oppressed* (M. Ramos, Trans.). New York, NY: Herder and Herder.

12.2 Films

12.2.1 GEMS—*Making of a Girl* film short

12.2.2 *Beast of No Nation* (film about child soldier)

12.2.3 *Girl Rising*

13. Research/Project Assignments/Homework/Exam Exercises

13.1 Primary Source Application: Exploring Risks

Ask students to use the Verité (2015) report *Strengthening Protections Against Trafficking in Persons in Federal and Corporate Supply Chains* as a primary source and assign students to use the key risks for human trafficking applied to one of the commodities that the agency expects to explore for labor trafficking (p. 4). How far has the organization gotten in its research on this commodity? What else is known worldwide about the product? How relevant are the risk factors for understanding labor trafficking?

13.2 Application of Critical Race Theory

Assign students to write a paper that considers Critical Race Theory and intersectionality (gender, race and ethnicity, socioeconomic status, nativity, and immigration status, for example) and vulnerabilities to human trafficking. Broad questions to address: Identify three to five ways that CRT and intersectionality apply to this vulnerable group. Identify three to five ways in which these concepts may not be applicable. What is learned about micro and macro interventions when CRT and intersectionality are used as a framework?

14. References

Alter, A. (2010). Why it's dangerous to label people: Why labeling a person "black," "rich," or "smart" makes it so. *Psychology Today*. Retrieved from https://www.psychologytoday.com/blog/alternative-truths/201005/why-its-dangerous-label-people

Barak, A. (2015). Critical consciousness in critical social work: Learning from the theatre of the oppressed. *British Journal of Social Work*. doi:10.1093/bjsw/bcv102

Barrick, K., Lattimore, P. K., Pitts, W. J., & Zhang, S. (2014). Labor trafficking victimization among farmworkers in North Carolina: Role of demographic characteristics and acculturation. *International Journal of Rural Criminology, 2*(2), 225–243. Retrieved from https://kb.osu.edu/dspace/handle/1811/61593

Batsyukova, S. (2012). Human trafficking and human smuggling: Similar nature, different concepts. *SCS Journal, 1*(1), 39–49. Retrieved from http://dialnet.unirioja.es/servlet/articulo?codigo=4045928

Beauregard, P., Houston, J., & Coleman, C. (2005). It's hard out here for a pimp. On *Hustle and flow soundtrack* [CD, Digital Download]. Atlanta, GA: Atlantic Grand Hustle.

Blagbrough, J. (2008). Child domestic labour: A modern form of slavery. *Children & Society, 22*(3), 179–190. doi:10.1111/j.1099–0860.2008.00149.x

Brown, W. (2015). An intersectional approach to criminological theory: Incorporating the intersectionality of race and gender into Agnew's general strain theory. *Ralph Bunche Journal of Public Affairs, 4*(1), 229–243.

Busch-Armendariz, N., Nsonwu, M., & Cook Heffron, L. (2009). *Understanding human trafficking: Development of typologies of traffickers phase II.* Paper presented at the First Annual Interdisciplinary Conference on Human Trafficking, Lincoln, NE.

Busch-Armendariz, N., Nsonwu, M., Cook Heffron, L., & Mahapatra, N. (2013). Trafficking in persons. In J. L. Postmus (Ed.), *Sexual violence and abuse: An encyclopedia of prevention, impacts, and recovery.* Santa Barbara, CA: ABC-CLIO.

Busch-Armendariz, N., Nsonwu, M., Cook Heffron, L., & Mahapatra, N. (2014). Human trafficking: Exploiting labor. In C. Franklin (Ed.), *Encyclopedia of social work online.* New York, NY: Oxford University Press.

Busch-Armendariz, N., Nsonwu, M. B., & Heffron, L. C. (2014). A kaleidoscope: The role of the social work practitioner and the strength of social work theories and practice in meeting the complex needs of people trafficked and the professionals that work with them. *International Social Work, 57*(1), 7–18. doi:10.1177/0020872813505630

Chuang, J. A. (2014). Exploitation creep and the unmaking of human trafficking law. *American Society of International Law, 108*(4), 609–649. Retrieved from http://www.iilj.org/courses/documents/JChuangdraft.pdf

Clawson, H., Layne, M., & Small, K. (2006). *Estimating human trafficking into the States: Development of a methodology.* Washington, DC: National Institute of Justice. Retrieved from https://www.ncjrs.gov/pdffiles1/nij/grants/215475.pdf

Covenant House. (2013, May). *Homelessness, survival sex and human trafficking: As experienced by the youth of Covenant House New York.* Retrieved from https://traffickingresourcecenter .org/resources/homelessness-survival-sex-and-human-trafficking-experienced-youth- covenant-house-new-york

Crenshaw, K. (1991). Mapping the margins: Intersectionality, identity politics, and violence against women of color. *Stanford Law Review*, 1241–1299.

Department of Homeland Security. (2016). *Blue campaign domestic servitude awareness poster* [Online image]. Retrieved from https://www.dhs.gov/blue-campaign/materials/ posters-general-awareness

Department of Homeland Security. (2016). *Blue campaign sex trafficking awareness poster* [Online image]. Retrieved from https://www.dhs.gov/blue-campaign/materials/posters- general-awareness

Durchslag, R., & Goswami, S. (2008). *Deconstructing the demand for prostitution: Preliminary insights from interviews with Chicago men who purchase sex.* Retrieved from Chicago, IL: http:// www.slaverynomore.org/wp-content/uploads/2011/07/Deconstructing-the-Demand- for-Prostitution.pdf

Estes, R., & Weiner, N. (2001). *The commercial sexual exploitation of children in the U.S., Canada, and Mexico.* Retrieved from Washington, DC: http://www.gems-girls.org/Estes%20Wiener% 202001.pdf

Fedina, L. (2014). Use and misuse of research in books on sex trafficking: Implications for inter- disciplinary researchers, practitioners, and advocates. *Trauma, Violence, & Abuse, 16*(2), 188–198. doi:10.1177/1524838014523337

Finklea, K. M., Fernandes-Alcantara, A. L., & Siskin, A. (2015). *Sex trafficking of children in the United States: Overview and issues for Congress.* (R41878). Washington, DC: Congressional Research Service. Retrieved from http://www.fas.org/sgp/crs/misc/R41878.pdf

Forth District. (2014, March 25). Sex trafficking 101, pt. 2: Terms & conditions of business. Retrieved from http://forthdistrict.com/sex-trafficking-101-pt-2-terms-conditions-business/

Freire, P. (1972). *Pedagogy of the oppressed* (M. Ramos, Trans.). New York, NY: Herder and Herder.

Haltiwanger, J. (2014, October 7). We are all human: 10 labels we need to stop using to describe people. *Elite Daily.* Retrieved from http://elitedaily.com/life/culture/we-are-human-words- we-need-to-stop-using-to-describe-people/787711/

International Labour Organization (ILO). (2012). *ILO global estimate of forced labour: Results and methodology*. Retrieved from http://www.ilo.org/global/topics/forced-labour/publications/WCMS_182004/lang--en/index.htm

Kappelhoff, M. J. (2011). Federal prosecutions of human trafficking cases: Striking a blow against modern day slavery. *University of St. Thomas Law Journal, 6*(1), 3. Retrieved from http://ir.stthomas.edu/ustlj/vol6/iss1/3

Karger, H. J., & Stoesz, D. (2002). *American social welfare policy* (4th ed.). Boston, MA: Allyn and Bacon.

Kotrla, K. (2010). Domestic minor sex trafficking in the United States. *Social Work, 55*(2), 181–187. doi:10.1093/sw/55.2.181

Lloyd, R. (2011). *Girls like us: Fighting for a world where girls are not for sale, an activist finds her calling and heals herself* (1st ed.). New York, NY: HarperCollins.

Lloyd, R. (2015). Commentary on "Human trafficking and domestic violence: Etiology, intervention, and overlap with child maltreatment." *Journal of Applied Research on Children: Informing Policy for Children at Risk, 6*(1), 9. Retrieved from http://digitalcommons.library.tmc.edu/childrenatrisk/vol6/iss1/9

Lutnick, A. (2016). *Domestic minors sex trafficking: Beyond victims and villains*. New York, NY: Columbia University Press.

Lynch, M. J., & Michaelowski, R. 2006. *Primer in radical criminology: Critical perspectives on crime, power & identity*. (4th ed.). Monsey, NY: Criminal Justice Press.

Mattsson, T. (2014). Intersectionality as a useful tool: Anti-oppressive social work and critical reflection. *Affilia, 29*(1), 8–17. doi:10.1177/0886109913510659

Menaker, T. (2015). The sex trafficking of youth in America. *Human Trafficking Series, 1*(3), 1–4. Retrieved from http://www.researchgate.net/profile/Tasha_Menaker/publication/271588805_The_Sex_Trafficking_of_Youth_in_America/links/54cd79b50cf24601c08d92c0.pdf

Mitchell, K. J., Finkelhor, D., & Wolak, J. (2010). Conceptualizing juvenile prostitution as child maltreatment: Findings from the national juvenile prostitution study. *Child Maltreatment, 15*(1), 18–36. doi:10.1177/1077559509349443

National Center for Homeless Education. (2014). *Sex trafficking of minors: What schools need to know to recognize and respond to the trafficking of students*. Retrieved from http://center.serve.org/nche/downloads/briefs/trafficking.pdf

Neumann, V. (2015). Never mind the metrics: Disrupting human trafficking by other means. *Journal of International Affairs, 68*(2), 39–53.

Ortiz, L., & Jani, J. (2010). Critical race theory: A transformational model for teaching diversity. *Journal of Social Work Education, 46*(2), 175–193.

Polaris. (2015a). *2015 Statistics*. Retrieved from http://polarisproject.org/sites/default/files/2015-Statistics.pdf

Polaris. (2015b). *Sex trafficking in the U.S.: A closer look at U.S. citizen victims*. Retrieved from https://polarisproject.org/resources/sex-trafficking-us-closer-look-us-citizen-victims

Popple, P. R., & Leighninger, L. (2004). *The policy-based profession: An introduction to social welfare analysis for social workers* (3rd ed.). Boston, MA: Person Allyn and Bacon.

President's Interagency Task Force to Monitor and Combat Trafficking in Persons. (2014, January). *Federal strategic action plan on services for victims of human trafficking in the United States 2013-2017*. (NCJ 244569). Washington, DC: Office for Victims of Crime. Retrieved from http://www.ovc.gov/pubs/FederalHumanTraffickingStrategicPlan.pdf

Reid, J. A. (2010). Doors wide shut: Barriers to the successful delivery of victim services for domestically trafficked minors in a southern U.S. metropolitan area. *Women & Criminal Justice, 20*(1/2), 147–166.

Sakamoto, I., & Pitner, R. O. (2005). Use of critical consciousness in anti-oppressive social work practice: Disentangling power dynamics at personal and structural levels. *British Journal of Social Work, 35*(4), 435–452. Retrieved from https://www.researchgate.net/profile/Izumi_Sakamoto2/publication/31106089_Use_of_Critical_Consciousness_in_Anti-Oppressive_Social_Work_Practice_Disentangling_Power_Dynamics_at_Personal_and_Structural_Levels/links/0f317533cd67c98ddb000000.pdf

Schrover, M. (2015). History of slavery, human smuggling and trafficking 1860–2010. In G. Bruinsma (Ed.), *Histories of transnational crime* (pp. 41–70). New York, NY: Springer New York.

Shelley, L. I., Picarelli, J. T., Irby, A., Hart, D. M., Craig-Hart, P. A., Williams, P., . . . Covill, L. (2005). *Methods and motives: Exploring links between transnational organized crime & international terrorism*. (211207). Washington, DC: Department of Justice.

The Schapiro Group. (2009). *Men who buy sex with adolescent girls: A scientific research study*. Retrieved from http://prostitutionresearch.com/wp-content/uploads/2014/04/The-Schapiro-Group-Georgia-Demand-Study-1.pdf

Swepston, L. (2014). *Forced and compulsory labour in international human rights law*. Retrieved from Geneva, Switzerland: http://www.ilo.org/wcmsp5/groups/public/---ed_norm/---declaration/documents/publication/wcms_342966.pdf

Thomas-Lester, A. (2006, March 7). Oscar winner hits angry chord. *Washington Post*. Retrieved from http://www.washingtonpost.com/wp-dyn/content/article/2006/03/06/AR2006030601461.html

Trafficking Victims Protection Act of 2000, Pub. L. No. 106–386, 114 Stat. 1464 (2000).

Trafficking Victims Protection Reauthorization Act, Pub. L. No. 108–193 (2003).

Trafficking Victims Protection Reauthorization Act, 22 USC § 7104 (2005).

Trafficking Victims Protection Reauthorization Act, 22 USC § 7311 (2008).

Trafficking Victims Protection Reauthorization Act of 2013, 22 USC § 7109 (2013).

U.S Department of State (2010). *The facts on child soldiers and the CSPA* [Online image]. Retrieved from http://www.humanrights.gov/dyn/the-facts-on-child-soldiers-and-the-cspa/

U.S. Department of State. (2013, October 4). *Four "Ps": Prevention, protection, prosecution, partnerships*. Retrieved from http://www.state.gov/j/tip/4p/index.htm

U.S. Department of State. (2015). *Trafficking in persons report*. Retrieved from http://www.state.gov/j/tip/rls/tiprpt/2015/

United Nations. (2000). *Protocol to prevent, suppress and punish trafficking in persons, especially women and children, supplementing the United Nations convention against transnational organized crime*. Retrieved from http://www.refworld.org/docid/4720706c0.html

United Nations Office of Drugs and Crime. (2009). *Global report on trafficking in persons*. Retrieved from https://www.unodc.org/unodc/en/data-and-analysis/glotip_2009.html

United Nations Office on Drugs and Crime. (2012). *Global report on trafficking in persons*. Retrieved from http://www.unodc.org/documents/data-and-analysis/glotip/Trafficking_in_Persons_2012_web.pdf

United Nations Office on Drugs and Crime. (2014). *Global report on trafficking in persons*. Retrieved from http://www.unodc.org/documents/data-and-analysis/glotip/GLOTIP_2014_full_report.pdf

United States v. Elnora Calimlim, No. 04 C 0248 U.S. Dist. (2006).

United States v. Supawan Veerapol, No. 98-CR-00334, Lexis Search (1999).

The University of Michigan Law School. (2016a). Case View. United States v. Elnora Calimlim. Retrieved from https://www.law.umich.edu/clinical/HuTrafficCases/Pages/CaseDisp.aspx?caseID=82

The University of Michigan Law School. (2016b). Case View. United States v. Supawan Veerapol. Retrieved from https://www.law.umich.edu/clinical/HuTrafficCases/Pages/CaseDisp.aspx?caseID=102

Verité. (2015). *Strengthening protections against trafficking in persons in federal and corporate supply chains*. Retrieved from http://www.verite.org/sites/default/files/images/Verite-Executive_Order_13627.pdf

Wachter, K., Cook Heffron, L., Busch-Armendariz, N., Nsonwu, M. B., Kerwick, M., Kellison, B., . . . Sanders, G. M. (2016). Responding to domestic minors sex trafficking (DMST): Developing principle-based practices. *Journal of Human Trafficking*. doi:10.1080/23322705.2016.1145489

Wolfer, T. A., & Scales, T. L. (2006). Decision cases for advanced social work practice: thinking like a social worker. Belmont, CA: Thomson Brooks/Cole.

Zhang, S. (2012). *Looking for a hidden population: Trafficking of migrant laborers in San Diego County*. San Diego, CA: San Diego State University.

4

The Economics of Human Trafficking

Bruce Kellison and Matt Kammer-Kerwick

In few other spheres is the need for courageous and committed leadership so critical. Personally, I unashamedly use business to help end slavery and I ask every chairman and chief executive to join me. Organizations that don't actively look for forced labor within their supply chains are standing on a burning platform. These leaders, like all of us, need support and empowerment to make major change. This is where governments can play a leading role.

—Andrew Forrest[1]
Founder and Chairman of Walk Free Foundation

I. Learning Objectives

1.1 Students will examine the two main economic aspects of human trafficking: slavery's economic impact (or size) and the cost to victims and society when victims are exploited.

1.2 Students will explore economic theories that explain the existence of markets for human bondage and products made with slave labor.

1.3 Students will be introduced to all of the points in the supply chain for goods produced with slave labor, from production to retail.

---

[1]Walk Free Foundation (2016).

1.4 Students will learn and be able to use economic arguments and to support the most efficient and effective interventions in the marketplace to disrupt and eliminate modern slavery.

2. Key Ideas

The central ideas of this chapter include:

2.1 Supply and demand factors of human trafficking are critical to building effective antitrafficking interventions and policies.

2.2 Understanding the role of the International Labour Organization in the fight against human trafficking, especially estimating prevalence.

2.3 Industry characteristics, economic sectors, and steps in global supply chains that are at increased risk for human trafficking activity as well as areas of opportunity for prevention.

2.4 Globalization's role and impact on human trafficking.

2.5 The methodologies used to estimate the economic impact of human trafficking, including both incidence- and prevalence-based approaches.

2.6 The methodologies used to estimate the size of vulnerable populations.

3. Decision Case

Hidden in Plain View[2]

At 4:45 p.m. Friday afternoon, Nora Gardner had one hand on the door frame, lifting her heavy bag to her shoulder, when one of her several graduate students asked to speak to her. Nora needed to be on the road to pick up her son from day care. "Do you need to talk to me right now?"

Bai Ch'en wore a panicked expression. "Yes." She nodded yes, too, her long black ponytail bouncing with emphasis.

Nora gave an internal sigh thinking "why, why" but she was tremendously close to Bai. "Talk fast, Bai. I have to pick up Peter."

"I have to go to court Monday," Bai began. "I was arrested for domestic violence."

Whatever Nora thought Bai might have to tell her late on Friday afternoon, that wasn't in any of her thoughts. As of that afternoon, Nora had known Bai for two years.

---

[2]This decision case was prepared solely to provide material for class discussion and not to suggest either effective or ineffective handling of the situation depicted. While based on field research regarding an actual situation, names and certain facts have been disguised to protect confidentiality. The authors wish to thank the case reporter for cooperation in making this account available for the benefit of students and practitioners (Wolfer & Scales, 2006, p. 29).

Not only was Bai one of her graduate research assistants, Bai had worked for several months as Nora's family helper when her son Peter was an infant. They saw each other nearly daily, and Bai often came to Nora's home for meals and to play with Peter. Nora was concerned about Bai's overly jealous boyfriend and they had conversations about their relationship, but nothing she knew about the young woman fit with the words she was hearing.

Nora Gardner

Nora Gardner was an aspiring assistant professor at Arizona State University. A Licensed Master Social Worker (LMSW) PhD with years of social work experience working in sexual assault agencies and domestic violence shelters, Nora's research and scholarship centered on the legal aspects of these two issues. A prolific researcher, Nora had already built an impressive resume on campus and within the response agencies in town. By crafting research projects aimed at producing concrete interventions, she kept in touch with the service delivery system she cared about while pursuing her academic career. She met her husband Greg when they were both 40 and pondered adoption when she became pregnant a couple of years later.

Nora and Greg both worked quite a bit from home and doted on their infant son. To help support them, they sought to hire someone who could be with the baby while they worked. The university employment services sent three applicants for them to vet. Intent on hiring a student, Nora and Greg were delighted with Bai's demeanor and energy. It was a definite plus for them to be able to help support an international student with employment.

Bai was a great addition to the Gardner household. Unflaggingly cheerful and energetic, Bai loved Peter. An extra set of hands, eyes, and ears in the house made life far more productive. Nora and Greg worked in their home offices while Bai played with Peter, kept him clean, and ferried him up and down the stairs to nurse or gather kisses. She helped keep up with laundry and the group often shared meal times.

It was clear to Nora that Bai would be better off with a job on campus. On-campus employment is accompanied by tuition assistance and health benefits that the Gardners couldn't provide as private employers. Bai wasn't eligible for any non-school-sponsored employment on her student visa. Nora made the offer, and Bai was appreciative. The Gardners found day care for Peter, and Nora offered a research assistant position to Bai.

Despite no longer working in the Gardner home, Bai came over for meals and celebrations regularly. Between seeing Bai during the day at work and on more social occasions, Nora felt well informed about Bai's life. Nora and Greg knew Bai quite well.

Bai Ch'en

Bai Ch'en was the product of China's one-child policy. She grew up in a sheltered environment where she was cherished and was very close to her parents. After college in China, Bai recognized that work opportunities in China weren't going to be very lucrative for her. Knowing she needed to support her parents and ensure them a safe and comfortable old age, she applied to schools in the United States for graduate programs. At 22 years old, she arrived in Arizona at Arizona State University (ASU) on a student visa, ready to earn a PhD in psychology.

Bai was young, cute, had long dark hair, a big smile, and big, dark eyes. She was always impeccably dressed. She didn't have much money, but she liked fashion. She worked very hard in school in China in order to get to the United States.

The arrangement for many international students at ASU was living in apartment complexes, leasing a room that was part of a large four or five bedroom apartment. There were shared living spaces, bathrooms, and kitchens, but the bedrooms were private and padlocked. One of her roommates was a man, Luk, also a Chinese international graduate student, whom she dated.

Once settled in school, Bai began looking for work. She was intent on making money to send home to her parents. Legal work opportunities were through school. Through the graduate school, she posted her resume on a website where employers could hire students; she also applied for any university position for which she thought she was qualified. She really liked the idea of working for a professor, taking care of kids, and doing light housework. Her school work was very challenging and required a lot of hard work. The possibility of having a job in a relaxed home setting was very welcome.

Bai quickly fell in love with Peter Gardner. The 4-month-old was a round, feisty, fearless baby with a ready laugh. Nora and Greg Gardner were incredibly nice and very generous. Bai called her parents often and she talked about her new "family" with affection and humor. She and her parents felt really lucky; Bai's parents told her often how proud they were of their adventurous daughter.

Graduate school did not go as well as Bai planned. Though her spoken English was strong, she struggled to express herself in writing. Professors and advisors found her confusing and she didn't know how to communicate to them well with the respect she knew they were due. She worked very hard in her classes, though she didn't get very good grades. She came to the United States from a very sheltered upbringing. Her critical thinking skills were not strong. She was a little naïve. Despite her struggles, Bai was always positive. Nora asked her about it one day. Bai explained that her mother told her that people don't want to be around people who are blue or down. She said she learned to always put on a happy face. Her parents were blue-collar workers. Her father worked in a factory and they saved every penny to send her to the United States. The compliance so invaluable to her at home became a barrier within a U.S. university, where the rules of communication were often baffling. At the end of her first year, her advisor recommended she leave the PhD program and attempt a master's degree. Bai transferred from the PhD program in psychology to the master's program in education. The Gardners found a day school for Peter, but Nora offered Bai a graduate assistant appointment with a research project.

The school of education was much friendlier and less competitive than the psychology department. Students and professors were patient communicators who understood Bai and enjoyed working with her. And everyone at the Research Center on

Violence loved Bai. Bai always had a huge smile on her face. Everything was "super" and she always offered to help. Year two in the United States was more fun, more successful, and Bai made more money. She had health insurance and with her tuition stipend she was able to send more money home. She graduated with a master of education (M.Ed.) degree. ASU employed her under a special visa for a little while after she had graduated. But eventually, it couldn't employ her anymore under that particular visa and she didn't have the skills the team needed. So Nora had encouraged her to continue looking for jobs. She had a master's degree in education, and she wanted to work for a tech company.

Bai lived pretty frugally and saved money to send home to her parents. She had not been home to China since she had arrived. She hoped she would bring her parents to the United States for her graduation. That didn't happen. Nora asked why not, and Bai never wanted to explain why or how. It seemed that it was just too expensive. She talked with her parents all the time. She was close with both her parents. It was important to her and very stressful for her to always stay employed and not get into immigration trouble. She felt like her prospects in China were slim.

A Revelation

No amount of surprise or concern was going to change the time Nora needed to arrive at the day care center. She asked Bai to walk with her to her car and give her more information.

Bai described an argument with her boyfriend that escalated into a confrontation that included raised voices and broken household items. During this argument, her boyfriend tried to strangle her. Bai took her long, manicured fingernails and dug them into his cheek to get him off of her. In the process, she hurt him pretty badly. But she didn't tell the police that.

Bai Called 911

In the moments waiting for the police to arrive, Bai's boyfriend convinced her to say they had been joking around. The police separated them. Bai told the police the story upon which she and her boyfriend had agreed. He told the police that she had taken a broken broomstick after him and she was the aggressor. She was arrested and spent the night in jail. They stayed living with one another until the court date. She hired an attorney. The lawyer's recommendation to her was that she attend batterer intervention and her record would be expunged. Nora told Bai she would be at the court with Bai. Bai's boyfriend did not want to press charges, so he wasn't part of the court hearing. He told the prosecutor that he wanted her held accountable but he didn't want her to go to jail.

Nora drove away from campus fuming. She had been talking to Bai about this boy for weeks, months perhaps, and Bai described a jealousy that Nora found unattractive in a young man.

Nora called a friend at the DA's office. She called JoLynn Smith (who now works at the Research Center on Violence). Nora knows the judges and prosecutors, and some of them know her. Bai was a complete wreck in court. JoLynn tried to get a conversation with the assistant DA and Nora. They went in a back hall. Nora said that she had been concerned about Bai's boyfriend and his extreme jealousy and had had multiple conversations with Bai about their relationship. The agreement in the end of that case was the DA was going to drop the charges, ignore the charges. They were not going to tell the boyfriend that. The boyfriend was telling Bai a different story the whole time.

The day of the court hearing, she moved out of the shared apartment. The agreement with the prosecutor had no legal binding at all. The agreement was based on back-office conversations among folks who had prior relationships. Bai agreed to move out and find another place to live. The DA called her boyfriend to say that they ordered her to stay away from him. This wasn't a court order but a note in the file. They also told him that she was to not have any contact with him at all. It was as if he was the victim, but everyone knew that she was the victim. Bai moved out, moved in with a friend, and ceased contact with him.

Nora and Greg continued to have Bai over for dinner often. The affection between the family and Bai was stronger than it had ever been. When Bai went out of town, she would bring things back for Peter. Although Bai was no longer an employee or student, she remained an integral part of the Gardners' lives.

Over dinners, Bai told them about her job searches and finally about working for a mortgage mogul in Austin, Mr. Xiāo. This owner was Chinese and hired only Chinese workers. There were a dozen or so other workers. It wasn't clear whether the job was a stroke of good fortune or a situation that would further isolate Bai from the potential of steady employment.

Over several months, Nora would hear bits and pieces. Mr. Xiāo wanted the women in the office to look a certain way. He wanted only young women like Bai. Bai would say that and giggle. He also had a daughter to whom he was mean. Nora thought his daughter was extremely anxiety ridden. Bai would talk about having to do more and more for the Xiāo family, picking the children up from school, for example.

One day at dinner, Bai mentioned, "Mr. Xiāo had me fill out identification documents that are falsified." She explained all the visa documents for the employees of this mortgage business were falsified. Much of what Bai talked about didn't make entire sense to Nora or Greg. All they knew about the mortgage business was what they learned from buying houses. But, when Bai told them she wasn't getting paid, they did know something about employment laws in the United States. Nora explained U.S. laws around work hours and pay requirements. Bai was intently interested in learning what the law said; she was always trying to make sure she was employed under the right status.

"We aren't earning vacation," Bai added. She also confided that as a whole group of Chinese worried about keeping their status. "We're not going to ask a lot of questions."

Through the evening, Bai shared more and more information. Prompted by Nora's questioning, not everything Bai shared was coherent. Nora thought Bai wasn't aware that some of the things described were not legal. Nora guided the conversation, saying,

"Bai, you are entitled to earn leave. Work hours should be understood between employers and employees. Do you have anything that says this is an equal opportunity employer from the Department of Labor? Have you ever seen anything in your company that says what your rights are and where to go if you have a complaint?" Bai did not know her rights as a worker and couldn't comprehend that she could refuse things Xiāo asked of her.

But, when Mr. Xiāo started having Bai take care of his kids, she witnessed him not treating his kids or wife well. She thought he was having an affair with someone in the office. He used foul language. She said it was a horrible place to work with sexual harassment, labor violations with leave time, hostile environment, not knowing how and when they would be paid, and getting money deducted from pay for things that didn't make sense. She said they got paid based on the number of mortgages they sold. It seemed to Greg that Xiāo was selling mortgages. The business sold to only Chinese customers.

As Nora delved deeper, it came out that Bai never got paid directly. When she got paid, the funds were deposited to her parents' account in China. It was one of the things that scared her the most. Xiāo had a concrete connection to Bai's parents. It wasn't just the responsibility she felt being the breadwinner to aging parents or as an only child. She was also afraid about the implicit threats Xiāo gave about what he would do if staff left, about blowing the whistle.

"He might be a nobody in the United States but would be considered powerful in China," Bai explained. Xiāo never said that if she left him he would kill her parents, but that's what she was afraid of. It kept her from leaving but also kept her from aligning with anyone else in the organization. Xiāo was an expert at ensuring people felt isolated, afraid, and trapped.

Late in the evening, Nora said, "It sounds like a really difficult place to work. The environment is really difficult. It sounds like not only he is difficult, but you find difficulty finding support in each other." Bai admitted that was true. People were immobilized. Xiāo had these pieces of control over them all.

Finally, Nora asked, "Do you feel physically safe?"

Bai shook her head. She said she feared the situation would result in Xiāo sexually assaulting her. One day at his house, he told her to take off all her clothes. She refused. But she didn't know what would happen in the future. That fear was what allowed her to talk to Nora and Greg about the situation fully. Bai was feisty by nature, in spite of being raised to be compliant. Fighting back against this guy who was powerful was not something she would do until it threatened her personal safety. Now, she was sure she never wanted to go to his house again. She was afraid of picking up his kids and having to go by his home.

Nora felt Xiāo targeted Bai in particular, though he was probably exploiting all of the workers. Bai got special and extra attention, it seemed. Nora would not normally make up someone's mind for them. But in this instance, she suspected Bai wanted out of the situation and was communicating with Nora as respectfully as she could. Nora said, "Today needs to be the last day you work there." They started to do safety planning immediately. They discussed what Bai could tell Xiāo about not coming to work.

During the past year, after the domestic violence arrest, Bai was asked to attend support groups at the local battered women's shelter. But she never fully engaged with the agency. Nora wanted to ensure Bai was connected with services this time around. Two days later, Nora and Bai sat in Nora's office and Bai called the International Rescue Committee Agency (IRC). Bai gave them formal permission to talk with Nora as well. They opened a case on Bai's behalf. Bai went to meet with a caseworker at IRC, and she was referred from there to SAFE for South Asians, a program for battered women from Asia. She started seeing a social work counselor referred by SAFE and an immigration attorney at Services & Charities.

Knowing Bai well, Nora and Greg knew she would struggle thinking through her choices. Many long conversations included talking through the possible risks. Bai worried about taking the gamble on reporting the trafficking to law enforcement. No one could fully assure her that the case would be successful. If the case failed, Bai would be deported. Claiming status as a trafficking survivor would exempt Bai from working in the United States until she obtained a visa, which might take up to a year. During that time, who would support her or her family? If she was deported back to China, the work possibilities were terrible and low paying. They did other problem solving. If it wasn't going to be a trafficking case, were there other immigration relief options? The information Nora got back from Bai didn't make sense in terms of what was or wasn't available. Eventually, Nora asked Bai to sign release of information forms with the various agencies that would allow Nora to talk directly with the staff.

In the meantime, Bai told the IRC staff she had been forced to falsify work documents and had remained in the United States working under false pretenses. Yet, without the certification as a trafficking victim, she was out of options for a visa. Eventually, as a human trafficking victim, one can become a permanent citizen. "That is gold," Nora commented. There was no other way Bai could become a citizen, unless she married a citizen, so she thought, "Let me make the best of this." She had no idea she was a trafficking victim until Nora started asking questions. "Bai was opportunistic, not in an evil way, but in a go-getting way. She came halfway across the world as a 20-something and made it in this country, all by herself." Weighing the risks of her current situation against the possibility of U.S. citizenship and being able to bring her parents to the United States as well were her decisions. Bai asked Nora to talk to both her attorney and her counselor at SAFE. Bai didn't think she (Bai) understood why law enforcement wasn't considering it a slam-dunk case. She wanted Nora to talk to these folks for more clarity. Bai may have been making statements that were inconsistent with what Nora knew was the usual progression of human trafficking cases.

It was agonizing for Nora talking through the decision with Bai. Nora knew something about the power (real or perceived) that this Chinese employer had over Bai's parents. She understood Bai's need to support her parents and the real possibility that if she formally reported the trafficking that she would not be certified and would be deported. It took several months to work through everything.

One important element to Nora at this stage was that Xiāo continued to exploit other employees and was abusing his daughter. Those concerns were compelling to Bai as well. Bai also felt some guilt about helping his family. She couldn't do anything without reporting the trafficking: How to stay in this country, how to report or not report, how to hold Xiāo accountable, how to continue working, how to care for her coworkers—she couldn't do all that at the same time.

Bai's distress was also about saving face. "You would not want to bring any shame to your family, no matter how exploited you were. You would not be telling people about that. You would just endure it. This is what we do. We stay at work until the boss leaves. And the boss doesn't have to tell you what time he is leaving. And everybody is still sitting there. It can be 9:00 at night and people don't leave."

At one point, Nora expressed the oddness of the situation to Greg. "I just happened to be a trafficking researcher and social work professor and former employer of this survivor," Nora said. And she had all the connections to providers. It defied the imagination that, despite Nora's work and scholarship on the issues of interpersonal violence and trafficking, a victim of both was hidden in plain sight. Bai worked in Nora's home and at the university, hearing about these issues regularly, and yet no one knew any of this.

The IRC social worker and Nora wondered about possibly vetting the case with a U.S. Immigration and Customs Enforcement (ICE) agent to see if it would fly as a human trafficking case. This practice was done regularly for clients who are on the fence about whether or not to report. The IRC social worker and Nora had talked about first making sure the physical safety issues were taken care of, that Bai's parents understood enough of what was happening (it was better not to tell them everything), and that this consult would happen after Bai was connected with services. The social worker and Nora talked about the next steps, the complexities of reporting, and what details law enforcement would need to open a case and start an investigation, how long that investigation might take, and what it would mean for Bai during that time.

One phone conversation in particular kept circling in Nora's memory. Bai said, "Nora, you have to tell me what to do." Bai's words felt like they were trying to choose between Bai staying in the country under false pretenses or reporting the abuse and jeopardizing her whole future in the wake of trauma.

Nora asked the IRC social worker directly, "Do you think this is labor trafficking?" She felt like she was wearing mother-bear, protective glasses. That was the first question she asked the social worker.

The social worker answered yes, she did think it was labor trafficking, and she didn't know if law enforcement would see it the same way or be able to certify Bai as a trafficked person. She said, "We will have to see, from a law enforcement perspective, if it meets the elements of human trafficking."

They decided to attempt the half-step of vetting the case anonymously with ICE. They had a good relationship with an ICE agent and felt like they could trust him. Nora got a report back, by phone, from the social worker, saying that the ICE agent was not sure it met the elements and would not investigate further. Without the victim coming forward, it would be difficult to determine whether or not trafficking happened.

Nora then got a panicked call from Bai, "What should I do? They want me to make a decision. They cannot make a determination unless I come forward. But if I tell my story and they decide it is not human trafficking, even though you say it is and my social worker says it is, they can say it is not."

Nora and the social worker had been preparing Bai the whole time for the potential that law enforcement may differ on identifying her situation as trafficking. "If they say it is not trafficking, what am I left with? Even if they do say it is trafficking, what are the real benefits of me doing this? Let me get this straight. We're not sure law enforcement will agree it is trafficking. If not, I get deported. If they do decide it is trafficking, I can't work for a year. Once I get a T visa I can work, but how can I find a job if I haven't worked for a year? And who will send my parents money that whole time?" Bai's voice betrayed all the risks she feared taking.

"This is really important, Bai," Nora said. "You need to think this through clearly. The other risk is you continuing to work under false pretenses in the United States."

Epilogue

Ultimately, Bai decided not to risk reporting the workplace abuses to law enforcement. She also decided to stay in the country and look for other jobs. She later moved to Houston and kept in touch with the Gardners through phone calls and occasional visits.

Bai eventually found a job at a mobile phone carrier, where her fluent Chinese was a valued asset. She asked Nora to give her a job reference as her former employer.

The IRC social worker and Nora both knew Bai's student visas were expired and her current visa documents were false, as did Bai's parents, former employer, and friends. Nora didn't know what her duty regarding reporting the information to a prospective employer was. The ethical question of giving Bai the stellar reference she deserved was a difficult one. While Bai was a student, the university held the responsibility for her visa. But an employer assumes the visa status of a visiting employee in the United States by becoming the person's sponsor. "It is complicated," Nora explained. Hiring Bai on false papers was a crime for both Bai and the company. It was not solely a matter of Nora being honest; it was also a question about whether or not Nora could be held criminally liable for knowingly putting the new employer at risk of legal trouble.

In addition to requesting confirmation of Bai's dates of employment, the company representative wanted to speak directly with Nora for references.

4. Selected Theories

There are several economic theories that provide useful conceptual frameworks to understand human trafficking including demand theory, cost-benefit economic theory, and migration theory. While these theories do not provide "cause and effect" explanations, they offer a behavioral economic lens through which to better understand their existence and work more effectively toward their containment and eventual eradication.

Demand theory considers the relationship among supply, demand, and price. This economic theory focuses on the volume of buyers and threshold of willingness by those buyers to spend their assets on purchasing services. Wheaton, Schauer, and Galli (2010) suggest a cost-benefit economic theory for human trafficking in which traffickers consider the benefits of the crime weighed against the costs. Grounded in cost-benefit theories, human trafficking exists because the potential profits (benefits) outweigh the risks (costs). Traffickers may consider costs as the financial investment (e.g., payment for the assistance of facilitators, expenses related to basic needs of enslaving people, etc.) or hazards related to potential criminal penalties.

Others have studied the economics of human trafficking from a risk analysis viewpoint. Mahmoud and Trebesch (2010) studied the micro-level economic factors that drive human trafficking and consider risk for human trafficking related to victims' willingness to partake in undocumented migration. Their research demonstrates that awareness campaigns and information about this risk may reduce the potential risk for exploitation by traffickers. Similarly, Kara (2011) focused on global economic factors (e.g., globalization, migration, etc.) that increase vulnerabilities to human trafficking. He suggests that antitrafficking interventions focus on measures specifically aimed at increasing the risks to traffickers while reducing profitability.

5. Scientific Knowledge/Literature

5.1 Introduction

The research literature on human trafficking is not extensive. Because of its complexity, human trafficking has been difficult to categorize conceptually and to analyze methodologically. The basics are easy enough to grasp: Demand for cheap labor on farms, in factories, in the underground sex economy, or in households is being met by a labor supply. While supply and demand may be important, a more thorough investigation of the economics of human trafficking considers international labor and capital flows, supply-chain management and consumer behavior, and the economic impact on victims, including their physical and mental health and the cost of lost productivity and wages over a lifetime. This chapter explores economic forces at work in modern-day slavery.

5.2 Economic Size of the Problem

Economists quantify the size of firms and industries so they can describe how resources are allocated in an economy. Quantifying the size of illicit economic activity like human trafficking is important because policy makers can assess the economic impact of the problem and allocate resources necessary to fight the activity. The gross world product (the combined gross national product of all the countries in the world) was about USD 77 trillion in 2014 (World Bank, 2016). The value of illegal activity, by its nature, is difficult to calculate precisely. However, the United Nations estimated in 2003 that the global value of illicit drug sales at retail was USD 322 billion, about 1% of gross world product at the time (United Nations Office on Drugs and Crime, 2005, p. 16). Because the world economy has grown since then and the global drug trade has similarly expanded, the value of illegal drugs in 2013 could be as high as USD 750 billion, making it the largest of the top three most lucrative illegal markets in the world (authors' calculation). Human trafficking is second, valued at USD 150 billion world-wide per year (International Labour Organization, 2014). Illegal arms trafficking is widely believed to be worth at least USD 6 billion per year (Schroeder and Lamb, 2006). Clearly, in human trafficking, the world confronts a significant economic crime with dramatically large human costs. And it is growing: One of the world's most influential antitrafficking organizations, the Walk Free Foundation, commissioned the Gallup polling organization in 2016 to survey a random sample of 42,000 people in 53 languages worldwide and estimates that 45.8 million people are trapped in some form of human trafficking, including an estimated 57,700 in the United States (Walk Free Foundation, 2016).

5.3 International Labour Organization (ILO)

The International Labour Organization (ILO) is a nongovernmental organization founded in the wake of World War I as a global organization to connect governments, employers, and workers to "secure the permanent peace of the world" by promoting humanitarian working conditions (International Labour Organization, 2010, p. 5). After World War II, it became a specialized agency of the United Nations, where it remains today. It was one of the first global groups to examine systematically the problem of modern slavery, and in 2005 it published the first quantitative estimate of human trafficking worldwide (International Labour Organization, 2014, pp. 5–6).

To build its latest economic estimate, the ILO collected and analyzed data on the annual profits from three types of labor: forced sexual labor (sex trafficking), domestic work, and nondomestic labor (labor trafficking). It estimated that of the 21 million people trapped in slavery worldwide, 18.7 million were laboring in the private sector, and 2.2 million were trapped in state-sponsored labor trafficking schemes like forced prison labor and victims enslaved by paramilitary and military forces. Due to a lack of transparent data, the ILO omitted from its estimate an analysis of the value of the work output from state-sponsored human trafficking. Breaking down the private-sector exploitation figure further, the ILO estimated that 4.5 million people were sex trafficking victims worldwide, and 14.2 million were labor trafficking (ILO, 2014).

To estimate the global value of trafficking worldwide, the ILO combined two common approaches to economic estimation in a hybrid methodology. The first approach involved a "profit-and-loss" estimation based on revenues generated by each slave, minus the cost of running the forced-labor operation (Kara, 2009). For example, if 100 forced laborers produced bricks for home building and the brick factory owner sold those bricks for a total of $35,000 but it cost the owner $5,000 to feed and house (but not to pay) the slaves, plus another $5,000 in raw materials, the "profit-and-loss" estimation methodology would arrive at $25,000 as the amount of revenue generated by all 100 slaves (or $250 per slave).

ILO researchers then combined the first approach with a second "value-added" methodology that looked at wages in industrial or agricultural sectors known to be vulnerable to trafficking activity. They then discounted those wages by the percentage of a trafficked worker's wages that was estimated not to have been paid to that worker who had been caught in a situation of forced labor. This approach accounts for an important economic aspect of human trafficking: Victims often are paid at least a portion of the wages they earn or are trapped in a situation of forced labor in which they are paid no wages for only short periods of time. "Victims usually lose much [but not all] of their earnings due to wage retention, debt repayments, and underpayment of wages" (ILO, 2014, p. 12). Variations in employment rates and wages were made to build regional estimates.

The estimate that resulted from this combined approach is presented in Table 4.1 below.

5.4 Industrial Characteristics That Increase Risk for Human Trafficking Activity

Human trafficking victims are difficult to identify and in some regions the challenges to identification are formidable. Nevertheless, experts have identified a number of industries with certain characteristics that are more prone than others to human trafficking (Verité, 2015). The U.S. Department of State and other sources point to industries including the following:

- Hazardous/undesirable work
- Vulnerable, easily replaced, and/or low-skilled workforce
- Migrant workforce
- Presence of labor contractors, recruiters, agents, or other middlemen in labor supply chain
- Long, complex, and/or nontransparent supply chains

However, this is one typology of the common characteristics among investigated cases of human trafficking, including sex trafficking. As a cautionary note, not all low-skilled workers or industrial operations with work or workforces marked by these characteristics necessarily always function as human trafficking hubs. By the same token, this is also not meant to imply that trafficking is never found in other economic sectors without these characteristics. Ultimately, heterogeneity is a factor in human trafficking and among traffickers that demands a collaborative response from governments, corporations, and citizens.

5.5 Identified Industries at Higher Risk for Human Trafficking Activity

Researchers and advocates have identified the following industries around the world with significant risk of labor trafficking (Verité, 2015):

- Agriculture
- Construction
- Electronics and Electrical Products Manufacturing
- Extractives/Mining and Basic Metal Production

Table 4.1 Estimated Annual Profits From Forced Labour (US$ Billion)

Region	Forced Sexual Exploitation	Domestic Work	Non Domestic Labour	Total
Asia-Pacific	31.70	6.30	13.80	51.80
Latin America and the Caribbean	10.40	.50	1.00	12.00
Africa	8.90	.30	3.90	13.10
Middle East	7.50	.40	.60	8.50
Central and South-Eastern Europe and CIS	14.30	.10	3.60	18.00
Developed Economies and EU	26.20	.20	20.50	46.90
World	99.00	7.90	43.40	150.20

SOURCE: *Profits and poverty: The economics of forced labour* (p.13) by The International Labour Office, 2014, Geneva: International Labour Organization ILO. Copyright 2014 by International Labour Organization. Reprinted with permission.

- Fishing and Aquaculture
- Health Care
- Hospitality
- Housekeeping/Facilities Operation
- Textile and Apparel Manufacturing
- Transportation and Warehousing

Again, this is not to argue that a majority or even a sizeable fraction of firms in these sectors engage in modern slavery. Rather, where human trafficking cases have been reported, investigated, and prosecuted around the world, firms in these sectors have frequently appeared. Likewise, human trafficking found in one sector in a particular global region does not mean it will translate across regions.

5.6 Tensions Among Wages, Wage Theft, and Human Trafficking

The boundary between slavery and liberty is not always clearly defined, and the differences among wages, wage theft, and human trafficking can be blurry. As previously discussed, there are disincentives for workers (and victims) to come forward and seek help, not to mention to be emancipated. For example, up to one third of all human trafficking victims are enslaved from 1 to 3 years, while half of victims are exploited for labor purposes for less than 6 months, holding out hope that they will eventually earn some money for their work (ILO, 2014, p. 9).

A recent study conducted in San Diego, California (Zhang, Spiller, Finch, & Qin, 2014), used respondent-driven sampling (RDS) to estimate the percentage of unauthorized immigrant laborers at risk for being trapped in human trafficking. The percentages indicate the risk for human trafficking in that industry in San Diego County:

- Construction (35%)
- Janitorial and Cleaning (36%)
- Landscaping (27%)
- Agriculture (16%)
- Food Processing (32%)
- Manufacturing (38%)

Signal International, Labor Trafficking Case: 2006–2015

Overview

Signal International, a privately held marine-services company, perpetrated one of the largest single cases of human trafficking in U.S. history. Signal was based in Alabama but had operations in Mississippi and Texas. The trafficking case was centered at Signal's Gulf Coast port operation in Pascagoula, Mississippi, where it built ships and repaired offshore oil drilling platforms.

Recruitment

After Hurricane Katrina devastated the Gulf Coast and its economy in 2005, many businesses were eager to take advantage of federal recovery funds and rebuild their operations. In 2006, Signal hired recruiters based in India to identify workers to bring to Pascagoula. The recruiters posted ads seeking 500 pipefitters and welders at wages up to $18 an hour, including the promise of a Green Card and permanent residence in the United States. As is often the case in human trafficking, the recruiter charged each worker up to $20,000 for brokering the deal, so workers who accepted Signal's job offer were immediately in debt. Some of the workers borrowed the recruiting fee from friends and family and in some cases sold their wives' gold jewelry. In addition, Signal's promise of the Green Card was fraudulent; it warned the workers, who were actually applying to come to the United States on temporary 9-month H-2B visas, not to mention the Green Card in their U.S. Embassy interviews or disclose that they had paid fees to recruiters.

(Continued)

(Continued)

Working and Living Conditions

The work camp was set up on the edge of Pascagoula at Signal's shipyard. Working as ship welders in round-the-clock shifts, the Indian guest workers were essentially prisoners, not guests, in the United States. Upon arrival, the workers were coerced into signing a "lease" to cover their room and board at the facility. The exorbitant and nonnegotiable lease payment was far above local rental market rates and up to a third of most workers' monthly salary. If they had not signed the "lease" with Signal, workers faced deportation and loss of their recruitment fee.

The guest workers lived in cramped, unsanitary trailers, 24 to a room. Signal called the trailers "man camps" and the workers could not have visitors on site. Internal company documents later revealed that Signal executives saw the man camps as a "profit" center for the company that generated $731,000 in 2007 for the company. Security guards checked the workers in and out of the camps, frisking them each time. Signal believed that these conditions would be acceptable to the Indian workers, making assumptions about these skilled workers' living conditions back in India. There was no economic alternative for the workers that made sense; leaving the camp or returning to India were not viable sociocultural or economic options.

Escape

On Sundays, workers were able to attend worship services at Sacred Heart Catholic Church in Pascagoula. Soon, in discussions with parishioners there, it became clear that the workers were in a desperate, illegal situation. Members of the congregation contacted the National Guestworker Alliance, a labor rights organization in New Orleans, Louisiana, which began investigating and, with the help of the Southern Poverty Law Center and other lawyers working pro bono, took up their case in 2008. Signal found out they were meeting with lawyers and threatened them with terminating "the visa extensions," which of course was a fraud. Signal tried to fire and deport two workers they believed were organizing the rest of the workers against the company, one of whom attempted suicide. The company contacted local U.S. Immigration and Customs Enforcement (ICE) agents for advice on how to fire the workers, which ICE received without somehow raising alarm bells about human trafficking going on at the Mississippi shipyard. The workers staged protests, and one worker went on a hunger strike to protest his working and living conditions. Local media picked up the story. Signal withdrew its illegal offer of Green Cards for the workers, so hundreds of workers quit their jobs and left the camp. Desperate to remain in the United States but now without a legal right to do so, the guest workers were in a difficult position.

Justice

The U.S. government finally stepped in and granted many of the workers special visas under new human trafficking statutes that enabled them not only to stay in the United

States but also to bring their families to the United States. In addition, the government joined the lawsuit against Signal. A judge initially denied the workers class action status, which meant that each worker would have to bring suit against Signal for his grievance, but was later overruled. In 2015, Signal lost a 7-year legal battle and paid the workers it trafficked $20 million in damages. Following its defeat in court, Signal immediately filed for Chapter 11 bankruptcy protection. Many of the workers remained in the United States, living and working on their own.

SOURCE: Brickley, July 13, 2015; Rather, 2011.

5.7 The Supply Chain

A supply chain is the economic path a good or service travels from the point of production to its end consumer, involving more than one business or group of people and multiple steps of production, transportation, marketing, and selling. Supply chain analysis follows the product from "mine to market" or the connected path of the good from producers to consumers. In the context of human trafficking, this chain has links of relevance for advocates seeking to end modern slavery.

Human traffickers are often the first link in the modern slavery supply chain. In many industries, traffickers deliver streams or groups of slave laborers to "producers" or manufacturers who are in charge of making goods or supplying services with whatever labor supply they can procure (legal or illegal). The producer pays a one-time fee to the trafficker, or a fee every time a new victim in procured. For example, in the commercial sex industry, recruiters will fraudulently advertise for "models" to deceive young women and later entrap them in commercial sex. Similarly, in farm work or an industrial sector, recruiters may advertise well-paying jobs but then ensnare them (see the Signal case presented earlier in this chapter) through the use of exorbitant and illegal "recruiting fees" that the workers either pay up front or are forced to repay over time in a modern form of "peonage" or debt bondage.

Producers or manufacturers (the people in charge of making goods or providing services), the next step in the human trafficking supply chain, often obtain their labor force from traffickers and then put them to work. Producers buy raw materials and assemble partial or completely finished products with a labor force. In commercial sex work, a producer would be the brothel owner who "employs" trafficked sex workers. In other industries, a producer would be the business owner or production foreman in charge of managing a labor force for the business. Producers engaged in human trafficking understand that cheap labor lowers their cost of production: The cheaper the labor, the more profits producers retain when sending their goods to the next link in the supply chain. But another benefit for producers working with slave labor is to be able to reduce the cost of their goods and drive out other, legal, producers from the market. Producers who compete fairly in a legal labor market and pay market-based wage rates to their workers cannot lower their cost of production to compete with goods produced by traffickers. They are at a competitive disadvantage in the market.

Wholesalers in many markets act as so-called middlemen between producers and retailers. They purchase goods from producers, often help transfer goods between producers and retailers, and help "make a market" between them. Sometimes, but not always, they knowingly participate in a human trafficking enterprise by moving goods they know were produced with exploited labor.

Retailers are farther down the supply chain and often are not aware that the products they purchase from wholesalers or producers were made with slave labor. This is often the case with apparel or electronics sold in developed economies but produced in less-developed countries or regions. Globalization (described elsewhere in the chapter) exacerbates the disconnect between retailers and producers. Under liberal trade regimes in which retailers and wholesalers are able to search the globe for products and are under tremendous pressure to hold down costs, producers who can provide low-cost goods made with slave labor have an economic advantage over legal producers. Retailers contract directly not with producers but with wholesalers for the goods they sell and often argue that they were unaware of human trafficking in the supply chains of goods they sell in their stores or under their brand names.

Consumers are the final link in the supply chain. They purchase goods almost always without full knowledge, let alone understanding, of the links in the supply chain for goods that may have been produced with slave labor. And yet, once consumers are aware that the products they buy and use every day, from tuna farmed with trafficked labor in Thailand to soccer balls made in Pakistan, they can act to stop human trafficking. Consumers have a lot of power to intervene in the market for goods made with slave labor. They can boycott retailers and producers. They can organize awareness campaigns. They can lobby governments, write to company shareholders and executives, and refuse to spend their money on such products.

Globalization and liberalized free-trade regimes have contributed to modern slavery by creating economic turmoil and greater vulnerability for marginalized social groups at risk of being caught up in human trafficking. But social media, travel, and the greater cultural awareness brought on by other aspects of globalization have produced, somewhat ironically, the tools and the leverage that consumers can use to combat trafficking.

Siddharth Kara (2009) and Alicja Jac-Kucharski (2012) argue that by inverting the risk-reward ratio and making it more expensive to operate human trafficking operations, reformers and advocates can use economics against traffickers. There may be "push" factors, like low socioeconomic status of women in certain countries, which contribute to the available pool of victims. But there are other "pull" factors, like traffickers' profits, ease of transit, and lack of a functioning and effective law enforcement and judicial system that make it attractive for traffickers to operate. Economic analysis and a more thorough understanding of the supply chain may help advocates and law enforcement identify market disruption points on which to focus in order to produce the most change for the least effort. For instance, it may not be very cost-effective to try to catch intermediaries who actually transport trafficking victims. Modes of transport are cheap, borders are porous, and the costs of transport are low. Alternatively, it may be more cost-effective to raise the costs on employers who use slave labor. Producers who cannot run their slave labor operations with impunity but who are constantly harassed by law enforcement operating with integrity and threatened with a functioning legal system and substantial fines or jail time may not be able to lower unit production costs enough to drive out legal market competitors.

5.8 Globalization

Joseph Stiglitz, Nobel Prize winner in economics, has defined globalization as "the closer integration of the countries and peoples of the world . . . brought about by the enormous reduction in transportation and communication costs, and the breaking down of artificial barriers to the flows of goods, services, capital, knowledge, and, to a lesser extent, people across borders" (Stiglitz, 2002, p. 9).

Globalization often seems like a beneficial by-product of global economic growth and modernity, and it may often appear inevitable, like the weather, something that cannot be controlled. Some of the economic effects of globalization have been productive: increased foreign direct investment, expanded trade, the spread of the knowledge economy, and technology transfer.

By disrupting traditional economic arrangements, however, globalization has exacerbated all of the factors that have contributed to the supply of slave labor throughout history:

- Poverty
- Bias against a gender or ethnicity
- Lawlessness
- Military conflict
- Social instability
- Economic breakdown

Radical economists and social scientists like Kamala Kempadoo (2015) argue that neoliberal trade relations imposed on less-developed countries and enforced by global economic institutions like the World Bank, the International Monetary Fund, and others have opened up once-restricted markets and purposefully destabilized the global economy for the benefit of developed countries. They argue that this, in turn, has further widened the economic gap between the global north (e.g., advanced capitalist economies) and the global south (e.g., developing economies). Critics of globalization and economic neoliberalism often wonder whether capitalism itself is responsible for poverty and underdevelopment, and whether slavery is simply an unintended consequence of the normal, brutal functioning of global capitalism (McNally, 2011).

5.9 Methodologies Used to Estimate Economic Impact of Human Trafficking

In this section, we introduce some of the methodologies used to assess economic impact. As discussed earlier, the human trafficking victims suffer economically as well as physically and emotionally from their traumatization. Adverse effects on victims' medical and mental health, lost wages, and lost productivity over their lifetimes are just a few of the economic impacts they suffer. The discussion here is narrower than the full methodology used by the ILO, and the intent is to provide a broad sense of what has been done and the challenges that remain. After a general review of different approaches to estimation, two specific impact studies are reviewed. This section closes with some additional consideration and a discussion of some of the challenges faced by society relative to assessing the impact of human trafficking.

To start, there are two main aspects to human trafficking's economic impact:

- Measuring the value of the economic output, including the value of the labor, produced by human trafficking activity
- Quantifying the costs to provide care to victims and survivors of human trafficking, including costs related to law enforcement, prosecution, and social services

Quantifying the costs to provide care helps policy makers estimate the amount of public funds it might take to prevent vulnerable populations from being victimized in the first place. And measuring the value of economic output produced by human trafficking activity will help place the problem of modern-day slavery into perspective by comparing it to other forms of legitimate and illegitimate economic activity in the state.

Both of these approaches to quantifying the economic impact of human trafficking can be further classified in terms of whether the quantification looks at the total costs incurred during some narrow time period, (e.g., annually), or looks at the total costs incurred over a time horizon, e.g., over a number of years. Further, quantification can be assessed on a per person basis or as a total societal impact over all people involved. The third aspect of economic impact considered in this chapter is whether the impact is viewed in terms of the costs incurred by individuals who are newly victimized at a particular point in time, (e.g., within a given year), or if the impact is viewed across all victims at that point in time. The choice between these perspectives is often determined by the objectives of the economic impact analysis.

Two common perspectives that combine these various approaches are often referred to as incidence- and prevalence-based estimates of impact (Fang, Brown, Florence, & Mercy, 2012). Incidence-based economic impact typically looks at the costs incurred over a lifetime by individuals victimized in a given year. Prevalence-based economic impact typically attempts to look at the total cost impact across all individuals impacted by trafficking in any given year. Both perspectives are valuable. Incidence approaches factor in long-term impact beginning with the start of victimization and can provide a perspective that is valuable to policy makers when making decisions about program funding, (e.g., for new interventional initiatives). Prevalence approaches address the total impact felt by victims and society annually and can be useful to policy makers when allocating resources and setting annual budgets for programs.

Incidence- and prevalence-based approaches share common informational needs: the number of individuals who have been victimized, the associated costs of that victimization, the benefit of any interventional programs utilized, and the like-lihoods for various events and outcomes within the time period being studied. The difference in informational needs between these two approaches has to do with the population focus of each method. Incidence-based approaches require information about the number of new victims and all of the events, outcomes, and associated likelihoods for what they will experience from the present onward. Prevalence-based approaches require similar information but are based on understanding the number of victims currently experiencing each type of event or outcome in the current year.

One difference between these two approaches is that incidence-based approaches can be utilized without knowing the total number of individuals victimized. Planning, albeit partial, can occur based on an understanding of the number of new victims who might be impacted by a new program or intervention being considered. An example of such an incidence-based analysis is presented next. Prevalence-based approaches ulti-mately are constrained by information about the number of total victims in the popu-lation. Challenges associated with estimating the number of individuals victimized by trafficking are profound.

5.10 Examples

5.10.1 Example Cost-Benefit Analysis of an Intervention

Martin and Lotspeich (2014) assess the effectiveness of an intervention designed to reduce sex trafficking by using a methodology known as the net present value (NPV) that allows the costs and benefits of activities and decisions that occur over time to be viewed as a total impact at a single point in time. The main elements of their study include:

- Net Present Value (NPV) model to assess the expected effectiveness of early intervention designed to divert minors from sex work in Minnesota (the Runaway Intervention Program, RIP);
- The model looks at investment cost versus benefits, where benefits can include things like avoided costs to society and lost work potential among victims.

Before reviewing their specific approach, we will introduce and summarize NPV analysis. NPV is a systematic way of establishing the value of programs, activities, or events that occur over time. It is often used to evaluate the appeal of alternative eco-nomic programs or investments. The name, NPV, is descriptive of how the analysis works. Costs are subtracted from benefits and are summed over time in a manner that allows them to be compared in the present. This net value means that alternative pro-grams can be compared in the present even if the related costs and benefits of those programs would be seen over different time horizons. The value of costs and benefits that are seen in the future needs to be adjusted by a discount factor when compared to the value of costs and benefits seen in the present. This discount adjustment can, in some situations, be thought of as accounting for inflation. When economic programs are being considered, the appropriate discount is the cost of obtaining the funds needed to invest in the program. Referred to as the cost of capital, this discount rate can be thought of as the interest rate that would be paid if funds were borrowed in order to pay for the program or programs under consideration. A consequence of this discounting process is that benefits seen in the future are worth less than benefits seen today. Alternatively, costs that can be deferred until a future time have less impact than costs incurred today. All of the concepts discussed above are incorporated into the formula shown below.

$$NPV = \sum_{t=1}^{T} \frac{Benefit_t - Cost_t}{(1+r)^t}$$

The subscript t on the Benefit and Cost terms is an index for time periods from 1 to some endpoint T and r is the cost of capital. In practice, this can be indexed over any unit of time, like months or years, and r is a rate appropriate for that time unit. For example, time units are often in years and the cost of capital is then often an annual interest rate on funds that might be borrowed to invest in the program.

Martin and Lotspeich (2014) use a slightly different formulation of NPV in their research that recognizes that most of the costs of implementing the intervention program to divert minors from sex work would occur in the present, viz. the time that the intervention program is created. Further, the benefits to society over time can be conceptualized as can future costs that would be avoided if the intervention program were implemented. This allows the NPV to be expressed as shown in the formula below.

$$NPV = \sum_{t=1}^{T} \frac{Benefit^t}{(1+r)^t} - Intervention\ Cost$$

The specific intervention considered by the authors is the Runaway Intervention Program (RIP), which, as described by the authors, focuses on stabilizing girls aged 15 or younger who are at risk for sexual exploitation by providing services based on the level of risk and need (Martin, Lotspeich, & Stark, 2012). RIP is an established program with both funding and program evaluation data that allowed the authors to make detailed calculations about the cost of implementation as well as the efficacy of the program. That known efficacy allowed the authors to make additional calculations about the costs avoided by girls predicted to avoid falling victim to sexual exploitation. The types of avoided costs included public health expenditures, criminal justice expenditures, child foster care expenditures, and forgone income tax revenue. These avoided costs included both short- and long-term costs, and the calculations for each time period included the likelihood of the cost being incurred.

This modeling methodology allowed the authors to calculate the NPV of RIP on a per person basis and conclude that about USD 26 in harm could be avoided for every dollar invested in the program (Martin, et al., 2012).

It is worth noting that the RIP intervention is only one of many different possibilities in which society might invest to reduce trafficking. Other possible interventions include:

- Increase victim rescue rates by increasing law enforcement staffing and budgets
- Increase effectiveness of rescue efforts by improving services to rescued victims
- Decrease the supply of victims by reducing recruitment effectiveness
- Decrease demand through prosecution of johns
- Decrease demand through education of johns
- Decrease demand through education of males in general
- Increase operating costs of traffickers by disrupting or destabilizing locales for conducting business
- Increase penalties for conviction and plea agreements
- Increase victim participation during investigation and prosecution phases through improvements to services provided after rescue
- Decrease supply of domestic minors in active sex trafficking situations by providing incentives to self-rescue
- Shrink the system by coordinating human trafficking efforts with other coincident criminal activities like murder, drugs, porn, and gang activity in general

5.10.2 Example of Cost Impact Only

The previous example involved assessing the economic impact of trafficking in terms of costs that could be avoided through an intervention. Alternatively, economic impact can be assessed as the impact of all costs without the mitigating effect of an intervention. There are no known estimates of the total economic impact of human trafficking, but Fang et al. (2012) use this approach to estimate the NPV of the cost of child maltreatment. Their study presents average lifetime costs per child maltreatment victim and total lifetime costs for all new child abuse cases in 2008. Similar to the Martin and Lotspeich (2014) study, this study included short- and long-term medical costs, lifetime productivity losses, child welfare costs, criminal justice costs, and special education costs. In addition to cost data, this study also utilized available information about the number of children who were determined by child protective services (CPS) to be victims of child maltreatment. The authors estimated the NPV of average lifetime cost per victim of nonfatal child maltreatment to be USD 210,000 in 2010 dollars. In addition, the researchers estimated that the lifetime economic impact from all new cases of fatal and nonfatal child abuse in the United States in a single year (2008) to be $124 billion (Fang et al., 2012).

While many of the cost impacts of human trafficking have been estimated, the viability of this methodology for human trafficking depends on one of the greatest unknowns about trafficking: an estimation of the number of individuals victimized. The next section discusses methods of addressing this challenge.

5.10.3 Estimating the Size of Vulnerable Populations

Many of the cost impacts of human trafficking have been estimated, but the viability of the NPV methodology for estimating the economic impact of human trafficking depends on one of the greatest unknowns about trafficking: an estimation of the number of individuals victimized. Tyldum and Brunovskis (2005) and Zhang (2012) describe victims of trafficking as an example of a hidden population because the size and boundaries of the population are unknown and trafficking victims are often stigmatized and are therefore reluctant to cooperate in research. The next section introduces methods of addressing this challenge. We review two promising methods that have been applied with some success by researchers to estimate the number of trafficking victims in specific settings. Each method has strengths and weaknesses and is included as much to explore methodological limitations as to illustrate its potential.

The first method, respondent-driven sampling (RDS), focuses on the development of a representative sample from a hidden population by enlisting members of the population who are encountered as part of a research project to encourage other members of that same population to participate (Zhang, 2012). The second method, multiple systems estimation (MSE), utilizes probability theory and multiple independent samples to estimate the size of a hidden population. Originally from ecology, MSE samples from a population, tags or identifies members of a sample before releasing them back into the population, and subsequently resamples the same population. During subsequent samples, previously identified sample members are tracked along with those encountered for the first time (Zhang, 2012).

Zhang, Spiller, Finch, and Qin (2014) utilized respondent-driven sampling (RDS) to develop estimates of the extent of trafficking among undocumented migrant workers in San Diego County, California, estimating that 30% of undocumented migrant workers were victims of labor trafficking. Their application of RDS used 18 initial "seed" respondents to start the referral process and 16 interview sites to ultimately generate a sample of 826 respondents from a fieldwork process that lasted 77 weeks. Their research team included 7 bilingual interviewers. As incentives, the researchers provided $30 honoraria for participation and three $10 coupons that participants could distribute to others in the community to encourage them to participate.

RDS is a very attractive method for accessing a hidden population, but it does require time for the referral process to gain momentum. Additionally, the selection of seed respondents and sites are critical factors in both the rate and extent of the referral process throughout the population.

Bales, Hesketh, and Silverman (2015) used multiple systems estimation (MSE) to estimate that there were between 10,000 and 13,000 potential human trafficking victims in the U.K. The authors examined existing data from the U.K. National Crime Agency (NCA) Strategic Assessment that had "identified 2,744 unique potential victims of human trafficking from a wide range of sources." The Strategic Assessment data set included personal information that allowed potential victims to be assigned a unique identification number. Additionally, the more than 100 data sources for the Strategic Assessment data set were grouped into 6 separate samples based on the different roles and responsibilities, including, for example, local authorities, police forces, and nongovernmental organizations. The MSE process involved looking at the overlap in identification among these 6 samples to estimate the number of potential victims not encountered in any of the samples.

MSE is a very attractive prevalence methodology if independent samples are either available or can be created for a population. However, a critical assumption of MSE is that the identification of victims and the "release" of said victims once encountered occur in a way that does not influence the probability that the victim will be seen in one of the other samples. Due to client privacy concerns, human trafficking victim identification may or (more likely) may not result in identification in a way that allows for re-identification in some future sample. Also, encounters with victims of trafficking are often accompanied by the offer of support or a set of services to victims, and that intervention will influence the probability that the same victim remains in their victimized status in a subsequent sample.

The broad availability of samples that identify victims (like the U.K. NCA Strategic Assessment) is a significant limitation of MSE that requires the development of multiple independent and overlapping samples of trafficking victims for the method to be successful. Bales, Hesketh, and Silverman (2015) describe MSE as cost-effective, but that is based on the pre-existence of multiple samples like those available in the U.K. If samples need to be collected, victim privacy concerns aside, it is an easy intellectual jump to envision combining RDS with MSE. RDS would provide deeper access into a hidden population through the referral process, and MSE would compensate for the limitations of RDS relative to rate and extent of the referral process by providing multiple independent sampling efforts for the population of interest.

6. Chapter Summary

This chapter focuses on the economic impact of human trafficking and reviews important considerations in the attempt to measure and quantify the cost of these crimes for individual victims and for society at large. Perhaps counterintuitively, the same markets and economic forces that exacerbate the vulnerability of marginalized peoples to become trapped in modern slavery also can be the same tools, used by advocates and reformers, harnessed to reduce human trafficking's prevalence. Students will better understand the global economic structures that have produced conditions conducive to trafficking and be better able to use economics to understand the impact that modern-day slavery has on victims and society.

7. Key Terms

7.1 Product supply chain

7.2 Globalization

7.3 Neoliberalism

7.4 Demand theory

7.5 Gross world product

7.6 Cost-benefit economic theory

7.7 Net present value (NPV)

7.8 Respondent-driven sampling (RDS)

7.9 Capture and recapture estimation methods

8. Active Learning Exercises or In-Class Discussion Questions

8.1   What economic sectors in my region might harbor human trafficking activity?

Start with labor characteristics and the industry list in the text and then discuss whether a city/region/state/country contains those characteristics and industries.

8.2   What are the links in the supply chain for a good made with slave labor that would be most effective and efficient for advocates to disrupt to have the maximum effect on ending the use of slave labor in the creation of that product?

8.3   How has globalization exacerbated the trafficking and exploitation of workers? How has globalization assisted in the movement against human trafficking?

9. Suggestions for Further Learning

9.1   **Reading Materials**

9.1.1   International Labour Organization. (2015, March 30). *The fair recruitment initiative: Fostering fair recruitment practices, preventing human trafficking and reducing the costs of labour migration.* Retrieved from http://www.ilo.org/global/topics/fair-recruitment/WCMS_320405/lang—en/index.htm

9.1.2   National Crime Agency. (2014). *UKHTC: A strategic assessment on the nature and scale of human trafficking in 2012.*

9.1.3   Me, A. (2014). *Global report on trafficking in persons.* United Nations Office on Drugs and Crime. Report.

9.1.4   Shelley, L. (2010). *Human trafficking: A global perspective.* Cambridge, U.K.: Cambridge University Press.

9.2   **Websites**

9.2.1   National Guestworker Alliance—http://www.guestworkeralliance.org

9.2.2   Southern Poverty Law Center—https://www.splcenter.org

9.2.3   Coalition of Immokalee Workers—http://www.ciw-online.org

9.2.4   Fair Food Program—http://www.fairfoodprogram.org

9.2.5   U.S. Department of Labor—List of Goods Produced by Child Labor or Forced Labor—http://www.dol.gov/ilab/reports/child-labor/list-of-goods/

9.3   **Films and Other Media**

9.3.1   *Tricked*

9.3.2   *True Cost*

10. Suggestions for Further Research or Projects/Homework/Exams

10.1 Examine the product supply chain involving tomatoes grown in southern Florida in the United States. Why are most of the tomatoes available in the United States during the winter months grown in southern Florida, where the soils are not well suited for growing tomatoes? How are the tomatoes harvested, and by whom? What companies are marketing them? Who is buying them in the winter?

10.2 Choose <u>one</u> product made and consumed in any region of the world and analyze its supply chain. There are many products that have been associated with human trafficking. Use Google or the U.S. Department of Labor's resources to identify a product that has been associated with human trafficking. Visiting a local supermarket or other store can help you to identify an interesting or unknown product. You might also find ideas by looking around your bedroom or kitchen.

11. References

Bales, K., Hesketh, O., & Silverman, B. W. (2015). Modern slavery in the UK: How many victims? *Significance*, *12*(3), 16–21. http://doi.org/10.1111/j.1740–9713.2015.00824.x

Brickley, P. (2015, July 13). Accused of Labor Trafficking, Oil-Rig Repairer Files for Bankruptcy. *Wall Street Journal*. Retrieved from https://www.wsj.com/articles/signal-international-files-for-bankruptcy-1436787503

Fang, X., Brown, D. S., Florence, C. S., & Mercy, J. A. (2012). The economic burden of child maltreatment in the United States and implications for prevention. *Child Abuse & Neglect*, *36*(2), 156–165. doi:10.1016/j.chiabu.2011.10.006

International Labour Organization. (2010). *Constitution of the International Labour Organisation and selected texts*. Retrieved from Geneva: http://www.ilo.org/public/english/bureau/leg/download/constitution.pdf

International Labour Organization. (2014). *Profits and poverty: The economics of forced labour*. Retrieved from Geneva, Switzerland: http://www.ilo.org/global/topics/forced-labour/publications/profits-of-forced-labour-2014/lang—en/index.htm

Jac-Kucharski, A. (2012). The determinants of human trafficking: A US case study. *International Migration*, *50*(6), 150–165.

Kara, S. (2009). *Sex trafficking: Inside the business of modern slavery*. New York, NY: Columbia University Press.

Kara, S. (2011). Supply and demand: Human trafficking in the global economy. *Harvard International Review*, *33*(2), 66.

Kempadoo, K. (2015). The modern-day white (wo)man's burden: Trends in anti-trafficking and anti-slavery campaigns. *Journal of Human Trafficking*, *1*(1), 8–20. http://doi.org/10.1080/23322705.2015.1006120

Mahmoud, T. O., & Trebesch, C. (2010). The economics of human trafficking and labour migration: Micro-evidence from Eastern Europe. *Journal of Comparative Economics*, *38*(2), 173–188.

Martin, L., & Lotspeich, R. (2014). A benefit-cost framework for early intervention to prevent sex trading. *Journal of Benefit-Cost Analysis*, *5*(1), 43–87. doi:10.1515/jbca-2013-0021

Martin, L., Lotspeich, R., & Stark, L. (2012). *Early intervention to avoid sex trading and trafficking of Minnesota's female youth: A benefit-cost analysis.* Retrieved from http://www.castla.org/templates/files/miwrc-benefit-cost-study-summary.pdf

McNally, D. (2011). *Monsters of the market: Zombies, vampires and global capitalism.* Chicago, IL: Haymarket Books.

Rather, D. (Producer). (2011, November 8). An American Nightmare [Podcast transcript]. *Dan Rather Reports* [Episode 637]. Retrieved from http://www.axs.tv/transcripts/?t=danrather&n=Dan%20Rather%20Reports

Schroeder, M., & Lamb, G. (2006). The illicit arms trade in Africa. *African Analyst, 1*(3). Retrieved from https://fas.org/asmp/library/articles/SchroederLamb.pdf

Stiglitz, J. (2002). *Globalization and its discontents.* New York, NY: W.W. Norton.

Tyldum, G., & Brunovskis, A. (2005). Describing the unobserved: Methodological challenges in empirical studies on human trafficking. *International migration, 43*(12), 17–34.

United Nations Office on Drugs and Crime. (2005). *World drug report.* Retrieved from https://www.unodc.org/unodc/en/data-and-analysis/WDR-2005.html

Verité. (2015). *Strengthening protections against trafficking in persons in federal and corporate supply chains.* Retrieved from http://www.verite.org/sites/default/files/images/Verite-Executive_Order_13627.pdf

Walk Free Foundation. (2016). *Global slavery index 2016.* Accessed June 28, 2016, from http://www.globalslaveryindex.org/findings/

Wheaton, E. M., Schauer, E. J., & Galli, T. V. (2010). Economics of human trafficking. *International Migration, 48*(4), 114–141. doi:10.1111/j.1468–2435.2009.00592.x

Wolfer, T. A., & Scales, T. L. (2006). Decision cases for advanced social work practice: thinking like a social worker. Belmont, CA: Thomson Brooks/Cole.

World Bank. (2016). *World development indicators, GDP ranking 2014.* Retrieved April 11, 2016, from http://data.worldbank.org/data-catalog/GDP-ranking-table

Zhang, S. X. (2012). Measuring labor trafficking: A research note. *Crime, Law and Social Change, 58*(4), 469–482. doi:10.1007/s10611–012–9393-y

Zhang, S. X., Spiller, M. W., Finch, B. K., & Qin, Y. (2014). Estimating labor trafficking among unauthorized migrant workers in San Diego. *The ANNALS of the American Academy of Political and Social Science, 653*(1), 65–86. http://doi.org/10.1177/0002716213519237

A Holistic Approach at Micro, Mezzo, and Macro Levels

Understanding, Disruption, and Interventions at the Micro Level

Education is the most powerful weapon which you can use to change the world.

—Nelson Mandela

1. Learning Objectives

1.1 Students will understand a micro-level intervention framework.

1.2 Students will explore the strengths-based perspective and trauma-informed approach as they relate to human trafficking.

1.3 Students will be introduced to key concepts and terms used in the identification of human trafficking victims.

1.4 Students will become familiarized with the immediate and long-term service needs of victims.

1.5 Students will be introduced to best practices used in identification, protection, and provision of support and services to human trafficking victims.

1.6 Students will understand the different perspectives on the use of "victim versus survivor" language.

1.7 Students will become familiar with the typologies of victims and traffickers and will be introduced to a profile of johns, or consumers of sex services.

2. Key Ideas

These are the central ideas of this chapter:

2.1 Responses to and interventions with trafficked individuals must take into account the wide range of complex experiences and needs of those who have experienced exploitation.

2.2 Two conceptual frameworks to support and respond to the needs of human trafficking survivors, a strengths-based and a trauma-informed approach, offer insights that are valuable to micro-level practice and program development.

2.3 There is not a one-size-fits-all intervention to support victims of human trafficking. However, there are indelible values that underpin best practice models.

2.4 Trauma-informed and victim-centered interventions are considered best practices. Utilizing these models will minimize revictimization.

2.5 Despite their experience of trauma, victims have the capacity to be incredibly resilient. A strengths-based approach should be utilized when working with human trafficking survivors.

2.6 Traffickers manipulate and assert power and control over their victims to exploit them for financial gains.

2.7 johns are not a homogenous group. Research indicates that consumers of sex services have a wide variety of educational, socioeconomical, faith, and geographical backgrounds. However, johns may hold values that are different from other men including the role of women in society or gender roles.

3. Selected Theories/Frameworks

3.1 A Strengths-Based Approach

Responses to and interventions with trafficked individuals must take into account the wide range of complex victimization experiences and needs of human trafficking victims. A strengths-based approach, although it is not considered a fully developed theory, is a useful foundation on which to base intervention with human trafficking survivors and program development. Professionals working in the human trafficking field have incorporated the strengths-based approach because of its application and underpinning values (Busch-Armendariz, Nsonwu, & Heffron, 2014; Saleebey, 1996). Attorneys, social workers, law enforcement, policy makers, and other practitioners benefit hugely from utilizing a strengthens-based approach that emphasizes the notion that all individuals have a wide range of capacities, skills, resources, hopes, talents, and possible futures. In a direct and intentional move away from a deficit-based model or medical model, the strengths-based perspective offers a new framework with which to view individuals and their connections to social problems. Deficit-based thinking, on the other hand, defines individuals by their disease, deficit, problem, disorder, or victimization and presumes that problems experienced by an individual denote a deficiency in that person. A deficit-based model also supports the view that professionals (e.g., mental health professionals or teachers) are better equipped to define the problems that face individuals than the individuals themselves.

A strengths-based approach, on the other hand, does not focus on the fixing of an individual's externally defined problem or deficit. Rather, it supports an environment in which individuals define their own needs, goals, dilemmas, and relationships with their

Table 5.1 Comparison of Pathology and Strengths

Pathology	Strengths
Person is defined as a "case"; symptoms add up to a diagnosis.	Person is defined as unique; traits, talents, resources add up to strengths.
Therapy is problem focused.	Therapy is possibility focused.
Personal accounts aid in the evocation of a diagnosis through reinterpretation by an expert.	Personal accounts are the essential route to knowing and appreciating the person.
Practitioner is skeptical of personal stories, rationalizations.	Practitioner knows the person from the inside out.
Childhood trauma is the precursor or predictor of adult pathology.	Childhood trauma is not predictive; it may weaken or strengthen the individual.
Centerpiece of therapeutic work is the treatment plan devised by practitioner.	Centerpiece of work is the aspirations of family, individual, or community.
Practitioner is the expert on clients' lives.	Individuals, family, or community are the experts.
Possibilities for choice, control, commitment, and personal development are limited by pathology.	Possibilities for choice, control, commitment, and personal development are open.
Resources for work are the knowledge and skills of the professional.	Resources for work are the strengths, capacities, and adaptive skills of the individual, family, or community.
Help is centered on reducing the effects of symptoms and the negative personal and social consequences of actions, emotions, thoughts, or relationships.	Help is centered on getting on with one's life, affirming and developing values and commitments, and making and finding membership in or as a community.

NOTE: "The strengths perspective in social work practice: Extensions and cautions" by D. Saleebey, *Social Work*, p. 298. Copyright 1996 by Oxford University Press. Reprinted with permission.

experiences of exploitation or violence. In doing so, this approach requires that those working with survivors of human trafficking meet on an even playing field, in a spirit of equality, and pay attention to addressing power differentials between survivor and provider. A strengths-based approach, first developed by social work, also incorporates the notion of person-in-environment that involves understanding individuals, their needs, and their behaviors in the context of the community and environment in which they operate (Rawana & Brownlee, 2009). Importantly, this perspective does not attempt to discount or negate the reality of social or psychological problems faced by individuals—be it exploitation, violence, oppression, addiction, or illness. Saleebey (1996) notes "In the lexicon of strengths, it is as wrong to deny the possible as it is to deny the problem" (p. 297). Strengths and resilience often emerge directly from, and/or are distorted by, social problems and experiences of violence, trauma, and oppression. And yet, our identities are not equated with the problems, traumas, or oppressions we face. According to Saleebey (1996), a strengths-based perspective rejects the idea that "all people who face trauma and pain in their lives inevitably are wounded or incapacitated or become less than they might" (p. 298). Rather, it focuses on the possibility for, and commitment to, resilience and transformation.

3.2 Trauma-Informed Theoretical Framework

A trauma-informed approach is a valuable conceptual framework in micro-level practice. As a theory, it seems to have recently reemerged in the literature as highly relevant for working with sexual assault survivors. This approach recognizes the broad impact of trauma on individuals, their families, and the organizations that come into contact with trauma survivors. The Substance Abuse and Mental Health Services Administration (SAMHSA, 2014) defines trauma as resulting from "an event, series of events, or set of circumstances that is experienced by an individual as physically or emotionally harmful or life threatening and that has lasting adverse effects on the individual's functioning and mental, physical, social, emotional, or spiritual well-being" (p. 7).

Fully embracing a trauma-informed approach entails recognition of the signs and symptoms of trauma in individuals, families, and those who work with them. It also necessitates the broad integration of knowledge about trauma into organizational policies and procedures, in addition to active attention to the prevention of retraumatization (SAMHSA, 2014). Principles that are fundamental to a trauma-informed approach include: safety; trustworthiness and transparency; peer support; collaboration and mutuality; empowerment, voice, and choice; and cultural, historical, and gender issues.

There are thorny issues in the application of these theories that are related to traumatized individuals. Victims and survivors may have developed strategies to survive and cope with ongoing victimization or past abuse that may challenge professionals in the full application of these theories (Rawana & Brownlee, 2009). For example, the experience of facing chronic trauma or persistent abuse may result in a survivor distrusting or acting defensively or angry toward those in the helping professions, including social workers, counselors, or law enforcement. Past experiences could also result in a survivor withholding information that may be deemed as fundamental to the criminal case or to service provision. It is crucial that these responses are understood in the context of an individual's experience of abuse and the overall environment in which they live.

Additionally, responses to trauma may be considered autonomic, or uncontrollable, and are thought to be evolutionarily wired into us to protect our own survival. Responses to trauma often involve hormonal fluctuations in the brain.

> This is a classic example of where our body can sometimes be working at cross-purposes. On the one hand . . . all of these hormones are very, very helpful for the emotional aspects and the physical safety of the organism. On the other hand, these same hormones are going to make it very difficult for the brain to lay down the encoding and consolidation that needs to happen to record the traumatic event in the brain.
>
> —Rebecca Campbell, Transcript,
> The Neurobiology of Sexual Assault.

4. Decision Case

Family Business[1]

As the telephone conversation with her client ended, novice social worker Araceli Aguilera felt stunned by new information. Araceli's client, Maria Perez, was a victim of sex trafficking. She had left her two daughters—Isabella and Jimena—in the guardianship of her father, Xavier Perez, when she fled sexual abuse by other family members. Now, Xavier was dead and the two girls were at risk of trafficking themselves.

As Araceli walked down the long hallway to her supervisor's office, she wondered, *How do we keep the girls safe while processing the paperwork for reunification? And who will help us with that now?*

International Organization for Migration (IOM)

The International Organization for Migration (IOM) was established in 1951 with a mission to advance awareness about migration and increase economic and social sustainability for migrants globally. IOM was the leading intergovernmental organization in the field of migration, partnering with 157 member states and operating offices in more than 100 countries. IOM worked to ensure an orderly and humane management process of migration, including the cooperation of international agencies on migrant issues and service provision for migrants in need, including refugees and internally displaced people (International Organization for Migration, 2015).

---

[1]This decision case was prepared solely to provide material for class discussion and not to suggest either effective or ineffective handling of the situation depicted. While based on field research regarding an actual situation, names and certain facts have been disguised to protect confidentiality. The authors wish to thank the case reporter for cooperation in making this account available for the benefit of students and practitioners (Wolfer & Scales, 2006, p. 29).

World Assistance of North Carolina

Established in 1944, World Assistance of North Carolina (WA) was the leading local nonprofit social service agency that provided services to refugees who resettled in North Carolina. With branches in High Point and Winston Salem, WA sought to provide services to refugees and other displaced persons "fleeing persecution" based on race, religion, nationality, and social and/or political affiliation. Through the Ending Human Trafficking (EHT) Program, WA worked with local law enforcement agencies to provide 24-hour support to identified survivors. This support included short- and long-term services to ensure the survivors' safety and success.

Additionally, WA offered services for unaccompanied children (UAC), counseling, immigration assistance, social adjustment services, job readiness training and placement, medical case management, and English language training services. All of these services were available to any WA clients.

WA was the initial referral center for victims of trafficking identified by law enforcement within the state of North Carolina. WA provided an initial assessment and screening to determine whether a client was appropriate for the EHT program.

To seek permanent residence within the United States, human trafficking victims must disclose their experiences of being trafficked. The information is needed to complete a Trafficking Visa or T visa. Created in 2000, the T visa allowed immigrants who were victims of human trafficking or a violent crime to apply for permanent residency, so as long as they cooperated with any ongoing investigations.

Similarly, a T visa *derivative* provided nonimmigrant status for the applicant's spouse, children, parents, and siblings if the human trafficking victim and family members met the qualifications. Family members could qualify for T visa derivatives in several ways. Trafficking victims under 21 years of age could apply on behalf of their spouses, children, parents, and unmarried siblings under age 18. Trafficking victims 21 years old and older could apply on behalf of their spouses and children. In each case, trafficking victims needed to apply for a T visa derivative for each qualifying family member using Form I-914, Supplement A, Application for Immediate Family Member of T-1 Recipient, and needed to submit it within a time frame specified by the United States government.

Araceli Aguilera

Araceli Aguilera was a 24-year-old Mexican American from Winston Salem, North Carolina. As a bright student growing up in a lower socioeconomic household, Araceli had the opportunity to choose between a failing local school district and a more successful school outside of her district. Because education was a priority, Araceli attended prep school, a private high school located in Greensboro, North Carolina, that provided an advanced college preparatory education. Through her experience at Bishop High School, Araceli met Dr. Patrick Greene, the president and CEO of Serving Youth at Risk, a nonprofit research institute that focused on issues affecting the welfare of North Carolina children. Araceli leveraged her networking skills to obtain a prestigious summer job working with Serving Youth at Risk, where she first learned about research addressing human trafficking.

After high school, Araceli entered the University of North Carolina as a computer science major. But, as a rising junior, she felt a faith-related calling to work in cross-cultural social work. Her initial field placement was at International High School, a three-year program where students with English as a second language could take the appropriate standardized test in preparation for higher education. After graduating with a bachelor of social work (BSW), she continued directly in the master of social work (MSW) program. As an MSW student, she had an international field experience in Central America. Through this placement, Araceli learned advanced clinical skills by providing group sessions and case management for parents of children experiencing malnutrition as well as community social work by creating the social work protocol for a local child welfare project. Her work in this international social service organization prepared her for the complexity of government systems involved with international family permanency plans.

Araceli's passion for working with international clients was reinforced when she began working for North Carolina World Assistance. Her job consisted of comprehensive case management with victims of sex trafficking. In addition, Araceli was responsible for coordinating and facilitating the permanency paperwork needed for victims seeking asylum from human trafficking.

An Outing With Maria

Araceli's initial encounter with her first client, Maria Perez, was unconventional because it occurred while the two were traveling to their first Immigration and Customs Enforcement (ICE) check-in. Araceli understood the importance of keeping her client safe and calm during this check-in, but this was Araceli's first interaction with ICE, too. She would need all of her social work practice skills for building rapport. As a new social work case manager, Araceli wanted to make sure she did everything right for her supervisor Lauren and for Maria.

First, we'll meet the officer. Araceli mentally rehearsed the checklist Lauren provided. *Then we'll walk through the detector. I show the papers and then we wait in the waiting room.* They walked into the check-in and it was just as she was instructed. First, they met the officer, walked through the metal detectors, and found the waiting room. Everything was as planned except the papers. *Was I supposed to keep the papers? Do I ask for them back?* Araceli couldn't remember what happened after they took the papers. Her furrowed brow softened as she noticed Maria's concerned stare fixated on her face. Araceli reassured Maria, "I know that this is a long process, but you are doing great."

After the check-in, as they returned to the car, hunger pangs reminded Araceli to ask, "Maria, are you hungry?"

Maria shrugged, uncertain.

As they drove past a sign advertising a Starbucks at the next exit, Araceli asked again, "Is Starbucks okay?"

Maria nodded and agreed to stop there for a light lunch. Araceli thought this would be a good time to say more about herself and some of the services provided by WA. As they waited for their food, Araceli began, "Maria, thank you for the bravery you showed in the meeting with ICE today. You were able to explain everything so effectively. You answered all of the questions appropriately. You should be very proud of yourself."

"No," Maria began shaking her head in objection, "I don't want to talk about my case here."

"Okay," Araceli responded, "well, can you tell me what you need?"

"Yes, I can tell you what I need," Maria answered hurriedly.

After the food arrived, Maria took a bite of her chicken wrap and grimaced. But she began identifying resources she needed to become more stable and independent. "I want to have my own place. My own person, that, umm," Maria paused to find the right words, "you know, that person that talks to you?"

The person that talks to you, Araceli wondered. *Who is the person that talks to you?* "The counselor? Do you mean a counselor?"

"Yes," Maria affirmed, "a counselor."

"Okay, we can see what services will be the best fit for you." Araceli thought of all of the counseling services available to Maria, as well as the other services she requested. As they left Starbucks and headed home, Araceli felt the tension of riding with someone unfamiliar. Araceli wondered if she should make small talk or continue the hour-long drive in silence.

Maria appeared exhausted and finished the ride with her head against the window. With no conversation, it felt like a long ride home. Araceli's thoughts were interrupted only by the low hum of the latest top-40 hits playing on the local radio station.

"You can come by the office to get the food vouchers," Araceli explained, as she pulled into Maria's apartment complex. "I'll be in contact about the therapeutic and case management referrals, and we will check about assisting with the other resources soon, okay?"

Maria nodded as she left the car.

Affidavit Sessions

Araceli would later learn about Maria's experience with human trafficking in much greater depth. Pieces of her story were revealed during subsequent ICE interviews (different from her initial ICE check-in) and later during conversations with Maria's immigration attorney. Maria would recount several occurrences of unlawful detainment of her identification documents, forced servitude, and coerced sexual encounters. Araceli would come to learn that Maria's boyfriend told her stories of freedom and prosperity in the United States, only to coerce her into a bonded labor arrangement that made her incapable of making any decisions regarding her life. Maria was advised by an immigration attorney that they would need to gather documentation.

"Maria, in order to complete your T visa packet we need an I-914 application for nonimmigrant status, passport photographs, a personal statement of the applicant's human trafficking experience, and other documentation that addressed victimization. Today you began this process by reporting your experience with human trafficking, but the process isn't complete. Do you understand this?" the attorney asked.

"Yes," Maria responded.

"You will provide the remaining documentation to Araceli, okay?" the attorney clarified. The immigration attorney ended the meeting by handing Maria a list of the remaining documentations needed.

In order to complete the I-914 form, Maria had to recount her incidents of sex trafficking again, this time to immigration attorney Hilda Fong. These sessions were similar to the ICE interviews, but Fong typically spread the process over several sessions to reduce retraumatization of clients. It had taken several weekly sessions to capture enough of Maria's story, and the 90-day application due date was swiftly approaching.

It was the fourth meeting to complete the I-914 form. Like the others, this meeting would include Maria; Araceli, to provide support; and Hilda, who had worked really well with Maria in the other three interviews. Hilda showed great ability to connect with Maria and make her comfortable in sharing stories of her human trafficking past. In response, Maria had been very forthcoming about her experiences and Araceli was excited that she would be one step closer to gaining asylum in the United States.

To begin, Hilda reminded Araceli and Maria of the purpose for the meeting and summarized the last interview to refresh everyone's memory. "Maria, you stopped right before you met Jose Gutierrez," Hilda concluded. "Do you mind beginning when you met him?"

Araceli knew this would be a hard interview for Maria. As Araceli prepared Maria for this final interview, Maria began to disclose her initiation into sex trafficking and the grooming that took place while she lived with Jose.

"Yes," Maria affirmed, "he had connections in Houston and Raleigh. He contacted a coyote that smuggled me from Tijuana through Juarez, Mexico. We crossed the border in El Paso, stopped in Houston, and finally in Charlotte. It took just over a month to get here. I had to leave my dear father and two little daughters, but I made it."

"Maria, can you tell why you ran away with your boyfriend?" Araceli encouraged.

"Yes. I needed to get away from my past. My mother sold me," Maria recounted, "sold me to everyone who wanted me. That's what my family does. It's like the family business. And that's why I moved in with my father, to get away. That's how I moved from Vera Cruz to Tijuana—and that's where I met Jose. And when I met him—I fell in love," Maria remembered.

"Thank you, Maria. This is very helpful," Hilda interjected, "but we need a little more information about how you were trafficked and why you are petitioning to have your daughters join you in the United States. We want to ensure that we provide as much detail as possible so that your visa meets the criteria for approval."

With her head bowed, Maria began to describe how she was trafficked across the border and her decision to leave her daughters with her father.

"I didn't think Jose would hurt me. He said he loved me—and after being sold by my mother, for sex—I just wanted someone to love me," Maria stated, shifting in her seat. "He promised we would make a life together in America. He said to leave my babies and we would send for them when we were settled. But it took longer than he thought to get to Charlotte. It took a whole month to get here."

"Okay," Hilda encouraged. "What happened when you finally arrived in Charlotte?"

"He found us an apartment and I found a job. Everything was fine. I paid the bills and began making friends. We were living the American dream—until he got mad. He said he didn't like me hanging out with my friends. He made me give him all the money I made at my job. He kept saying, 'You owe me, you owe me.'"

"What happened after he began taking your money?" Hilda probed.

"At first he made me, you know, have sex with his friends," Maria stuttered. "He would beat me if I refused, so I did it. And then he wanted me to have sex with men I didn't know. He would offer me up like I was for sale. He'd force me in a room with a man and lock the door. I couldn't come out until we had sex—and they would pay him." Suddenly, Maria began sobbing. "It was just like my mother all over again."

She's shaking, Araceli observed. *Should we keep going?* Araceli questioned. *We need to complete the affidavit if she wants to achieve her goal of independence, and we're running out of time to file the paper work.* Then Araceli's social work professional skill began flashing through her brain: *Ensure the client's safety. Meet her where she is. De-escalate the situation.*

"Thank you for being so brave," Araceli said, leaning over to comfort her client, "thank you for trusting us with your story." *This is too much for her*, Araceli thought. *It's too much for anyone.*

Araceli and Hilda waited a few moments while Maria calmed herself.

"Can you tell Hilda," Araceli encouraged, "how you got connected to WA?"

"Well, one night after he forced me to have sex with some guy," Maria confessed, "we started fighting. He was beating me up and someone called the police."

"How did that connect you to WA?" Hilda asked for clarification. "Did the police take you to World Assistance?"

"No. The police asked me for documentation and I didn't have any. They heard my accent and arrested me for deportation. They sent me to—detention," Maria explained. "They said I had assault, umm, charged with assault from the fight."

Maria sunk down in her seat. "I didn't assault him. I just couldn't stay with him anymore. I never tried to assault him," Maria said weeping. "I just wanted to save my life."

"I know it's tough, Maria," Araceli comforted. "Do you need a break?"

Maria nodded.

"Hilda, is it okay if we take a 15-minute break?" Araceli asked.

"Sure. I'll get some coffee. Would either of you like coffee?" Both nodded. "I'll walk slowly," Hilda whispered.

When the door closed Araceli hugged Maria. "You're doing a great job. What can I do to help make this interview easier for you?

In a moment of clarity, Maria looked up and asked, "Can we do some grounding meditation? I have my sea meditation sounds on my phone."

"Sure," Araceli agreed, "we can do a grounding meditation while we wait. Is that one of the coping skills you're learning with your counselor?

"Yes," Maria said nervously. "And I've been practicing my coping skills—walking, listening to music, lighting my candles—I just don't want to take any medicine."

"Okay, we'll do this grounding exercise—and then we'll get back to the affidavit. Is that okay?"

Maria nodded.

Fifteen minutes later, Hilda returned with two cups of coffee.

As Maria slowly ended her grounding exercise, Araceli questioned, "Are you feeling better? Do you think you can finish the interview today?"

"Yes," Maria whispered through her last deep exhale. "I can finish the interview now."

"That's great, Maria," Araceli encouraged. "We're hoping that soon we'll be able to submit your T visa derivatives, you know, the papers to bring your girls over."

"I know," Maria sighed.

Maria began to recount her most recent sexual exploitation at the hands of Jose. "Maria, can you explain why you continued living with Jose, after all this abuse?" Hilda inquired.

"He said he'd kill me," Maria said in a muffled voice. Her head was bowed with her gaze fixed on the table, as she repeated it again. "I was really scared. I didn't have anywhere I could go because he knows where my family lives. I knew that if I left him, he would really hurt my family to get to me."

"Thank you, Maria, I really appreciate you sharing all of that with us," Hilda responded, after further elaboration. "I know it wasn't easy. I just needed to clarify the force, fraud, and coercion aspect of your trafficking case and you helped me with that." Hilda added, "Thank you for being so brave." With that closing statement, Hilda concluded the interview and notarized the I-914 form.

Family Reunification

Araceli was excited when they received formal notification that Maria's T visa was approved and she was granted asylum in the United States. Her excitement grew because they could now finalize the application for a T-3 visa derivative to allow reunification with Maria's daughters. Araceli telephoned Lorenzo Gutiérrez with the International Organization for Migration (IOM) to learn the final steps needed in the permanency placement plan to include in Maria's case plan.

"I just wanted to update you on Maria's visa status," Araceli began. "We received Maria's T visa approval, so we don't have to worry about deportation anymore."

"Great, Araceli," Lorenzo exclaimed. "Do you have any recent information about the girls' documentation? We're still waiting on their passports and birth certificates. Has Maria given them to you?"

"No. You should have received all of that information from Maria's father, Xavier Perez," Araceli responded. "Has he not provided that information? That should have happened months ago."

"We haven't received any paperwork," Lorenzo sounded impatient. "It's holding up our paperwork and, as you know, if we miss the submission deadline we will have to start all processes from the beginning. Have you heard anything from Ms. Perez?"

"No," Araceli offered, "but she'll be coming in for a meeting, so I can ask for an updated status. Will you be in the office later for a possible conference call?"

"Absolutely. Thanks for taking care of this, Araceli. We want to ensure the safe procurement of Isabella and Jimena. I'll be looking forward to your update."

Later that afternoon, Maria arrived on time for her case management session with Araceli. This surprised Araceli because Maria routinely arrived 20 minutes late for sessions.

"Hey Maria, come on in," Araceli greeted her client with a smile. "How are you feeling today?"

"I'm doing okay," Maria responded. "How are you?"

"I'm good. Thanks for asking. I'm so glad you were able to come in today," Araceli said as she motioned Maria over to her seating area. "I know it hasn't been easy for you to get off work for our meetings, so I just wanted you to know how appreciative I am that you could make it today."

"Yeah," Maria shrugged.

"We just want to make sure we can get all of the documentation to process your daughters' T-3 visas," Araceli reiterated. "Does that make sense? Have you been able to contact your father about the documents? If we don't get those documents it will hold up the process."

"You didn't get them?" Maria responded with apparent surprise. "I sent my father money. He said he would send them."

"When I asked you about this during our phone check-in a few weeks ago, you said the same thing. Did you send more money since then?"

"Yes," Maria affirmed. "I sent him more money, specifically for the birth certificates."

"Have you talked with him again?"

"Yes," Maria nodded, "he said he needed 50 dollars to get the documents."

"Fifty dollars? He doesn't need 50 dollars. Lorenzo from IOM stated that because we're using the IOM services, document processing is free." *Something's not adding up.* Araceli was puzzled by this information. *I remember telling you that all of the services with IOM were free. That's why we chose to partner with IOM,* she thought, *so that it wouldn't be a financial hardship on you.* Araceli caught herself shaking her head as she heard Maria respond.

"My father says that it costs 50 dollars to get the certificates," Maria reported, "so I sent him the money."

"Maria, let me check with Lorenzo. I think the processing should be free."

Araceli telephoned Lorenzo. "Hi Lorenzo, this is Araceli again. I'm with Maria Perez. Do you have time for a conference call?"

"Sure. Hi, Maria. How are you doing today?"

"I'm doing fine, Mr. Gutiérrez. How are you?"

"I'm well. We wanted to touch base with you regarding your daughters' identification cards and birth certificates. Were you able to contact your father to let him know that we need that information?"

"Yes. I sent him the money to pay for it and everything."

"Money? Ms. Perez, these services are free. We contacted the front desk to determine if your father dropped off any packages and his name is not in the visitor's log. Are you sure he's coming to the correct address?"

Maria assured them that she gave the correct address and showed the money wire receipt proving that she'd sent money for the purpose of securing her daughters' documentation.

"Well, Ms. Perez," Lorenzo interjected, please follow up on your end and we will see if anything comes in the mail. Please remember that all services with IOM are completely free. No charges at all."

"Yes, Mr. Gutiérrez," Maria agreed. "I'll see what happened."

"Thank you. Have a good rest of your visit with Ms. Aguilera and I'll touch base with you soon. Good-bye."

"Maria, do you think your father knows how to get to the IOM offices in Mexico?" Araceli asked, after hanging up the phone. "Does he need the money for transportation to the office?"

"No, no," Maria stuttered. "He has a ride. My aunt said she'd give him a ride if he couldn't get there."

"Do you have any idea why he might need the money since we have now confirmed that IOM's services are free?"

"No, I don't. I do know that there is a lot of corruption and violence in his area. That's why I wire the money directly to him instead of sending a money order in the mail. It's safer that way."

"Do you think he's in any danger?" Araceli probed.

"He didn't tell me that," Maria shook her head no. "He would have told me that." Maria's breathing became more stifled as her brow furrowed. Her gaze seemed distant, as if she were searching for something in the next room.

"What's going on, Maria?"

"I don't understand how he could do this to me," Maria nearly shouted. "I send him money to get the documents and he doesn't even need it. Why would he take money from me when he doesn't need it?"

Araceli couldn't understand why Xavier had asked for 50 dollars but attempted to deescalate her client.

"Just contact your dad for me, one more time," Araceli instructed, "to make sure he's safe and understands what we're asking of him. Remind him that if he uses the IOM Mexico offices, all of the services are free. Tell him to ask the IOM worker to call you when he's in the office so that you can explain all of the needed documentation. Can you do that for me, Maria?"

"Yes, Araceli. I promise, I will."

"Thank you. You have been so helpful during this entire process," Araceli reassured. "I'll follow up with our offices about next steps."

"Yes. I can do that."

"Good. I'll write that into your case plan and follow up with you next week. Is there anything else you need from us this week?"

"No, Araceli. You all have helped with so much. Now that I have my visa I can get a better job. You all have done more than enough."

"Well, you've done all of the hard work. I like the way you are progressing with your case plan. As soon as we can finalize this reunification visa we will be on the road to reuniting you with your girls."

"Thank you so much, Araceli." Maria could barely contain the tears welling up her eyes. "It's been five years since I've seen my daughters. I can't return to Mexico to visit and I'm afraid to try and smuggle them over."

Before leaving they summarized the list of things that needed to be completed before their next visit, Maria wrote herself a list as a reminder, and she left.

The Final Call

Over the next few weeks, with a new job and new apartment, Maria's appointments were more sporadic. But one day she came to Araceli's office in a panic. "He's dying, he's dying!"

"Who's dying?" Araceli asked, confused.

"My father. He's sick. I didn't know. No one told me." The information spilled out.

"How did you find out?" Araceli asked.

"When I called to inquire about the documents," Maria explained, "my Tia Letty answered the phone and told me he was in the hospital."

"What happened, what's wrong?" Araceli asked. "How serious is it?"

"I don't know," Maria began sobbing uncontrollably. "No one wants to tell me anything—and I can't even go and see him. What if he dies and I never get to see him? What if he dies?" Maria's voice drifted off.

Araceli just sat with Maria as she cried. After several minutes, she asked, "Maria, why don't they want to tell you?"

"They said they didn't want me to worry. They know I can't return to Mexico because of the T visa. They know if they told me I would try to go see him. They said they didn't have money for the phone calls, so they wanted to wait to see if he got better before letting me know he was sick. They didn't want me to worry about my daughters."

She went on, "It helps to explain a lot though—about why I didn't hear from him."

Maria was talking so fast that Araceli could hardly keep up. Araceli knew that Maria was stuck in America even if her father died, as required by the T visa. *Who's watching the kids? Are they eating or going to school?* Araceli's thoughts quickly turned to Maria's children. *Who would be the guardian of her daughters? Who could get clearance to keep them if Xavier is sick? We've got to create a safety plan and update contact information for Maria's relatives in Mexico*, Araceli thought.

After Maria told Araceli what she knew, they began to work on a safety plan for Isabella and Jimena and to update IOM on identifying another guardian for Maria's daughters. The safety plan would assist IOM in identifying responsible relative placements should the girls need to be moved. The safety plan outlined names and numbers of Maria's relatives who lived in the area as well as her understanding of "fit for placement." Maria was extremely concerned about placing her daughters with her maternal side of the family due to her own history of sexual abuse and sexual exploitation by those family members. After completing the safety plan, Maria left to try to contact her father and gather updated information regarding his medical condition.

Despite repeated attempts, Araceli was unable to reach Maria by phone for three weeks. Finally, Maria answered her call.

"He's dead, Araceli," Maria announced abruptly.

"What?!" Araceli replied.

"My dad is dead," Maria clarified.

"I'm so sorry, Maria," Araceli responded. "I know how much he meant to you. What can I do to help you in this process?"

"Nothing. I'm working on it. I went to church, lit some candles, and said my prayers. Some days it's so hard to get out of bed. Some days I think going back to Mexico is worth risking all of my residential status just to get my girls." Maria paused, then added, "I need to get my girls!"

"That's what we're trying to do through IOM," Araceli reassured. "Maria, who's going to care for your girls now that your father has passed? Do you have any thoughts on who might be able to take care of your girls right now?"

"I don't know." Maria paused. "I have two aunts who might be able, Delores and Letty, but they're older and I'd have to send money to help them."

Araceli knew that if the girls went into the foster care system there would be no way to track them in Mexico. Araceli's communication was already limited in Mexico because IOM's communication protocol required that only IOM could communicate on behalf of her client. *Keeping the girls with a family member was the safest option for a fast procurement procedure, but who could keep the girls?*

"You have a sister, Teresa. Could she watch the girls?" Araceli asked, recalling the family members Maria had mentioned previously.

"No, no!" Maria exclaimed. "Her husband is the one who abused me—three times! I don't want my girls with him—or her."

"Do you have any other relatives?" Araceli asked again. "Anyone at all?"

"None other than my mother. But she will never get my girls!" Maria stated emphatically.

What do I do? How do I place these girls until the paperwork can be completed for the T-3 visa? Do I advocate for the placement of the kids with her sister, whose husband abused Maria, if only on a short-term basis? Questions raced through Araceli's mind. *If IOM would only let me do a quick home visit or at least talk to a fostering agency, I could put safety and communication plans in place to make the procurement easier.* The weight of these decisions was almost too much for Araceli to bear. *How do I make sure the girls are okay? What happens if the girls disappear and Maria can't be reunited with them?*

As Araceli walked down the long hallway to her supervisor's office, she wondered, *How do we keep the girls safe while processing the paperwork for reunification? And how can we facilitate or support the coordination and decision making between Maria and IOM?*

5. Scientific Knowledge/Literature

5.1 Micro-Level Practice That Supports and Protects Victims of Human Trafficking

Providing protection to those who have been trafficked entails the procurement of short-term and long-term services to address diverse bio-psycho-social-spiritual needs of victims. In addition to perhaps the need for immediate safety often provided by law enforcement, victims may also need medical, legal, educational, and mental health services to begin the process of recovery. Self-sufficiency and independence are often the goals of social service organizations. Best practices require understanding and exploring the similarities and differences among various groups of human trafficking victims with special attention to assessing unique needs and appropriate resources for the protection of and service to this vulnerable population.

5.2 Identification of Victims

The identification of human trafficking victims (both those born in and outside their home countries) is the first step in providing for their protection; and the origins of the victims play a significant role in identification. To review the various definitions and types of human trafficking see Chapter 3.

Identifying victims is extremely complex because of the clandestine nature of the crime; perpetrators always socially isolate victims and frequently keep victims underground or invisible, including moving them to various locations in order to keep them out of public view and prevent detection (Goździak, 2010; Okech, Morreau, & Benson, 2012; Sigmon, 2008). Fundamentally, awareness and recognition of the populations that are most vulnerable to human trafficking are critical to their identification by agencies and individuals charged with their protection. Our understanding begins with describing the vulnerabilities that exist.

5.3 Victims in the United States

The National Human Trafficking Resource Center (NHTRC) is a national antitrafficking hotline and resource center serving victims and survivors of human trafficking and the antitrafficking community in the United States since December 2007 (NHTRC, 2016). This hotline provides personal assistance in over 200 languages, 24 hours a day 7 days a week, 365 days a year to victims and concerned reporters. The NHTRC hotline offers referrals to victims in accessing direct

Figure 5.1 *Labor trafficking poster.*

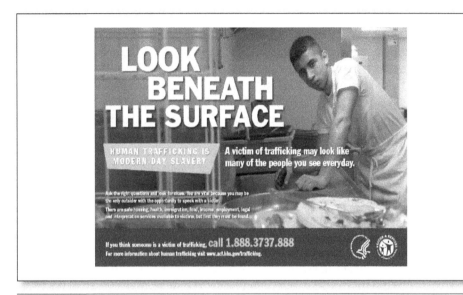

SOURCE: *Administration for Children and Families, Office on Trafficking in Persons, Rescue and Restore Victims of Human Trafficking Campaign,* 2012. Retrieved from https://www.acf.hhs.gov/otip/resource/labor-trafficking-poster. In the public domain.

services and helps to facilitate victim rescue by working with law enforcement in reporting tips on suspected human trafficking operations. NHTRC maintains data on the number of reports they receive via their call data, demographics from their case data, and the location of potential human trafficking cases where known. Statistical data collected from the NHTRC from December 7, 2007 to December 31, 2015, determined 25,696 cases of human trafficking, of which 24,920 survivors were identified with high indicators and 27,533 survivors with moderate indicators of human trafficking. A case is categorized as "High" when it contains a high level of indicators of human trafficking and "Moderate" when several indicators of human trafficking are identified but the case lacks important information in regard to elements of force, fraud, or coercion (Polaris, 2014b). The NHTRC's 2015 statistical report indicated that 20,673 were female victims, 3,487 were male victims, and 200 were transgender victims; 7,768 cases were identified as minor victims and 15,724 were adult victims; and 7,885 victims were foreign nationals while 8,676 victims were identified as U.S. citizens. The NHTRC 2015 report rated the top three sex-trafficking venues as commercial-front brothel, hotel/motel-based brothel, and residential brothel. The same report identified the top three labor-trafficking industries as domestic work, traveling sales crews, and restaurant/food service (Polaris, 2014b). Industries with a high risk for human trafficking can be found in Chapter 2.

5.4 Victim Vulnerabilities: Consider Gender, Age, History of Abuse, and Homelessness

Domestically and internationally, women and children are disproportionately represented as victims in the sex trafficking industry (Faulkner, Mahapatra, Heffron, Nsonwu, & Busch-Armendariz, 2013); poverty, crime, and corruption further exacerbate this risk factor in low-resource countries (Goździak, Bump, Duncan, MacDonnell, & Loiselle, 2006; Macy & Johns, 2011). A 2012 International Labour Office report estimates that 98% of the victims of forced labor worldwide are women and girls trafficked for the purpose of forced commercial sexual exploitation, and they make up 55% of total forced labor victims (11.4 million) relative to men and boys (45% at 9.5 million) (International Labour Office [ILO], 2012). In low-resource countries, especially where there is a caste system or inequity among indigenous groups, families are often subjected to generational debt bondage, falling into further debt with duplicitous employers, in an attempt to free themselves from bonded labor (ILO, 2005). Other times, vulnerable women and children are forced into prostitution to merely survive, as they are financially and psychologically dependent upon their traffickers. These circumstances occur because of systemic conditions that leave individuals marginalized with no other means of legitimatized employment or self-sufficiency (ILO, 2005).

Children are especially vulnerable to being trafficked both in the United States and abroad. Internationally, youth may be "sold" into slavery by their parents or family members for financial gain, the promise of procuring an education, or obtaining better opportunities; sometimes the exchange of the child and money is with the knowledge that the child will be trafficked and other times family members are misled by facilitators and traffickers who prey on marginalized communities. Other children are conscripted into human trafficking due to war and political upheaval leaving gaps in the social infrastructure that previously protected them. Worldwide, children are subjected to labor trafficking through forced begging or involuntary work, typically in the agriculture and fishing industries or the manufacturing of goods such as garments, rugs, and charcoal (Sigmon, 2008). The United States Department of Labor issued a 2009 report that identified 4,734 youth who were illegally employed during 2008; these findings indicated child labor violations that included dangerous conditions, unsafe environments, and improper use of equipment as well as noncompliance by employing children under 16 years old (United States Department of Labor, 2009).

In the United States, at-risk youth often have circumstances that increase their vulnerability. Youth who are victimized have a history of being raised in chaotic homes (e.g., domestic violence; parents with substance abuse, mental health needs, or limited cognitive ability); some victims may already be victimized by physical or psychological abuse of a parent/caretaker and may remain in this abusive environment; other youth may be placed in foster care or are aging out of the child welfare system and are at risk for being solicited, tricked, or exploited by traffickers. Numerous studies report a correlation between childhood sexual abuse and sex trafficking victimization (Kotrla, 2010; Reid, 2010; Smith, Healy Vardaman, & Snow, 2009). Research funded by the Administration for Children, Youth and Families in 2013 showed that the majority of commercially sexually exploited children (CSEC) report histories of childhood abuse in the 70 to 90 percentage range, and those with a history of sexual abuse were 28% more likely to be charged with prostitution during their lifetimes (Goodman & Laurence, 2014). Norton-Hawk (2002) conducted a study in Boston of 106 adult females arrested for prostitution; 68% reported a history of sexual abuse before 10 years of age and approximately half reported being raped before the same age. In a four-year study of National Incident-Based Reporting System (NIBRS) data for the years 1997 to 2000, the majority of juvenile victims involved in prostitution incidents were female (72%), and of all juvenile victims, the majority (77%) were age 15 years or younger (Finkelhor & Ormrod, 2004). Some youth may be vulnerable due to naiveté or lack of protection due to a special needs diagnosis. Foreign-born youth and their families who are in legal jeopardy may be threatened or coerced into human trafficking because of their undocumented status (Reid, 2014, 2016; Task Force on Trafficking of Women and Girls, 2014). Understanding the economic drivers of human trafficking as detailed in the previous chapter as well as the risk factors and vulnerabilities that traffickers exploit are necessary in order to fully address this complex social justice issue. In the United States, runaway youth are at increased risk and often targeted by traffickers because of their vulnerability due to limited resources and dependence on noncaregivers to provide for basic needs (food, shelter, etc.). According to the National Alliance to End Homelessness 2015 report *The State of Homelessness in America*, "On a single night in January 2014, 578,424 people were experiencing homelessness—meaning they were sleeping outside or in an emergency shelter or transitional housing program" (p. 3). Of those, 45,205 represented unaccompanied youth and children who are at "particular risk for being unsheltered" (p. 7). Many homeless youth rely on staying temporarily with friends, extended family, or acquaintances, exchanging sex for shelter, otherwise known as "survival sex." Survival sex requires victims to exchange sex acts for something that they need (e.g., water, shelter, food, etc.) in order to survive (Smith et al., 2009). This arrangement may take place for days, weeks, or sometimes years as an alternative to residing outside or in shelters. According to Smith et al. (2009), "In the absence of a trafficker/pimp selling the youth, the perpetrator paying for the sex" act with food, a bed, or a ride can become the trafficker (p. 5). In an earlier study of domestic minor sex trafficking in Utah, Snow reported that 32% ($n = 39$) of homeless youth victims of commercial sex exploitation were coerced in return for food, drugs, or shelter (e.g., survival sex), with 50% indicating that they had been solicited by an adult perpetrator (Snow, August 2008). Unaccompanied youth have often run away from home due to traumatic experiences resulting from child abuse and/or witnessing interpersonal violence. A random sample study of 174 young adults (aged 18 to 23) at Covenant House New York reported that 48% of youth who engaged in commercial sex acts did so because they did not have a place to stay (Covenant House, May 2013, p. 6).

Lesbian, gay, bisexual, transgender, and queer (LGBTQ) youth are at an elevated risk for homelessness (Rosario, Schrimshaw, & Hunter, 2012; Estes & Weiner, 2001) and at considerable risk of being trafficked because of their overrepresentation in the homeless youth population (Gordon & Hunter, 2013; Schwarz & Britton, 2015). In "coming out" about their sexual orientation, LGBTQ youth may be rejected and stigmatized by their families and communities, leading to homelessness (Gordon & Hunter, 2013), and many may be forced to leave home due to parental/caregiver reaction to their gender or sexual-minority identity (Ream & Forge, 2014). Sexual abuse and early nonmajority sexual development may also put youth at risk for homelessness (Rosario, Schrimshaw, & Hunter, 2012). In order to survive and secure shelter, food, and clothing, homeless LGBTQ youth have often been subjected to sexual victimization (Ferguson-Colvin & Maccio, 2012; Schwarz & Britton, 2015).

Homelessness was also identified as a risk factor for drug-dependent adult men who were labor trafficked in an agricultural setting. In addition to drug dependence, individuals who experience debilitating mental health issues have been vulnerable to being trafficked (Busch-Armendariz, Nsonwu, & Cook Heffron, 2009).

The populations most at risk globally are females, children, and the poor. In the United States, individuals at risk include these groups as well as individuals who experience drug dependence, who are homeless, or who are LGBTQ community members alienated by their family and other support systems.

5.5 Barriers to Identifying Victims

On a global scale, the identification of victims worldwide mirrors challenges of the United States system. However, Rafferty (2015), in her article titled *Challenges to the Rapid Identification of Children Who Have Been Trafficked for Commercial Sexual Exploitation*, noted several cultural and national differences. Rafferty concluded that some children who have been identified as potential victims of human trafficking never have their official status confirmed. Rafferty (2015) also reported that "failure to identify child victims is linked with varying legal definitions and government policies and responses surrounding the definition of 'trafficking' and 'child'" (p. 161) and that the age of the child can affect the prosecution of the trafficker. Other national variations include differences in how gender influences the identification process; in many parts of the world, human trafficking victims are viewed as only women and girls. Rafferty's (2015) findings revealed that males in Vietnam, India, and Laos were not recognized as victims of human trafficking and, therefore, no services were made available; this means that victims are "imminently more at risk of revictimization, and the lack of access to care inhibits recovery from the abuse" (p. 4).

Clawson and Dutch (2008a) assert two primary reasons for victims remaining unidentified—the general public misses the opportunities to identify victims and because of the lack of information about crime victims, victims themselves do not identify as victims. Victims are often threatened or coerced by their traffickers to remain silent (Clawson & Dutch, 2008a) and therefore do not seek help. Traffickers use psychological control tactics, intimidation, and threats of continued or intended physical abuse (Sigmon, 2008) to mute victims. There are a variety of other reasons that victims may not initially identify themselves as being trafficked even after being questioned by law enforcement or helping professionals (e.g., physicians, nurses, social workers, etc.) or when they have sought assistance for needs such as medical care or help with domestic violence (Brennan, 2005; Clawson & Dutch, 2008a). Some foreign-born victims may have a general distrust of law enforcement both in their homelands and in the countries where they are victimized, and they may also be fearful of deportation if they are undocumented (Brennan, 2005; Roby, Turley, & Cloward, 2008). Others may fear incarceration for crimes committed while being trafficked (Logan, Walker, & Hunt, 2009; Macy & Graham, 2012). Such fear is part of a process of coercion and intimidation that traffickers employ to keep victims silent.

Some victims are misidentified by first responders and "viewed first as undocumented, or illegal immigrants and treated as criminals and subjected to deportation hearings" while other victims have initially been perceived as "prostitutes and charged with solicitation and placed in jail or detention (even in cases involving minors)" (Clawson & Dutch, 2008a, p. 3). This inaccurate labeling further perpetuates the victim's mistrust of the system and prevents adequate protection.

Still, in other cases, such as the domestic sex trafficking of minors, victims often fall prey to emotional manipulation from their traffickers (Hardy, Compton, & McPhatter, 2013; Lloyd, 2011; Macy & Graham, 2012). This emotional control by the trafficker further complicates the work of first responders (e.g., law enforcement) to assist and intervene as many victims may resist their support (Clawson & Dutch, 2008a). The trafficker often exploits the victim to falsely defend their relationship to others, instructing her to claim that they are dating, married, or related to each other. Victims who have developed a strong emotional bond with their traffickers are at high risk for returning to the abuse after rescue (Bokhari, 2008; Muraya & Fry, 2015); this strong emotional connection with their captors is often referred to as trauma bond or Stockholm syndrome (Carnes, 1997; Clawson & Dutch, 2008a; Kalergis, 2009; Reid,

Table 5.2 Countering Trauma Bonds

Trafficker Provides	Response
Traffickers/pimps seek to fill emotional voids and needed roles.	Find out what needs are being met or are trying to be met, such as love and self-esteem.
Traffickers/pimps provide hope, which they later exploit.	Give hope through a variety of ways, such as skill-building, education, and advocacy.
Traffickers/pimps fill physical needs.	Provide holistic programs and services.
Traffickers/pimps thrive off fear and intimacy creating instability.	Create a safe pace to stabilize and long-term care.
Traffickers/pimps manipulate, lie, betray, and let the victims down, but they are always there.	Set realistic and honest expectations. Be consistent.

NOTE: *The National Report on Domestic Minor Sex Trafficking: America's Prostituted Children* (p. 70) by L. A. Smith, S. Healy Vardaman, and M. A. Snow, 2009, Arlington, VA: Shared Hope International. Copyright 2009 by Shared Hope International. Reprinted with permission.

2014). A trauma-informed response could integrate tactics to countering trauma bonds that may have developed between victim and trafficker. Smith et al. (2009) suggest that service providers make an assessment of the needs that the trafficker may be providing and offer alternate, and more beneficial, replacements (for more information see Table 5.2). Zimmerman, Hossain, and Watts (2011) reported that the risk of a return by the victim to the perpetrator within the first two years after rescue was especially prevalent among youth who had been trafficked.

Foreign-born individuals are especially vulnerable due to language and cultural barriers and may not recognize that they have been victimized by their traffickers (Goździak, 2010). Victims, who may have initially sought or agreed to be smuggled, may be duped into thinking that their labor or sex trafficking is expected for repayment of their smuggling debt. Additionally, their inability to communicate in a foreign language further limits their ability to understand their rights as a crime victim and seek assistance.

5.6 Screening for Victims

Frequently, individuals who have been trafficked are initially identified by local law enforcement or by a community service organization (Kappelhoff, 2008; Okech et al., 2012). Increased education and awareness programs for professionals on the indicators or "red flags" of human trafficking and the implementation of screening protocols have improved identification of victims (Kotrla, 2010; Okech et al., 2012). Logan et al. (2009) list three ways that victims exhibit red flags: (a) situational

Figure 5.2   *Social service screening poster.*

SOURCE: *Administration for Children and Families, Office on Trafficking in Persons, Rescue and Restore Victims of Human Trafficking Campaign, 2012.* Retrieved from http://www.acf.hhs.gov/orr/resource/download-campaign-posters-and-brochures. In the public domain.

indicators, (b) story indicators, and (c) demeanor (p. 19). Situational indicators include "lack of English-speaking persons in an establishment, frequent movement of individuals through an establishment, many people living together in a private residence, or people living where they work" (Logan et al., 2009, pp. 19–20). Story and demeanor indicators consist of attending to the often subtle nuances of what people say in an interview and how they act (e.g., are they fearful and anxious). Behavioral indicators and client's responses to questions may reveal concerns or threats to safety or well-being (Okech et al., 2012). Medical, educational, and social services providers will better evaluate risk and vulnerability if screening tools are incorporated in agency protocols. Polaris (2016) developed *Recognize the Signs* as a supplement to already existing intake forms that probe about human trafficking victimization. This tool can be found in Chapter 1 (see box titled Red Flags for Human Trafficking).

In 2014, the Vera Institute for Justice developed another tool, the Trafficking Victim Identification Tool (TVIT), to aid service providers and law enforcement in screening for potential human trafficking (see link under 9.2 Websites later in this chapter). Additionally, Nsonwu et al. (2015) developed a survey tool that assesses the perception of social work students regarding human trafficking and can be found in Appendix B.

Screening tools for educational settings also exist since teachers, school counselors, and administrators are in positions to uncover students who are being exploited or are vulnerable to being trafficked. School-based screening tools help educators and school personnel to longitudinally assess and recognize changes in a student's behavior, physical appearance, educational achievements, living situation/environment, and support systems, for example. Also, teachers and counselors in particular often have developed trusting relationships with students.

Many law enforcement programs have also implemented awareness programs and specialized training to recognize victims of human trafficking and identify human trafficking situations in ongoing investigations (Logan, 2007; Logan et al., 2009). To provide adequate protection for human trafficking victims, law enforcement professionals engaged in human trafficking raids must be well trained and acutely aware of the complexity of the identification process, which can often be confusing and unclear (Sigmon, 2008). Shared Hope International published a 2009 report, *Domestic Minor Sex Trafficking: America's Prostituted Children,* to call attention to the misidentification of victims, one of the obstacles in providing holistic responses to domestic minor sex trafficking victims. The concern is that "misidentification occurs at all levels of first responses from law enforcement arrest on the streets to homeless and runaway youth shelters' intake process, to court adjudication of the victim as a delinquent for habitual runaway or drug possession, or other offense occurring as a result of the prostitution of the child" (Smith et al., 2009, p. v). Victims of domestic minor sex trafficking are at risk for mistakenly being processed as juvenile delinquents or adult prostitutes, which can have compounding legal and emotional consequences for the victim. Legally, charges for prostitution or lesser crimes of a delinquency offense may cause a victim to be ineligible from utilizing crime victim funds in some states while the emotional results of misidentifying a victim can ostracize a victim from trusting the system and

Figure 5.3 *Human trafficking assessment tool for educators.*

Tools for Educators | National Human Trafficking Resource Center

This tool is designed to help educators identify the risk factors and indicators of human trafficking in their students and to offer guidelines on how to respond and access resources. **Disclaimer: This protocol does not substitute for internal or mandated reporting requirements and does not guarantee safety. For emergencies, please contact 9-1-1.**

Red Flags & Indicators
- **Exhibits changes in behaviors or school participation**, i.e. spike in truancy; or performs severely under grade level.
- Student's family shows **signs of frequent migration, periodic homelessness**, disorientation, uncertainty of surroundings.
- **History of homelessness or running away from home.**
- **Reveals signs of abusive or inattentive caregivers**, such as untreated illness or injury, bruises, or scars.
- Displays **heightened sense of duty or obligation to family**, has **unreasonable or inappropriate chores or duties**.
- **Works for little or no pay**, or the **employer keeps identification documents and/or confiscates wages.**
- **Accumulates debt to employer** while at work or recruited for work with promises of easy money.
- Exhibits **sexual behavior that is high risk and/or inappropriate for his/her age.**
- Has an explicitly sexual online profile via internet community or social networking sites.
- **Involved in relationship with an older man**, receives frequent gifts, may be picked up from school by controller.
- **Engages in sexual activity in exchange for money or anything of value** (can include clothing, food, shelter, other goods and resources). No force, fraud, or coercion necessary if the student is under 18.
- **Knowledge of the commercial sex industry.** Uses lingo: "The Life," "The Game," "Daddy," for boyfriend, "Track" or "Stroll," refers to dates as "Johns" or "Tricks.

Consult Polaris Project's Red Flags & Indicators for a complete list.

YES
- I have a safe space to talk with the student privately.
- I am acting within the role designated for me by my school's protocols.

First Response
If any of the above indicators is present, follow all relevant school protocols, specifically those for discussing potential abuse with students and reporting abuse to appropriate authorities.

Is your next step to talk with the student?

NO
- I am looking for resources, referrals, or general support.
- My school's protocols require me to follow a different course of action.

Contact the National Human Trafficking Resource Center
Call the hotline at **1-888-3737-888,** 24 hours a day/7 days a week.

Ask for assistance with assessment questions, safety planning, resources & referrals, specialized reporting options, and next steps, **even if you are not sure if this is a case of human trafficking.**

Assess Safety and Needs
Speak to the student alone or privately, and follow her/his cues.
- Is the student a minor (under 18 years of age)?
- Is it safe for the student to talk right now?
- Is anyone watching, listening, calling, or texting her/him?
- Is the controller present or nearby, i.e. at the school, waiting outside, at the home [of the student]?
- Does the controller know where the student attends school or lives?
- What would happen if the student tried to leave the controller? Refuse to continue working or engaging in commercial sex?
- Is the student or a family member in danger?
- Do the parent(s)/legal guardian(s) know about the situation?

See Polaris Project's Safety Planning & Prevention for more Safety Planning tips.

Basic Trafficking Assessment
- How did you meet your boyfriend/find out about your job?
- Have you ever tried to break up with your boyfriend/leave your job? Is anyone preventing or threatening you?
- Do you want help leaving?
- Are your family members or friends are in danger if you try to leave?
- Have you ever been forced to do work that you didn't want to do?
- Were you ever lied to about the type of work that you would do?
- Has anyone ever given you money or offered it to you for having sex? Does anyone make you have sex?

See Polaris Project's Comprehensive Trafficking Assessment for more.

This publication was made possible in part through Grant Number 90XR0012/02 from the Anti-Trafficking in Persons Division, Office of Refugee Resettlement, U.S. Department of Health and Human Services (HHS). Its contents are solely the responsibility of the authors and do not necessarily represent the official views of the Anti-Trafficking in Persons Division, Office of Refugee Resettlement, or HHS.

POLARIS PROJECT   Polaris Project | National Human Trafficking Resource Center | 1-888-3737-888 | NHTRC@PolarisProject.org
www.PolarisProject.org © Copyright Polaris Project, 2011. All Rights Reserved.

SOURCE: "Tools for Educators: National Human Trafficking Resource Center" by Polaris and the National Human Trafficking Resource Center, 2011 (https://traffickingresourcecenter.org/resources/human-trafficking-assessment-tool-educators). Copyright 2011 by Polaris and the National Human Trafficking Resource Center. Reprinted with permission.

Table 5.3 Warning Signs of Domestic Minor Sex Trafficking	
Homelessness	Chronic running away (three or more times)
Presence of an older boyfriend	Tattoos often serve to mark a victim as the property of a particular pimp
Signs of violence and/or psychological trauma	Multiple sexually transmitted diseases
Masking charges such as curfew violations, truancy, and other status offenses	Substance abuse
Travel with an older male who is not a guardian	Access to material things the youth cannot afford

NOTE: *The National Report on Domestic Minor Sex Trafficking: America's Prostituted Children* (p. 49) by L. A. Smith, S. Healy Vardaman, and M. A. Snow, 2009, Arlington, VA: Shared Hope International. Copyright 2009 by Shared Hope International. Reprinted with permission.

make him or her even more codependent on the trafficker (Smith et al., 2009). There are some warning signs and victim vulnerabilities that may help to identify minors vulnerable to sex trafficking, which can be found in Table 5.3.

Misidentification also occurs with foreign-born victims. Adult victims may be initially arrested and taken into custody because there may be an immediate lack of clarity about victimization and/or perpetration where traffickers have "hidden" in the victim group after a police sting. Language and cultural barriers can further complicate these conclusions.

Identification of foreign-born child victims of human trafficking must be a coordinated and collaborative effort by government and nongovernment agencies (Goździak, 2010). Since minor victims often come into contact with a variety of service providers (e.g., school officials, medical providers, child welfare workers, etc.) or may be interviewed or apprehended by a variety of law enforcement entities (e.g., juvenile detention, local police, border patrol, etc.), accurate and timely identification is dependent upon a thorough assessment and screening process, as well as efficiently shared communication between and among various professionals and their agencies. Failure to properly and consistently identify child victims of human trafficking has resulted in their increased harm if victims fall through the system cracks. Coordination among the various federal, state, and local resources will help to protect and serve victims.

5.7 Immediate and Long-Term Needs of Victims

These next sections include discussion of the immediate and long-term needs of victims. Some sections pertain to people victimized in the countries in which they were born as well as those who were transported to another country. One section specifically addresses the unique needs of foreign-born victims.

5.8 Immediate Needs

Victims of human trafficking often need immediate safe housing, food, clothing, and medical care, particularly if they made a quick escape from their trafficker or were emancipated by law enforcement. All victims, regardless of their country of origin, share these basic needs. Hodge (2014) reports, "Survivors often have pressing needs for medical treatment given that traffickers tend to neglect routine medical care to avoid detection and to maximize victims' working time to obtain as much profit as possible" (p. 115). Health concerns in survivors of human trafficking are significantly increased (Zimmerman, 2003) as a result of the physical abuse, rape, and beatings that victims sustain while enslaved. Victims who are trafficked for labor are required to work in horrendous conditions for long periods of time, and victims who have been trafficked for sex are forced to engage in unsafe sexual practices; these conditions, coupled with poor nutrition, put the victims at risk for contracting disease and illness (Hodge, 2014; Zimmerman et al., 2011). Addressing basic short-term survival needs is crucial in assisting victims to rebuild their lives (Busch-Armendariz et al., 2009). The United States federal government created grants administered through the Office of Victims of Crime (OVC) to deliver essential services to newly identified victims of human trafficking (Caliber Associates, 2007). This funding, dispersed through community agencies, provides victims of human trafficking immediate needs of food, clothing, and housing, as well as ongoing and long-term support for medical, mental health, legal aid, and advocacy services (Busch-Armendariz et al., 2009; Caliber Associates, 2007).

5.9 Service Needs of Trafficking Victims

Nongovernmental organizations (NGOs), faith-based agencies, and governmental agencies across the country are providing social services to human trafficking victims. Often, these services have been situated in organizations that provide support to the homeless population, victims of domestic violence and sexual assault, and refugees. Child welfare organizations such as shelter services may be providing services to children and youth victims of human trafficking. Several U.S. cities with progressive anti–human trafficking community programs have developed services to specifically meet the short-term and long-term needs of human trafficking victims (Busch-Armendariz et al., 2009).

Securing a victim's physical safety is an essential need at the primary stage of case management. In some cases, the trafficker may not initially be apprehended and may seek to abduct or coerce the victim into fleeing with him or her. In other cases, the trafficker may be incarcerated but may employ facilitators who can directly threaten victims or intimidate the victim's family members (Busch-Armendariz et al., 2009; Hopper, 2004; Roby et al., 2008). Safe housing with clear safety guidelines for its residents is a critical service for human trafficking victims. Similarly, safety planning is paramount to a victim's physical and emotional wellbeing (Clawson & Dutch, 2008b; Gluck & Mathur, 2014; Okech et al., 2012).

Human trafficking survivors may need extra support during the transition from agency-based housing to independent living. Their anxieties are compounded by the

Figure 5.4 *Needs of victims of human trafficking.*

Needs of Victims of Human Trafficking			
	International		Domestic Minors
	Adults	Minors	
Emergency			
Safety	X	X	X
Housing	X	X	X
Food/clothing	X	X	X
Translation	X	X	
Legal guardianship		X	X
Short-/Long-term			
Transitional housing	X		X
Long-term housing	X		X
Permanency placement		X	
Legal assistance	X		X
Advocacy			
Translation	X	X	X
Medical care	X	X	X
Mental health/counseling	X	X	X
Substance abuse treatment			X*
Transportation	X		X
Life skills	X	X	X
Education	X	X	X
Financial assistance/management	X		X
Job training/employment	X	X	X
Child care	X	X	X
Reunification/repatriation	X	X	X

SOURCE: *Addressing the needs of victims of human trafficking: Challenges, barriers, and promising practices,* by H. J. Clawson and N. Dutch, 2008. Retrieved from https://aspe.hhs.gov/basic-report/addressing-needs-victims-human-trafficking-challenges-barriers-and-promising-practices. In the public domain.

*While substance abuse treatment may be a need for international victims, it was identified as a need for only domestic minor victims continued level of fear, retribution, or concern about abduction by their trafficker. Social workers and mental health professionals must assist victims in successfully adapting during these transitions.

The case management for children and youth who were previously homeless and experienced deprivation of their basic needs being met (e.g., food, shelter, and clothing) will require a mental health assessment and support. Trauma-informed approaches are necessary to address their traumatic experiences during the exploitation and those circumstances that initially led to their homelessness. Health and well-being issues need to be treated such as injuries, sexually transmitted infections, pregnancy, immunizations, dental care, and many others. The attention to emotional safety and fostering a sense of self-sufficiency are also a central necessity for children and youth to begin the restoration and healing process (Schwarz & Britton, 2015).

5.10 Service Needs of Foreign-Born Victims

Foreign-born victims of human trafficking may have certain needs that are unique because they have been victimized in a country that is not their country of origin. There are specific services and benefits available for foreign-born human trafficking victims. First, programs that support foreign-born victims of human trafficking should be culturally responsive, where social service providers recognize that there is not a "one size fits all" model (Schwarz & Britton, 2015).

Foreign-born victims of human trafficking may be detained or incarcerated without the system recognizing their status as victims. These failures often occur because of language and cultural barriers, the victims' mistrust or misperception of the law enforcement, or the inability to disclose because of fear of retribution by their traffickers. In instances with a lack of proper documentation (Logan et al., 2009) and in circumstances where police have raided a business or brothel and later detained both victims and perpetrators, disclosure decisions are compounded.

Refugee resettlement agencies are often contracted to serve foreign-born victims of human trafficking because these organizations may have trained interpreters and culturally competent staff already on board. The basic needs for foreign-born victims of human trafficking are similar to those of other victims (Busch-Armendariz, Nsonwu, & Heffron, 2011; Nsonwu, Busch-Armendariz, & Heffron, 2014). However, foreign-born victims may have been kept from any contact with their family members, so phone cards or other means of communication are immediately needed (Busch-Armendariz et al., 2011). These victims and their family members have wondered about the safety and whereabouts of one another. Initial counseling services in the first language of the client are also an essential component for healing and recovery (Busch-Armendariz et al., 2011).

5.11 Long-Term Needs

The long-term needs of human trafficking victims include affordable and safe housing, viable employment or schooling, culturally sensitive counseling (including trauma-informed mental health services), and assistance with family reunification and legal services. These services are essential components of a holistic plan of integration process and recovery for victims of human trafficking (Busch-Armendariz et al., 2011; Faulkner et al., 2013; Nsonwu et al., 2014).

In particular, legal representation is critical for foreign-born victims. In the United States, certified victims of human trafficking may be eligible for a T visa that includes benefits such as temporary immigration status with a legal path for permanent residency, work authorization, and family reunification (Busch-Armendariz, 2012; Faulkner et al., 2013). Family reunification, a complex legal process, means that victims can be reunited with minor children and dependents in the United States. Certification may be granted after the victim agrees to assist law enforcement and prosecutors in their human trafficking case (Bishop, 2003).

5.12 Needs and Challenges After Family Reunification

Family reunification can be a time of both joy and adjustment. After extended periods of separation between family members, it is reasonable to expect a period of adjustment. Professionals and communities should anticipate both ease and turbulence for newly reunited family members. By the time family members are brought together, many foreign-born victims have exhausted their entitlement services through the refugee resettlement program. They must navigate complex bureaucracies on their own. Mental health resources are frequently needed because of the stress of acculturation and integration processes for their newly arrived family members. Victims who are parents may have been physically separated from their minor children for many years. Consequently, the emotional bonds and relationships that would have naturally developed when living together are absent because of the physical separation. This is especially challenging in situations where mothers have been apart from very young children for many years and now must assume a parental role with a child who may not recognize them after years of separation. In a study about foreign-born victims of human trafficking, Busch-Armendariz and her colleagues (2011) found that many of the children of the exploited women had been raised by another family member and when they were reunited had difficulty relating to their mothers as parents (Busch-Armendariz et al., 2011). This research also concluded that older school-age children who reunited with their mothers faced added hardships including struggles with integrating into school, learning a new language, and often finding employment to financially assist the family. These expectations can cause additional stress; the child often feels overwhelmed by the need to quickly adjust to a new culture and burdened by extra responsibilities, and the parent often experiences feelings of guilt in witnessing their child's struggle (Busch-Armendariz et al., 2011).

5.13 Immigration Status of Victims

Another factor that can cause considerable stress for foreign-born victims of human trafficking is the realized inequity of family members in a mixed legal status family.

A mixed-status family is composed of individual family members who have varying immigration statuses in the same household (e.g., unauthorized immigrant, temporary residency, permanent residency, or naturalized citizen). These differences provide opportunities and liabilities. Individuals and families may qualify for social service benefits although there is fear about family members being apprehended by immigration services. In the United States, the governmental agency is Immigration and Customs Enforcement (ICE). Certified victims of human trafficking are ensured legal protection; however, this may not extend to other undocumented household members who may have joined the family. When this occurs, it causes an imbalance among household members and may contribute to fear and strain within the family group. Such stress may permeate the family relationships and make members wary of trusting outsiders.

World Hope International—Aid for Africa

Sub-Saharan Africa

http://www.aidforafrica.org/member-charities/world-hope-international/
    World Hope International—Aid for Africa alleviates suffering and injustice in Africa and elsewhere through education, microfinance, and community health programs. It builds wells, provides HIV/AIDS education and orphan care, and works to prevent human trafficking.

5.14 Mental Health Needs of Victims

Foreign-born victims of human trafficking experience significant mental health stressors. Initially, victims experience emotional trauma as a result of being deceived by perpetrators and the conspirators who recruited them; oftentimes, these facilitators are people whom they knew and trusted, possibly even family. This violation of trust causes the person who has been trafficked to deeply question the motives of others as well as their own sense of self. Traffickers intimidate victims by threatening harm to their family members in their homelands if victims attempt to escape, seek protection, and cooperate with law enforcement. This puts a considerable amount of stress on the victim and is a valid concern. International traffickers have a well-developed communication network that crosses borders. Victims are keenly aware that family members have been murdered or beaten as a result of their enslaved family member's resistance (Sigmon, 2008). A lack of trust in law enforcement or government officials contributes to victims' silence and mental health problems. In some countries, government representatives are complicit in human trafficking, either participating in the crime or accepting bribes from traffickers to turn a blind eye (Hodge, 2014). Sigmon (2008) reports, "Police corruption is reported as a key factor impeding efforts to combat human trafficking in many countries" (p. 254). The victim often links a corrupt law enforcement system in their homeland with a deep distrust of law enforcement officials everywhere.

5.15 Need for a Continuum of Care

It is crucial that the extended team of service providers, including law enforcement, legal aid, medical providers, and social services, understands that trust building is at the foundation of effective service delivery when working with victims (Busch-Armendariz, Nsonwu, & Heffron, 2014). Victims may be wary of being revictimized by duplicitous individuals. Foreign-born victims may be especially vulnerable since they may not be aware of their rights or understand local norms, customs, and laws that could protect them (Sigmon, 2008). The various roles of collaborating professionals and clients' rights to confidentiality, legal representation, and self-determination in the case management process may be entirely new concepts for foreign-born victims since other countries may not operate under the same set of legal assumptions or may not have the same service delivery resources as the United States. Therefore, educating foreign-born victims about this process and their rights is a fundamental component in addressing their immediate and long-term needs.

5.16 Best Practice in the Delivery of Services

Developments in the field of antitrafficking work have begun to evaluate the efficacy of service delivery systems to victims of human trafficking and have created a forum for research on evidence-based practice that includes the voices of survivors to guide first responders and practitioners in the firsthand perspectives of victims. The President's Interagency Task Force and the Federal Strategic Action Plan on Services for Victims of Human Trafficking determined that best practices involve comprehensive, survivor-centered, and trauma-informed services (President's Interagency Task Force, 2014) by multi-agencies to leverage limited resources.

5.17 Survivor-Centered Approach

Service providers are beginning to understand that we must employ a *survivor-centered approach* in planning prevention programs and when offering protection to victims of human trafficking. Specialized, innovative, and evidence-based strategies are compulsory if we are to work toward preventing human trafficking while simultaneously offering protection through programs that specifically serve the needs of individuals who have been trafficked. Best practices in the service delivery system call on providers to individualize case plans and to utilize *client-first, survivor-first*, or *victim-centered* models since each human trafficking case is uniquely different from one another and possesses individual characteristics. Although these paradigms utilize various names (e.g. *client-first, survivor-first*, or *victim-centered*), they all encompass the philosophical principle of placing the client at the center of the decision-making process and in valuing the rights and self-determination of clients. "An adaptable 'survivor-first' model allows for survivors to opt in and out of services and resources as they need during times of vulnerability, while allowing them to build resilience skills during times of security and self-sufficiency" (Schwarz & Britton, 2015, p. 64). This client-first approach appreciates that "survivors move in and out of risk and security and that there is no single package of mechanisms for each survivor" (Schwarz & Britton, 2015, p. 64).

5.18 Trust Building From the Victim's Perspective

Building trust with clients is at the bedrock in providing best practices. Victims of human trafficking, regardless of whether they were native born or foreign born or were trafficked for labor or sex, have been lied to by their captor(s) as fraud is a key element of initially gaining trust and/or maintaining control. It is imperative that all professionals working with victims of human trafficking acknowledge that since their client's trust has been violated, they may be reluctant to trust others. The trust-building process is facilitated by creating an atmosphere where victims are recognized as "the experts of their own experience" (Hom & Woods, 2013, p. 78). Trust is further developed when professionals provide a judgment-free zone and are accepting of the decisions and choices that their client has made and will make.

5.19 The Need for Case Management Collaboration

Interdisciplinary teams and case collaboration and coordination are crucial components to providing best practices to victim of human trafficking. Multidisciplinary teams will think through a variety of issues and challenges during all aspects of the service provision. This team of professionals from different disciplines will synchronize services for clients to be holistic and avoid the possibility of secondary trauma. The ability to develop open communication and trust is essential between professionals and survivors. The most comprehensive interdisciplinary teams have developed professional coalitions with representatives from local, state, and federal law enforcement agencies and professionals from social service agencies serving the homeless, refugees, juvenile justice, sexual assault and domestic violence, and medical and housing assistance (Busch, Fong, Heffron, Faulkner, & Mahapatra, 2007; Office for Victims of Crime, September 2012).

5.20 Putting the Victim's Needs First

Best practices in social services are those that purposefully design programs with a victim-centered approach to meet the specific needs of individual survivors. Busch-Armendariz and colleagues make the point that "the mission and program services are developed through a survivor's lens rather than what might be best for professionals or the structures in which they work" (Busch-Armendariz et al., 2014). Another important aspect of providing specialized intervention strategies involves utilizing a single point-of-contact service delivery paradigm, especially in conjunction with a coalition-based model. This framework provides clients with one social worker or provider whose job is to act as a conduit in facilitating wraparound services while maintaining a client-first or victim-centered approach; the provider also functions as the point of contact for the other professional team members. This model allows the social worker to easily pivot and meet the needs of their client as well as shift newly identified priorities as a result of interdisciplinary collaboration (Busch-Armendariz et al., 2014). This is different from other traditional case management models because the social worker is "privy to guarded and confidential law enforcement operations and other policy decisions . . . allowing her to be proactive and initiate innovative strategies and new developments" (Busch-Armendariz et al., 2014, p. 13).

5.21 The Need for Cultural Competency

A survivor-centered approach recognizes and affirms that culturally competent services for clients are essential. Busch-Armendariz and colleagues suggest that "to be effective, specialized intervention strategies need to be culturally grounded and consider age and developmental stage, type and length exploitation, relationship with traffickers, nationality, previous history of victimization, and many other factors." (Busch-Armendariz et al., 2014, p. 17). When working with foreign-born victims of human trafficking or survivors with language skills different from the professionals' providing services to them, it is especially important to utilize interpreters (translates speech orally) and translators (changes written text from one language to another) who have received training for these positions. Ideally, social service agencies are moving to employing bilingual and bicultural professionals so that miscommunication is minimized. Correctly utilizing an interpreter in an interview, becoming proficient in another language, and becoming verbally adept in communicating with others are all important components of cultural competence. However, cultural competence should be "defined broadly (extending beyond ethnicity and race) to encompass learning specifically about the crime of human trafficking and its impact on its survivors (psychological coercion and trauma, cultural practices of survivors and their families, risk factors of vulnerability, etc.)" (Busch-Armendariz et al., 2014, p. 15).

The service delivery process can be multifaceted and complex. In working to facilitate the most effective, efficient, and survivor-centered approach,

> the social worker's attention to coordination of services (affirmative ecological approach in social work), understanding of trust building (affirmative strengths-based perspective in social work), and cultural competency (affirmation of survivor-centered focus) provide for a thoughtful and thorough catalyst towards survivor restoration. (Busch-Armendariz et al., 2014, p. 13)

5.22 Perspective on the Process of Recovery

A Language of Recovery

The language used to describe clients of human trafficking services—*survivors* or *victims*—is typically defined in professional context. For example, law enforcement and legal services tend to use the terminology *victim* to indicate that a crime that has been committed. Victim is also used in these settings because in many states, being a crime victim opens up possibilities to services and support from the criminal justice

Awareness Against Human Trafficking (HAART)

Kenya

http://haartkenya.org/

HAART is a Kenyan nongovernmental organization (NGO) dedicated to ending human trafficking—also known as modern slavery—in Kenya. We work with creating awareness against human trafficking in the grassroots communities in Nairobi and its environs, assisting victims of trafficking, prosecuting offenders, and working in partnerships with other organizations and networks to end modern slavery. Moreover, we are involved with research to better understand trafficking in Kenya.

system (Kalergis, 2009). Social service providers tend to use *survivor* as a term that invokes empowerment and resiliency. The lexicon that is used by professionals may or may not accurately correspond to the language that clients prefer when describing their experience, as this differs with each client.

It is evident from survivor testimonies and accounts from law enforcement, first responders, as well as trial affidavits, that survivors of human trafficking have experienced traumatic events due to the horrific nature of this crime. These life-changing events impact the victims' emotional, physical, spiritual, social, and mental health well-being and their capacity to function (SAMHSA, 2014). Leitch, Vanslyke, and Allen (2009) state, "Traumatic stress causes both mental health problems and a variety of serious somatic symptoms, including loss of bowel and bladder control (Solomon, Laor, & McFarlane, 1996); shaking, trembling, and increased heart rate (Bernât, Ronfeldt, & Calhoun, 1998; Shalev et al., 1998); myofascial pain (Scaer, 2006); diabetes (Golden, Williams, & Ford, 2004); heart disease (Musselman & Nemeroff, 2000); and a continuum of stress-related diseases (Green, Grace, & Glesser, 1985; Scaer, 2006)" (p. 10) in addition to psychological pain and suffering. Victims may experience a range of psychological disorders and mental health issues as a result of being trafficked. Traumatic experiences can manifest in changes or disturbances in victims' eating, sleeping, and behavior, as exposure to prolonged violence disrupts the neurological system (Smith et al., 2009).

Smith et al. (2009) describe hyperarousal and hypoarousal as two psychological states that minor victims of commercial sex trafficking may experience (although these emotional reactions may also be experienced by adult and labor human trafficking victims). The symptoms of hyperarousal include anger, panic and phobias, irritability, and hyperactivity; and hypoarousal symptoms include a flat affect, inability to bond with others, and inattention (Smith et al., 2009).

5.23 Confidentiality and Telling Their Story

Along the journey of healing and restoration, the desire or reluctance among survivors to share their experiences as a guest speaker or educator or join the antitrafficking movement as an advocate may emerge. A survivor's decision to disclose will vary considerably. Many survivors may be reticent because of the fear of retaliation from their traffickers, and others may be concerned about being judged, blamed, or belittled by the public or family members. There are many other reasons that survivors are hesitant to discuss their experiences. Brennan (2005) recounts that trauma counselors who have worked with

Table 5.4 Potential Mental Health Issues Facing Victims of Sex Trafficking	
Psychological Disorders	
1. Anxiety and Stress Disorder	
2. Attachment Disorder	
3. Attention Deficit/Hyperactivity Disorder (ADHD)	
4. Conduct Disorder	
5. Depression (Major, Dysthymia)	
6. Developmental Disorders	
7. Eating Disorders	
8. Learning Disorders	
9. Acute Stress Disorder	
10. Post Traumatic Stress Disorder (PTSD)	
11. Anxiety Disorders	Panic Attacks
	Agoraphobia
	Social Phobia
12. Dissociative Disorders	
13. Eating Disorders	Anorexia Nervosa
	Bulimia Nervosa
14. Impulse Control Disorders	
15. Mood Disorders	Major Depression
	Dysthymia
	Bipolar
	Hypothymia

(Continued)

Table 5.4 (Continued)

16. Personality Disorders	Borderline P.D.
	Histrionic P.D.
	Narcissistic P.D.
	Paranoid P.D.
	Anti-Social P.D.
	Avoidant P.D.
	Dependent P.D.
	Obsessive Compulsive P.D.
17. Self-Harming Disorders	Self-Mutilation
18. Sleep Disorders	Insomnia
	Hypersomnia
19. Somatic Disorders	
20. Substance Abuse Disorders	Often DTMs use substances to cope

SOURCE: *The national report on domestic minor sex trafficking: America's prostituted children* (p. 42) by L. Smith, S. Healy Vardaman, and M. Snow, 2009, Arlington, VA: Shared Hope International. Copyright 2009 by Shared Hope International. Reprinted with permission.

NOTE: The above are possible disorders common among domestically trafficked minors. Due to the nature of domestic minor sex trafficking and the multiple traumas victims sustain, it is common for victims to have a multidiagnosis.

foreign-born victims of human trafficking in the United States reported "the larger community of immigrants where trafficked persons settle (usually composed of co-ethnics) often stigmatizes and rejects trafficked persons" (p. 42–43); therefore, many victims do not feel adequate social support from within their own culture or ethnic communities. Kleinman and Kleinman (1996) address the pressures that many victims feel to publically share their "trauma stories" in the media that becomes "currency" or "symbolic capital" (p. 10). The expectation to constantly talk about their experiences may inadvertently make it difficult for survivors to rewrite their futures without an overfocus on their victimization. Additionally, sharing one's intimate experience of being traumatized may have unintended consequences of revictimization or retraumatization. Manz (2002) cautions, "The act of remembering, let alone of retelling, is a highly charged, politicized event, fraught with danger" (p. 299).

Sill, others may be emotionally ready to share their experiences. Often, survivors find that sharing their experiences is empowering. Reclaiming through disclosure can be therapeutic, as with narrative therapy, because it allows survivors to speak their truth as a means for healing from the trauma and abuse (Brennan, 2005). Survivors have also embraced sharing their experiences as a platform to promote education and awareness, to assist in prevention program planning, and to contribute to program evaluation. As consumers of social services, survivors can provide firsthand accounts about receiving services. Kalergis (2009) interviewed Rachel Lloyd, a former victim of child sexual exploitation and founder/executive director of Girls Educational & Mentoring Services (GEMS), who suggests that survivors "move past just recounting their stories and being [sic] able to give an analysis of the issue, recognizing that with their voice they have a lot more to say than just their stories" (p. 323). A survivor's testimony is based on appalling experiences and a unique understanding of trafficker's motives, maneuvers, and manipulation tactics, as well as on a perspective of needed services. Survivors are positioned well to be valuable partners in taskforces and community coalitions.

5.24 The Journey From Victim to Survivor

Partnership between professionally trained practitioners and former victims of human trafficking in providing services has been found to be an effective practice strategy. Survivors are able to connect with other survivors in a unique way because of their shared, lived experiences. The former victim of human trafficking may be better equipped to keep the process of recovery authentic and to recognize and bypass any attempts by victims to obfuscate or deny the truth, even if for self-protection. Most importantly, survivors working with survivors give a glimpse into the possibility of healing and recovery. Kalergis (2009) also interviewed Lisa Goldblatt Grace, program director for My Life My Choice project, a program that utilizes survivors as mentors to victims of child sexual exploitation. Mentors provide supportive services to survivors during the initial referral and time of crisis, and Goldblatt Grace contends, "This connection increases the likelihood that the girl will use other services" (Kalergis, 2009 p. 321).

5.25 Traffickers and Typologies of Human Traffickers

As discussed, human trafficking is a complex crime that affects all ages, genders, nationalities, and regions of the country and world. Traffickers and their methods and strategies for enslaving people also vary such that research indicates there is not a single typology of trafficker. A study conducted by Busch-Armendariz, Nsonwu, and Cook Heffron (2009), *Understanding Human Trafficking: Development of Typologies of Traffickers PHASE II,* established four typologies of human traffickers. The study involved reviewing 67 prosecuted cases and conducting in-depth interviews with professionals working in the field of human trafficking. Six variables were considered for the case review (demographics of traffickers; demographics of victims; the nature of the victimization; the methods of the recruitment; methods of control and coercion; and the location, scope, and size of the operation) (Busch-Armendariz et al., 2009, p. 3). The typologies may serve as a tool to assist first responders, prosecutors, and other professionals who work with victims to examine, analyze, and explore the various mechanisms of how traffickers recruit victims and engage in covert operations. However, these typologies are not necessarily an exhaustive classification, so it should be noted that the strategies that traffickers use to deceive victims and "thwart law enforcement's efforts are dynamic and ever-changing" (Busch-Armendariz et al., 2009, p. 2).

Traffickers were categorized in two broad groups and two subgroups to illustrate the similarities and differences among human traffickers. The first broad group, *Shattering the American Dream*, includes labor trafficking cases with two subsets, Organized Labor Exploitation for Profit and Family-Based Domestic Servitude. The second broad typology is *johns' Demand*, represented by sex trafficking cases with two subgroups: Sex Trafficking of U.S. Citizens and Sex Trafficking of Foreign-Born Victims (Busch-Armendariz et al., 2009).

Shattering the American Dream: Traffickers in Organized Labor—Exploitation for Profit

Traffickers in the Organized Labor Exploitation for Profit subgroup represented family-based operations to large organized crime entities. Labor trafficking may take the form of forced labor in restaurants/food service, nail shops, janitorial work, agriculture/fishing industry, entertainment business, garment/manufacturing industries, and hotels/motels. Labor trafficking includes forced labor and debt bondage (Logan et al., 2009). A United Nations Office on Drugs and Crime (UNODC) 2015 report found that forced labor trafficking cases are rising, accounting for 40% of all detected human trafficking victims during the 3-year period ending 2012, and including industries such as domestic work, construction, restaurant/service, textile work, and manufacturing. In the United States, women and girls are trafficked for purposes of forced labor at 56%, a higher rate than men and boys, who make up 44% (Hepburn & Simon, 2010). In some cases, the trafficker recruits victims through a series of networks and in other cases the trafficker has established a previous relationship with the victim and/or his or her family. Traffickers exploit vulnerabilities, such as poverty, substance abuse, and mental illness, to recruit American-born victims; they make false promises of travel to the United States and offer promises of educational opportunities and financial security to foreign-born victims (Busch-Armendariz et al., 2009). Communities that experience chaos and disorder as a result of natural disasters, coupled with the need for inexpensive labor to begin to rebuild damaged infrastructures, produce an environment that can yield deceitful labor practices, thereby generating labor trafficking for the vulnerable and marginalized (Hepburn & Simon, 2010). Control and coercion may take the form of physical abuse, sexual assault, or continued dependence on drugs or alcohol; foreign-born victims are threatened with deportation.

Shattering the American Dream: Traffickers in Family-Based Domestic Servitude

Traffickers in the Family-Based Domestic Servitude subgroup typically come from the same culture as the victim and understand the cultural nuances and vulnerabilities

Prosecuted Organized Labor Exploitation For-Profit Cases

United States. v. Evans—a case where traffickers facilitated addiction to crack cocaine for homeless men working in the agricultural field

United States v. Kaufman—a case where a couple provided "therapeutic residential treatment," which included nude therapy and working nude in fields, to patients with mental illness

United States v. Ramos—a case where labor contractor brothers supplied undocumented migrant workers to citrus growers in order for workers to pay off smuggling debt

SOURCE: Busch-Armendariz et al., 2009, p. 7.

of victims and their circumstances. "The motivations of traffickers seem to be closely related to the traffickers' family needs and somewhat detached from direct economic gain" (Busch-Armendariz et al., 2009, p. 7). Victims with limited social and financial capital (e.g., death of a breadwinning spouse, an ill child, or a large number of children to provide for) are often recruited by family members or community contacts in their villages to fraudulently travel abroad under the auspices that the trafficker will employ them. Often, the trafficker agrees to financially compensate the victim's family members for their employment and often gives the victims empty promises of a better life or the opportunity to receive an education. Typically, the victim's family receives little to none of the earned income that has been pledged to them and many times all communication is severed once the victim leaves their homeland. Victims are expected to serve as in-home domestic servants, providing child care and housekeeping services for their traffickers; therefore, "operations are generally small, involving only a single victim at a given time, although the duration of victimization can be lengthy" (Busch-Armendariz et al., 2009, p. 7). The apprehension of traffickers can be difficult as victims of family-based servitude are often hidden away for years despite living in mainstream communities. Control and coercion tactics include confiscating of travel documents; threats of deportation; risk of humiliation or harm to family members back in the victim's homeland; isolation; and physical, sexual, and psychological abuse.

Prosecuted Family-Based Servitude Cases

United States v. Calimlim—a case where a couple brought a 19-year-old Filipina woman to their home in Wisconsin where she was enslaved in domestic servitude for 19 years

United States v. Mubang—a case where Theresa Mubang brought an 11-year-old girl from Cameroon for housecleaning and child care and denied her education

SOURCE: Busch-Armendariz et al., 2009, p. 8.

johns' Demand: Sex Trafficking of United States Citizens

The sexual exploitation of victims has become an economically profitable industry worldwide; "globally, hundreds of thousands—perhaps millions—are forced or coerced into commercial sex acts" (Sangalis, 2011, p. 1). This social problem has also been more widely publicized in the media over labor trafficking (Hepburn & Simon, 2010) and is usually what most novice individuals associate with human trafficking. Using the Busch-Armendariz and colleagues (2009) *johns' Demand*, Sex Trafficking of U.S Citizens typology, most traffickers who exploit victims for sex tend to be men, although remarkably women's involvement in this crime is an overrepresentation of women in other types of crimes. Sex traffickers may be single pimps, small-scale operations, or have connections with gangs (Busch-Armendariz et al., 2009). Traffickers who are involved in commercial sex trafficking and/or the sex trafficking of domestic minors are often referred to as pimps. Pimps create a culture that governs the environment, language, and lifestyle of "the game" (Smith et al., 2009), and some traffickers have published books describing their "pimpology" or rules of "the game" that detail their success and demonstrate their vernacular in "pimptionary" (Smith et al., 2009). Although general principles or "rules of the game" are followed by traffickers in this typology, the recruitment, and initial coercion, and control strategies may vary within this category as they are closely tied to the idiosyncratic nature of the individual pimp. The single pimp is sometimes referred to as the Romeo pimp or lover-boy tactic, as he initially grooms his victim into believing they are in an intimate relationship where he "institutes a cycle of intimacy and violence" (Smith et al., 2009, p. 37). The intention is to foster emotional dependency with the victim, preying upon her vulnerabilities and need for belonging, love, and security. Traffickers are skilled at building trust with their victims; they use tactics of romance, isolation, violence/intimidation, and involvement in criminal activities to become their victim's ally against the outside world (Reid, 2014). Many times, the victim will refer to the trafficker with terms of endearment such as her "boyfriend" or "daddy." The emotional connection or trauma bonding makes it particularly challenging for law enforcement and first responders to build trust and rapport with the victim. Reid (2014) also outlines how the "entrapment and enmeshment tactics used by sex traffickers shared several commonalities with exploitive tactics of batterers such as controlling victims through violence, shame, and intimidation" (p. 14).

Other single pimps are referred to as Guerrilla pimps as their recruitment tactics, or "seasoning process," begin as brutal and violent acts (e.g., rape, beatings, confinement) to dominate and control their victim (Administrative Office of the Courts, 2012). Traffickers assert power and control over their victims with calculated methodologies and strategies that indoctrinate their victims and leave them emotionally and physically dependent on the trafficker for survival. These methods, highlighted in the Domestic Minor Sex Trafficking Power and Control Wheel as illustrated below, elicit isolation and economic dependence of the victim. Traffickers forcibly control the victim through the use of physical and sexual violence to restrict their decision-making ability and freedom. Traffickers systematically manipulate their victim through humiliation, shame, threats, blackmail, or exploiting the victim's vulnerabilities. Although

Figure 5.5 *Domestic minor sex trafficking power and control wheel.*

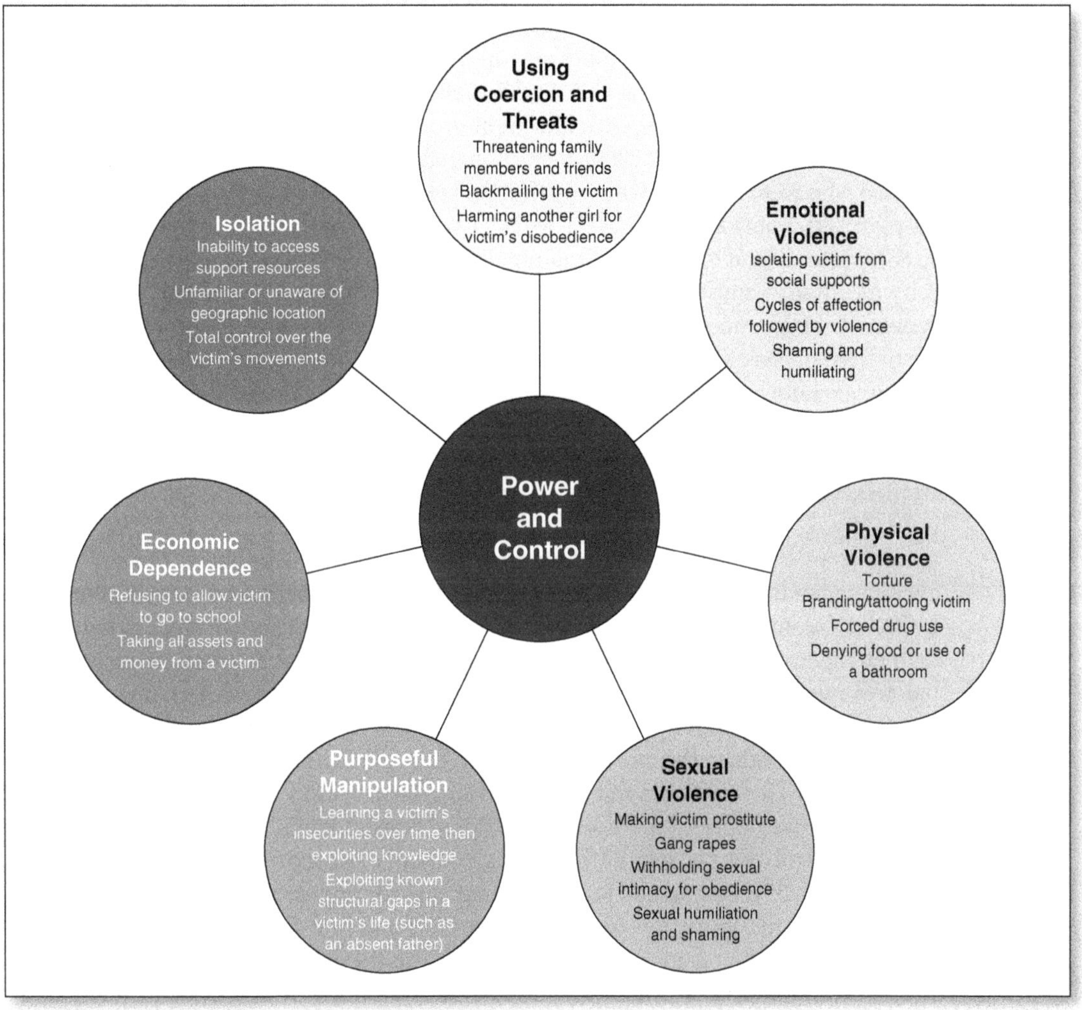

SOURCE: *The National Report on Domestic Minor Sex Trafficking: America's Prostituted Children* (p. 37) by L. Smith, S. Healy Vardaman, and M. Snow, 2009, Arlington, VA: Shared Hope International. Copyright 2009 by Shared Hope International. Reprinted with permission.

the initial enlistment strategies differ between the two single pimps, the intention of both pimps is to control and sexually exploit their victims for economic gain.

Many traffickers have shifted from former criminal practices of manufacturing and selling drugs to the commercial sexual exploitation of people as a business due to its lucrative financial results. An increase in violence against victims of human trafficking has been noted by law enforcement and prosecutors who attribute this change to the ruthless and cruel practices of gangs and organized crime members who have entered the commercial sex trafficking industry as an alternative from their past criminal drug-trade industry (Administrative Office of the Courts, 2012). Another method that traffickers use to increase their revenue is to exploit children; "there is evidence that pimps may specifically recruit minors, since minors may be at increased vulnerability and easier to recruit. In addition, johns pay more for sex with a child, and the traffickers' primary motivation is making a profit. Virtually all pimps will prostitute children, given the opportunity, because they make money, and that's what it's all about—money" (Busch-Armendariz et al., 2009, p. 9). One study found that "at least 70% of adult women who were involved with prostitution were introduced to the sex industry before 18 years old, many as young as 11 to 14" (Administrative Office of the Courts, 2012, p. 16). Victims tend to represent marginalized or high-risk groups (e.g., runaways, victims of physical/emotional/sexual assault, youth in or aging out of the child welfare system, drug dependent, LGBTQ youth, and homeless) who have little social capital and are in need of basic safety and resources. The pimp uses the victim's vulnerabilities to his advantage, knowing the victim has no other viable options to maintain self-sufficiency (Reid, 2014; Reid & Piquero, 2014). Control and coercion take the form of physical, psychological, and sexual abuse of the victim or withdrawal of love and affection as "traffickers are supported by broad societal culture of abuse, exploitation, [and] unhealthy relationships" (Busch-Armendariz et al., 2009, p. 10). The trafficker systematically traps the victim into thinking that her behavior is delinquent, thereby further alienating her from attempts to seek or receive help from others (Smith et al., 2009). The traffickers' control and manipulation of victims is a sophisticated process with well-defined hierarchies within the pimp framework. Traffickers often rotate giving preferential treatment to one victim over another. "This method establishes hierarchy and ensures constant competition with each other [victims] for rewards and promotions to the girls who produce the most money and follow the 'rules of the game'" (Smith et al., 2009, p. 40). The trafficker may assign a long-term victim the role of "bottom girl" (Administrative Office of the Courts, 2012), or "bottom bitch," to recruit and "maintain internal control over his 'stable' (the children or adults being prostituted by him)" (Smith et al., 2009, p. 39). Despite the fact that it may initially appear as though the bottom girl is complicit in the abuse, it is important to understand that she is held emotionally hostage by the trafficker. A former police sergeant who has worked with human trafficking victims describes it as a "kind of battered-child syndrome. It happened to them. They hated it. And then they do it to someone else" (Hepburn & Simon, 2010, p. 10).

In the pimp framework, traffickers use facilitators (taxi drivers, unscrupulous security personnel, and middle men) to promote, coordinate, and protect their industry (Smith et al., 2009); they use the Internet, social media, and cell phone contact as methods to advertise and communicate with one another. Busch-Armendariz et al. (2009) contend that "there is some evidence that supports an alliance between pimps and gangs. Gangs may become involved in the protection of a pimp, in extorting a pimp, and in using a pimp's services. Sex-related services may also be integral to the social and member initiation activities of the gang" (p. 9). Victims may be branded with tattoos signifying their association with a specific gang or pimp; this symbol identifies victims as property and further labels them as economic commodities.

Prosecuted Sex Trafficking Cases of U.S.-Born Victims

U.S. v. Brice—a case where Jaron Brice exploited girls as young as 14 in a prostitution operation that spanned the Eastern seaboard

U.S. v. Doss, et al.—a case where Doss and his wife trafficked two underage girls throughout California

SOURCE: Busch-Armendariz et al., 2009, p. 10.

johns' Demand: Sex Trafficking of Foreign-Born Victims

Sex trafficking of foreign-born victims tends to be large, organized prostitution rings that run brothels, clubs, massage parlors, and spas. The Trafficking in Persons Report (2003) brings attention to the connection between global trafficking in persons and organized crime networks, due in part to human trafficking's high profitability and low risk of punishment or sanctions (U.S. Department of State, 2003). The global commercial sexual exploitation is estimated to generate USD 99 billion in profits (International Labour Organization, 2014). Although conclusive prevalence numbers on sex trafficking are lacking, it is estimated that "45,000 to 50,000 women and children are trafficked annually to the United States" (Richard, 1999). The majority of sex trafficking victims come from Southeast Asia, Latin America, Central and Eastern Europe, and independent former Soviet states, with the United States as one of the major destination countries for these victims (Richard, 1999). Traffickers, who often share similar nationalities or ethnicities with their victims, work on a global scale to recruit victims, often luring naïve women from low-resource countries to come to the United States under the auspices that they will be employed in legitimate businesses (e.g., restaurants, the food industry, providing home or child care services, modeling, or entertainment industry). Some victims arrive in the United States legally with valid travel documents (e.g., fiancée, student, or visitor visas) that are quickly confiscated by the traffickers to gain power and control; victims are forced to overstay their visa limitations, thereby placing them in jeopardy after violating immigration regulations. Beare (1999) reports that victims may be smuggled into the United States as "human cargo," requiring victims to repay a debt to the traffickers for their travel; this debt often is unable to be paid off as the trafficker imposes interest and additional fines to the debt, essentially holding victims captive as sex slaves indefinitely (as cited in Rieger, 2007). Travel fees "ranged from $2,000–$47,000 and often varied by countries of origin: e.g., $40,000–$47,000 for Chinese, $35,000 for Koreans and $2,000–$3,000 for Mexican women" (Raymond & Hughes, 2001). These victims may initially agree to travel to the United States, without the knowledge that they will be forced to work in the sex industry (Rieger, 2007). Traffickers lure victims with offers and promises of foreign, better-paying jobs that do not exist, often trapping them without their consent once they arrive in slave-like conditions and debt bondage (Miko, 2004). It is important to remember that individuals may be considered human trafficking victims regardless of whether they "previously consented to work for a trafficker, or participated in a crime as a direct result of being subjected to trafficking" (U.S. Department of State, 2015, p. 7). Some victims are deceived into believing that they are beginning a relationship through a mail-order bride or match-making service (*Human trafficking: Mail order bride abuses: Hearing before the subcommittee on East Asian and Pacific affairs,* 2004; Miko, 2004); the trafficker's tactics may be similar to the Romeo pimp's strategies of conning the victim by appealing to her need for security. Organized criminal networks often procure victims by kidnapping girls and young women in order to sell them globally to traffickers and intermediaries (Shannon, 1999). Once a victim is in the stronghold of the trafficker, she is forced into the commercial sex industry, often-times working in cantinas, massage parlors, karaoke bars, brothels, or transported for sex trafficking to residential sites or motels/hotels (Busch-Armendariz et al., 2009). Traffickers may employ facilitators (e.g., taxi drivers, security personnel) to move victims to various locations to either serve clientele or protect their covert operations. Some family and community members of the victim in her homeland may be complicit in the human trafficking scheme; other times, the family may be in jeopardy, receive threats, or encounter retaliation by the trafficker if/when the victim resists, attempts to escape, or requests assistance. Oftentimes, victims and traffickers/facilitators are from the same community and victims risk being retraumatized and revictimized if they are deported and/or if their perpetrators are not prosecuted to the fullest extent of the law. One study details that 50% of victims who have been deported to their homelands are retrafficked (Bailliet, 2006). In addition to threatening to harm family members, traffickers maintain control and coercion through drugging their victims, inflicting physical and sexual abuse, and imposing a fear of deportation (Busch-Armendariz et al., 2009).

Prosecuted Cases of Sex Trafficking of Foreign-Born Victims

U.S. v. Chang and Chang—South Korean women were forced to work in a karaoke bar, drinking with customers, to pay off their smuggling debts.

U.S. v. Malcolm—A Korean Madame forced Korean women into prostitution in a network of three "spas" in Dallas, Texas.

U.S. v. Mondragon, et al.—Almost 90 victims from Central America were involved in forced prostitution in a network of cantinas.

SOURCE: Busch-Armendariz et al., 2009, p. 11.

5.26 johns or the Buyers

There is research about johns or the buyers/consumers of sex services; however, little research has been conducted on johns who purchase the services of human trafficking victims. The research that exists concludes that johns "can be anyone— professionals, students, tourists, military personnel, a family member" (Smith et al.,

2009, p. 17). There is also a correlation between the demand and supply for commercial sexual services; "the supply of women and children in the sex industry serves as the fuel for this criminal slave trade" (Smith et al., 2009, p. 16), and the demand from johns/buyers drives this industry. Busch, Bell, Hotaling, and Monto (2002) found johns may hold values that are different from other men, especially around beliefs in regard to the role of women in society and gender roles. johns may be introduced to the commercial sex trafficking of women and children through Internet pornography, the marketing tool of choice among traffickers, especially to exploit children and minor victims. The availability to access pornography has become quite easy because of easy access to the Internet, and "individuals viewing child pornography have found comfort in the cyber community which brought justification and normalcy to their thoughts and desires, bonding the group together" (Smith et al., 2009, p. 19). Predators who seek to exploit naïve or vulnerable individuals (e.g., mail-order brides, teenagers, etc.) may use the Internet as the initial contact with victims as well as a tool for recruitment of johns. Traffickers also "market" their victims to johns at large entertainment events, tourist attractions, and airports; schools or shopping centers that youth frequent are also areas that are conducive to recruiting minor victims and making connections with johns. Smith et al. (2009) contend that "in a sexually charged society that both encourages promiscuity and covets the innocence of youth, it follows that the demand for young victims will rise to meet the cultural glorification of underage sexuality" (p. 16).

Prosecution and penalties against johns have been statistically low. Smith et al. (2009) report that "most buyers of sexual services from minors receive little or no punishment, while many of the victims are arrested and charged with the crime committed against them" (p. 20). Even in cases with adult victims of sex trafficking, johns have notoriously been given lenient sentences or not charged at all, while the adult victim has been charged with prostitution; in some egregious cases, the john/buyer has testified against the victim (Smith et al., 2009).

6. Chapter Summary

This chapter provides an overview of strengths-based and trauma-informed approaches to the identification, protection, and provision of support and services to human trafficking victims. Best practices in meeting the immediate and long-term needs of victims are discussed as well as important terminology and typologies of victims and traffickers.

7. Key Terms

7.1   Trafficking Victims Protection Act (TVPA)

7.2   T visa

7.3   U visa

7.4   Domestic minor sex trafficking

7.5   Trauma bond

7.6   Stockholm syndrome

7.7   Screening protocols

7.8	Behavioral indicators	7.18	Coalition-based model
7.9	Short-term needs	7.19	Wraparound services
7.10	Office of Victims of Crime (OVC)	7.20	Culturally competent services
7.11	Long-term needs	7.21	Interpreter vs. translator
7.12	Foreign-born victims	7.22	Ecological approach
7.13	Self-determination	7.23	Strengths-based perspective
7.14	Survivor-centered approach	7.24	Cultural competency
7.15	Client-first, survivor-first, or victim-centered models	7.25	*Victim* vs. *survivor* terminology
		7.26	Trauma
7.16	Resilience skills during times of security and self-sufficiency	7.27	Story telling as *currency* or *symbolic capital*
7.17	Single point-of-contact service delivery paradigm	7.28	Strengths-based perspective
		7.29	Trauma-informed approach

8. Active Learning Exercises or In-Class Discussion Questions

8.1 What do you think about the terminology "rescue" when working with victims of human trafficking? How does this term feel in a values-laden field?

8.2 Consider the ways you see the strengths-based perspective reflected in programs that serve survivors of human trafficking (or conversely a deficit-based model).

8.3 How might a trauma-informed approach impact the way social workers or counselors interact with a survivor of human trafficking? A law enforcement investigator? An immigration attorney?

8.4 What do you think about the term *john* when working with customers of prostituted women? How does this term feel in a values-laden field?

8.5 Go to the National Human Trafficking Resource Center website (http://traffickingresourcecenter.org/states) and review data on human trafficking reports in your state. Compare and contrast these reports to statistics in neighboring states. What factors might contribute to high or low numbers in specific states? What do you understand about your state as a source, transit, or destination state?

9. Suggestions for Further Learning

9.1 **Books**

9.1.1 Bales, K. (2012). *Disposable people: New slavery in the global economy, Update with a new preface* (3rd ed.). Berkeley, CA: University of California Press.

9.1.2 Bales, K. (2000). *New slavery: A reference handbook*. Santa Barbara, CA: ABC-CLIO.

9.1.3 Bales, K., & Soodalter, R. (2009). *The slave next door*. Berkeley, CA: University of California Press.

9.1.4 DeStefano, A. M. (2007). *The war on human trafficking: U.S. policy assessed*. New Brunswick, NJ: Rutgers University Press.

9.1.5 Kara, S. (2009). *Sex trafficking: Inside the business of modern slavery*. New York, NY: Columbia University Press.

9.1.6 Lutnick, A. (2016). *Domestic minors sex trafficking: Beyond victims and villains*. New York: Columbia University Press.

9.1.7 Lloyd, R. (2011). *Girls like us: Fighting for a world where girls are not for sale, an activist finds her calling and heals herself* (1st ed.). New York, NY: HarperCollins.

9.2 **Websites**

9.2.1 https://polarisproject.org/sites/default/files/2014Statistics.pdf

9.2.2 Substance Abuse and Mental Health Services Administration [SAMHSA], www.samhsa.gov (concept of Trauma and Guidance for a Trauma-Informed Approach)

9.2.3 VERA Screening Trafficking Victim Identification Tool (TVIT) http://www.vera.org/sites/default/files/resources/downloads/human-trafficking-identification-tool-and-user-guidelines.pdf

9.3 **Films and Other Media**

9.3.1 "Stockholm Syndrome" by One Direction

9.3.2 *Playground* by Libby Spears

9.3.3 *Girl Rising*

9.3.4 *Girl Trouble*

9.3.5 *Miss Representation*

9.3.6 *Hip-Hop: Beyond Beats & Rhymes*

9.3.7 *Not My Life*

9.3.8 *Half the Sky*

9.3.9 *Sex & Money*

9.3.10 *NOW on PBS*: "Fighting Child Prostitution" with David Brancaccio

10. Research/Project Assignments/ Homework/Exam Exercises

10.1 Survey pop culture and media to identify examples of where human trafficking is being glorified or accepted. How does pop culture or the media's adoption of the objectification of women play a role in being complicit with human trafficking?

10.2 Examine the philosophical and policy changes that have occurred over time in the domestic violence/sexual assault field and the anti–human trafficking field. Compare and contrast these two fields, taking into special consideration how the anti–human trafficking field is relatively new.

10.3 Research the symptoms of Stockholm syndrome. Does the song/video "Stockholm Syndrome" by One Direction accurately portray this psychological condition?

11. References

Administration for Children and Families. (2012). *Rescue and restore victims of human trafficking campaign labor trafficking poster* [Online image]. Retrieved from http://www.acf.hhs.gov/orr/resource/download-campaign-posters-and-brochures

Administration for Children and Families. (2012). *Rescue and restore victims of human trafficking campaign social service poster* [Online image]. Retrieved from http://www.acf.hhs.gov/orr/resource/download-campaign-posters-and-brochures

Administrative Office of the Courts. (2012). *AOC briefing: Human trafficking cases in California's courts: Successful practices in the emerging field of human trafficking.* Retrieved from San Francisco, CA: http://www.courts.ca.gov/cfcc-publications.htm

Bailliet, C. M. (2006). Responsibilities of the destination country. *Forced Migration Review, 25,* 28–30.

Beare, M.E. (1997) Illegal Migration: Personal Tragedies, Social Problems, or National Security Threats? *Transnational Organized Crime, 3*(4), 11–41.

Bernat, J. A., Ronfeldt, H. M., & Calhoun, K. S. (1998). Arias I: Prevalence of traumatic events and peritraumatic predictors of posttraumatic stress symptoms in a nonclinical sampling of college students. Journal of Traumatic Stress, 11, 645–665.

Bishop, C. (2003). The Trafficking Victims Protection Act of 2000: Three years later. *International Migration, 41*(5), 219–231. Retrieved from http://ncat.idm.oclc.org/login?url=http://search.ebscohost.com/login.aspx?direct=true&db=a9h&AN=11953080&site=ehost-live

Bokhari, F. (2008). Falling through the gaps: Safeguarding children trafficked into the UK. *Children & Society, 22*(3), 201–211. doi:10.1111/j.1099–0860.2008.00151.x

Brennan, D. (2005). Methodological challenges in research with trafficked persons: Tales from the field. *International Migration, 43*(1/2), 35–54. doi:10.1111/j.0020–7985.2005.00311.x

Busch, N. B., Bell, H., Hotaling, N., & Monto, M. A. (2002). Male customers of prostituted women exploring perceptions of entitlement to power and control and implications for violent behavior toward women. *Violence Against Women, 8*(9), 1093–1112.

Busch, N. B., Fong, R., Heffron, L. C., Faulkner, M., & Mahapatra, N. (2007). *Assessing the needs of human trafficking victims: An evaluation of the Central Texas Coalition Against Human Trafficking.* Retrieved from The Institute on Domestic Violence and Sexual Assault website: https://socialwork.utexas.edu/dl/files/cswr/institutes/idvsa/publications/evaluation_of_trafficking-2007.pdf

Busch-Armendariz, N. (2012). T visas. In S. Loue & M. Sajatovic (Eds.), *The encyclopedia of immigrant health.* New York, NY: Springer.

Busch-Armendariz, N., Nsonwu, M., & Cook Heffron, L. (2009). *Understanding human trafficking: Development of typologies of traffickers phase II.* Paper presented at the First Annual Interdisciplinary Conference on Human Trafficking, Lincoln, NE.

Busch-Armendariz, N., Nsonwu, M. B., & Heffron, L. C. (2011). Human trafficking victims and their children: Assessing needs, vulnerabilities, strengths, and survivorship. *Journal of Applied Research on Children: Informing Policy for Children at Risk, 2*(1), Article 3. Retrieved from http://digitalcommons.library.tmc.edu/childrenatrisk/vol2/iss1/3

Busch-Armendariz, N., Nsonwu, M. B., & Heffron, L. C. (2014). A kaleidoscope: The role of the social work practitioner and the strength of social work theories and practice in meeting the complex needs of people trafficked and the professionals that work with them. *International Social Work, 57*(1), 7.

Caliber Associates. (2007). *Evaluation of comprehensive services for victims of human trafficking: Key findings and lessons learned.* Retrieved from http://www.ojp.usdoj.gov/nij/

Campbell, R. (2012, December 3). *The neurobiology of sexual assault: Implications for first responders in law enforcement, prosecution and victim advocacy* [Video transcript]. (NCJ 240953). Retrieved from http://www.nij.gov/events/pages/research-real-world.aspx

Carnes, P. (1997). *The betrayal bond: Breaking free of exploitive relationships.* Deerfield Beach, FL: HCI.

Clawson, H. J., & Dutch, N. (2008a). *Identifying victims of human trafficking: Inherent challenges and promising strategies from the field.* Washington, DC: Office of the Assistant Secretary for Planning and Evaluation (ASPE). Retrieved from http://aspe.hhs.gov/hsp/07/HumanTrafficking/

Clawson, H. J., & Dutch, N. (2008b). *Addressing the needs of victims of human trafficking: Challenges, barriers, and promising practices.* Department of Health and Human Services, Office of the Assistant Secretary for Planning and Evaluation. Retrieved from https://aspe.hhs.gov/basic-report/addressing-needs-victims-human-trafficking-challenges-barriers-and-promising-practices

Covenant House. (2013, May). *Homelessness, survival sex and human trafficking: As experienced by the youth of Covenant House New York.* Retrieved from http://traffickingresourcecenter.org/sites/default/files/Homelessness%2CSurvivalSex%2CandHumanTrafficking-CovenantHouseNY.pdf

Estes, R. J., & Weiner, N. A. (2001). *The commercial sexual exploitation of children in the U. S., Canada and Mexico.* Retrieved from http://www.gems-girls.org/Estes%20Wiener%202001.pdf

Faulkner, M., Mahapatra, N., Heffron, L. C., Nsonwu, M. B., & Busch-Armendariz, N. (2013). Moving past victimization and trauma toward restoration: Mother survivors of sex trafficking share their inspiration. *International Perspectives in Victimology, 7*(2), 46–55. doi:10.5364/ipiv.7.2.46

Ferguson-Colvin, K., & Maccio, E. (2012). *Toolkit for practitioners/researchers working with lesbian, gay, bisexual, transgender, and queer/questioning (LGBTQ) runaway and homeless youth (RHY).* Retrieved from New York, NY: National Resource Center for Permanency and Family Connections Silberman School of Social Work: http://www.hunter.cuny.edu/socwork/nrcfcpp/info_services/download/LGBTQ HRY Toolkit September 2012.pdf

Finkelhor, D., & Ormrod, R. (2004). Prostitution of juveniles: Patterns from NIBRS. *Juvenile Justice Bulletin.* Retrieved from https://www.ncjrs.gov/pdffiles1/ojjdp/203946.pdf

Gluck, E., & Mathur, R. (2014). *Child sex trafficking and the child welfare system.* Retrieved from http://childwelfaresparc.org/wp-content/uploads/2014/07/Sex-Trafficking-and-the-Child-Welfare-System.pdf

Golden, S., Williams, J., & Ford, D. (2004). Depressive symptoms and the risk of type 2 diabetes: The atherosclerosis risk in communities study. Diabetes Care, 27, 429–435.

Goodman, M., & Laurence, J. (2014, July). Child trafficking victims and the state courts. In *A guide to human trafficking for state courts* (pp. 77–88). State Justice Institute (SJI). Retrieved from http://www.htcourts.org/wp-content/uploads/00_EntireGuide_140726_v02.pdf

Gordon, D. M., & Hunter, B. A. (2013). *Invisible no more: Creating opportunities for youth who are homeless.* Retrieved from New Haven, CT: The Consultation Center Yale University School of Medicine http://www.pschousing.org/files/InvisibleNoMoreReport.pdf

Goździak, E., Bump, M., Duncan, J., MacDonnell, M., & Loiselle, M. B. (2006). The trafficked child: Trauma and resilience. *Forced Migration Review* (25), 14–15.

Goździak, E. M. (2010). Identifying child victims of trafficking. *Criminology & Public Policy, 9*(2), 245–255. doi:10.1111/j.1745–9133.2010.00623.x

Green, B. L., Grace, M. C., & Glesser, G. C. (1985). Identifying survivors at risk: Long-term impairment following the Beverly Hills Supper Club fire. Journal of Consulting and Clinical Psychology, 53, 672–678

Hardy, V. L., Compton, K. D., & McPhatter, V. S. (2013). Domestic minor sex trafficking: Practice implications for mental health professionals. *Affilia, 28*(1), 8–18. doi:10.1177/0886109912475172

Hepburn, S., & Simon, R. (2010). Hidden in plain sight: Human trafficking in the United States. *Gender Issues, 27*(1/2), 1–26. doi:10.1007/s12147–010–9087–7

Hodge, D. R. (2014). Assisting victims of human trafficking: Strategies to facilitate identification, exit from trafficking, and the restoration of wellness. *Social Work, 59*(2), 111–118. doi:10.1093/sw/swu002

Hom, K. A., & Woods, S. J. (2013). Trauma and its aftermath for commercially sexually exploited women as told by front-line service providers. *Issues in Mental Health Nursing, 34*(2), 75–81. doi:10.3109/01612840.2012.723300

Hopper, E. K. (2004). Underidentification of human trafficking victims in the United States. *Journal of Social Work Research & Evaluation, 5*(2), 125–136. Retrieved from http://ncat .idm.oclc.org/login?url=http://search.ebscohost.com/login.aspx?direct=true&db=sih&AN =16014420&site=ehost-live

Human trafficking: Mail order bride abuses: Hearing before the subcommittee on East Asian and Pacific affairs, Senate, 108th Cong. 1 Sess. (2004).

International Labour Office. (2005). Forced labour today. *World of Work,* 4–6.

International Labour Office (ILO). (2012). *ILO global estimate of forced labour: Results and methodology.* Retrieved from http://un-act.org/publication/view/ilo-global-estimate-forced-labour-2012/

International Labour Organization. (2014). *Profits and poverty: The economics of forced labour.* Retrieved from Geneva, Switzerland: http://www.ilo.org/wcmsp5/groups/public/---ed_norm/---declaration/documents/publication/wcms_243391.pdf

International Organization for Migration. (2015). Retrieved from http://www.iom.int

Kalergis, K. I. (2009). A passionate practice: Addressing the needs of commercially sexually exploited teenagers. *Affilia, 24*(3), 315–324. doi:10.1177/0886109909337706

Kappelhoff, M. J. (2008). Federal prosecutions of human trafficking cases: Striking a blow against modern day slavery. *University of St. Thomas Law Journal, 6*(1), 9–20.

Kleinman, A., & Kleinman, J. (1996). The appeal of experience; the dismay of images: Cultural appropriations of suffering in our times. *Daedalus, 125*(1), 1–23. doi:10.2307/20027351

Kotrla, K. (2010). Domestic minor sex trafficking in the United States. *Social Work, 55*(2), 181–187. doi:10.1093/sw/55.2.181

Leitch, M. L., Vanslyke, J., & Allen, M. (2009). Somatic experiencing treatment with social service workers following Hurricanes Katrina and Rita. *Social Work, 54*(1), 9–18. doi:sw/54.1.9

Lloyd, R. (2011). *Girls like us: Fighting for a world where girls are not for sale, an activist finds her calling and heals herself* (1st ed.). New York, NY: HarperCollins.

Logan, T. K. (2007). *Human trafficking in Kentucky.* Retrieved from Lexington, KY http://www.cdar.uky.edu/CoerciveControl/docs/Human Trafficking in Kentucky.pdf

Logan, T. K., Walker, R., & Hunt, G. (2009). Understanding human trafficking in the United States. *Trauma, Violence, & Abuse, 10*(1), 3–30. doi:10.1177/1524838008327262

Macy, R. J., & Graham, L. M. (2012). Identifying domestic and international sex-trafficking victims during human service provision. *Trauma, Violence, & Abuse, 13*(2), 59–76. doi:10.1177/1524838012440340

Macy, R. J., & Johns, N. (2011). Aftercare services for international sex trafficking survivors: Informing U.S. service and program development in an emerging practice area. *Trauma, Violence, & Abuse, 12*(2), 87–98. doi:10.1177/1524838010390709

Manz, B. (2002). Terror, grief, and recovery. In A. L. Hinton (Ed.), *Annihilating difference: The anthropology of genocide* (Vol. 2, pp. 292). Berkeley, CA: University of California Press.

Miko, F. T. (2004). *Trafficking in women and children: The U.S. and international response— Updated March 26.* Washington, DC: Congressional Research Service. Retrieved from http://digitalcommons.ilr.cornell.edu/cgi/viewcontent.cgi?article=1059&context=key_workplace

Muraya, D. N., & Fry, D. (2015). Aftercare services for child victims of sex trafficking: A systematic review of policy and practice. *Trauma, Violence, & Abuse.* doi:10.1177/1524838015584356

Musselman, D., & Nemeroff, C. (2000). Depression really does hurt: Stress, depression, and cardiovascular disease. Progressive Brain Research, 122, 43–59

National Alliance to End Homelessness. (2015). *The state of homelessness in America.* Retrieved from http://www.endhomelessness.org/page/-/files/State_of_Homelessness_2015_FINAL_online.pdf

National Human Trafficking Resource Center (NHTRC). (2016). NHTRC Mission. Retrieved from http://traffickingresourcecenter.org/mission

Norton-Hawk, M. (2002). The lifecourse of prostitution. *Women, Girls & Criminal Justice, 3*(1), 7–9.

Nsonwu, M., Busch-Armendariz, N., & Heffron, L. C. (2014). Human trafficking. In L. H. Cousins (Ed.), *Encyclopedia of human services and diversity* (pp. 672–675). Thousand Oaks, CA: SAGE.

Nsonwu, M. B., Welch-Brewer, C., Heffron, L. C., Lemke, M. A., Busch-Armendariz, N., Sulley, C., . . . Li, J. (2015). Development and validation of an instrument to assess social work students' perceptions, knowledge, and attitudes about human trafficking questionnaire (PKA-HTQ): An exploratory study. *Research on Social Work Practice.* doi:10.1177/1049731515578537

Office for Victims of Crime. (2012, September). *National victim assistance academy resource paper: Human trafficking.* (NCJ 240570). Retrieved from http://www.ncdsv.org/images/OVCTTAC_HumanTraffickingResourcePaper_2012.pdf

Okech, D., Morreau, W., & Benson, K. (2012). Human trafficking: Improving victim identification and service provision. *International Social Work, 55*(4), 488–503. doi:10.1177/0020872811425805

Polaris. (2014). *A look back: Building a human trafficking legal framework.* Retrieved from https://polarisproject.org/sites/default/files/2014-Look-Back.pdf

Polaris. (2016). Recognize the signs. Retrieved from http://polarisproject.org/recognize-signs.

Polaris and the National Human Trafficking Resource Center (NHTRC). (2011). *Human trafficking assessment tool for educators.* Retrieved from https://traffickingresourcecenter.org/resources/human-trafficking-assessment-tool-educators

President's Interagency Task Force. (2014). Retrieved from https://www.ovc.gov/pubs/FederalHumanTraffickingStrategicPlan.pdf

Rafferty, Y. (2015). Challenges to the rapid identification of children who have been trafficked for commercial sexual exploitation. *Child Abuse & Neglect.* doi:http://dx.doi.org/10.1016/j.chiabu.2015.11.015

Rawana, E., & Brownlee, K. (2009). Making the possible probable: A strength-based assessment and intervention framework for clinical work with parents, children and adolescents. *Families in Society: The Journal of Contemporary Social Services, 90*(3), 255–260.

Raymond, J. G., & Hughes, D. M. (2001). *Sex trafficking of women in the United States: International and domestic trends.* (NCJ 187774). Retrieved from https://www.ncjrs.gov/pdffiles1/nij/grants/187774.pdf

Ream, G. L., & Forge, N. R. (2014). Homeless lesbian, gay, bisexual, and transgender (LGBT) youth in New York City: Insights from the field. *Child Welfare, 93*(2), 7–22.

Reid, J. A. (2010). Doors wide shut: Barriers to the successful delivery of victim services for domestically trafficked minors in a southern U.S. metropolitan area. *Women & Criminal Justice, 20*(1/2), 147–166.

Reid, J. A. (2014). Entrapment and enmeshment schemes used by sex traffickers. *Sexual Abuse: A Journal of Research and Treatment,* 1–21. doi:10.1177/1079063214544334

Reid, J. A. (2016). Sex trafficking of girls with intellectual disabilities: An exploratory mixed methods study. *Sex Abuse: A Journal of Research and Treatment.* doi:10.1177/1079063216630981

Reid, J. A., & Piquero, A. R. (2014). On the relationships between commercial sexual exploitation/prostitution, substance dependency, and delinquency in youthful offenders. *Child Maltreatment, 19*(3–4), 247–260. doi:10.1177/1077559514539752

Richard, A. O. N. (1999). *International trafficking in women to the United States: A contemporary manifestation of slavery and organized crime.* Washington, DC: Center for the Study of Intelligence. Retrieved from https://www.cia.gov/library/center-for-the-study-of-intelligence/csi-publications/books-and-monographs/trafficking.pdf

Rieger, A. (2007). Notes—Missing the mark: Why the Trafficking Victims Protection Act fails To protect sex trafficking victims in the United States. *Harvard Women's Law Journal, 30*(1), 231.

Roby, J. L., Turley, J., & Cloward, J. G. (2008). U.S. response to human trafficking: Is it enough? *Journal of Immigrant & Refugee Studies, 6*(4), 508–525. doi:10.1080/15362940802480241

Rosario, M., Schrimshaw, E. W., & Hunter, J. (2012). Risk factors for homelessness among lesbian, gay, and bisexual youths: A developmental milestone approach. *Children and Youth Services Review, 34*(1), 186–193.

Saleebey, D. (1996). The strengths perspective in social work practice: Extensions and cautions. *Social Work, 41*(3), 296–305. Retrieved from http://ncat.idm.oclc.org/login?url=http://search.ebscohost.com/login.aspx?direct=true&db=rzh&AN=107389421&site=ehost-live

Sangalis, T. R. (2011). Comment elusive empowerment: Compensating the sex trafficked person under the trafficking victims protection act. *Fordham Law Review, 80*(1), 403–439.

Scaer, R. (2006). The traumatic spectrum: Hidden wounds and human resiliency. New York: W. W. Norton.

Schwarz, C., & Britton, H. E. (2015). Queering the support for trafficked persons: LGBTQ communities and human trafficking in the Heartland. *Social Inclusion, 3*(1), 63–75. doi:10.17645/si.v3i1.172

Shannon, S. (1999). Prostitution and the mafia: The involvement of organized crime in the global sex trade. In P. Williams (Ed.), *Illegal immigration and commercial sex: The new slave trade.* New York, NY: Frank Cass.

Sigmon, J. N. (2008). Combating modern-day slavery: Issues in identifying and assisting victims of human trafficking worldwide. *Victims & Offenders, 3*(2/3), 245–257. doi:10.1080/15564880801938508

Smith, L., Healy Vardaman, S., & Snow, M. (2009). *The national report on domestic minor sex trafficking: America's prostituted children.* Retrieved from http://sharedhope.org/wp-content/uploads/2012/09/SHI_National_Report_on_DMST_2009.pdf

Snow, M. (2008, August). *Domestic minor sex trafficking Salt Lake City, Utah. Salt Lake City Assessment: Identification of domestic minor sex trafficking victims and their access to services.* Retrieved from http://sharedhope.org/wp-content/uploads/2012/09/SaltLakeCity_PrinterFriendly.pdf

Solomon, Z., Laor, N., & McFarlane, A. C. (1996). Acute posttraumatic reactions in soldiers and civilians. In B. A. van der Kolk, A. C. McFarlane, & L. Weisaeth (Eds.), Traumatic stress: The effects of overwhelming experience on mind, body, and society (pp. 102–114). New York: Guilford.

Substance Abuse and Mental Health Services Administration [SAMHSA]. (2014). *SAMHSA's concept of trauma and guidance for a trauma-informed approach.* (HHS Publication No. (SMA) 14–4884). Retrieved from http://store.samhsa.gov/shin/content/SMA14–4884/SMA14–4884.pdf

Task Force on Trafficking of Women and Girls. (2014). *Report of the task force on trafficking of women and girls.* Retrieved from Washington, DC: http://www.apa.org/pi/women/programs/trafficking/report.aspx

United States Department of Labor. (2009). *U.S. Department of Labor's 2008 findings on the worst forms of child labor.* Retrieved from http://digitalcommons.ilr.cornell.edu/key_workplace/648

U.S. Department of State. (2003). *Trafficking in persons report.* Retrieved from http://www.state.gov/documents/organization/21555.pdf

U.S. Department of State. (2015). Trafficking in persons report. Retrieved from https://www.state.gov/documents/organization/245365.pdf.

Vera Institute of Justice. (2014, June). *Guidelines for administering the Trafficking Victim Identification Tool (TVIT).* (NCJ #246713). Retrieved from http://www.vera.org/pubs/special/human-trafficking-identification-tool

Wolfer, T. A., & Scales, T. L. (2006). Decision cases for advanced social work practice: thinking like a social worker. Belmont, CA: Thomson Brooks/Cole.

Zimmerman, C. (2003). *The health risks and consequences of trafficking in women and adolescents: Findings from a European study.* London, UK: London School of Hygiene & Tropical Medicine.

Zimmerman, C., Hossain, M., & Watts, C. (2011). Human trafficking and health: A conceptual model to inform policy, intervention and research. *Social Science & Medicine, 73*(2), 327–335. doi:http://dx.doi.org/10.1016/j.socscimed.2011.05.028

Understanding, Disruption, and Interventions at the Mezzo Level

Human trafficking ought to concern every person, because it is a debasement of our common humanity.

—Barack Obama[1]
President of the United States of America
September 25, 2012

I. Learning Objectives

1.1 Students will appreciate the deeply value-laden expressions of the current antitrafficking movement.

1.2 Students will recognize the mezzo-level root causes of human trafficking.

1.3 Students will understand the importance of mezzo-level responses to ending human trafficking.

1.4 Students will become acquainted with organizations whose missions are to end slavery in the United States and around the world.

1.5 Students will become acquainted with current-day abolitionists in the United States and globally.

---

[1]*Fordam Law Journal*, 2013

Figure 6.1 *Human trafficking poster.* You don't need to specialize in human trafficking to serve its many victims.

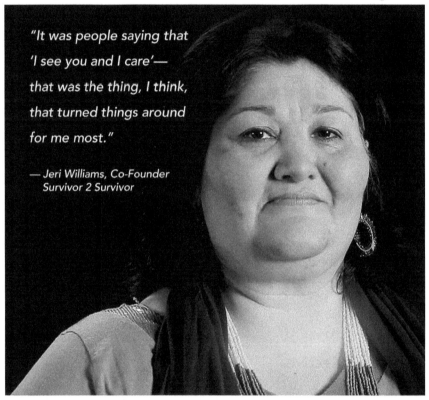

Know the Faces of Human Trafficking

"It was people saying that 'I see you and I care'— that was the thing, I think, that turned things around for me most."

— Jeri Williams, Co-Founder Survivor 2 Survivor

You don't need to specialize in human trafficking to serve its many victims. By knowing what human trafficking is, looking for indicators in the clients you serve, and referring potential victims to appropriate services, you can play an important role in identifying and supporting victims.

For more information, visit the human trafficking section of the Office for Victims of Crime website at www.ovc.gov/trafficking or call the National Human Trafficking Resource Center at 888–373–7888.

SOURCE: *Office for Victims of Crime, Know the Faces of Human Trafficking Poster Gallery, 2014.* Retrieved from http://ovc.ncjrs.gov/humantrafficking/Public_Awareness_Folder/images/final_poster_jeri.jpg. In the public domain.

2. Key Ideas

These are the central ideas of this chapter:

2.1 In the United States, much of the early anti–human trafficking movement has been framed within the criminal justice system context. This emphasis influenced the early perspectives of this crime including the development of programs and services.

2.2 Trafficking in persons exists because of its lucrativeness. It is driven by the demand for sexual services and cheap labor.

2.3 Human trafficking is deeply value-laden and grounded in the context of organization missions and individual perspectives.

2.4 First responders, practitioners, and professionals who serve human trafficking victims often experience compassion fatigue, vicarious trauma, and secondary trauma; they must be vigilant with their self-care to sustain their professional well-being, resilience, and ethical practice.

3. Selected Theories/Frameworks

3.1 Ecological Systems (Eco-Systems) Theory

In its early development in the 1970s, the ecological perspective offered a departure from individualistic and deficit-based interpretations of human behavior (Neal & Neal, 2013). In exploring social behavior, Uri Bronfenbrenner (1979) wrote about mezzosystem, exosystem, and macrosystem. By microsystem, Bronfenbrenner described settings in which individuals have direct interaction with other individuals. In terms of a survivor of human trafficking, the microsystem may include the survivor's parent, child, teacher, or trafficker. Interactions between microsystems represent the mezzosystem. An example of a mezzosystem is the connection between the family system and the school setting of a minor involved in commercial sexual exploitation. Exosystems involve settings in which an individual may not have direct engagement but nonetheless influence the individual's experience. For example, the exosystem of child welfare and foster care policies may impact an individual's vulnerability to human trafficking. Likewise, immigration policies at the exosystem level play a role in an exploited worker's access to protection and legal immigration status. The macrosystem includes the larger cultural, legal, and political contexts within which individuals are embedded, such as racism, patriarchal gender norms, nativist or xenophobic beliefs. Later, Bronfenbrenner added the chronosystem to include the element of time or the sociohistorical context (Neal & Neal, 2013). Others have subsequently argued that individuals interact with a network of systems, or "an overlapping configuration of interconnected ecological systems," rather than nested systems (Neal & Neal, 2013, p. 735).

Regardless of whether systems are understood as nested or networked, it is important to understand how the experiences and needs of survivors

> may impact and be impacted by the criminal justice system; legal, social and medical service providers; the survivor's family; social service eligibility policies; and social and political movements about immigration, to name a few. This model also incorporates these impacts in a chronological manner, gaining insight into and preparing for how survivors' needs may change over time due to future employability, predicted changes in legal status, and possible reunification with children. (Busch-Armendariz, Nsonwu, & Cook Heffron, 2014a, p. 16)

These interactions between individuals and the various systems are both continuous and fluid. Furthermore, those working with survivors and/or perpetrators of human trafficking must understand that these interactions may be recognized by individuals themselves, or they may remain unidentified and operate more covertly (Busch-Armendariz et al., 2014a). Such analyses inform the adaptation and delivery of services and advocacy efforts among interacting systems, and support efforts toward increased coordination between providers and survivors and among providers.

3.2 Transnational Theory

Our understanding of human trafficking through the lens of an ecological systems theory may be complemented and furthered by transnational theory. While an ecological perspective considers the human experience across scales (microsystem, mezzosystem, etc.) and across time (chronosystem), a transnational perspective adds a definitive spatial component to the analysis, particularly related to migration.

Transnational theory attempts to dismantle antiquated ideas about unidirectional migration experiences. In other words, transnational migration implies that migration may be unidirectional, multidirectional, or circular. Individuals and families do not always have simple migration journeys of leaving a home country and permanently resettling in a second location. Transnationalism also suggests that "immigrants live their lives across borders and maintain their ties to home, even when their countries of origin and settlement are geographically distant" (Schiller, Basch, & Blanc-Szanton, 1992, p. ix). Economic responsibilities, parenting roles, and communication often continue to exist across boundaries after an individual has migrated (Furman, Negi, Schatz, & Jones, 2008). The "linkages between and across time and space are complex, and the notion of transnationalism involves an expansive and fluid sense of place, belonging, identity, and responsibility" (Cook Heffron, Snyder, Wachter, Nsonwu, & Busch-Armendariz, 2016, p. 172).

Levitt and Jaworsky (2007) describe the ways in which transnational migrants simultaneously occupy and act within multiple spaces. Transnational migrants maintain

> a variety of ties to their home countries while they became incorporated into the countries where they settled. Migration has never been a one-way process

of assimilation into a melting pot or a multicultural salad bowl but one in which migrants, to varying degrees, are simultaneously embedded in the multiple sites and layers of the transnational social fields in which they live. More and more aspects of social life take place across borders, even as the political and cultural salience of nation-state boundaries remain clear. (p. 130)

Transnational theory further suggests that parenting from afar, in the context of migration, is a prime example of the ways that the transnational self spreads across both social and physical space (Soerens, 2015). Transnational mothers, in particular, struggle with the basic question of "how to be socially and emotionally present while physically absent" (Carling, Menjívar, & Schmalzbauer, 2012, p. 203).

While transnational theory is often utilized to investigate international migration, it is also applicable to human trafficking, in that the crime often (though not always) involves the movement of people from one location to another. For example, this may involve the transportation or movement of individuals across geopolitical borders, through force, fraud, or coercion, in pursuit of monetary profit. The application of transnational theory is straightforward and useful in exploring the ways in which the human trafficking of people across international borders impacts family systems and the vulnerabilities inherent in being a newcomer. A transnational approach is useful, for example, in responding to immigrant survivors of human trafficking, particularly those who prepare for and navigate the complex array of needs related to reunification with children through the T visa process (Busch-Armendariz,

Figure 6.2 *Sex trafficking poster.*

SOURCE: Reprinted from *Administration for Children and Families, Office on Trafficking in Persons, Rescue and Restore Victims of Human Trafficking Campaign Posters, 2012.* Retrieved from http://www.acf.hhs.gov/orr/resource/download-campaign-posters-and-brochures. In the public domain.

Nsonwu, & Cook Heffron, 2011). Furthermore, a transnational lens can also be applied to human trafficking that occurs within the border of a country or of a state and the ways that survivors' identities, relationships, and needs may be maintained and impacted by exploitation in the context of successive mobility. Consider the movement of youth who are trafficked for commercial sexual exploitation up and down the Atlantic seaboard or the movement of exploited migrant farmworkers from one harvest region to another.

4. Decision Case

...To the Rescue?[2]

> I live with a guy who's a lot older than I am. He makes me act out in porn videos. He beats me up if I don't. I'd really appreciate some ideas about how to get out of this.
>
> —Survivor Network Services Facebook page

The Community

Located in Southern California, Santa Teresa was the county seat of Visa County. Santa Teresa was the 11th-most populous city in the United States and the fourth-most populous city in California. It was also the third-fastest-growing large city in the nation from 2000 to 2006. The city was the cultural and economic center of Southern California, which had an estimated population of 1,883,051 as of July 1, 2013.

News reports on trafficking in Santa Teresa, November 2014:

In Santa Teresa specifically, the detective said the victims are primarily domestic, meaning from here in the United States. They've also noticed an increase in under-age victims.

"As of late, we've seen a lot of kids from 14 to 17. The vast majority of our domestic sex trafficking, especially with minors, occurs in or around hotels or motels."

He says it happens particularly in hotels along the I-5 corridor often close to downtown.

Detectives also tell news reporters that is can be difficult to spot a victim of human trafficking because it's not always obvious that they are being used against their will.

---

[2]This decision case was prepared solely to provide material for class discussion and not to suggest either effective or ineffective handling of the situation depicted. While based on field research regarding an actual situation, names and certain facts have been disguised to protect confidentiality. The authors wish to thank the case reporter for cooperation in making this account available for the benefit of students and practitioners (Wolfer & Scales, 2006, p. 29).

"A lot of ours (cases) involve a coercion or a fraud. A coercion can be a spoken or implied threat, a threat of violence. 'I'm going to kill your kids, I'm going to kill your grandma.'"

It's an increasing problem that these detectives are trying to stop online and undercover. They also rely on tips from the public.

Santa Teresa Police Department

The Santa Teresa Police Department (STPD) was a government department of 2,547 sworn law enforcement and support personnel who carried out police operations within the City of Santa Teresa, as well as at the Santa Teresa International Airport, city parks and lakes, and municipal courts. It had an annual general fund budget of $369 million. Its mission statement was: To keep you, your family, and our community safe; and its vision statement was: To be respected and trusted by all segments of Santa Teresa's diverse community. In addition, the department had written values:

We C.A.R.E.

- Wellness—promoting wellness within the police force and across the community
- Courage—to make the right professional decision
- Accountable—to the community, the department, and coworkers
- Respect—of the community, the department, and most importantly, self
- Ethical—professional actions and decision making

The Human Trafficking and Vice Unit

The Human Trafficking and Vice Unit was housed in the downtown Santa Teresa Police Department Headquarters building in an open bay where the detectives worked side by side. The unit of seven detectives, a civilian, and a sergeant. The task of the unit was to investigate cases involving human trafficking, vice, and child exploitation.

Detective Michael Daniel

Michael Daniel grew up in a small town in Oklahoma. He stumbled upon policing as a career in his early 20s when a gang-connected crime unfolded outside his home. A large man and not easily intimidated, he stepped outside his apartment to see what was happening. Amidst gunfire and confusion, he saw two young men running from the scene. Without a second thought, Michael gave chase. He managed to slow the men down enough for police officers to catch up. Based on Michael's information, the men were arrested. During the arrest process, Michael watched what he perceived were "terrible officer safety" procedures. Instead of feeling relieved that officials were taking care of the situation, Michael actually wanted to help the officers. "I don't want to rubber neck," Michael quickly realized, "I want to be part of it."

The following day, still fascinated by the incident and hoping to prove what he'd seen, Michael searched for shell casings and bullet holes as well as the gun used in the crime. After presenting testimony in court, he was hooked. Everything about the law enforcement world he saw unfolding around him was interesting. After the court hearing, one of the police officers told him, "Hey, we'll pay for school if you come work for us." He bit. That was in 1991.

By 2011, Michael had worked three cities and several crime areas. He moved to Santa Teresa because his second love was painting. Attracted by the vibrant art community and hoping to paint when he wasn't policing, a close friend asked Michael once why he didn't just give up being a cop and be a full-time artist. "I want to save the world, trust me," Michael answered. "It's a learning curve for all of us and I've certainly made mistakes, but there's nothing more rewarding than to sit down with someone who's young and get an outcry." He explained that helping a young victim recognize that what happened to them was actually a crime brought him deep satisfaction. Even more than art did.

As a seasoned police officer and supervisor who often worked undercover, he was usually in plain clothes, regularly sported shades on his shaved head, a leather bracelet, and silver rings. He was sun weathered, fair skinned, and quick to blush with strong emotion. His twinkling blue eyes were assessing. Michael also easily engaged with people, talking with his hands always in motion. Although he worked a variety of shifts, sectors, and crimes over his 20-year career, he consistently strove to make a contribution. He brought passion, experience, and a commitment to make a difference to the Human Trafficking and Vice Unit as a detective. Michael's work kept him in contact with nonprofit organizations, providing services to victims of trafficking. Through teaching and public speaking, he educated professionals and community members about the crime of trafficking. Not jaded by experience, Michael remained optimistic concerning his cases.

A Phone Call

It was mid-August 2011 when Michael picked up a phone call from Sharon Morgan. She introduced herself as a new employee at Survivor Network Services, a small nonprofit that provided outreach to trafficked persons in the community.

"Hey, I've got this situation," Sharon said. "I want to run it past you and see what you think."

"Sure, what've you got?" Michael asked.

Sharon explained that a young woman had contacted her organization through social media. The woman's post described the situation of living with a much older man who was forcing her to participate in porn. Sharon had communicated further and discovered the story also involved a victimized roommate. Both women were University of California undergraduate students in their early 20s. Sharon made it clear the women didn't want to talk to the police. But Sharon wanted to know, based on the story, what Michael advised.

Michael listened carefully, thinking, *Well, that sounds strange*. It wasn't unusual to have people make outlandish claims or false reports. It wasn't unusual that the women were not yet interested in talking with police. It sounded as if the situation was in a holding pattern and Michael assured Sharon he was available to speak to the women when they were ready to make a report.

The next day, Michael received a call from Dr. Diane Green, a colleague at the university. Michael and Diane had worked on the human trafficking task force for the city for the past two years and had given a few talks together. Diane explained having gotten a call from Sharon asking if the university had resources to help Alexandra. "Do you know about the women posting online with Survivor Network Services?" Though Michael wasn't sure why Sharon was calling researchers about an active situation, he assured Diane he had heard about the situation; he again commented that he was ready and willing to take a statement. When he hung up, he wondered if anything in the situation had changed but reminded himself that Sharon would call if the women wanted to talk to law enforcement. Perhaps they were trying to work something out about the women being students.

Two days later, while leaving a Trafficking Task Force meeting, Michael overheard an FBI agent mention the same situation to another colleague. They also wanted to know if Michael had heard. *Who all has Sharon called about this?* he wondered. Concerned about confusing or jumbled reporting, at best, and even embellished reports, at worst, Michael put in a call to Sharon.

"What's happening with the two girls you were in touch with the other day?" Michael asked.

Sharon gave him a long, convoluted ramble about talking to the school, Assistance Support Services for Refugees staff, the FBI, and a church. Michael closed his eyes.

"Listen, Sharon," he finally interrupted, "when you come to me with something, then you go to someone else, it suggests I didn't do my job. What do you need?"

"I need to know how to help these girls," Sharon said. "What if they don't want to talk to the police? They still need help."

"I agree with you. But, here's the deal. The more people talking about the situation or trying to investigate," Michael pointed out, "the higher the chances of getting something entangled in ways that can hurt the victims. Tell you what. Let me talk to Tilda over at the bureau, compare stories, and see who needs to do what. In the meantime, maybe you can help the girls understand that I'm not scary. They can talk to me. This is a crime."

They talked for a few moments longer, smoothing over the edges of a sharp conversation. As soon as he ended the call, Michael dialed Tilda Garvis with the FBI. He and Garvis commiserated about the confusion and agreed that when the girls were ready to report, they would both participate in an interview to determine where the jurisdiction lay.

Michael made note of both conversations with what little information he had. He also opened a pending file as a reminder that the situation, definitely trafficking of some sort, existed in space.

A Visit

In late October, Michael was at his desk in the bullpen when Sergeant Litch waved him over to the office.

When they stepped in Litch's office, FBI Agent Garvis sat in the sergeant's office guest chair. Apparently, there was a meeting under way. Michael grabbed a chair and joined the meeting, his curiosity definitely piqued.

"We've looked into this and we're not interested in pursuing it," Garvis said, handing Sergeant Litch a case file. Litch passed the folder directly to Michael.

Michael looked over the file in his hands. Agent Garvis offered a quick tutorial on what was where in the file and how the case notes were organized. It was immediately clear he was looking at an FBI jacket on the case from Survivor Network Services. Despite the previous agreement to work the case together if and when the victims were ready to report, Garvis had interviewed the victims, vetted the case, and decided the case didn't meet the requirements for a federal investigation.

Wasn't the case shiny enough for you? Michael wondered but didn't say. He scanned notes about a single interview with two potential victims, Alexandra Smith and Kathryn Lucas, identification of Frank Harris as a suspect, and some background information including the suspect's social media activity. Agent Garvis was still talking when Michael looked up.

"There's a case, but I thought it would fit better with you guys," Garvis said, this time speaking directly to Michael.

Michael was tempted to give Garvis a polite lecture on follow-through and collaboration to let her know he was annoyed. Instead, he nodded. He had a question. "I see on the suspect's Facebook page that he's posted that a cold case unit from North Carolina interviewed him and executed a DNA search warrant. What's that about?"

Garvis shook her head dismissively. "No idea."

"Okay. I'll take it from here." Michael shrugged.

Litch and Garvis made some small talk about working together. Michael's interest returned to the file in his hands. The outline of the situation was sketched in the file, greatly expanding the version of the story he'd heard two months back. Alexandra Smith was 21 years old and a student at the university. She was also married to this Frank Harris, who was 49 years old. Alexandra reported that Harris ran some kind of porn site on the Internet. He forced her to perform sex on video and displayed it on his site.

After the courtesy good-byes, Michael jumped up and went to his desk to call North Carolina. Two tries got Michael connected with Detective Stan Rob with the cold case unit in North Carolina. Michael introduced himself and then explained, "We're investigating this guy, Frank Harris, for possibly trafficking a young woman. I've got some information here that you guys are investigating him, too. Is that right?"

"Oh, yeah," Detective Rob responded, "that's my partner's case, I can tell you we have a DNA match." Rob explained that Frank Harris was wanted in a 19-year-old homicide. "We fully anticipate an indictment for murder within a few weeks."

After the call, Michael took several minutes to do the mundane work of slotting the FBI data into his own case file along with a note about the information from North Carolina. As he did so, Michael began to realize the level of danger that Alexandra Smith and Kathryn Lucas might face should they attempt to leave Harris. *How did Alexandra end up married to this guy?* He began plotting his next phone call to Survivor

Network Services and sorting through the information in front of him for ideas about how best to communicate with Alexandra and Kathryn.

He called Sharon, seeking insight into how to have a conversation with one or the other victim. It turned out that the girls' willingness to talk to the FBI agent didn't automatically translate into willingness to talk to Michael. Sharon had a lot of questions about why the FBI had handed over the case to STPD. Michael had a lot of questions about why the girls were hesitating now that the FBI had spilled the beans.

After several days of back-and-forth calls, Sharon called Michael to report, "Alexandra and Kathryn want to get out of the situation with Frank."

"Great," Michael responded, "that's a game changer."

"Yes. Alexandra is ready to make a report and move somewhere Frank can't find her," Sharon explained. "We can provide the shelter."

"That's terrific. It might be best to get them out first," Michael immediately began thinking ahead, "and make the reports afterward. Harris's a pretty dangerous guy. If we're planning to take Harris's wife and his primary source of income, we should have a really tight plan."

"Okay," Sharon agreed. "How do we do that?"

Michael remembered how new Sharon was to this work. "Next time you talk to them, can you find out when and how they might be able to leave safely? When is he regularly out of the house and for how long? Might be best if there's a time they are both on campus without him." Michael paused. "Find out what they need for transportation."

"I can try," Sharon said.

It turned out Sharon's planning with the women was complicated by several factors. The safe place that Survivor Network Services had available for the women was not in Santa Teresa and had very strict rules about staying in the shelter, with no contact to the outside world for several months. Alexandra was only weeks away from graduating with three bachelor degrees with high honors and unwilling to miss classes or postpone her graduation. Negotiations between university staff, Survivor Network Services staff, and the women unfolded slowly. There was a lot to work around. The university required students finish their last semester in residence, and arrangements were made with professors and administrators. Survivor Network Services required isolation for victims, and the staff needed to arrange safe transport for Alexandra to take finals and computer communication for Alexandra and the school. Sharon kept Michael informed of the conversations and compromises. Two weeks crawled by while the deliberating continued.

During the planning period, Michael had planning of his own to do. He informed his team a rescue was imminent. The various officers available for a rescue operation included Michael's fellow detectives on the unit, their sergeant, and Victim Services counselors. Those folks had all been working their own cases over the past three months, only hearing bits and pieces of this case along the way. Michael communicated a shell of an armed plainclothes operation plan—briefing the team with pictures of the victims and suspect, and providing some history.

The unit had the capacity to arm up and physically rescue someone if needed. In a perfect world, the team would meet Alexandra and Kathryn on campus during school hours. But Sharon reported that the girls didn't want that to happen. As November approached, timing became the crucial issue. Finally, Sharon called Michael with a rough plan and some dates. The women had complicated ideas about what they would need to leave. Michael repeatedly encouraged Sharon to help the women take only bare necessities and get out safe.

Over the next week, Sharon also coordinated with Alexandra's aunt and uncle to help with the move. Michael learned the location of the women's apartment and details of Frank's habits and routines that would make a rescue difficult. Frank mainly worked from the apartment and was very strict about the women staying in the apartment unless they were at school. Frank also supplemented his online business with occasional irregular day labor jobs. Finally, Michael and Sharon decided to pick up the women when Frank was working a temporary day labor job.

The Rescue

The women's apartment complex was located across the street from a restaurant. Told that Frank was likely going to work a temp job on Wednesday morning, Michael decided to carry out the rescue during that small window of opportunity. Michael and a team of six detectives, all in plain clothes and unmarked SUVs, began Wednesday by putting Frank under surveillance. With protective gear in their cars and in constant radio contact, the team moved into proximity. When Frank left the apartment, a team of detectives followed him to work and kept him under constant surveillance during the operation. Michael and Det. Matt Jacob went straight to the restaurant.

Sharon was in the parking lot when Michael and Jacob pulled in with two suburban-style vans. Sharon was leaning on her car, talking on her phone. She waved the detectives over. An older couple got out of a station wagon as they approached.

"This is Detective Daniel," Sharon said to the older couple. "These are Alexandra's aunt and uncle."

The older man held out a hand. "Ted Smith; pleased to meet you."

Michael shook hands and introduced Jacob.

"Here they are." Sharon tugged on Michael's sleeve.

Because of her appearance, Michael immediately recognized Alexandra Smith crossing the street. A striking young woman with long white-blonde hair, her skin was nearly transparent and her eyes almost clear. She had two cats under her arms. The woman with her was also extremely fair and carried a small dog. The startling appearance of the women actually caused passersby to stare.

Sharon made very quick introductions while the aunt and uncle cooed over the animals. Michael got on the radio and brought the rest of the team in to keep watch and begin fetching and carrying. Five of them made three trips from the apartment to the vans. The belongings the women took with them filled the two Suburbans, Sharon's car trunk, and the uncle's pickup bed.

It was clear the two young women wanted to travel with Sharon. They said good-bye to Alexandra's family. Sharon offered to bring both woman and some food down to the station.

The Interviews

Back at police headquarters, the four of them had lunch together in one of the interview rooms. Though it took only 15 minutes to wolf down burgers, there was an opportunity to describe the interview process to Alexandra and Kathryn, let them get accustomed to Michael's voice, and begin building rapport. As soon as they were done eating, Sharon and Kathryn settled in a nearby interview room, and Michael turned on the recording equipment and sat down to interview Alexandra.

STPD policy was to video record victim interviews. Michael preferred the process because it provided the most thorough record of everything happening in the interview room. Because they had just met, Michael began the interview by building rapport. With her it wasn't hard. She expressed effusive gratitude. "You're a hero; you just saved me." Michael factored that into his approach, aware that her reaction to him was a form of influence he didn't want to misuse while talking with her.

"What do you want me to know about your situation, Alexandra?" Michael began.

"I was born in LA." Alexandra began. "That's where I grew up." She described a comfortable upbringing. An only child, her parents were divorced, her dad was a defense attorney in Los Angeles, and her mom worked as a probation officer. Alexandra talked about her parents with detachment, obviously a kid who'd been shuttled back and forth a lot between busy parents. Michael listened carefully, prompting occasionally, although as Alexandra warmed up, she spoke easily.

"Look, Mr. Daniel. This isn't easy." She gestured to herself. "Looking like this. I mean, my parents didn't know what to do about this. When I got teased at school, my mom took me to karate lessons." She shook her head. "Karate doesn't make you look like everyone else. I . . . look, my folks never really had much use for me. But, I'm smart. I figured out I had to go to college. If I don't have higher education, then look at me, I'm not worth anything."

Michael wanted to protest this assessment. Alexandra's unique looks had to have made her childhood and teen years challenging. Very few people with albinism look exotic; rather they often appear ill and Alexandra was no exception. As she talked, Michael soon realized Alexandra was smart and articulate with excellent recall for detail. She explained to Michael in no uncertain terms that given how she looks her only chance for success as an adult was to get a college education.

"My parents didn't—don't—see the point," Alexandra said. "They weren't offering any financial support. Which I get, I mean, they have a lot of medical to deal with because of . . ." She gestured at herself again. "Anyway, I got a one year scholarship to the University of California."

"How did you meet Frank?" Michael asked.

"Hmmm. I was in this volunteer group and we worked at alumni events. There was this builder's group; we helped host a couple of events." Alexandra described being befriended by a married couple, both of whom were business owners. She was subsequently invited into their social life in Southern California by the wife, Veronica. They introduced Alexandra to their friends, including Frank. Alexandra talked very briefly about enjoying having this older, parental couple take an interest in her.

Michael was impressed by Alexandra's honesty and her insight.

Near the end of the fall semester, Alexandra began looking for financial support for her sophomore year at school. She already knew her parents would not pay for school and she discovered they had too much income for her to qualify for financial aid. She was heartbroken and desperate.

At the end of a day she had spent at the financial aid office, she came home and got online, seeking support. Frank was online in a chat forum they both frequented. Alexandra explained her terrible day and her distress about the school situation. Frank was interested and offered to marry her so she would qualify for aid. He also talked about the ways she could help him with the clerical end of his import business in return for him paying for school incidentals. Alexandra scoffed at the idea as ridiculous.

As the semester slowed toward the winter break, she stayed in touch with her friends, including Frank, and he kept the option of marriage open. He made it sound quite businesslike and expressed wanting to help her out. They chatted and talked about the potential of getting married as friends, in a kind of arranged relationship solely for the purpose of her attaining financial aid for school. Eventually Alexandra accepted Frank's offer of an arranged marriage. When the fall semester ended, Alexandra married Frank at the justice of the peace's office in nearby San Jose, where he lived and had a business. That day, she went home with Frank.

When they arrived at the house, Frank summarily ordered Alexandra to have sex with his roommate. Shocked, Alexandra refused. Alexandra was surprisingly matter-of-fact in describing the events of the evening. Frank physically attacked her and beat her until she conceded to have sex with the roommate. Under continued threat from Frank, Alexandra had sex with the roommate and other men Frank brought to the house. Alexandra didn't recall when she first became aware Frank was getting money from the guys with whom he forced her to have sex.

In January, Frank relocated them to an apartment in Santa Teresa in order for Alexandra to return to school. He demanded total control of Alexandra, except as regarded school. During the spring semester, he forced her to provide phone sex and continued bringing men to the house to have sex with her. After the semester ended, he took her to a hotel, where Veronica was the madam of a BDSM (Bondage and Discipline, Dominance and Submission, Sadism and Masochism) community. Veronica and Frank set up a video shoot with multiple men in the room with Veronica and Alexandra. During a particularly painful and brutal scene, they used a machine to sexually violate Alexandra.

Although Frank allowed Alexandra to attend school and do school work, the forced prostitution continued. Frank posted sex-for-sale ads online and sold the porn videos online. Alexandra's albinism made her fit neatly into a very profitable porn subculture. To cut costs, he forced her to pick up free condoms from school.

Frank also had sex with Alexandra, labeling their relationship as Dom/sub. Alexandra lived with Frank for 3 years. Her knowledge about the small tight-knit group of porn producers was clearly extensive.

The information spilled out of Alexandra over 3 hours. Alexandra showed little reserve in trusting Michael with the details of her situation. There was a lot of context about Alexandra she didn't provide in that first interview. But Michael inferred pieces of the sources of Alexandra's vulnerability. Her albinism fit the profile for a specific subset of porn fetish. In the way she talked about her father, Michael also suspected her father sexually abused her as a child in a BDSM setting. While his instincts were telling Michael there was a likely history of abuse, Alexandra did not seem ready for that kind of conversation.

Michael ended the interview with Alexandra by telling her a little bit about what the next steps in the investigation might be and describing the process they would use to make her written statement. Given her level of honesty and directness, Michael also felt she needed to know about the charges against Frank in North Carolina. While he didn't want to scare her, he wanted her to understand how seriously she would have to safeguard her security until Frank was behind bars.

Michael and Alexandra joined the others in the squad room for a bite and a break before he sat down with Kathryn. Kathryn had been living with Alexandra and Frank for several months. She was a couple of years older than Alexandra and more reserved. She offered vague details about how she came to be in the circumstances, leaving Michael feeling as if she was more consenting to the arrangement. There was no physical violence or threats in her account of the relationships. She seemed quite concerned about Alexandra.

After Michael's interview with Kathryn, Sharon took the women to the Survivor Network Services safe house. Everything was fixed for one day. In the following days, Michael knew he and his team could unpack the situation and figure out what needed to happen next.

Ensuring Alexandra's Safety

The goal of the tactical operation was to create the impression that the women vanished off the face of the earth. It worked brilliantly. Frank had absolutely no idea where they went.

"We wanted to reset his OODA[3] loop enough so he couldn't begin to look for them," Michael said. "We call it the fruit loops."

The team continued monitoring Frank, mainly through his social media use. It was apparent Frank had no idea what happened.

As days passed, unlike some of his other cases, Alexandra was safe for now. In the short term, Alexandra had secure shelter and the team could maintain surveillance on

---

[3]A SWAT term for the decision cycle of *observe, orient, decide, and act*, developed by military strategist and USAF Colonel John Boyd. In tactical operations, the goal is to disrupt the suspect's OODA loop in order to safely resolve a potentially dangerous situation (Fallows).

Frank. But long term, something would need to be done about Frank. Michael had to spread his attention among several cases but continued to field phone calls about Alexandra's situation. He also kept in touch with Alexandra. Kathryn left the sheltered situation a week after they moved in. Alexandra needed consistent reassurance that she was believed. Michael felt responsible for providing that.

The charges Visa County could file against Frank were all second-degree felonies, with penalties of up to 20 years. If convicted in California, Frank could be out of prison in 4.

But North Carolina was on the verge of filing capital murder charges. Frank was potentially facing death or a life sentence. Investigators in North Carolina continued to reassure Michael they were moving forward. They wanted to interview Alexandra and Kathryn, too.

A second week passed. Michael felt torn between filing charges against Frank and waiting for North Carolina to charge him with the more serious crime. Alexandra's trust weighed heavily on him as time dragged by. She was weeks away from the college graduation she had sacrificed so much for and he didn't know if he could provide her the safety to walk across the stage. Michael had a decision to make: Are we going to ramp up an investigation or are we going to let the issues in North Carolina take precedence? Although no one in the DA's office wanted to waste the time and resources to charge a man who was about to be extradited, Michael felt an obligation to get justice for Alexandra.

5. Scientific Knowledge at the Mezzo Level

5.1 Value-Laden Work

Individual Values

Professionals working in the antitrafficking field must have a clear understanding of their professional and personal belief systems as well as continuously engage in the self-reflective practice of examining their own values while working with clients. The value-laden work of human trafficking is emotionally taxing, and many professionals experience compassion fatigue, secondary trauma, or vicarious trauma as a result of hearing their victims' stories. The work may be as a law enforcement investigator, attorney, social worker, or within the counseling process or in witnessing a client's horrific human trafficking experience at the time of a rescue.

Experiencing Secondary Trauma—Take Quiz

In the process of learning about human trafficking, have you experienced the following symptoms, feelings, or occurrences? Irritability, anger/rage, or cynicism; tearfulness, emotional outbursts, or a flat/labile affect; stress eating or the loss of appetite; bad dreams, an inability to sleep, or an increased amount of sleep; a state of hyperarousal or being highly suspicious of others; an avoidance of participating in events that once brought you pleasure; or any of the other reactions in Lipsky's *A Trauma Exposure Responses* (see Figure 6.3.)?

If you answered "yes," then this may be a result of being exposed to the trauma in the literature that you read in this textbook. O'Halloran and O'Halloran (2001) assert that "individuals who encounter traumatic material or who work with traumatized clients can be profoundly impacted by their experiences" (p. 93). Now, consider how you might feel if your professional life consistently reflected the trauma in readings that you have been exposed to in this textbook. What if you were regularly surrounded by stories of others' pain, suffering, violence, and oppression in your daily work? Salston and Figley (2003) assert that this work environment can be "an occupational hazard of caring service providers" (p. 173). Helping service practitioners (e.g., social workers, law enforcement, attorneys, and medical providers) who are either first responders or ongoing support systems for victims of human trafficking are at high risk for experiencing emotional, physical, and spiritual exhaustion. In order to be ethical and professionally resilient, it is crucial that practitioners understand the psychological constructs that affect their work as well as what is required to sustain their well-being.

5.2 Compassion Fatigue, Vicarious Trauma, and Secondary Trauma

Compassion fatigue (Figley, 1989; Joinson, 1992), vicarious trauma (Pearlman & Saakvitne, 1995) and secondary trauma/traumatic stress (O'Halloran & O'Halloran, 2001; Pryce, Shackelford, & Pryce, 2007), and trauma exposure (Lipsky & Burk, 2009) have often been used synonymously as they are similar concepts that address the consequences that many helping professions experience when they engage in emotionally taxing work with vulnerable and marginalized clients. Compassion fatigue is used interchangeably with secondary traumatic stress disorder, which Figley (1995) defines as "the natural consequent behaviors or emotions resulting from knowing about a traumatizing event experienced by a significant other—the stress resulting from helping or wanting to help a traumatized or suffering person" (p. 7); while vicarious trauma has been described as "the transformation in the inner experience of the therapist that comes about as a result of empathic engagement with client's trauma material" (Pearlman & Saakvitne, 1995, p. 31). A study by Hollingsworth (1993) revealed symptomology in therapists in relation to trust, safety, intimacy, and connectedness issues as well as feelings of anger, disgust, sadness, distress, and somatic responses as a result of their work with survivors of incest. Some noted that a difference between compassion fatigue and vicarious trauma is that vicarious trauma tends to happen over an extended time period (Pearlman & Saakvitne, 1995), whereas compassion fatigue has a quicker beginning and ending of symptoms (Figley, 1995). The term trauma exposure relates to "anyone who interacts with the suffering, pain, and crisis of others" (Lipsky & Burk, 2009, p. 11).

Figure 6.3 *A trauma exposure response.*

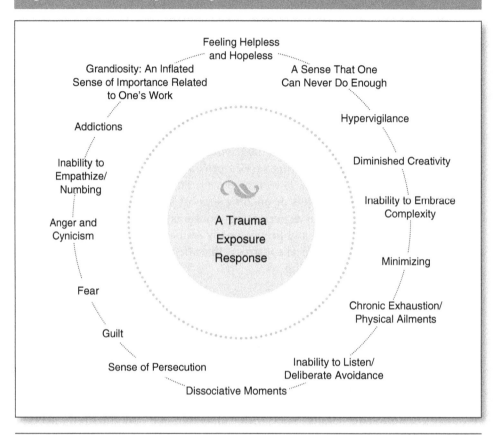

Practitioners who work in the health care field have long recognized that their profession is susceptible to the stress of caring for others, sometimes referred to as nurse burnout (Joinson, 1992). Richard Cabot, a physician and medical social work pioneer in the early 1900s, wrote about a condition that he called "breathlessness" in social workers that would equate to our modern-day terminology of secondary or vicarious trauma, burnout, or compassion fatigue (Nsonwu, Casey, Cook, & Busch-Armendariz, 2013); he further described a "dulling [of] the social worker's soul" (Rappaport, 2006, p. 6) to describe what Figley (1995) calls "a cost to caring" (p. 1). Pryce et al. (2007) report a high incidence of secondary trauma in child welfare workers; and Salston and Figley (2003) affirm an increase of secondary traumatic stress effects with professionals who work with crime victims. Whether professionals are working with clients who have been or continue to be victimized by oppressive persons or systems (e.g., human trafficking, domestic violence, hate crimes), clients who have suffered from traumatic events (e.g., experiencing or witnessing violence/sexual assault, natural disasters), or clients who have debilitating physical ailments (e.g., diagnosis of a terminal or chronic disease), there is a normal reaction to interfacing with the emotional, cognitive, and spiritual pressures of caring for others. Malakh-Pines, Aronson, and Malakh-Pines (1988) describe burnout as "a state of physical, emotional and mental exhaustion caused by long-term involvement in emotionally demanding situations" (p. 9). Helping professionals who are consistently subjected to trauma, whether firsthand trauma (e.g., witnessing emotional outbursts/violence or viewing graphic crime scene/evidence pictures) or secondary trauma (e.g., listening to violent details/accounts from victims), can experience secondary traumatic stress disorder (STSD). STSD, according to Figley,

> is a syndrome of symptoms nearly identical to Post Traumatic Stress Disorder (PTSD) except that exposure to knowledge about a traumatizing event experienced by a significant other is associated with the set of STSD symptoms, and PTSD symptoms are directly connected to the sufferer, the person experiencing primary traumatic stress. (1995, p. 8)

Students are often drawn to helping professions such as medicine, policing, law, and social work and often speak of being "called" to their vocations. In social work in particular, students are willing to describe being called "because of their love and desire to help others, their strong commitment to social change, and a dedication to work for disenfranchised individuals and communities" (Nsonwu et al., 2013, p. 5); this can most likely be attributed to other helping professional disciplines (medical/mental health providers, attorneys, policy advocates) as well. Many of these students may also bring with them painful, personal experiences of their own victimization (e.g., domestic violence, child abuse, rape, sexual assault) and trauma. O'Halloran and O'Halloran (2001) contend that 40%–50% of their students self-report as survivors of trauma (p. 94); this victimization history may increase a student's secondary traumatic stress. Alpert and Paulson (1990) contend that there is a significant need for specialized training and support for students and practitioners who plan to work with victims of trauma, specifically those affected by child abuse.

5.3 The Importance of Self-Awareness

Nsonwu et al. (2015) suggest that educators and faculty assess student knowledge, attitudes, and perceptions of human trafficking as an educational component to acquiring the necessary skills and self-awareness to work with survivors of human trafficking. In addition to students, both novice and seasoned professionals need to prepare themselves educationally, emotionally, and spiritually for their chosen field by understanding how they are susceptible to compassion fatigue, secondary trauma, vicarious trauma, or worker burnout. If practitioners fail to realize their vulnerabilities and the need to practice self-care, they will inadvertently compromise ethical care and jeopardize their own well-being (Figley, 1995; Pearlman & Saakvitne, 1995; Way, VanDeusen, & Cottrell, 2007).

Self-awareness and reflection are key elements in developing strategies for self-care. O'Halloran and O'Halloran (2001) classified self-care strategies for graduate students preparing to work with victims of trauma and violence; however, these strategies can also be utilized by experienced practitioners as a self-assessment plan. These strategies were delineated into four categories—biobehavioral, affective-cognitive, relational, and spiritual. The biobehavioral strategy focuses on eating nutritious meals, maintaining physical fitness, and health; the affective-cognitive plan develops self-care strategies and self-awareness of strengths and challenges; the relational strategy component is used to assess trauma history and current support systems—it also explores ways to increase social capital when needed; and the spiritual strategy or "connection to a greater source" (p. 95) is individually defined and focuses on "peace and renewed hope" (p. 95). This holistic approach offers the practitioner a blueprint for self-reflection so that they can become aware of their strengths, challenges, and needs. This framework echoes the practice wisdom that implementing enjoyable activities into a practitioner's lifestyle will help in maintaining work/life balance (Crothers, 1995; Figley, 1989; Sexton, 1999). Figley (1989) also contends that therapists need to set healthy boundaries and be cautious not to fall into the "savior" syndrome, where they assume that they are solely responsible for the success of their client.

Working with vulnerable populations requires understanding the factors that cause stress for the practitioner; it is additionally important to put strategies into place that provide caretaker resilience. Individual and group supervision, peer and staff support, as well as continued educational training are essential components in assisting practitioners who work with victims of trauma and violence (Crothers, 1995; Hollingsworth, 1993; Sexton, 1999). Practitioners need to understand that their feelings are normal, receive support, and be encouraged to utilize their vacation and time off to provide self-care and professional sustainability.

5.4 Principle-Based Practice for Organizations

Trauma stewardship is the self-care model for those who have experienced trauma exposure. The belief is "that both joy and pain are realities of life, and that suffering can be transformed into meaningful growth and healing when a quality of presence is cultivated and maintained even in the face of great suffering" (Lipsky & Burk, 2009, p. 11). Trauma stewardship is a model that can be used with individuals and organizations, particularity practitioners and agencies who work with victims of human trafficking, since this work causes emotional, physical, and spiritual fatigue. Many times, organizations reflect the stress of the social problems they are tasked to restore and are in need of organizational healing. Lipsky and Burk (2009) convey practical applications to practice trauma stewardship at either an individual or organizational level through five directions—inquiry, focus, compassion, balance, and centering. In their book *Trauma Stewardship: An Everyday Guide to Caring for Self While Caring for Others*, Lipsky and Burk (2009) offer some concrete steps to focus on self-care:

1. "We ask ourselves where we're putting our focus, and we expand range of possibilities by imagining a Plan B. We gain a new sense of freedom by understanding that we have the ability to shift our perspective. When we open ourselves to inspiration, we may also rediscover our passion" (p. 172).

2. Reconnect with former clients/patients who are currently doing well to affirm the work that I/we are currently doing.

3. Practice compassion for myself and others.

4. "We may alter systems by 'altering' the way we interact with them" (p. 200).

5. Work toward balance.

Symptoms of Secondary Traumatic Stress and Secondary Stress Disorder

Feelings of anger, disgust, sadness, distress, difficulty maintaining relationships or boundaries, trust of others, intimacy, feelings of agitation or irritability, hyperarousal, difficulty concentrating, high startle response, hypervigilance, sleep disturbances, experiencing intrusive thoughts or images, beginning to dream the clients' dreams, feelings of helplessness or hopelessness, development of a negative attitude and/or self-concept, lack of empathy for others, cynicism

NOTE: Adapted from "Secondary Traumatic Stress Effects of Working With Survivors of Criminal Victimization" by Mary Dale Salston and Charles R. Figley, 2003, *Journal of Traumatic Stress, 16(2)*, p. 171. Copyright 2003 by the International Society for Traumatic Stress Studies. Adapted with permission.

Responding to Secondary Traumatic Stress

1. Mindfulness

2. Meditation

3. Critical Incident Stress Debriefing (CISD) (Harris, 1995; McCammon & Allison, 1995)

4. Multiple Stressor Debriefing Model (Armstrong, O'Callahan, & Marmar, 1991)

5. Sensory-Based Therapy (Harris, 1995; Ogden & Minton, 2001)

6. Vicarious Trauma Treatment Approach (Pearlman & Saakvitne, 1995)

7. Accelerated Recovery Program for Compassion Fatigue (Gentry, Baranowsky, & Dunning, 1997)

NOTE: Adapted from "Secondary Traumatic Stress Effects of Working With Survivors of Criminal Victimization" by Mary Dale Salston and Charles R. Figley, 2003, *Journal of Traumatic Stress, 16(2)*, p. 171. Copyright 2003 by the International Society for Traumatic Stress Studies. Adapted with permission.

If professionals and volunteers strive for longevity in the antitrafficking field, they need to consider self-care and work-life balance for sustainability. Similarly, it can be quite challenging for the novice professional who has unrealistic expectations of their limited role and expects to be able to "rescue" their client without considering the complicated and multifaceted variables that lead to human trafficking. Rachel Lloyd in Kalergis (2009) asserts that when working with youth, her agency "talk[s] about it in terms of empowerment versus rescuing. If you frame it as 'rescuing' them from trafficking, it's sensational, but 'empowering' them is better in terms of helping them heal" (p. 319). Most importantly, it is the realization that the client's self-determination should take precedence over the values of the professional. This can be especially problematic when working with youth who are at risk and continue to make poor judgments.

Engaging in advocacy/prevention efforts, providing direct practice, developing policies and programs, or conducting research in the area of human trafficking all confront the complex issue of addressing the value-laden areas of this subject. The potential for continued harm may be great, beyond the initial trauma inflicted by the trafficker, when the structure of response systems is not culturally grounded to understand the impact of trauma that victims experience. A compounded situation is when the system procedures and those who work in this system assign some level of culpability to victims for their victimization. Kotrla (2010) describes a demoralizing macro-level example for sex trafficking victims as a "culture of tolerance, fueled by the glamorization of pimping, (that) is embodied in multiple venues of daily life, including clothing, songs, television, video games, and other forms of entertainment" (p. 183). These distorted messages permeate society, conveying an acceptance of the objectification of women and the normalizing of human trafficking. Vulnerable and impressionable youth who are abused and neglected are at particular risk. Child sexual abuse is oftentimes a precursor to the future exploitation of human trafficking by creating emotional and physical susceptibility from being homeless, troubled, and noncompliant. While perceptions are changing, youth and children have been labeled "delinquent" by social service and criminal justice systems charged with their care (Mitchell, Finkelhor, & Wolak, 2010). For example, the language may incorrectly describe sex trafficking victims in ways that is demoralizing such as "child prostitute" (Mitchell et al., 2010). A systemic paradigm shift to reframe pejorative "blaming the victim" terms is needed. The terms commercial sexual exploitation (CSE) or, in cases of minors, the commercial sexual exploitation of children and youth (CSEC) or domestic minor sex trafficking (DMST) (Reid, 2010) are value-laden terms that acknowledge the victimization of this crime.

Wachter et al. (2016) suggest that organizations serving survivors of domestic minor sex trafficking (DMST) integrate principle-based practices into their service responses and organizational frameworks, especially given the myriad of victim needs and vulnerabilities and the significant increase in organizations with untrained staff providing services to human trafficking survivors (Wachter et al., 2016).

This research suggests organizational grounding in five principle-based practices including nurture the humanity and dignity of clients; contextualize survivor needs within a social justice framework; prioritize the immediate and practical needs of clients; support of the dynamic nature of survivors' healing; and help identify and engage essential community and professional partners (Wachter et al., 2016).

5.5 Understanding Prosecution and Conviction Efforts

Criminal justice officials have made clear links from human trafficking crimes to other crimes, including crimes involving illegal drugs and weapons (Busch-Armendariz, Nsonwu & Heffron, 2014). Busch-Armendariz et al. (2014) write, "traffickers who exploit U.S. citizens tend to be associated with small criminal groups, gangs, and criminal entrepreneurs, human traffickers who move victims across international borders are more likely to be linked with national or transitional organized crime syndications" (p. 9).

To steer national and international antitrafficking efforts, the Trafficking Victims Protection Act (TVPA) is broad in scope as it provides definitions for human trafficking and the provision of resources; for example, a major thrust has been to encourage criminal justice reforms.

Worldwide, criminal justice systems have been hindered by the complexity of this crime, delaying the goals of identifying victims and holding human traffickers accountable, which is exasperating for law enforcement. The *Global Report on Trafficking in Persons* (2014) investigated convictions in 128 countries and found that between 2010 and 2012, 40% had fewer than 10 convictions and 15% reported no convictions (United Nations Office on Drugs and Crime [UNODC], 2014). Similarly, the *Trafficking in Persons Report* (2015) reported 10,051 prosecutions and 4,443 convictions worldwide (U.S. Department of State, 2015). However, the worldwide prosecutions have been trending up, while conviction rates have stayed relatively stable over the last seven years. Governments are prosecuting at nearly twice the rate; worldwide, 5,682 and 10,051 prosecutions were tallied in 2007 and 2014, respectively. Nevertheless, the counts for convictions are not impressive: 3,427 and 4,443 convictions in 2007 and 2014, respectively (U.S. Department of State, 2015). After a quick comparison of the estimated prevalence worldwide of trafficked people (27 million), Chuang (2014) explains, "If one accepts, as the U.S. TIP Reports suggest, prosecution and conviction rates as the most important signifiers of success, then today's global anti-trafficking movement has been a failure" (p. 642). While it appears to be difficult to achieve positive verdicts, investigative and accountability efforts have increased worldwide.

5.6 Strategies for Filling the Gaps

We have little empirical data available about federal or state prosecutions of human trafficking in the United States. Although the Office of Research and Evaluation is exploring efforts that will likely inform the prosecutorial processes, what we know is that State and local prosecutors have made steady but slow progress because they have fewer resources than federal prosecutors. Clawson, Lyne & Small (2006) also cite the lack of accountability for traffickers as another concern. Research from Europe, Australia, and North America indicates a clear need to develop collaborations among law enforcement entities, from the federal to local level (David, 2008; Reichel, 2008). Law enforcement agents and service providers in the United States have cited the need for creating and improving mechanisms for such collaborative efforts (Busch-Armendariz et al., 2008). In the United States, federally funded task forces have a positive impact on the delivery of services to victims (Busch-Armendariz et al., 2008), yet identification, investigation, and prosecution remain complex undertakings (Farrell, McDevitt, & Fahy, 2008). Despite recent increases in the identification and prosecution of traffickers (Busch-Armendariz, Nsonwu, Cook Heffron, & Mahapatra, 2013), the numbers for each remain dismally low in relationship to the extent of the crime.

Several explanations for low investigation and prosecution rates have been cited: a) lack of precedence and case law; b) victim reluctance to testify; c) lack of institutional infrastructure; and d) lack of training for detectives to investigate and prosecutors to litigate human trafficking cases (Farrell et al., 2008). On the other hand, law enforcement and prosecutors should also work to develop effective strategies to engage traumatized victims moving through the criminal justice system (Frazier & Haney, 1996; Patterson & Campbell, 2010).

The TVPA set forth the three pillars (referred to as the three Ps) of antitrafficking work that included prevention, prosecution of traffickers, and protection of victims. A decade later, partnership was added as a fourth pillar (Busch-Armendariz, Nsonwu, Cook Heffron, & Mahapatra, 2014; Busch-Armendariz, Nsonwu, Heffron, & Mahapatra, 2012). Although the antitrafficking efforts were working toward the same end, pragmatically, prevention, prosecution, and protection were not well synced. Schwarz and Britton (2015) assert that one "cannot separate protection from prevention, given the cyclical nature of vulnerability among populations" of victims (p. 64).

As an example of local efforts, Busch-Armendariz et al. (2008) conducted a statewide analysis in Texas that considered 11 state statutes (Alcoholic Beverage, Business and Commerce, Civil Practices and Remedies, Criminal Procedure, Family, Government, Health and Safety, Human Resources, Labor, Occupations, and Penal) that might be used to address antitrafficking accessibility and utility. Specifically, two factors were used to evaluate current laws: services for victims and remedies for prosecution of traffickers. The project goal was to understand the current statutes and guide future legislation toward strengthening services while being more stringent in accountability of traffickers. As a mezzo-level analysis, these efforts were useful to change course.

The 4-Ps framework has lost much of its influence as a guide to our understanding and efforts. A focus on addressing the root causes of human trafficking and efforts that discourse about the strategies used by traffickers, industries at high risk for exploitation, goals to reduce demand, and victim-centered and victim-driven services are replacing local and national conversations about the 4-Ps framework. Efforts to strengthen the criminal justice system are important, and yet many abolitionists advocate that our success will be built on creating *trafficking-resistant* societies that are locally and transnationally focused, that systematically address root causes, and that fully integrate prevention and intervention efforts.

Figure 6.4 *Human trafficking power and control wheel.*

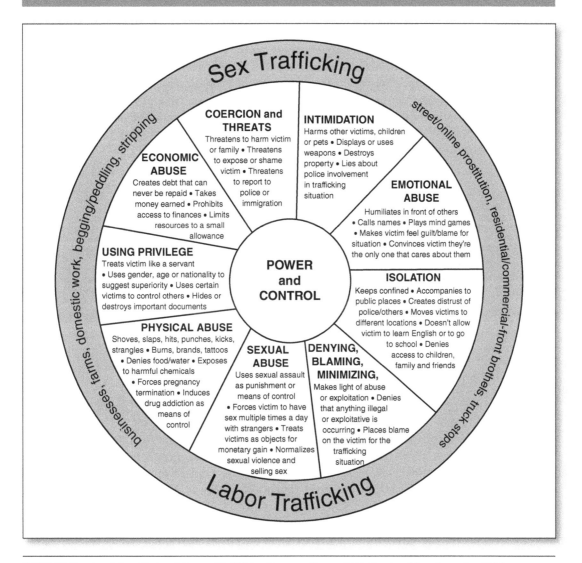

SOURCE: Reprinted from National Human Trafficking Resource Center, 2010. Retrieved from https://traffickingresource-center.org/resources/human-trafficking-power-and-control-wheel Copyright 2010 by Polaris. Reprinted with permission.

5.7 Understanding Mezzo-Level Causes of Human Trafficking

After many years of advocacy, the violence against women's movement shifted culture to describe victims in nonjudgmental and nonvictim-blaming ways and saw a recent surge for the adoption of victim-centered approaches. Busch-Armendariz et al. (2014) proposed that the antitrafficking movement learn from the practical lessons and effective methodological strategies of the long-established domestic violence and sexual assault movements with the goal to improve awareness about human trafficking. To their credit, early antitrafficking efforts acknowledged that the needs of human trafficking victims were best met utilizing an interdisciplinary approach. In the review of programs for human trafficking victims, Ferguson et al. (2009) urged that the most effective programs acknowledge and understand "differences among professions in their codes of ethics, roles, legal responsibilities, and proximity to victims and perpetrators [that] can complicate collaborative efforts" (p. 571).

Teaching Human Rights

East Asia and Pacific

http://teachinghumanrights.org/content/humantraffickingorg
The goal of this platform is to provide the opportunity for government and non-government stakeholders in East Asia and the Pacific to collaborate and learn from each other on the topic of human trafficking.

5.8 Root Causes of Human Trafficking

From a prevention perspective, it is essential to examine "push and pull factors" that result in the existence of modern slavery. The underlying premise is a deep understanding of the complex decision making and factors that victims confront. This knowledge allows antitrafficking advocates and practitioners new insight into how to protect victims from being sent "back to those intolerable conditions, and indeed expose them to further trafficking" (Hoyle, Bosworth, & Dempsey, 2011, p. 327; Hoyle, Bosworth, & Dempsey, 2012).

Economic vulnerabilities place individuals at risk for exploitation by traffickers. However, as information garnered from survivors of sex trafficking in the United States demonstrates, not all victims of human trafficking are trafficked across international borders (Polaris, 2015). Jac-Kucharski (2012) proposes that although poverty, economic disparity, and political unrest may influence human trafficking in terms of vulnerabilities from which to exploit potential victims, other factors such as logistics/geographic proximity, corruption in both source and destination countries, and organizational structure of the criminal networks are perhaps more important factors to understand since these factors influence the cost-benefit analysis of traffickers.

Kristof and WuDunn (2009), in their book *Half the Sky*, address the prevalence of violence against women around the world and its intersection with human trafficking.

They contend, "It's hard not to see something more sinister than just libido and prurient opportunism. Namely: sexism and misogyny" (p. 67) and argue that the key to ending violence against women and girls (and human trafficking of women and girls, in particular) is a brave conversation and culture shift about the worth and value of women. Kristof and WuDunn specifically advocate for increased access to education for all girls and women globally. More to the point, as discussed earlier, "we sometimes think that Westerners invest too much effort in changing unjust laws and not enough in changing culture . . . laws matter but typically the law by itself accomplishes little" (Kristof & WuDunn, 2009, p. 66).

5.9 Understanding Mezzo-Level System Responses

In this research we wrote, "Although the legislative response over the past 12 years to address human trafficking in persons has been impressive, the literature about the needs of survivors of human trafficking and the efficacy and effectiveness of services to meet those needs is relatively scarce. Current focus should be to develop and expand effective prevention strategies and responsive short- and long-term health, legal, and social services for survivors" (Busch-Armendariz et al. 2014, p. 10).

5.10 Considerations and Current Controversies About Social and Legal Services

As discussed earlier, micro-level interventions include addressing the needs of human trafficking victims through a single point-of-contact social work perspective grounded in survivor-centered, trauma-informed practice that empowers victims toward healing and recovery. Busch-Armendariz et al. (2014) suggest that the interventions with individuals and families are also grounded in mezzo strategies and viewed in an ecological perspective that includes advocacy, interdisciplinary coordination, and cross-cultural and disciplinary competency.

Anecdotal evidence points to an upsurge of interest in providing direct services to survivors of domestic minor sex trafficking and a proliferation of small-scale shelters organized by faith-based groups. According to one report (Cooper, 2010), "All over North America, faith-based organizations similar to Eagles Wing [a Christian ministry to women], are rising up" (p. 19) to address human trafficking. Kim Kern, one of the organizers, stated, "Maybe it's not [God's] plan that the government do more; maybe it's his plan that his church do more. When the government gets involved, you can't talk about Jesus" (Cooper, 2010, p. 19).

In the United States, government, social services, and communities have long relied on faith-based and religious organizations to meet immediate and critical human needs (Mink, 2001). Nonetheless, questions and criticisms have focused on the readiness of both untrained professionals and well-meaning nonprofessionals to meet the complex needs of traumatized populations such as DMST survivors (Wachter et al., 2016; Zimmerman, 2010, 2011).

In addition, the proliferation of state agencies and private organizations serving human trafficking victims requires the establishment of minimal standards and the understanding of what works and what does not work to assist survivors in their recovery and healing (Wachter et al., 2016). Our lack of understanding about program effectiveness increases the possibility that victims receive services from ineffective, perhaps even harmful, programs and that limited resources will be squandered. Organizational self-reflection and standard setting will ultimately inform the development and evaluation of programs with the end goal to improve services to survivors (Wachter et al., 2016).

Two other unresolved issues have emerged in the field: the inclusion of formerly trafficked survivors as mentors and organizational leaders and the need for residential shelter beds versus the effectiveness of community-based services (Wachter et al., 2016). The subject of peer mentoring was a contentious issue, with some organizations inviting formerly trafficked survivors to serve as mentors, peer counselors, and leaders within the organizations, while others rejected such practices. Untrained, religiously affiliated staff working in the field also fuels the debate about best practices. These debates are not new; the same conversations emerged within grassroots organizations serving sexual assault and domestic violence survivors during the second wave of the women's movement. The historical trend has moved toward professionalizing survivors through credentialing, licensing, and formal education (Wies, 2008). It will be interesting over the next 10 years to observe the conclusions of the antitrafficking field on these issues.

A case study of one residential treatment program for sexually exploited adolescent girls reported:

> From our experience, a combination of contact with staff such as clinicians, administrators, and milieu counselors who are nurturing but maintain professional boundaries, with survivor mentors who share their own personal stories, has been an effective way to both engage youth in treatment and provide necessary continuing support after graduation. (Thomson, Hirshberg, Corbett, Valila, & Howley, 2011, p. 2295)

Safe shelter and meeting basic needs are essential to assist domestic minor victims of sex trafficking (Busch-Armendariz et al., 2014a; Clawson & Goldblatt Grace, 2007). However, shelter services compared to nonresidential programs are resource intensive and require well-trained, competent staff to safely operate the program. Understanding the extent to which nonresidential interventions (programs and services) are successful and cost-effective, vis-à-vis residential programs, is needed.

5.11 Strategies by Law Enforcement

Across the globe, citizens "understand more about modern slavery because of antitrafficking legislation and policy, the rescue of survivors, and the prosecution of traffickers" (Busch-Armendariz et. al., 2014, p. 9). Law enforcement and other criminal justice efforts have been a large part of the increased awareness. Yet standardized measures that accurately estimate the prevalence, rates, and descriptive specificity of victimization remain relatively elusive. The elusiveness is due in part to barriers faced by law enforcement regarding identification, investigation, and prosecution of these crimes and a broad understanding that this crime is not static. Mezzo-level criminal justice strategies that promote and hinder the understanding of human trafficking can effectively guide future policies, laws, and programs about human trafficking.

Law enforcement responses to human trafficking are varied and complex. Challenges to a criminal justice response are related to perceptions about human trafficking prevalence, investigation, prosecution, and (lack of) collaboration. Research indicates that many U.S. law enforcement professionals have previously perceived human trafficking as rare or nonexistent (Farrell et al., 2008). A United States Department of Justice, National Institute of Justice–sponsored study found that 32% of trafficking cases were discovered as a result of the investigation of cases other than human trafficking (Clawson et al., 2006), highlighting the need for broadly trained law enforcement. Law enforcement officials themselves have called for more training, knowing that well-crafted investigations are central to successful prosecution (H. Clawson et al., 2006). However, it is known that human trafficking investigations are time- and resource-intensive for law enforcement (David, 2008), and specific techniques and resources for investigating human trafficking cases, including dedicated agents and new technology (Busch-Armendariz et al., 2012; Busch-Armendariz et al., 2014a; Clawson et al., 2006), are needed.

Law enforcement task forces have provided important criminal justice insights, and progress has been made with the implementation of these multidisciplinary task forces. The U.S. Department of Justice, Office of Justice Programs, Bureau of Justice Statistics (2008–2010) tracks human trafficking incidents by federally funded law enforcement human trafficking task forces. Banks and Kyckelhahn (2011) found that 80% were suspected sex trafficking cases, 10% were labor trafficking cases, and 10% were identified as other or unknown forms of trafficking. In total, 2,515 incidents were investigated; 389 cases were confirmed as human trafficking, with 488 suspects and 527 victims identified. Of the sex trafficking victims, 83% were U.S. citizens. Of confirmed cases open for one year, 30% were later confirmed to be human trafficking, 38% were confirmed not to be human trafficking, and the remaining were still under investigation; 144 arrests were made. Of the cases that were open and confirmed as human trafficking, "64% involved allegations of prostitution or sexual exploitation of a child, and 42% involved allegation of adult prostitution. Most cases that were not confirmed as human trafficking involved allegation of adult prostitution" (Banks & Kyckelhahn, 2011, p. 8).

Law enforcement has benefited by further understanding the cunningness of traffickers' strategies to lure and deceive victims. In cases of sexual exploitation there is ample practice wisdom (Lloyd, 2011) and research evidence (Busch-Armendariz, et al., 2009) to suggest that traffickers or pimps control their victims by building a relationship with them, often an intimate relationship, that involves 'trust, love, and attention'

(Lloyd, 2011). There is also ample evidence suggesting that traffickers lure foreign nationals by promising them work, legitimate opportunities, and better wages when they reach their destination (Busch-Armendariz, 2012).

Busch-Armendariz (2012) reports that

> traffickers maintain control by using physical and sexual violence, isolation, entrapment, drug addiction, psychological and emotional abuse, and treats to other family members' well being; as well as exploiting victims' lack of knowledge of the legal process, their rights, or available services. Psychological coercion cannot be understated; many victims have endured years of enslavement because traffickers use fear and threats of retaliation against them and their family members (minor children and parents, etc.) if they attempt to escape. (p. 9)

Chapter 5 provides additional information on traffickers and typologies of traffickers.

5.12 Demand Reduction

Until now, antitrafficking efforts have mostly focused on intervening with traffickers and johns and providing support services to victims. Demand-reduction programs are gaining traction, and law enforcement agencies may be involved in demand-reduction programs aimed at preventing human trafficking crimes. As a primary prevention initiative, demand-reduction programs seek to eliminate the demand for sex services. Shively et al. (2008) suggest that primary prevention is an area that has been neglected efforts and few formal evaluations about the effectiveness of demand-reduction programs have been conducted, although there is some evidence that these programs are effective.

Demand-reduction programs are typically public awareness and educational programs directed toward men and boys. While the focus is to educate men about prostitution and sex trafficking, the real aim is to dissuade men and boys from contributing to sexual exploitation and perhaps the sex industry by refraining from purchasing sex. Areas of high incidents of prostitution have led to neighborhood and community action that includes providing tips to police, citizen patrols, citizen-led blogs, billboard campaigns, and community members participating in community-impact panels and/or giving presentations in john schools (Shively et al., 2012, p. 23). For a review of demand reduction efforts, see the Shively, Kliorys, Wheeler, and Hunt (2012) report *A National Overview of Prostitution and Sex Trafficking Demand Reduction Efforts*, Washington, DC: The National Institute of Justice.

5.13 john Schools

Law enforcement is also highly involved in or administers the small number of operating john schools around the United States. "'john school' is a generic term that is used to describe a wide range of programs that involve an education or treatment component" (Shively et al., 2012, p. 61). john schools are deferred-adjudication programs typically designed for first-time offenders who are arrested for solicitation of a prostituted person. Although the programs operate somewhat differently, the general structure includes first-time offenders paying a fee to attend an educational program in order to have their arrest records dismissed (Busch, Bell, Hotaling, & Monto, 2002). Accountability for customers, or johns, are typically structured as a sentencing option (coupled with other criminal sanctions) or as diversion programs that result in dismissed charges for johns (Shively, et al., 2012). The curriculum often includes content on health consequences of sex with a prostituted person, the impact of prostitution on prostituted people and communities through survivor testimony, victimization risks and other negative outcomes for johns, and legal consequences for hiring a prostituted person (Shively et al., 2012).

The longest-standing john school in the United States is operated by SAGE, a nonprofit organization founded by Norma Hotaling, a self-identified former street prostitute and drug addict. The SAGE program located in San Francisco has been evaluated and has shown promise as an intervention program for prostitution. The recidivism among johns who attended the one-day educational program was reduced by 40%, and after one year of the john school implementation, the recidivism rate for arrested johns dropped to 4.5% (from 8.8%) (Shively et al., 2008). This reduction was sustained over the next 10 years.

5.14 Reverse Stings

Law enforcement is also involved in reverse sting operations, with the aim to reduce prostitution. Reverse stings involve female police officers posing as prostitutes and targeting johns for arrest. In Jersey City, New Jersey, reverse sting efforts contributed to the reduction of prostitution by 75%. There are several venues and types of reverse stings including street-level, web-based, and brothel-based.

In particular, johns fuel the demand for sex with exploited adults and children (Shively et al., 2012). Although the hypothesis has not been empirically supported, law enforcement and practitioners opine that sporting events, entertainment and festivals, "conventions, and business meetings that bring large numbers of people together may increase the likelihood of the demand for sex services and provide opportunities for minor victims to be exploited" (Busch-Armendariz et al., 2014, p. 10).

Myths vs. Realities

MYTH: Prostitution Is Exclusively the Exchange of Money for Sex
REALITY: The majority of men exchanged something other than money for sex, such as drugs, shelter, food, clothes, or transportation.

MYTH: Men Do Not Feel Guilty About Purchasing Sex

REALITY: A majority of men expressed strongly conflicted feelings about their purchase of sex. Some men acknowledged the possibility that their purchase of a woman in prostitution might trigger her memories of childhood abuse. Other men dissociated during the sex act in order to avoid their feelings of guilt and shame.

MYTH: Men Who Buy Sex Are Unaware of the Harm Experienced by Women in the Sex Trade

REALITY: Most men who buy sex acknowledge that women in prostitution experience high levels of abuse, health issues, homelessness, and rape.

MYTH: Men Purchase Sex Because They Do Not Have Access to a Regular Sex Partner

REALITY: The majority of men who buy sex have a regular sex partner such as a girlfriend or a wife.

MYTH: Prostitution Decreases Rape

REALITY: Men who use women in prostitution frequently justify rape of women both in and out of the sex trade.

MYTH: There Is No Link Between Prostitution and Pornography

REALITY: For many men who buy sex, there is no difference between pornography and prostitution. Men purchased women in prostitution as a way to engage in specific sex acts they had seen in pornography. Pornography consumption influences men who buy sex to view women as objects and not individuals.

MYTH: Prostitution Will Never Disappear

REALITY: A significant number of men who buy sex believe that women would not be in the sex trade if they had greater economic opportunities and did not experience childhood sexual abuse.

MYTH: Men Who Buy Sex Think That It Is Appropriate to Purchase Sex at Any Age

REALITY: A majority of men who buy sex think that it is not appropriate for minors to do so. Stated reasons included that it is emotionally unfulfilling and that once someone buys sex they will never view women the same way again.

SOURCE: *Deconstructing the demand for prostitution: Preliminary insights from interviews with Chicago men who purchase sex* (p. 30) by R. Durchslag and S. Goswami, 2008, Chicago, IL: Chicago Alliance Against Sexual Exploitation. Copyright 2008 by Chicago Alliance Against Sexual Exploitation. Reprinted with permission.

5.15 Prostitution Courts

In recognition that many sex workers are victims of trafficking, some new prostitution diversion courts have emerged:

Several cities and counties have established *prostitution courts* that offer diversion or sentencing options for survivors that parallel those offered to male buyers through john school programs (e.g., Dallas, TX; Hartford, CT; Phoenix, AZ). Such programs can provide gender and role balance to the penalties and opportunities within a city that are provided to those selling and buying sex. (Shively et al., 2012, p. xvi)

5.16 Understanding Sociopolitical Responses

It is important to consider sociopolitical responses in the anti–human trafficking field. We cover the issues of legal and policy responses extensively in other chapters including Palermo Protocol, TVPA, T visas, and other country and organizational responses to this crime. Challenges are tied up in ideological perspectives and the will, or lack thereof, to end human trafficking. To this point, Kristof and WuDunn (2009) opine that at the heart of the sociopolitical stagnation is reckoning that sex trafficking is tied up in the "politics of prostitution . . . while the left and right each do important work fighting trafficking, they mostly do it separately. The abolitionist movement would be far more effective if it forged unity in its own ranks" (p. 25). They continue, "The tools to crush modern slavery exits, but the political will is lacking" (p. 24).

5.17 Responding by Building Knowledge Through Research and Practicing Wisdom

Millions of new, redirected, or reoccurring state, federal, and private dollars have become available to develop programs and services for victims and apprehend traffickers, facilitators, and buyers. Resources have also been directed to increase consumer awareness and provide tools to purchase slave-free products, and research funding to improve our understanding of the problem and evaluate solutions has increased exponentially.

More research is needed to fully understand the impact of victimization and exploitation in the short- and long-term. Understanding survivors' immediate needs, such as safety, basic needs, and establishing equilibrium in their lives through competent and holistic trauma-informed crisis management, has been established (U.S. Department of State, 2014; Busch-Armendariz et al., 2011; Faulkner, Mahapatra, Cook Heffron, Nsonwu, & Busch-Armendariz, 2013). Long-term services such as employment and family reunification are also relatively well understood. However, little is known about how to successfully lessen vulnerabilities, and little is known about how to lessen the risks of victimization either once a survivor has been identified or perhaps even before a person has become victimized. Even less has been written about how to successfully interrupt the supply networks of human traffickers. For additional information on victim vulnerabilities and risk factors as well as strengths-based and trauma informed approaches, please see Chapter 5.

Many nongovernmental organizations have emerged to address various aspects of human trafficking. Some of the most noteworthy are Walk Free, Free the Slaves,

Shared Hope International, Made in a Free World, and GEMS, just to name a few. Existing organizations have expanded their services or missions to include working with survivors or developing research agendas on human trafficking. As stated in an earlier chapter, domestic violence and sexual assault organizations, refugee resettlement, services for the homeless youth, and child welfare agencies are examples. Research organizations such as the International Labour Organization; the University of Texas at Austin, Institute on Domestic Violence & Sexual Assault; the Center on Violence Against Women at Rutgers University; and others are building empirical knowledge on human trafficking. Through these collective efforts, our understanding of human trafficking, its impact on victims and society, and strategies to eradicate it are bringing us ever closer to its end.

6. Chapter Summary

Mezzo-level interventions, ones that consider organization, program develop, and system changes, are important to address human trafficking. This chapter discusses root causes and push-pull factors as mezzo-level constructs. Programs in the criminal justice system such as demand reduction, john schools, and reverse stings are not new initiatives but have been applied to antitrafficking efforts.

7. Key Terms

7.1	johns	7.6	Value-laden
7.2	Demand reduction	7.7	Eco-systems perspective
7.3	Traffickers	7.8	Mezzosystem
7.4	Facilitators	7.9	Compassion fatigue, vicarious trauma, and secondary trauma
7.5	Four pillars of antitrafficking movement		

8. Active Learning Exercises or In-Class Discussion Questions

8.1   Show the film *Dying to Leave.*

Divide students into small groups and ask them to answer the questions below. Once you have separated students into groups, assign each group one case highlighted in the film. How does movement or traffic play into modern-day slavery? Do all these cases meet the definition of human trafficking? How or why or why not? Give specific criteria including the perspective that the group has taken (social worker or human service professional, law enforcement, border patrol agent, immigration attorney, etc.). Discuss and give examples, if appropriate, of force, fraud, or coercion. Discuss what these victims needed or need for services (immediate and long term). Have groups report back about their discussion for a larger class discussion. What are the push-pull factors?

8.2   Show *Now on PBS: Fighting Child Prostitution with David Brancaccio*. Ask students to consider and tease out the mezzo level initiatives that are being implemented in Atlanta, Georgia. How did the development of these address the vulnerabilities of domestic minors of sex trafficking? What should we know about their effectiveness or replicability? What are the shortcomings or limitations? Have the class discuss or take notes about what is out of date about this documentary?

9. Suggestions for Further Learning

9.1   **Books**

    9.1.1   *Pimpology: The 48 Laws of the Game* by Pimpin' Ken with Karen Hunter

9.2   **Websites**

    9.2.1   International Labour Organization

    9.2.2   Walk Free

    9.2.3   Shared Hope International

    9.2.4   Made in a Free World

    9.2.5   GEMS

    9.2.6   Free the Slaves

9.3   **Films**

    9.3.1   *Dying to Leave*

    9.3.2   *NOW on PBS*: "Fighting Child Prostitution" with David Brancaccio

10. Suggestions for Further Research or Projects/Homework/Exams

10.1 Fish Bowl and Book Club

Purpose

This assignment engages students in course readings, provides them an opportunity to practice small group work and presentation skills, and requires them to critically examine the salient points of a reading.

Introduction

Students work in small groups to take a collective deep dive into a popular press book (see examples below). Students will organize a book discussion and make a class presentation using a "fish bowl" experience.

Book Selection

Assign the popular press book randomly to small groups. As examples:

1. Kristof, N., and WuDunn, S. (2010). *Half the sky*. Knopf Doubleday Publishing Group: New York, NY.

2. Lloyd, R. (2011). *Girls like us: Fighting for a world where girls are not for sale, an activist finds her calling and heals herself.* Harper Collins: New York, NY.

3. Ken, P., & Hunter, K. (2008). *Pimpology: The 48 laws of the game*. Simon Spotlight Entertainment: New York, NY.

Fish Bowl (15 minutes)

Students should use a fish bowl technique to simulate a book club and present their assigned book to the class. A fish bowl teaching technique consists of two groups; one active inner group and one outer observing group. For this assignment, some members of the inner group will use the fish bowl as a role play/book club discussion and teach about the salient points of their book to the observing group of the fish bowl. In a fish bowl, the observing groups are all students not assigned to the book being presented. These students will be looking in and observing (like a fish bowl). There are many ways to develop the fish bowl to "teach."

There are several parts to this assignment:

1. Research the fish bowl technique.

2. Model the fish bowl in class using the contents of the assigned book (i.e., think about a series of questions that you will engage in as a book club might during the fish bowl).

3. Engage your classmates (those in the outer circle observing) in the discussion after the fish bowl experience in a meaningful discussion about the contents of the book (i.e., think about a series of questions that you will engage your peers in for the large discussion to continue to connect ideas, thoughts, learning, etc.).

Fish bowl experience	approximately 15–20 minutes
Large group discussion	approximately 20 minutes
Total group exercise	40 minutes (strictly timed by the group and instructor)

Evaluation

The evaluation should consist of two peer evaluations and an instructor evaluation. Each group member should evaluate themselves and each other on their contributions to the assignment. At the end of each fish bowl demonstration, the observing members should evaluate their peers on their ability to teach the book content and engage them in a discussion. Encourage creativity.

11. References

Administration for Children and Families. (2012). *Rescue and restore victims of human trafficking campaign social service poster* [Online image]. Retrieved from http://www.acf.hhs.gov/ orr/resource/download-campaign-posters-and-brochures

Alpert, J. L., & Paulson, A. (1990). Graduate-level education and training in child sexual abuse. *Professional Psychology: Research and Practice, 21*(5), 366–371. doi:10.1037/0735–7028.21.5.366

Banks, D., & Kyckelhahn, T. (2011). *Characteristics of suspected human trafficking incidents, 2008–2010.* (NCJ 233732). Washington, DC: U.S. Department of Justice, Office of Justice Programs, Bureau of Justice Statistics. Retrieved from http://www.bjs.gov/content/pub/pdf/ cshti0810.pdf

Bronfenbrenner, U. (1979). *The ecology of human development: Experiments by design and nature.* Cambridge, MA: Harvard University Press.

Busch, N. B., Bell, H., Hotaling, N., Monto, M. A. (2002). Male customers of prostituted women exploring perceptions of entitlement to power and control and implications for violent behavior toward women. *Violence Against Women, 8*(9), 1093–1112.

Busch-Armendariz, N. B., Heffron, L. C., Kalergis, K., Mahapatra, N., Faulkner, M., Voyles, L., Eaton, S. (2008). *Human trafficking in Texas: A statewide evaluation of existing laws and social services.* Austin, TX: the University of Texas. Retrieved from http://sites.utexas.edu/ idvsa/publications/technical-reports/

Busch-Armendariz, N., Nsonwu, M., Heffron, L. C., Garza, J., & Hernandez, M. (2009). *Understanding human trafficking: Development of typologies of traffickers.* Retrieved from Austin, Texas: http://digitalcommons.unl.edu/cgi/viewcontent.cgi?article=1008&context= humtraffconf

Busch-Armendariz, N., Nsonwu, M. B., & Cook Heffron, L. (2011). Human trafficking victims and their children: Assessing needs, vulnerabilities, strengths, and survivorship. *Journal of Applied Research on Children: Informing Policy for Children at Risk, 2*(1), 3. Retrieved from http://digitalcommons.library.tmc.edu/childrenatrisk/vol2/iss1/3/

Busch-Armendariz, N., Nsonwu, M. B., Heffron, L. C., & Mahapatra, N. (2012). Trafficking in persons. In J. Postmus (Ed.), *Encyclopedia of sexual violence and abuse.* Santa Barbara, CA: ABC-CLIO.

Busch-Armendariz, N., Nsonwu, M., Cook Heffron, L., & Mahapatra, N. (2013). Trafficking in persons. In J. L. Postmus (Ed.), *Sexual violence and abuse: An encyclopedia of prevention, impacts, and recovery.* Santa Barbara, CA: ABC-CLIO.

Busch-Armendariz, N., Nsonwu, M., Cook Heffron, L., & Mahapatra, N. (2014). Human trafficking: Exploiting labor. In C. Franklin (Ed.), *Encyclopedia of social work online.* New York, NY: Oxford University Press.

Busch-Armendariz, N., Nsonwu, M. B., & Cook Heffron, L. (2014). A kaleidoscope: The role of the social work practitioner and the strength of social work theories and practice in meeting the complex needs of people trafficked and the professionals that work with them. *International Social Work, 57*(1), 7–18. doi:10.1177/0020872813505630

Carling, J., Menjívar, C., & Schmalzbauer, L. (2012). Central themes in the study of transnational parenthood. *Journal of Ethnic and Migration Studies, 38*(2), 191–217. doi:10.1080/13691 83X.2012.646417

Chuang, J. A. (2014). Exploitation creep and the unmaking of human trafficking law. *American Society of International Law, 108*(4), 609–649. Retrieved from http://www.jstor.org/stable/10.5305/amerjintelaw.108.4.0609

Clawson, H., Layne, M., & Small, K. (2006). *Estimating human trafficking into the States: Development of a methodology.* Washington, DC: National Institute of Justice. Retrieved from https://www.ncjrs.gov/pdffiles1/nij/grants/215475.pdf

Clawson, H. J., & Goldblatt Grace, L. (2007). Finding a path to recovery: Residential facilities for minor victims of domestic sex trafficking. *Human trafficking: Data and documents,* 10. Retrieved from https://aspe.hhs.gov/basic-report/finding-path-recovery-residential-facilities-minor-victims-domestic-sex-trafficking

Cook Heffron, L., Snyder, S., Wachter, K., Nsonwu, M., & Busch-Armendariz, N. (2016). Something is missing here: Weaving feminist theories into social work practice with refugees. In S. Wendt & N. Moulding (Eds.), *Contemporary feminisms in social work practice.* New York, NY: Routledge.

Cooper, E. (2010). Sexual slavery on Main Street: Trafficking of teenagers in the U.S. is getting worse. Here's what some Christians are trying to do about it. *Christianity Today, 54*(5), 17–19.

Crothers, D. (1995). Vicarious traumatization in the work with survivors of childhood trauma. *Journal of Psychosocial Nursing & Mental Health Services, 33*(4), 9–13. doi:10.3928/0279–3695–19950401–04

David, F. (2008). *Trafficking of women for sexual purposes.* Canberra, ACT: Research and Public Policy Series. Retrieved from http://www.aic.gov.au/media_library/publications/rpp/95/rpp095.pdf

Durchslag, R., & Goswami, S. (2008). *Deconstructing the demand for prostitution: Preliminary insights from interviews with Chicago men who purchase sex* (p. 30). Chicago, IL: Chicago Alliance Against Sexual Exploitation.

Fallows, J. (2015, August 29). John Boyd in the News: All You Need to Know About the OODA Loop. *The Atlantic.* Retrieved from https://www.theatlantic.com/notes/2015/08/john-boyd-in-the-news-all-you-need-to-know-about-ooda-loop/402847/.

Farrell, A., McDevitt, J., & Fahy, S. (2008). *Understanding and improving law enforcement responses to human trafficking: Final report.* Washington, DC: National Institute of Justice. Retrieved from https://www.ncjrs.gov/pdffiles1/nij/grants/222752.pdf

Faulkner, M., Mahapatra, N., Cook Heffron, L., Nsonwu, M. B., & Busch-Armendariz, N. (2013). Moving past victimization and trauma toward restoration: Mother survivors of sex trafficking share their inspiration. *International Perspectives in Victimology, 7*(2), 46–55.

Ferguson, K. M., Soydan, H., Lee, S.-Y., Yamanaka, A., Freer, A. S., & Xie, B. (2009). Evaluation of the CSEC community intervention project (CCIP) in five U.S. cities. *Evaluation Review, 33*(6), 568–597. doi:10.1177/0193841x09346132

Figley, C. R. (1989). *Helping traumatized families* (1st ed.). San Francisco, CA: Jossey-Bass.

Figley, C. R. (1995). *Compassion fatigue: Coping with secondary traumatic stress disorder in those who treat the traumatized.* New York, NY: Brunner/Mazel.

Frazier, P. A., & Haney, B. (1996). Sexual assault cases in the legal system: Police, prosecutor, and victim perspectives. *Law and Human Behavior, 20*(6), 607–628.

Furman, R., Negi, N., Schatz, M. C. S., & Jones, S. (2008). Transnational social work: Using a wraparound model. *Global Networks, 8*(4), 496–503. doi:10.1111/j.1471-0374.2008.00236.x

Hollingsworth, M. A. (1993). *Responses of female therapists to treating adult female survivors of incest.* WorldCat.org database.

Hoyle, M. M., Bosworth, C., & Dempsey M. (2011). Labelling the victims of sex trafficking: Exploring the borderland between rhetoric and reality. *Social & Legal Studies, 20,* 313–329.

Hoyle, M. M., Bosworth, C., & Dempsey M. (2012). Defining sex trafficking in international and domestic law: Mind the gaps. *Emory International Law Review, 26,* 137–162.

Jac-Kucharski, A. (2012). The determinants of human trafficking: A U.S. case study. *International Migration, 50*(6), 150–165. doi:10.1111/j.1468-2435.2012.00777.x

Joinson, C. (1992). Coping with compassion fatigue. *Nursing, 22*(4), 116–121. Retrieved from http://search.ebscohost.com/login.aspx?direct=true&db=rzh&AN=107487653&site=ehost-live

Kalergis, K. I. (2009). A passionate practice: Addressing the needs of commercially sexually exploited teenagers. *Affilia, 24*(3), 315–324. doi:10.1177/0886109909337706

Kotrla, K. (2010). Domestic minor sex trafficking in the United States. *Social Work, 55*(2), 181–187. doi:10.1093/sw/55.2.181

Kristof, N., & WuDunn, S. (2009). *Half the sky: Turning oppression into opportunity for women worldwide.* New York, NY: Random House.

Levitt, P., & Jaworsky, B. N. (2007). Transnational migration studies: Past developments and future trends. *Annual Review of Sociology, 33,* 129–156.

Lipsky, L. V. D., & Burk, C. (2009). *Trauma stewardship: An everyday guide to caring for self while caring for others.* San Francisco, CA: Berrett-Koehler.

Lloyd, R. (2011). *Girls like us: Fighting for a world where girls are not for sale, an activist finds her calling and heals herself* (1st ed.). New York, NY: HarperCollins.

Malakh-Pines, A., Aronson, E., & Malakh-Pines, A. (1988). *Career burnout: Causes and cures.* New York, NY: New York Free Press.

Mink, G. (2001). Faith in government? *Social Justice, 28*(1), 5–10.

Mitchell, K. J., Finkelhor, D., & Wolak, J. (2010). Conceptualizing juvenile prostitution as child maltreatment: Findings from the national juvenile prostitution study. *Child Maltreatment, 15*(1), 18–36. doi:10.1177/1077559509349443

Neal, J. W., & Neal, Z. P. (2013). Nested or networked? Future directions for ecological systems theory. *Social Development, 22*(4), 722–737.

Nsonwu, M. B., Casey, K., Cook, S. W., & Busch-Armendariz, N. (2013). Embodying social work as a profession: A pedagogy for practice. *SAGE Open, 3*(3).

Nsonwu, M. B., Welch-Brewer, C., Heffron, L. C., Lemke, M. A., Busch-Armendariz, N., Sulley, C., . . . Li, J. (2015). Development and validation of an instrument to assess social work students' perceptions, knowledge, and attitudes about human trafficking questionnaire (PKA-HTQ): An exploratory study. *Research on Social Work Practice.* doi:10.1177/1049731515578537

Office for Victims of Crime. (2014). *Know the faces of human trafficking poster gallery* [Online image]. Retrieved from http://ovc.ncjrs.gov/humantrafficking/Public_Awareness_Folder/images/final_poster_jeri.jpg

Office on Trafficking in Persons. (2013). 2013 accomplishments on combating trafficking in persons. Retrieved from http://www.acf.hhs.gov/programs/endtrafficking/accomplishments/2013

O'Halloran, M. S., & O'Halloran, T. (2001). Secondary traumatic stress in the classroom: Ameliorating stress in graduate students. *Teaching of Psychology, 28*(2), 92–97. Retrieved from http://search.ebscohost.com/login.aspx?direct=true&db=a9h&AN=4758399&site=ehost-live

Patterson, D., & Campbell, R. (2010). Why rape survivors participate in the criminal justice system. *Journal of Community Psychology, 38*(2), 191–205.

Pearlman, L. A., & Saakvitne, K. W. (1995). *Trauma and the therapist: Countertransference and vicarious traumatization in psychotherapy with incest survivors* (1st ed.). New York, NY: W. W. Norton.

Polaris. (2010). *Human trafficking power & control wheel* [Image]. Retrieved from https://traffickingresourcecenter.org/resources/human-trafficking-power-and-control-wheel

Polaris. (2015). *Sex trafficking in the U.S.: A closer look at U.S. citizen victims.* Retrieved from https://polarisproject.org/resources/sex-trafficking-us-closer-look-us-citizen-victims

Pryce, J., Shackelford, K., & Pryce, D. (2007). *Secondary traumatic stress and the child welfare professional.* Chicago, IL: Lyceum Books.

Rappaport, C. D. (2006). Breathlessness: Richard Cabot's 1908 conceptualization of social work burnout. *Social Welfare History Group, 99.*

Reichel, P. L. (2008). *Cross-national collaboration to combat human trafficking: Learning from the experience of others.* National Institute of Justice. Retrieved from https://www.ncjrs.gov/pdffiles1/nij/grants/223286.pdf

Reid, J. A. (2010). Doors wide shut: Barriers to the successful delivery of victim services for domestically trafficked minors in a southern U.S. metropolitan area. *Women & Criminal Justice, 20*(1/2), 147–166.

Roby, J. L. (2012, March). Human trafficking in the United States: A case study of national policy and impact on victims. *Social Dialogue, 2*, 22–31. Retrieved from http://social-dialogue.com

Salston, M. D., & Figley, C. R. (2003). Secondary traumatic stress effects of working with survivors of criminal victimization. *Journal of Traumatic Stress, 16*(2), 167–174. doi:10.1023/A:1022899207206

Schiller, N. G., Basch, L., & Blanc-Szanton, C. (1992). Towards a definition of transnationalism. Introductory remarks and research questions. *Annals of the New York Academy of Sciences, 645*(1), ix–xiv. doi:10.1111/j.1749-6632.1992.tb33482.x

Schwarz, C., & Britton, H. E. (2015). Queering the support for trafficked persons: LGBTQ communities and human trafficking in the heartland. *Social Inclusion, 3*(1), 63–75. doi:10.17645/si.v3i1.172

Sexton, L. (1999). Vicarious traumatisation of counsellors and effects on their workplaces. *British Journal of Guidance & Counselling, 27*(3), 393–403. Retrieved from http://www.volunteertoday.com/Katrina/SecondaryTrauma2.pdf

Shively, M., Kliorys, K., Wheeler, K., & Hunt, D. (2012). *A national overview of prostitution and sex trafficking demand reduction efforts.* Washington, DC: The National Institute of Justice. Retrieved from https://www.ncjrs.gov/pdffiles1/nij/grants/222451.pdf

Shively, M., Kuck Jalbert, S., Kling, R., Rhodes, W., Finn, P., Flygare, C., . . . Wheeler, K. (2008). *Final report on the evaluation of the first offender prostitution program.* Washington, DC: National Institute of Justice. Retrieved from https://www.ncjrs.gov/pdffiles1/nij/grants/222451.pdf

Soerens, M. J. (2015). Violence in the borderlands: A dialogical approach to intimate partner violence among migrant women. *Psychology & Society, 7*(1), 64–81.

Thomson, S., Hirshberg, D., Corbett, A., Valila, N., & Howley, D. (2011). Residential treatment for sexually exploited adolescent girls: Acknowledge, commit, transform (ACT). *Children and Youth Services Review, 33*(11), 2290–2296.

United Nations Office on Drugs and Crime. (2014). *Global report on trafficking in persons.* Retrieved from https://www.unodc.org/unodc/en/human-trafficking-fund.html

U.S. Department of State. (2014). *The president's interagency task force to monitor and combat trafficking in persons.* Retrieved from http://www.state.gov/j/tip/response/usg/

U.S. Department of State. (2015). *Trafficking in persons report.* Retrieved from http://www.state.gov/j/tip/rls/tiprpt/2015/

Wachter, K., Cook Heffron, L., Busch-Armendariz, N., Nsonwu, M. B., Kammer-Kerwick, M., Kellison, B., . . . Sanders, G. (2016). Responding to domestic minors sex trafficking (DMST): Developing principle-based practices. *Journal of Human Trafficking.* doi:10.1080/23322705.2016.1145489

Way, I., VanDeusen, K., & Cottrell, T. (2007). Vicarious trauma: Predictors of clinicians' disrupted cognitions about self-esteem and self-intimacy. *Journal of Child Sexual Abuse, 16*(4), 81–98. Retrieved from http://ncat.idm.oclc.org/login?url=http://search.ebscohost.com/login.aspx?direct=true&db=rzh&AN=105927795&site=ehost-live

Wies, J. (2008). Professionalizing human services: A case of domestic violence shelter advocates. *Human Organization, 67*(2), 221–233.

Wolfer, T. A., & Scales, T. L. (2006). Decision cases for advanced social work practice: thinking like a social worker. Belmont, CA: Thomson Brooks/Cole.

Zimmerman, Y. C. (2010). From Bush to Obama: Rethinking sex and religion in the United States' initiative to combat human trafficking. *Journal of Feminist Studies in Religion, 26*(1), 79–99. doi:10.2979/FSR.2010.26.1.79

Zimmerman, Y. C. (2011). Christianity and human trafficking. *Religion Compass, 5*(10), 567–578.

7

Understanding, Disruption, and Interventions at the Macro Level

National responses to this problem must be aligned with international human rights standards. I call on all States to adhere to the treaties that aim to stop human trafficking, especially the United Nations Protocol to Prevent, Suppress and Punish Trafficking in Persons, especially Women and Children.

—General Ban Ki Moon[1]
United Nations Secretary 2012

One thing is clear: No nation can end modern slavery alone. Eliminating this global scourge requires a global solution. It also cannot be solved by governments alone. The private sector, academic institutions, civil society, the legal community, and consumers can all help to address the factors that allow human trafficking to flourish. But governments have a special responsibility to enforce the rule of law, share information, invest in judicial resources, and espouse policies that urge respect for the rights and dignity of every human being. Human trafficking is not a problem to be managed; it is a crime to be stopped.

—U.S. Secretary of State John F. Kerry 2015[2]

[1] Secretary-General's remarks to General Assembly Interactive Dialogue "Fighting Human Trafficking: Partnership and Innovation to End Violence against Women" http://www.un.org/sg/STATEMENTS/index.asp?nid=5974

[2] Kerry, J. F. (2015). *Trafficking in Persons Report 2015*. U.S. Department of State. Retrieved from: http://www.state.gov/documents/organization/243557.pdf

1. Learning Objectives

1.1 Students will examine policy responses to human trafficking at the international level, in federal policy, and in state-level approaches.

1.2 Students will examine federal policies that seek to provide immigration remedies to undocumented trafficking survivors.

1.3 Students will be introduced to three types of prostitution-related policy efforts: complete criminalization, partial decriminalization, and legalization/regulation.

1.4 Students will explore a variety of feminist perspectives on commercial sex and human trafficking.

2. Key Ideas

The ideas central to this chapter are:

2.1 The international community has long recognized exploitation as a human rights violation, as evidenced by United Nations instruments such as the Universal Declaration of Human Rights and the Palermo Protocol (Protocol to Prevent, Suppress and Punish Trafficking in Persons, Especially Women and Children).

2.2 Federal U.S. policy first formally recognized the crime of human trafficking with the passage of the Trafficking Victims Protection Act (TVPA) in 2000 to address emerging international and national recognition of the trafficking of persons for labor or sex.

2.3 A variety of legal remedies are available for undocumented victims of human trafficking, violence, and abuse: continued presence, T visas, U visas, VAWA self-petition, battered spouse waiver, cancellation of removal, and asylum.

2.4 By 2013, all 50 states and the District of Columbia had enacted state laws and programming to address human trafficking.

3. Selected Theories/Frameworks: Feminism as a Range of Theoretical Approaches to Human Trafficking

Policy responses at all levels have been the focus of considerable controversy and debate among scholars and theorists alike. The uninformed and uneducated may simply misunderstand feminism to mean "woman." The range of feminist movements and thinkers is broad and fluid and reveals multiple approaches to transformative social and structural change toward equality and social justice. There is not a single feminist approach and, in particular, feminist approaches in the context of human trafficking will invite a much-needed, complex, ongoing discussion and dialog.

Despite differences, there remain concepts and spaces of solidarity across feminisms. First, an overarching goal of feminism is to challenge or disrupt inequalities and address gender-based and other oppressions. By doing so, the person becomes political as a fundamental principle of feminism. The phrases "the personal is political" or "the private is political" have been influential in feminism since the 1960s. While Carol Hanisch is often credited with originating the phrase, it pre-existed her 1969 essay titled "The Personal is Political" (Hanisch, 2006). That is, the personal, everyday lived experience of those who experience discrimination and oppression is tied to, and must be understood as tied to, a larger political experience of discrimination and oppression. Kimberle Crenshaw, for example, notes the "process of recognizing as social and systemic what was formerly perceived as isolated and individual" (Crenshaw, 1991, pp. 1241–1242) is important to questions of gender, in addition to race and other sites of oppression. While this concept highlights the structural, systematic nature of oppression, it also promotes the need for public dialogue and analysis of the political structures that perpetuate oppression.

Several additional concepts can inform the ways we think about policy and practice on the topic of human trafficking and exploitation (Cook Heffron, Snyder, Wachter, Nsonwu, & Busch-Armendariz, 2016). Complementing the concept of intersectionality described in Chapter 3, feminism supports the notion of *intersectional and fluid identities*. That is, the social identities of those who experience oppression are not simple, fixed, or static. Instead, identities and experiences are multifaceted and may collide and shift over time. Secondly, feminism *recognizes heterogeneity*, or complex diversity, within and across groups. That is, while human trafficking survivors may have similar experiences of exploitation that are related to wider oppressive structures, we cannot expect survivors to be uniformly impacted by human trafficking. Furthermore, feminism generally affirms *agency*. That is, despite experiencing human trafficking and more generally oppression, survivors are not passive victims. Chandra Mohanty helps us understand the dangers in viewing women, in particular, as agency-less: "Defining women as archetypal victims freezes them into 'objects-who-defend-themselves,' men into 'subjects-who-perpetrate-violence,' and (every) society into powerless (read: women) and powerful (read: men) groups of people" (2003, p. 24). Furthermore, she states that women are "agents who make choices, have a critical perspective on their own situations, and think and organize collectively against their oppressors" (Mohanty, 2003, p. 72). Finally, linked to the idea of agency and power, feminism upholds the value of sharing power and dismantling unequal power relationships. This idea can be clearly viewed as relevant to the power relationships between those who exploit others by perpetrating human trafficking crimes. It is also useful in considering the relationships and power dynamics between those who are trafficked and those whose aim is to help, support, or rescue trafficked persons.

Figure 7.1 *Domestic servitude poster.*

SOURCE: Reprinted from *Administration for Children and Families, Office on Trafficking in Persons, Rescue and Restore Victims of Human Trafficking Campaign Posters, 2012.* Retrieved from http://www.acf.hhs.gov/orr/resource/download-campaign-posters-and-brochures. In the public domain.

4. Decision Case

Working Systems[3]

Driving home from a meeting between the Mayor's Commission on the Status of Women and the San Diego Police Department, Assistant District Attorney Kylea Clarke was steaming. Clarke made a phone call to her husband to vent. "They lied, and I was shocked!"

"Hey," he interrupted, "why are you yelling at me?"

"I'm not yelling at you," Clarke explained, "I'm just yelling! I'm so frustrated with what happened at that meeting." After describing the situation, Clarke concluded, "I just want to get home and see the kids before bedtime."

As she continued the drive home, Clarke knew her power was limited in this situation. *But,* she thought, *there's always a way to get things done, one way or the other. So the question is, what way would that be?*

---

[3] This decision case was prepared solely to provide material for class discussion and not to suggest either effective or ineffective handling of the situation depicted. While based on field research regarding an actual situation, names and certain facts may have been disguised to protect confidentiality. The authors wish to thank the case reporter for cooperation in making this account available for the benefit of students and practitioners. (Wolfer & Scales, 2006, p. 29)

San Diego, California

San Diego is located in the southwestern corner of California. According to the 2010 United States Census, it had a population of slightly more than 3 million people, making it the second-most-populous county in California and the fifth-most-populous in the United States (U.S. Census Bureau, 2015). San Diego is the largest metropolitan area between the United States and Mexico. The county's population was about 42.9% White, 6.0% African American, 29.9% Hispanic, 17.1% Asian, 3.3% two or more races, .4% Native Hawaiian and Other Pacific Islander, .3% American Indian, and .1% other races (U.S. Census Bureau, 2015). The median income is $63,456 and the median income in California is slightly lower at $60,190. The median house or condo value in 2013 was $444,200, and in California it was $373,100 (U.S. Census Bureau, 2015). San Diego is the county seat of San Diego County.

San Diego County Criminal District Attorney

The San Diego County Criminal District Attorney sought to establish a "team of dedicated prosecutors committed to aggressively seeking justice and the protection of the family, person and property of all the citizens of our community." In 2012, it was led by an elected attorney, Paul Andrews. Its large staff was organized into eight divisions, each of which was led by its own chief: Investigation, Grand Jury and Intake, Criminal Trial, Misdemeanor, Special Crimes, Juvenile, Appellate, and Civil.

Kylea Clarke

Kylea Clarke and her three sisters were raised in a military family and experienced several moves as a result. But their father died while Kylea was an adolescent, and she completed high school at San Diego Christian. After attending college at Brown University, she worked in the antitrust division of the U.S. Department of Justice in Washington, DC, for 2 years. That experience confirmed her interest in the legal profession, and she returned to California to attend the University of California-Berkeley School of Law. After earning her law degree, Kylea returned to Washington, DC, for several more years before moving back to San Diego.

By 2014, Kylea Clarke had worked for 14 years as an assistant district attorney in the San Diego County District Attorney's office. She spent 6 months as a misdemeanor attorney before switching to the Special Crimes Unit. There, she handled a full caseload of child abuse, domestic violence, and adult sex crimes.

Getting Started With Human Trafficking

Clarke's interest in human trafficking was sparked by a comment her mother made. One day, she said to Clarke and her three sisters, "You know, you need to do something that makes a difference in the world. I want you girls to look into human trafficking." She gave each of them a book and insisted they read it. After some preliminary investigation, they decided to start a nonprofit organization, Help the People Ministries (HPM). Because Clarke and their mother knew some lawyers at their own and other churches, HPM's first program was Legal Escape Team (LET). But 2 years later, they closed HPM and incorporated LET as its own nonprofit organization. Clarke's involvement with LET prompted questions for her about whether the district attorney's office had any trafficking cases.

Clarke eventually found two cases in another section and asked whether she could have them. Her boss, Elizabeth Spurling, agreed but was initially unable to persuade her superiors to permit this. A year later, however, Spurling walked in to Clarke's office and tossed the cases on her desk. "Nothing's getting done on these cases," Spurling explained. "I've been pestering them for a year, and they finally agreed to let you take them."

Eagerly, Clarke took the two cases on top of her normal duties. She began developing the cases, tried the first one in 2010 and the second one in 2012, and pled a third one in the interim. By 2012, Clarke was spending significant amounts of time on trafficking cases. Because of their novelty and complexity, these cases were especially labor intensive.

In September 2012, Clarke challenged her supervisor, Elizabeth Spurling. "I really need to do this full time. I'm not able to dedicate the amount of work necessary. As a result, I'm not doing a good job."

"Well, yeah," Spurling responded, "I wish you could, too."

"I'm doing too much," Clarke insisted.

But nothing changed.

Finally, in early December 2012, Clarke walked into Spurling's office and said, "You know I love you, Chief, but I need to let you know that I'm leaving at the end of 2012 if they decide they don't want me to do human trafficking full time."

"Okay," Spurling responded, "let me see what they say about that."

"Please, these victims need a real advocate," Clarke nudged, "and I need a new challenge."

"Yes," Spurling reported later that day, "you can do human trafficking full time."

That evening, when Clarke reported this ultimatum to her husband, he exclaimed, "Whoa! Did we talk about this? Had we already decided that?"

"Well, no, we hadn't decided," Clarke acknowledged, "but we've been talking about it. It just came out of my mouth."

Despite the new full-time assignment, Clarke was still called into numerous traditional cases because she was the senior lawyer in her section.

Nevertheless, Spurling agreed the emerging human trafficking work required the attention of a full-time, senior staff person. She encouraged Kylea to address trafficking in whatever way necessary, something unprecedented in the unit, and ran interference for her with administrators.

"I had done everything I felt called to do in my current position," Kylea later confided to several friends. "I had tried every kind of kid case there was. I had tried injury cases. I had tried baby death cases and capital murder cases. I was *done*. Either there's a new challenge out there and I'm going to be able to broaden my scope, or I'll leave for something else. I'm not content anymore. I'm done just having a docket, just trying cases, just going to court. Look, I've been working in this area, working with other attorneys in the state. When I'm working on human trafficking, I get to speak to legislators. I'm involved in our regional coalition. We started our own school education program. I was doing all these things that I needed to have as part of my own professional development and also to do my job well. I needed to have all these different aspects."

Over time, she slowly developed a larger caseload in trafficking. But she was dependent upon law enforcement for referrals and began pushing to have the San Diego Police Department (SDPD) dedicate detectives to human trafficking to generate cases. But the SDPD refused. The San Diego County Sheriff's Office had a grant-funded unit until it lost its grant funding. Because of limited support from law enforcement, the DA's office never had more than about 50 cases. Neither law enforcement unit had a squad car out looking for cases. However, the Juvenile Probation Office was screening youth for potential trafficking, and that generated some cases. But when the cases got turned over to law enforcement, they would often disappear. For whatever reason, the SDPD never prioritized human trafficking, perhaps because leaders did not emphasize and reward long-term case investigation. Instead, much to Clarke's consternation, Chief Daniels had his entire vice unit—18 detectives—on a year-long special project to ticket homeless people. At the same time, the captain viewed his unit as a misdemeanor unit. That meant they would repeatedly catch people engaged in prostitution. They had great case numbers. The SDPD would catch the same people, send them off to prison for 6 months—where they would get some medical care and gain weight—and then they would show up back on the streets.

To build relationships and press for change, Clarke began meeting over lunch with Sergeant John Schmidt. As head of the Sex Crimes Unit, he was also interested in human trafficking cases and acknowledged that SDPD was not finding and pursuing these cases effectively. With more than 25 years at SDPD, Schmidt was also a master at navigating the bureaucracy. When Clarke would say, "If something's not working, let's change the process, let's make it better," Schmidt would try to find an angle. He made several proposals to higher ups for re-allocating SDPD resources to address trafficking but without success. When one staff configuration would be rebuffed, he would try another.

Leading a Coalition

In her role as an assistant district attorney, Clarke began attending monthly meetings of a city coalition focused on human trafficking. Regular attendees at the coalition meetings included representatives from Juvenile Probation, San Diego Police Department (SDPD), the Federal Bureau of Investigation (FBI), the District Attorney's Office, and California Division of Juvenile Justice (DJJ). But she soon became frustrated by the coalition's lack of leadership and clear purpose and by its general inefficiency.

One day, when there was a particularly large gathering of more than 75 people, she thought, *I don't want to go to this meeting and I figure most other people don't want to either.* Knowing she had Spurling's support, Clarke decided to act. She stood up and said, "Hey, I don't know if anyone else is feeling the way I'm feeling, but I'm really wondering what we're all doing here and why it takes so long. What's going on?" With some encouragement, she continued. "Do we as a group want to set specific goals and then try to meet those goals? Do we want to combine resources and go forward? Or do we just want to talk? It's okay to talk, but I'm feeling like we should do something else."

In response to a swell of support, Clarke said, "Okay, I'll come back in a month, and I'll give you a mission and vision. We can vote on them, and let's get moving. I'll suggest a new structure for the coalition."

Over the next few months, Clarke quickly streamlined the coalition's operations. Instead of loosely structured, three-hour monthly meetings, she implemented coalition meetings that met on alternate months for one hour, received reports from workgroups, voted on any changes in policy or plan, made announcements, and offered congratulations for successes.

"It helped keep the crazy level down," Clarke said. "Believe it or not, that's a major challenge in the coalition. You've got your segment of people who feel very strongly and want to be involved but don't always use their passion in a productive way. Without a solid understanding of the group's goals and initiatives, they tend to take up a lot of time on side issues." While people could linger to talk after the meetings, and many did, most seemed to appreciate the more streamlined process.

Under Clarke's leadership, the coalition developed several initiatives, including a program in schools to train counselors, teachers, and social workers on human trafficking. In 2012, the coalition sponsored a play about human trafficking. It was presented by the La Jolla and California Division of Juvenile Justice (DJJ). Clarke helped by providing court transcripts and other information about a real case as the basis for the play and editing the script for accuracy. She attended the actual performance in her role as coalition chair, and that was where she first met Alejandra Ortiz, a high-ranking administrator from DJJ.

When they got acquainted, Clarke learned that Ortiz was also a member of the San Diego County Commission on the Status of Women. Ortiz explained that the County Commission had taken up the issue of human trafficking at a national level, and she wondered whether the local commission might want to adopt the issue as well. A few days later, Ortiz called Clarke and asked her to meet with the County Commission.

In the meantime, Ortiz also invited Clarke to speak to a group at her church. Clarke knew that telling some local stories about human trafficking could be most effective. As she liked to say, "That's what makes people care about it, when they hear stories of actual people."

Addressing the County Commission on the Status of Women

About a month later, after a few postponements, Clarke met with the County Commission on the Status of Women. She didn't make a formal PowerPoint presentation but simply explained what human trafficking is and isn't, and shared some cases. "Human trafficking is a subcategory of child sexual abuse but differs in significant ways. In child abuse, for example, we're looking for consistency. We usually have a victim with fairly clean hands, a kid in the family, and the perp is often a teacher, coach, or parent. The kid doesn't usually have problems, and the kids don't change their story so much as build on it as they become more comfortable talking to professionals. In contrast, human trafficking usually involves a troubled, noncredible kid, who initially lies or rather tells a partial truth embedded in a lie. You have to work your way around to what the truth is. You need to develop a lot of corroboration to take the case."

Then, Clarke told the story of her very first human trafficking case. "Karen's a 13-year-old girl," she reported, "the second of four children, whose parents are divorced. Her father has been in and out of prison, and her stepfather has also been in and out of prison for drugs and theft. Karen sometimes skipped school and hung out with a rough crowd. Sometimes, for example, she would dress for school and leave with her backpack but hang out with these kids. One day in January 2008, she skipped school and went to the corner store. She hung out with an older woman she knew and they went to a drug house nearby to purchase marijuana. The house was owned by two brothers, Leftie and Randy. The house was partly under construction, had no running water, and only sometimes had electricity. When Karen asked to use the bathroom, the brothers locked her in and told her the other woman she had left. Later, they took her across the hall, tied her on the bed spread eagle, and raped her. Then, they decided to keep her and sell her to others who had extra money after they bought drugs. Over the next week, they sold her to more than 20 guys for $25 each, who paid to rape a 13-year-old who was lying in her own urine and feces and was injected with drugs. She was rescued only because a guy from the corner store who knew her was offered the opportunity to rape her. He said, 'I know that kid,' and physically ran her out of that place and took her to a friend's house. They lived on the run for a week or two until she was picked up by juvenile probation. After she was assigned a new juvenile probation officer, out came her story. As with a lot of these cases, we had trouble gathering evidence. Robbie, the guy who rescued her, was himself a felon. Anyway, I eventually prosecuted both of her traffickers and two of her johns." Clarke's presentation captivated the commissioners. After she finished, they peppered her with questions.

"Where in San Diego is this happening?" they wanted to know, and "What's being done to stop it?" One asked Clarke directly, "What resources do you need? What do you want?"

"A dedicated unit in the SDPD that will investigate this stuff," Clarke responded.

"Why don't we have that?" the woman followed up.

"Well," Clarke said, "I don't know." *After months of concern about this, I'm glad that someone is finally paying attention.*

A lively discussion ensued with questions about the investigation process, budget cycles, and timing for allocations. One of the commissioners volunteered to write an official letter to the city manager requesting that she look into the issue of human trafficking and what SDPD resources were being devoted to it. The commissioners also decided they would each call the city councilman or councilwoman by whom they were appointed to raise these issues with the SDPD.

After the meeting, the Commission chairwoman approached Clarke to offer her personal assistance. "I'm a civil lawyer," she explained, "and if you ever have reason to sue someone on behalf of the victim, I will take your case pro bono."

A few days later, Spurling came to talk with Clarke. "Someone from the SDPD called to ask, 'Did your person go over to the Commission and say we need a designated unit to investigate?'"

"Yes," Clarke replied, "I did say that. They asked me what we needed, and I told them what we needed."

As a result, administrators from the District Attorney's Office and from the SDPD met to discuss the issues. "But," Clarke confided, "here's the problem. Once it gets to that level, nobody who really says anything out loud gets to go to those meetings."

Meanwhile, the Women's Commission called another meeting, this time with the SDPD and District Attorney's Office to, as Clarke explained, "create kerfuffle." This meeting included the captain of the Sex Crimes Unit, the person responsible for addressing human trafficking. Elizabeth Spurling attended with Clarke.

"I am so glad you have asked me to talk about human trafficking," the captain recited expressionless, "because I am so passionate about human trafficking that I could talk for days." As he proceeded to talk through a PowerPoint presentation, Clarke paged through the handout.

That's a big fat lie! she thought. *Does your superior know what you're saying? Did your superiors put you up to this or is this just you, Captain Marner, trying to make your unit look like you're on top of the problem?*

Glaring sideways at Spurling, Clarke pointed to some deceptive information on the handout.

Turning back to face the captain, she thought, *Oh my gosh, I'm going to kick you in the face! . . . But I can't kick you in the face.*

Then, checking one page after another, *These are lies, these are lies!*

Noticing her growing indignation and agitation, Spurling put her hand on Clarke's knee.

I'm just going to be quiet, Clarke tried to restrain herself, *because Elizabeth's really good at saying things that are controversial and getting away with it. I know she knows these are lies and she has my back. If there is a high-up comment that needs to be made, she's going to make it.*

Surveying the other participants, Clarke also knew she had at least two strong allies on the Women's Commission. Indeed, after the captain concluded his presentation, commissioners asked pointed questions to make it clear they did not believe what they were being told.

When the captain responded with an inaccurate answer, one commissioner asked Clarke directly, "Kylea, what do you think? What's your opinion?"

"Well," Clarke replied, "the cases aren't coming in! We're certainly not seeing those cases." *The tension is so thick,* Clarke reflected, *you could cut it with a knife.*

"If you give me more people," the captain interjected, "I want to dedicate them to the federal task force. That would generate more cases."

"The last thing we need is more federal resources," Clarke responded. "We need them on the state side."

At the end of the meeting, Assistant Deputy Chief Geraldine Maynard said to the Women's Commission, "Thank you for having us."

As Clarke walked out, Captain Marner approached her to say, "Oh, I brought you a copy of the SafeFlex curriculum. You helped write it, so you should have a copy."

At the moment, Clarke couldn't bring herself to say anything except, "Thanks." She took the report and walked out. She needed the fresh air and room to clear her head.

Meanwhile, Spurling lingered to talk with Maynard.

Debriefing With Her Boss

Still steaming, Clarke waited on the curb outside to talk with Spurling.

A few minutes later, Spurling rejoined her.

"Boss, they're lying!" Clarke exclaimed before Spurling could say anything. "I can't believe they're lying."

"I know," Spurling responded, "I didn't think they would do it so blatantly."

"What did Geraldine say?" Clarke asked.

"Geraldine asked, 'What the hell was going on in there?' I told her, 'Well, what was being presented by Captain Marner is not what is happening in actuality. That's not what we're seeing on the ground.' She said, 'Well, you need to come by my office next week, so we can sort this out.'"

"Okay," Clarke pressed, "are you going to call her?"

"Yes," she assured, "I'm going to call her and we'll have a meeting and maybe we'll get it straightened out at that level."

"How can he do that?" Clarke asked indignantly, as they turned to walk to the parking garage. "Just lie, blatantly lie?"

"I can't believe they did that either," Spurling replied, "but how can I get around that and still get what we need?"

"Okay, Boss. Use your magic," Clark encouraged, "go get it done. Whatever it is, use your magic and get it done."

"Well, I'm going to talk with her."

"What do you think is going on? What would make them do that?" Clarke persisted. "Why would they do that?"

"Well, they're dealing with an employment contract dispute and the budget cycle. Remember the concessions the police made on salary and health benefits a few years ago; that's why they're not willing to negotiate now. They cannot come in after presenting their budget and now say something different from that. They can't come back and say, 'We need more personnel.'"

"But why?" Clarke asked. "It doesn't make any sense to me. If they would say, 'We want to do more about human trafficking but we need more people,' you and me would be 100% behind them. We would be like, 'Absolutely, let me tell you about the wonderful results they have when they have the resources. They need at least five more detectives assigned 100% of the time . . .'"

"I hear you," Spurling interrupted, "but I'm telling you that they have a different game that they're playing. It's all about the budget strategy and the contract dispute. I think this is all about the budget."

"That's crazy," Clarke responded. "I know Sergeant John Schmidt has made several small requests for resources to address human trafficking. He even proposed starting with one or two detectives from Sex Crimes and one or two detectives from Vice. He offered to start with that group and enlist help from those units for occasional field operations. That wouldn't cost much."

"Yeah, I know," Spurling responded, "but the chief insisted on requesting a 10-man unit with a lieutenant, sergeant, analyst, and seven detectives, knowing full well that the city didn't have the money to give. It's a negotiating strategy, not about getting the job done."

"Politics," Clarke exclaimed, "how frustrating! Meanwhile, a lot of crime victims in the community get overlooked."

The Aftermath

Alone in her car, Clarke made a phone call to her husband. "They lied, and I was shocked!"

"Hey," he interrupted, "why are you yelling at me?"

"I'm not yelling at you," Clarke explained, "I'm just yelling! I'm so frustrated with what happened at that meeting." After describing the situation, Clarke speculated, "I'm going to tell Sergeant Schmidt that Captain Marner went in and lied. I want Schmidt to be armed, and I don't want him to get in trouble. There will probably be internal fallout." Concluding the telephone conversation, she said, "I just want to get home and see the kids before bedtime."

As she continued the drive home, Clarke knew her power was limited in this situation. *But*, she thought, *there's always a way to get things done, one way or the other. So the question is, what way would that be? I like to have multiple irons in the fire.* She wondered, *What do I do now?*

Epilogue

Later, Alejandra Ortiz called to ask about the meeting. At the end of their conversation, Clarke offered to type up a report and send it to her.

"That would be good," Alejandra said, "because the Public Safety and Livable Neighborhoods Committee of the City Council is going to have a closed-door meeting with the SDPD and they need to know what's going on."

"I can't have my name on it," Clarke explained, "but you're welcome to distribute it. I want people to know but don't want to get fired. They need to know what's going on in the Police Department, so I'll put that all down in the letter. I'll include Sergeant Schmidt's proposal, too."

When Clarke told her husband about the letter and the risk that she might get fired, he said, "So be it." Clarke's mother encouraged, "You've got to send it. It's the truth, send it!"

After writing and sending the letter, Clarke told Spurling, "By the way, I sent this information out while you were gone."

"Okay," she responded, "don't worry."

"It makes me very sad," Clarke reflected later, "I get very sad when systems that are supposed to work on behalf of people do not work. That's not right. I get very upset. If I don't do something, how can I complain about it? If I don't do something, who's going to? God will raise up people, I do believe that. But if I'm placed in that position, at that time, there's a purpose for it."

5. Scientific Knowledge

5.1 Introduction

This chapter provides an overview of global and United States policy responses that seek to address and respond to the problem of human trafficking. This section includes an overview of international policy, including the application of broader human rights instruments, major U.S. federal and state-level policies, immigration remedies related to human trafficking crimes, and global prostitution-related policies.

5.2 International Policy

While the more recent uproar in the United States around human trafficking has produced considerable response and action, the international response to the problem gained momentum decades ago. Early policies that indicate international agreement on the concept of human trafficking date back to the early part of the 20th century, through the United Nations, the League of Nations, and the International Labour Organization (Androff, 2011). The Universal Declaration of Human Rights, adopted in 1948 by the UN General Assembly, declared that "no one shall be held in slavery or servitude" and that "slavery and the slave trade shall be prohibited in all their forms" (The United Nations [UN], 1948, article 4). The UN further addressed human trafficking in the Convention for the Suppression of Traffic in Persons and the Exploitation of Prostitution of Others (UN, 1949).

More recent references to human trafficking in international human rights instruments include the United Nations Convention on the Elimination of All Forms of Discrimination against Women (CEDAW) (UN, 1979) and the United Nations Convention on the Rights of a Child (UN, 1989). It is important to note that the United States has not ratified either of these conventions.

During the World Conference on Human Rights in Vienna in 1993, the Human Rights Council created the Special Rapporteur on violence against women, its causes, and consequences. Special rapporteurs have subsequently been dispatched on missions to El Salvador and Guatemala, with a focus on the rights of women and violence against women. (UN, 2006; UN, 2011). In 1994, a special rapporteur on violence against women was further charged with investigating forced prostitution and trafficking (Farrell & Fahy, 2009).

In 2000, the United Nations adopted the Protocol to Prevent, Suppress and Punish Trafficking in Persons, Especially Women and Children, which has served as a catalyst for further action at the global level. This protocol, often referred to as the Palermo Protocol, defines trafficking in persons as

the recruitment, transportation, transfer, harboring or receipt of persons, by means of the threat or use of force or other forms of coercion, of abduction, of fraud, of deception, of the abuse of power or of a position of vulnerability or of the giving or receiving of payments or benefits to achieve the consent of a person having control over another person, for the purpose of exploitation. (Article 3)

5.3 Federal U.S. Policy

While antislavery legislation dates further back into the nation's history, the United States began to directly address the modern concept of human trafficking nearly concurrently with the passage of the United Nations' Palermo Protocol. The Trafficking Victims Protection Act (TVPA) was passed in 2000 to address emerging international and national recognition of the trafficking of persons for labor or sex. In tandem with the Palermo Protocol, the TVPA defines human trafficking as "the recruitment, harboring, transporting, provision, or obtaining of a person for labor or services, through the use of force, fraud, or coercion for the purpose of subjection to involuntary servitude, peonage, debt bondage, slavery, or forced commercial sex acts" (TVPA, section 103[8]). The law also aims to prevent trafficking in persons, to protect those who have been trafficked, and to prosecute traffickers (Polaris, 2016). In addition to creating a new crime of human trafficking, the TVPA enhanced penalties for related existing crimes such as slavery, peonage, and involuntary servitude (Farrell & Fahy, 2009). Furthermore, the TVPA developed a funding mechanism to support benefits and services for victims, in addition to legal immigration remedies for undocumented victims. The TVPA was reauthorized in 2003, 2005, 2008, and 2013. The most recent reauthorization of the TVPA is included within Title XII of the Violence Against Women Reauthorization Act of 2013.

The TVPA also established domestic and international standards for antitrafficking initiatives including prevention, prosecution, and victim protection. Since 2001, the United States Department of State has produced the Trafficking in Persons (TIP) Report, ranking countries (ranging from Tier 1 to Tier 3) based on efforts to comply with the TVPA's minimum standards for the elimination of trafficking. Tier 1 is the optimal goal and describes countries whose governments fully comply with the Trafficking Victims Protection Act's minimum standards. In the most recent TIP Report (2016), there were 36 countries in Tier 1, 78 in Tier 2, 44 in Tier 2 Watch List, and 27 in Tier 3. Table 7.1 provides a snapshot of selected countries' tier rankings. During the early years of the TIP Report, the United States did not rank itself. In 2010, the Department of State began to include the United States in the rankings, and it has consistently received Tier 1 ranking.

While the TIP Report has had considerable influence on global antitrafficking efforts, it has also been widely criticized, and some have questioned the methodology and empirical basis of the TIP Report (Gallagher, 2011).

Its very existence angers activists and governments alike, who object to the USA appointing itself supervisor and arbiter of a complex international issue that remains both contested and controversial. While firm friends take

Table 7.1 Tier Rankings for Selected Countries—2016 Trafficking in Persons Report

Tier	Description	Selected Countries (this is not an exhaustive list of ranked countries)
Tier 1	Countries whose governments fully comply with the Trafficking Victims Protection Act's (TVPA) minimum standards.	Armenia, Australia, Canada, Chile, Colombia, Czech Republic, Germany, Israel, Italy, Lithuania, Poland, South Korea, Spain, Sweden, Taiwan, United States of America
Tier 2	Countries whose governments do not fully comply with the TVPA's minimum standards but are making significant efforts to bring themselves into compliance with those standards.	Angola, Argentina, Bangladesh, Bosnia & Herzegovina, Botswana, Croatia, Indonesia, Liberia, Mexico, Mongolia, Nicaragua, Nigeria, Turkey, United Arab Emirates, Uruguay, Vietnam
Tier 2 Watch List	Countries whose governments do not fully comply with the TVPA's minimum standards but are making significant efforts to bring themselves into compliance with those standards AND: 1. The absolute number of victims of severe forms of trafficking is very significant or is significantly increasing; 2. There is a failure to provide evidence of increasing efforts to combat severe forms of trafficking in persons from the previous year; or 3. The determination that a country is making significant efforts to bring itself into compliance with minimum standards was based on commitments by the country to take additional future steps over the next year.	Afghanistan, Bolivia, China, Cuba, Pakistan, Saudi Arabia, Sri Lanka, Thailand, Ukraine
Tier 3	Countries whose governments do not fully comply with the minimum standards and are not making significant efforts to do so.	Algeria, Belize, Burma, Eritrea, The Gambia, Guinea-Bissau, Haiti, Iran, North Korea, Russia, Syria, Zimbabwe

SOURCE: U.S. Department of State. (2016). *Trafficking in persons report.* Retrieved from http://www.state.gov/j/tip/rls/tiprpt/2016/.

comfort in the glowing assessments they receive each year from Washington, the usual targets of U.S. disapproval point to their consistently poor ranking as evidence of entrenched bias. (Gallagher, 2011, p. 382)

In addition to the TVPA and institution of the TIP Report, multiple federal agencies have developed policies related to human trafficking. These include, but are not limited to, the Administration for Children and Families, the Federal Bureau of Investigation, the Department of Homeland Security (including Immigration and Customs Enforcement), and the Department of Justice.

"Know your rights" at the border

As a result of the 2008 reauthorization of the TVPA (William Wilberforce Trafficking Victims Protection Reauthorization Act), the Department of State began disseminating pamphlets and videos designed to help those entering the United States understand their rights, protections, and available resources if they encounter work-related concerns and need help in the United States. In particular, the pamphlet highlights basic workers' rights, regardless of status, such as the rights to: be treated and paid fairly; not be held in a job against your will; keep your passport and other identification documents in your possession; not be discriminated against; a healthy and safe workplace; leave an Abusive Employment Situation; report abuse without retaliation; request help from unions, immigrant and labor rights groups and other groups; and seek justice in U.S. courts. (U.S. Department of State, 2014, December 22)

5.4 Immigration Policies

Policies that seek to provide immigration remedies to undocumented trafficking survivors have been a hallmark of the federal efforts to support those impacted by human trafficking and related crimes. A variety of legal remedies are available to undocumented victims of violence and abuse. These include U visas, T visas, VAWA self-petition, battered spouse waiver, cancelation of removal, asylum, and continued presence. The original VAWA of 1994 and its 2000 reauthorization, paired with the Trafficking Victims Protection Act of 2000, made important strides in creating legal immigration avenues that protect and support women experiencing violence. Table 7.2 lists and describes the various avenues of legal immigration remedies for immigrant women who have experienced intimate partner violence, sexual violence, or human trafficking.

A prime example is the U visa, which provides immigration relief to individuals who have suffered substantial physical or mental abuse as a result of having been a victim of a qualifying criminal activity, including sexual assault, domestic violence, and human trafficking (U.S. Citizenship & Immigration Services [USCIS], 2013). The number of available U visas is capped each year at 10,000, and scholars and advocates argue that this is insufficient given the number of undocumented victims of violence and abuse (Levine & Peffer, 2012). Levine and Peffer (2012) estimate that in 2008, there

Table 7.2 Immigration Relief for Battered Immigrant Women

Immigration Relief	Description	Eligibility of Applicant	Date Established
U Visa	Victim cooperating with the investigation/prosecution of a crime may receive work authorization, temporary (4 years) immigration status, and an opportunity to apply for permanent residency after 3 years. The individual must have suffered substantial physical or mental abuse as a result of having been a victim of a qualifying criminal activity. The individual must have information concerning that criminal activity and must have been helpful, is being helpful, or is likely to be helpful in the investigation or prosecution of the crime.	Victim of criminal activity (such as sexual assault, sexual exploitation, trafficking, domestic violence, and rape) Stalking was added as a qualifying crime under VAWA reauthorization 2013	Battered Immigrant Women Protection Act of 2000
T Visa	Applicant must be a victim of trafficking, as defined by law, and be in the United States due to trafficking. Applicant must comply with any reasonable request from a law enforcement agency for assistance in the investigation or prosecution of human trafficking (unless under the age of 18 or unable to cooperate due to physical or psychological trauma). Applicant must demonstrate that she/he would suffer extreme hardship if removed from the United States. Benefits include work authorization, temporary (4 years) immigration status, and the opportunity to apply for permanent residency after 3 years.	Victim of human trafficking	TVPA 2000
Continued Presence	Temporary immigration status provided to individuals identified by law enforcement as victims of human trafficking. This status allows victims of human trafficking to remain in the United States temporarily during the ongoing investigation into the human trafficking–related crimes committed against them. Continued Presence is initially granted for 1 year and may be renewed in 1-year increments.	Victim of human trafficking	TVPA 2000

SOURCE: American Gateways, 2013; National Latino Network, 2013; National Network to End Domestic Violence, 2013; National Task Force to End Sexual and Domestic Violence, 2012; U.S. Citizenship and Immigration Services, 2013; U.S. Committee for Refugees and Immigrants, 2013; U.S. Department of Homeland Security, 2017.

were over 37,000 undocumented female victims of intimate partner violence in the United States and that by 2015, there may be as many as 100,000.

Virtually all legal immigration relief strategies involve women engaging formally with large systems such as the U.S. Citizenship and Immigration Services. Given that undocumented women experiencing abuse are unlikely to seek help from formal systems, these remedies often remain out of reach for women without legal documentation (Raj and Silverman, 2002; Mowder, 2010; Hass, Dutton, & Orloff, 2000; Salcido & Adelman, 2004).

Grupos Beta in Mexico

Grupos Beta were begun by the Mexican government in 1991 to protect migrants traveling through Mexico, primarily those migrating from Central America to the United States. This initiative recognizes Mexico as a possible transit country for human trafficking and highlights the protection of human rights of migrants. The purpose of the Grupos Beta is to provide migrants with humanitarian, medical, and legal assistance and to share information about migrant rights and dangers of the migration routes in Mexico. The IOM reports that in 2011 alone, the Grupos Beta assisted almost 300,000 migrants (International Organization of Migration, May 17, 2012). More information about the Grupos Beta can be found on the website of the National Institute of Migration of Mexico.

5.5 State-Level Policies

Many states have also since enacted state laws and programming to address human trafficking. Washington and Texas passed the first state criminal statutes in 2003, and by 2013, all 50 states and the District of Columbia had passed criminal statutes. In Figure 7.3, Polaris outlines the timeline of state-level human trafficking legislation. While early state legislation focused on increasing the ability of states to prosecute human trafficking crimes, more recent efforts target the protection of and assistance for victims and survivors of human trafficking. Similar to the U.S. Department of State's TIP Report, Polaris evaluates and ranks state initiatives to prevent and prosecute trafficking and to support those who are impacted by the crime (Polaris, 2014).

In general, federal and state policies have multiplied since the TVPA was originally passed in 2000. Overall, these policies originally targeted the problem of human trafficking crimes against immigrants/foreign-born communities. Later advocate groups began to address concerns and needs around crimes against U.S. citizens and residents, in particular domestic minors, and push for inclusion in policy, programming, and funding. Political advocacy efforts to date have also focused heavily on sex trafficking, and many argue that labor trafficking remains a problem with unique policy needs.

6. Complex and Critical Discourse: Prostitution-Related Policies

In addition to the broader antitrafficking policies developed at the international, federal, and state levels, it is important to also consider the realm of policy responses

Figure 7.2 *Migrant child poster.*

SOURCE: Reprinted from *Administration for Children and Families, Office on Trafficking in Persons, Rescue and Restore Victims of Human Trafficking Campaign Posters, 2012.* Retrieved from http://www.acf.hhs.gov/orr/resource/download-campaign-posters-and-brochures. In the public domain.

Figure 7.3 *Chronology of passage of first state criminal statute against human trafficking.*

	2005 (8 states)	**2007 (7 states)**			
2003 (2 states) Texas Washington	Arizona, Arkansas California, Illinois, Kansas, Louisiana Nevada, New Jersey	Delaware, Kentucky, Maryland, Montana, New York, Rhode Island, Oregon	**2009 (4 states)** New Hampshire, North Dakota, Vermont, Virginia	**2011 (2 states)** Massachusetts, South Dakota	**2013 (1 state)** Wyoming
2004 (2 states) Florida Missouri	**2006 (14 states)** Alaska, Colorado, Connecticut, Georgia, Idaho, Indiana, Iowa, Michigan, Minnesota, Mississippi, Nebraska, North Carolina, Pennsylvania, South Carolina	**2008 (7 states)** Hawaii, Maine, New Mexico, Oklahoma, Tennessee, Utah, Wisconsin		**2010 (3 states)** Alabama, District of Columbia, Ohio	**2012 (1 state)** West Virginia

SOURCE: "A look back: Building a human trafficking legal framework" by Polaris, 2014 (https://polarisproject.org/sites/default/files/2014-Look-Back.pdf). Copyright 2014 by Polaris. Reprinted with permission.

specifically related to prostitution. Prostitution is not synonymous with human trafficking, and the 2010 TIP Report states that "prostitution by willing adults is not human trafficking regardless of whether it is legalized, decriminalized or criminalized" (p. 8). However, the two are often conflated, and many countries rely on prostitution-related policies to address the supply and demand for commercial sexual exploitation (Deady, 2010). In fact, in its assessment of countries' efforts to eliminate human trafficking, the 2010 TIP Report also evaluates initiatives of countries with legalized prostitution to reduce demand for commercial sex.

This section explores three categories of this type of prostitution-related policy effort: 1) complete criminalization; 2) partial decriminalization; and 3) legalization/ regulation.

6.1 Complete Criminalization

On one end of the spectrum are policies that completely criminalize all aspects of prostitution in an effort to reduce supply and demand by deterring anyone engaged in the commercial sex industry. Criminalizing prostitution considers the buying and selling of commercial sex, in addition to third-party involvement, illegal. This strategy is thought to hinder human trafficking in particular, because it sets the risk of arrest for exploiting others as higher than any financial benefits of such activity. With a few regional exceptions, the United States serves as an example of policies on the complete criminalization end of the spectrum. In general, this type of response supports a distinction between those *voluntarily* involved in the commercial sex industry and those who are being *exploited* by the commercial sex industry and are forced or coerced into prostitution. In other words, those who are exploited are presumably not criminalized, as they are considered victims of a crime, not offenders. However, despite these intentions, many continue to incur criminal charges (Deady, 2010).

This style of policy response has a diverse array of proponents and opponents. Those in favor of criminalization often cite moral, religious, and feminist objections to prostitution (Deady, 2010; Weitzer, 2005). Proponents argue that prostitution threatens public health and opens the door for criminal activity, including human trafficking. Opponents argue that criminalization is not effective in reducing prostitution. In particular, having a conviction on one's record may limit future job opportunities and increase the likelihood of remaining in the commercial sex industry. In addition, some believe that criminalization may increase the opportunity for coercion, because if those working in the commercial sex industry are afraid of being arrested and punished, they may become more vulnerable to victimization and less likely to report human trafficking when they see it (Deady, 2010). Some argue that the policy is not evenly applied to sex workers, to clients, and to those facilitating commercial sex (such as pimps), despite similar culpability on the surface of the policy. Specifically, the ban on the sale of commercial sex is more rigorously enforced than the ban on the purchase of sex. In other words, those at highest risk of being criminally charged with prostitution-related offenses are sex workers themselves.

Furthermore, it is often the most marginalized of sex workers (such as women of color and the LGBTQ community) who are most likely to be arrested and suffer legal consequences (Hayes, 2008).

6.2 Partial Criminalization

Another tool involves partial criminalization of prostitution. In this form, most prostitution-related activities (such as buying sex and facilitating prostitution) become illegal, but the activities of sex workers themselves are *not* criminalized. Known as the Swedish or the Nordic model, Sweden instituted this approach in 1999. Proponents of this approach claim that the law enhances gender equality, reduces the demand for trafficked women, and has resulted in decreased street prostitution (Ekberg, 2004). However, opponents fear that this approach penalizes sex workers by decreasing their client base, which may encourage engagement in riskier activities. Furthermore, some believe that this approach will result in forcing human trafficking deeper underground (Ekberg, 2004).

6.3 Legalization/Regulation

Further along the spectrum, the Netherlands serves as an example of approaches that aim to legalize and regulate the commercial sex industry. In this model, prostitution is allowed in certain conditions, as specified by the government. Regulations may include banning street-based prostitution and/or requiring that sex workers be licensed and submit to mandatory health examinations. Exploitation and human trafficking are still criminalized under a legalization model. This model presumes that prostitution includes the consensual giving and receiving of sexual services and represents an inevitable component of the social order. This model views the commercial sex industry as a legitimate economic sector that contributes to employment and economic growth. The legalization and regulation of the industry is thought to protect the rights of sex workers and decrease instances of exploitation, violence, and abuse. Others argue that legalization increases the demand for prostitution, which will in turn increase human trafficking. In other words, setting up a regulation system makes it easier for traffickers to obtain valid work permits but then engage in exploitation. Some also claim that the exploitation of undocumented immigrants and of children have blossomed in areas using these approaches.

The Texas Alcoholic Beverage Commission

www.tabc.state.tx.us

The Texas Alcoholic Beverage Commission (TABC), a state governmental agency that regulates the alcoholic beverage industry in Texas, requires that all establishments that sell and/or serve alcoholic beverages post signs that include the following information in English and in Spanish: "Warning: Obtaining forced labor or services is a crime under Texas law. Call the national human trafficking hotline: 1–888–373–7888. You may remain anonymous."

Figure 7.4 *Suamhirs, survivor advocate.* **The signs of human trafficking are subtle.**

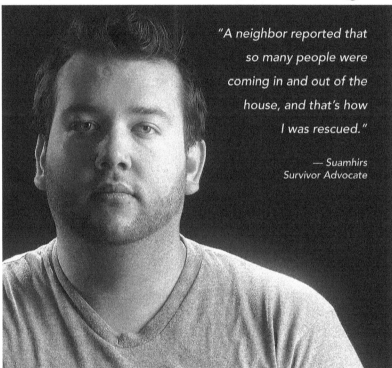

SOURCE: *Office for Victims of Crime, Know the Faces of Human Trafficking Poster Gallery, 2014.* Retrieved from http://ovc.ncjrs.gov/humantrafficking/Public_Awareness_Folder/images/final_poster_Suamhirs.jpg. In the public domain.

7. Implications for Practice: Applying Feminist Approaches to Sex Trafficking

Feminism's debate on the topics of sex trafficking, prostitution, and sex work is vibrant and often polarizing. In fact, feminist debates on these topics have been referred to as the feminist sex wars (Wahab & Panichelli, 2013). Controversy centers on the commercial sex industry, the often-conflated terms *sex trafficking* and *prostitution*, and the degrees to which those in the commercial sex industry are impacted by coercion, agency, and self-determination.

> On one side of the debate are sex workers and feminists who emphasize the importance of sex workers' rights and understand sex work as potentially liberating and empowering. On the other side are those who believe sex work is exploitive, casting sex workers as coerced victims. (Wahab & Panichelli, 2013, p. 344)

Figure 7.5 *Human Trafficking Hotline Number Sign.*

- WARNING -

OBTAINING FORCED LABOR OR SERVICES
IS A CRIME UNDER TEXAS LAW.
CALL THE
NATIONAL HUMAN TRAFFICKING HOTLINE
1-888-3737-888
YOU MAY REMAIN ANONYMOUS.

- ADVERTENCIA -

LA OBTENCIÓN DE SERVICIOS O TRABAJO FORZADO ES UN
DELITO SEGÚN LA LEY DE TEXAS. LLAME A LA LÍNEA DIRECTA
NACIONAL DE TRÁFICO HUMANO AL
1-888-3737-888
USTED PUEDE PERMANECER ANÓNIMO.

SOURCE: Texas Alcohol Beverage Commission, Publications, Signs, 2016. Retrieved from https://www.tabc.state.tx.us/publications/brochures/humanTrafficking .pdf. In the public domain.

Feminist scholars Sloan and Wahab (2000) provide a useful theoretical background on prostitution and sex work. First, Sloan and Wahab explore various feminist positions that claim prostitution to inherently involve violence and/or exploitation. For example, some radical feminists use domination theory to suggest that sex work is inherently oppressive, violent, and exploitative, serving to assert male dominance over women. Black feminist thought argues that prostitution must be viewed as sitting at the intersection of race, class, and gender (Collins, 2000). Furthermore, sex work represents the exploitation of Black women's sexuality for an economic purpose.

On the other hand, many feminists argue that prostitution is better understood as sex work. A liberal feminist contractarian position, for example, maintains that sex work is a social contract in which sex workers contract out a service for a certain amount of time and are free workers, similar to any other wage laborer. Related to this position is the sex worker rights movement, which appeals to the idea that most women working in the commercial sex industry made a conscious decision to do so after having looked at other work alternatives. In this vein, sex work should be viewed as legitimate work, and it is a violation of women's civil rights to be denied the opportunity to work as a sex worker. Advocates of sex worker rights argue for the enforcement of existing laws that prohibit kidnapping, assault, rape, and fraud. However, they also argue that initiatives that limit or prohibit sex work or prostitution have resulted in the isolation, increased vulnerability, abuse, and exploitation of sex workers and serve to control and stigmatize sex workers and deny the self-determination and autonomy of sex workers. In fact, a sex worker rights collective in India uses the slogan "Save us from our saviors, we're tired of being saved" (Bernstein, 2010, p. 65).

Elizabeth Bernstein uses the frame of carceral feminism to argue that modern U.S. antitrafficking initiatives and collaborations, particularly among radical feminists and evangelical Christian organizations, are part of a neoliberal (market-based and punitive) project of social control. Such efforts, she argues, are "successful at criminalizing marginalized populations, enforcing border control, and measuring other countries' compliance with human rights standards based on the curtailment of prostitution" (p. 57). Bernstein takes issue with current policy ramifications: "Pimps can now be given ninety-nine year prison sentences as sex traffickers and sex workers are increasingly arrested and deported for the sake of their 'protection'" (p. 57). She warns against the current trend in antitrafficking efforts that may further foment the incarceration of marginalized communities and obligatory services for survivors of human trafficking through prostitution diversion programs.

In general, the debates around the roles of exploitation and violence in prostitution will continue. Those making and analyzing policies at local, state, federal, and international levels must maintain a steady eye toward both the potential hidden agendas and the unintended consequences of antitrafficking policies. Policy makers must continue to ensure that those who are marginalized and experience a range of intersecting oppressions are not harmed by the very same policies designed to assist and support them.

8. Chapter Summary

Implications for practice, policy, and policy practice will continue to evolve as initiatives that address human trafficking continue to evolve over time at the international, federal, and state levels. The refinement of macro mechanisms to address prevention and intervention, accountability, and emerging trends for the human trafficking field is needed. Despite various philosophical perspectives, human rights remain the bedrock of political discourse around this social problem. It is crucial that in valuing a feminist perspective of affirming the victim's agency, professionals, advocates, and policy makers understand the lived experiences of victims and value them as experts in their own lives.

9. Key Terms

9.1	Universal Declaration of Human Rights	9.5	U visa
9.2	Palermo Protocol	9.6	T visa
9.3	TVPA	9.7	Continued presence
9.4	TIP Report	9.8	Personal is political
		9.9	Feminism

10. Active Learning Exercises or In-Class Discussion Questions

10.1 How are contemporary antitrafficking policies connected to, or reflective of, earlier abolitionist movements and policies to end slavery in the antebellum period of the United States?

10.2 Given that a variety of laws are already in place that criminalize kidnapping, sexual assault, and wage violations, what is the purpose of human trafficking–specific policies? What did the TVPA contribute, for example, that was not already made possible by existing laws?

10.3 How are international human rights instruments, such as the Universal Declaration of Human Rights or the convention on the Rights of the Child, included (or not included) in the approach to human trafficking in the United States?

10.4 What are the benefits and pitfalls of the U.S. Department of State's Trafficking in Persons report? What is left unstated in the United States' positions on and ranking of other countries' efforts?

10.5 What does our language tell us about our values around prostitution? Think of these phrases and terms: oldest profession, teen prostitute, sex worker, rescue, saving, and freedom? Is prostitution inevitable? Is prostitution equivalent to sex trafficking? Is all prostitution coerced, forced? How might feminist theory support this discussion?

In-Class Activities:

10.6   Review the human rights instruments by reading them together or watching a short video. Watch GEMS' video "Making of a Girl" and identify basic, universal human rights that are violated or are not protected.

10.7   In small groups, review the basic policy responses to prostitution and consider the pros and cons of each strategy. What values do the strategies illustrate? What is your group's assessment of an appropriate/useful strategy?

11. Suggestions for Further Learning

11.1   Readings

11.1.1   Wahab, S., & Panichelli, M. (2013). Ethical and human rights issues in coercive interventions with sex workers. *Work*, *28*(4), 344–349.

11.1.2   Bernstein, E. (2014). Militarized humanitarianism meets carceral feminism: The politics of sex, rights, and freedom in contemporary antitrafficking campaigns. *Signs*, *40*(1).

11.1.3   Trafficking Victims Protection Reauthorization Act of 2013 (Title XII of the Violence Against Women Reauthorization Act of 2013).

11.1.4   Hooks, B. (2000). *Feminism is for everybody: Passionate politics*. Pluto Press.

11.2   Websites

11.2.1   The United Nations. (1948). *Universal Declaration of Human Rights*: http://www.un.org/en/documents/udhr/

11.2.2   UNHCR (2008). Refugee Protection and Human Trafficking: http://www.unhcr.org/trafficking

11.2.3   United Nations Global Initiative to Fight Human Trafficking: http://www.ungift.org

11.2.4   International Organization for Migration: Counter-Trafficking: http://www.iom.int

11.2.5   U.S. Department of State (2016). *Trafficking in Persons Report*: http://www.state.gov/j/tip/rls/tiprpt/2016/

11.2.6   Polaris Project: www.polarisproject.org

11.2.7   GEMS—"Making of a Girl" video: http://www.gems-girls.org/media-center/music

11.3   Films

11.3.1   *Slavery Out of the Shadows: Spotlight on Human Trafficking*

11.3.2   *Sex + Money: A National Search for Human Worth*

12. Research Assignments/
Project Assignments/Homework/Exam Exercises

12.1 Review selected countries' profiles and rankings in the most recent TIP Report. What may be missing from the discussion and understanding of human trafficking in that context?

12.2 How is your home state doing in its response to human trafficking? Find and review Polaris Project's report of your home state's efforts. Where might your state be excelling/lacking in its response to human trafficking?

12.3 How do prostitution-related policies benefit and/or hinder the efforts to combat the crime of human trafficking? Consider two programs—Project Rose in Arizona and the Sonagachi project in India—and the ways these programs reflect underlying ideas and values around prostitution, and how prostitution-related policies impact those who are exploited in the commercial sex industry. To find out more about Project Rose and the community's response to it, do a simple Internet search for news articles on Project Rose. (For example, see Arizona State University's early press release on the project at https://asunow .asu.edu/content/asu-phoenix-police-team-help-victims-prostitution; see Mike Ludwig's article "Sex Work Wars: Project ROSE, Monica Jones and the Fight for Human Rights" at http://www.truth-out.org/news/item/22422-sex-work-wars-project-rose-monica-jones-and-the-fight-for-human-rights).

12.4 Read E. Bernstein's 2014 article titled *Militarized humanitarianism meets carceral feminism: The politics of sex, rights, and freedom in contemporary antitrafficking campaigns*. Discuss the roles of feminism and faith-based communities in the antitrafficking movement, the notion of the movement as a "moral crusade," and the role of incarceration.

13. References

Administration for Children and Families. (2012). *Look beneath the surface campaign domestic servitude poster* [Online image]. Retrieved from http://www.acf.hhs.gov/orr/resource/ download-campaign-posters-and-brochures

Administration for Children and Families. (2012). *Rescue and restore victims of human trafficking campaign migrant child poster* [Online image]. Retrieved from http://www.acf.hhs.gov/ orr/resource/download-campaign-posters-and-brochures

Androff, D. K. (2011). The problem of contemporary slavery: An international human rights challenge for social work. *International Social Work, 54*(2), 209–222. doi:10.1177/ 0020872810368395

Bernstein, E. (2010). Militarized humanitarianism meets carceral feminism: The politics of sex, rights, and freedom in contemporary antitrafficking campaigns. *Signs, 40*(1).

Collins, P. H. (2000). *Black feminist thought: Knowledge, consciousness, and the politics of empowerment*. New York, NY: Routledge.

Cook Heffron, L., Snyder, S., Wachter, K., Nsonwu, M., & Busch-Armendariz, N. (2016). "Something is missing here": Weaving feminist theories into social work practice with refugees. In S. Wendt & N. Moulding (Eds.), *Feminist social work: A reader*. Thousand Oaks, CA: Sage.

Crenshaw, K. (1991). Mapping the margins: Intersectionality, identity politics, and violence against women of color. *Stanford Law Review, 43*(6), 1241–1299. doi:10.2307/1229039

Deady, G. M. (2010). The girl next door: A comparative approach to prostitution laws and sex trafficking victim identification within the prostitution industry. *Washington and Lee Journal of Civil Rights and Social Justice, 17*, 515.

Ekberg, G. (2004). The Swedish law that prohibits the purchase of sexual services best practices for prevention of prostitution and trafficking in human beings. *Violence Against Women, 10*(10), 1187–1218.

Farrell, A., & Fahy, S. (2009). The problem of human trafficking in the U.S.: Public frames and policy responses. *Journal of Criminal Justice, 37*(6), 617–626. doi:http://dx.doi.org/10.1016/j.jcrimjus.2009.09.010

Gallagher, A. T. (2011). Improving the effectiveness of the international law of human trafficking: A vision for the future of the US Trafficking in Persons reports. *Human Rights Review, 12*(3), 381–400.

Girls Educational & Mentoring Services, & Buckley, J. (GEMS). (2006, November 11). *The making of a girl*. [Video file]. Retrieved from http://www.gems-girls.org/media-center/music

Hanisch, C. (2006). *The personal is political*. Retrieved from http://www.carolhanisch.org/CHwritings/PersonalIsPolitical.pdf

Hass, G. A., Dutton, M. A., & Orloff, L. E. (2000). Lifetime prevalence of violence against Latina immigrants: Legal and policy implications. *International Review of Victimology, 7*(1–3), 93–113.

Hayes, V. (2008). Prostitution policies and sex trafficking: Assessing the use of prostitution-based policies as tools for combatting sex trafficking. Retrieved from http://www.kentlaw.edu/perritt/courses/seminar/VHayes-final-IRPaper.pdf

International Organization of Migration. (2012, May 17). Mexican National Migration Institute, IOM workshop shares "Grupos Beta" experience [Press release]. Retrieved from https://www.iom.int/news/mexican-national-migration-institute-iom-workshop-shares-grupos-beta-experience

Levine, H., & Peffer, S. (2012). Quiet casualties: An analysis of U non-immigrant status of undocumented immigrant victims of intimate partner violence. *International Journal of Public Administration, 35*(9), 634–642.

Mohanty, C. T. (2003). *Feminism without borders: Decolonizing theory, practicing solidarity*. Durham, NC: Duke University Press.

Mowder, D. L. (2010). *The relationship between the undocumented immigrant battered Latina and US immigration policy*. Pullman, WA: Washington State University.

Office for Victims of Crime (2014). *Know the faces of human trafficking poster gallery* [Online image]. Retrieved from http://ovc.ncjrs.gov/humantrafficking/Public_Awareness_Folder/images/final_poster_Suamhirs.jpg

Polaris. (2014). *A look back: Building a human trafficking legal framework*. Retrieved from https://polarisproject.org/sites/default/files/2014-Look-Back.pdf

Polaris. (2016). *Current federal laws*. Retrieved from https://polarisproject.org/current-federal-laws

Raj, A., & Silverman, J. (2002). Violence against immigrant women: The roles of culture, context, and legal immigrant status on intimate partner violence. *Violence Against Women, 8*(3), 367–398. doi:10.1177/10778010222183107

Salcido, O., & Adelman, M. (2004). "He has me tied with the blessed and damned papers": Undocumented-immigrant battered women in Phoenix, Arizona. *Human*

Organization, *63*(2), 162–172. Retrieved from http://sfaa.metapress.com/content/ V5W7812LPXEXTPBW

Sloan, L., & Wahab, S. (2000). Feminist voices on sex work: Implications for social work. *Affilia,* *15*(4), 457–479.

Texas Alcohol Beverage Commission. (2016). *Human trafficking hotline number sign* [Online image]. Retrieved from https://www.tabc.state.tx.us/publications/brochures/ humanTrafficking.pdf

Trafficking Victims Protection Act of 2000, Pub. L. No. 106–386, 114 Stat. 1464 (2000).

Trafficking Victims Protection Reauthorization Act, 22 USC § 7311 (2008).

United Nations. (1948, December 10). The universal declaration of human rights. Retrieved from the United Nations website: http://www.un.org/en/universal-declaration-human-rights/

United Nations. (1949, December 2). *Convention for the suppression of traffic in persons and the* *exploitation of prostitution of others, GA Res 317A (IV).* Retrieved from http://www.ohchr .org/Documents/ProfessionalInterest/trafficpersons.pdf

United Nations. (1979). *Convention on the elimination of all forms of discrimination against* *women* (1249 U.N.T.S. 13). Retrieved from http://www.un.org/womenwatch/daw/cedaw/

United Nations. (1989). *Convention on the rights of the child* (1577 U.N.T.S. 3). Retrieved from http://www.ohchr.org/en/professionalinterest/pages/crc.aspx

United Nations. (2000). *Protocol to prevent, suppress and punish trafficking in persons, especially* *women and children, supplementing the United Nations convention against transnational* *organized crime.* Retrieved from http://www.refworld.org/docid/4720706c0.html

United Nations. (2006). *In-depth study on all forms of violence against women.* Retrieved from Geneva, Switzerland: https://documents-dds-ny.un.org/doc/UNDOC/GEN/N06/419/74/ PDF/N0641974.pdf?OpenElement

United Nations. (2011). *Report of the Special Rapporteur on violence against women, its* *causes and consequences.* Retrieved from Geneva, Switzerland: http://www.refworld.org/ docid/4ef1a8ae2.html

U.S. Census Bureau (2015). American Community Survey 1-year estimates. Retrieved from Census Reporter Profile page for San Diego, CA https://censusreporter.org/ profiles/16000US0666000-san-diego-ca/

U.S. Citizenship & Immigration Services (USCIS) (2013). *Immigration and citizenship data.* Retrieved from https://www.uscis.gov/tools/reports-studies/immigration-forms-data

U.S. Department of Homeland Security. (2017). *Immigration options for victims of crime.* Retrieved from https://www.dhs.gov/immigration-options-victims-crimes.

U.S. Department of State (2010). *Trafficking in persons report.* Retrieved from http://www.state .gov/documents/organization/142979.pdf

U.S. Department of State. (2014, December 22). *Rights, protections and resources* [Brochure]. Retrieved from http://travel.state.gov/content/dam/visas/LegalRightsandProtections/ Wilberforce Pamphlet English Online Reading Version 12–22–2014.pdf

U.S. Department of State. (2016). *Trafficking in persons report.* Retrieved from http://www.state .gov/j/tip/rls/tiprpt/2016/

Violence Against Women Act Reauthorization Act of 2013, Pub. L. No. 113–4, 127 Stat. 54 (2013).

Wahab, S., & Panichelli, M. (2013). Ethical and human rights issues in coercive interventions with sex workers. *Affilia, 28*(4), 344–349. doi: 10.1177/0886109913505043

Weitzer, R. (2005). The growing moral panic over prostitution and sex trafficking. *The* *Criminologist, 30*(5), 1–4.

Wolfer, T. A., & Scales, T. L. (2006). *Decision cases for advanced social work practice: Thinking like* *a social worker.* Belmont, CA: Thomson Brooks/Cole.

Section III

A Holistic Approach to Taking Actions

Understanding Collective Impact and Individual Action

This is not a problem that can be solved by one individual or one organization. Traffickers are increasingly sophisticated and well networked, making use of technology as a means of exploitation. Our response must be equally sophisticated and networked. It takes the whole community linking arms, taking a stand, and sending a message loud and clear that trafficking has no place in our city.

—John Nehme[1]
President and CEO of Allies Against Slavery
October 15, 2015

I. Learning Objectives

1.1 Students will examine collaborative responses and partnerships in the antitrafficking movement.

1.2 Students will explore fair trade practices and their role in the antitrafficking movement.

---

[1] Nehme, J. (2015). Austin City Council passes resolution approving "Human Trafficking Awareness Initiative." Retrieved from http://www.alliesagainstslavery.org/city-of-austin-resolution/.

Figure 8.1 *There is no one profile of a trafficked person.*

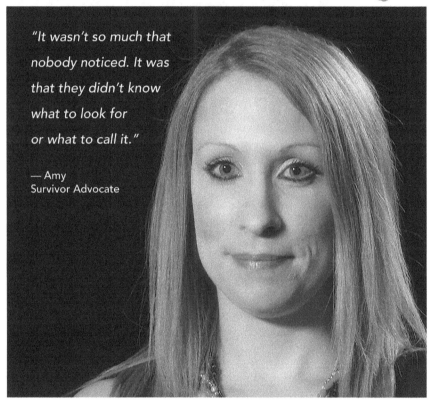

Know the Faces of Human Trafficking

"It wasn't so much that nobody noticed. It was that they didn't know what to look for or what to call it."

— Amy
Survivor Advocate

There is no one profile of a trafficked person; human trafficking can happen to anyone. So whether you are making a traffic stop, responding to a domestic violence call, or helping a homeless youth, remember to look for indicators of human trafficking and know whom in your department and your community to call for appropriate services.

For more information, visit the human trafficking section of the Office for Victims of Crime website at www.ovc.gov/trafficking or call the National Human Trafficking Resource Center at 888–373–7888.

SOURCE: *Office for Victims of Crime, Know the Faces of Human Trafficking Poster Gallery, 2014.* Retrieved from http://ovc.ncjrs.gov/humantrafficking/Public_Awareness_Folder/images/final_poster_amy.jpg. In the public domain.

1.3 Students will explore the collective impact approach to human trafficking.

1.4 Students will examine the role of individual action and explore practical suggestions for engagement at the individual level.

2. Key Ideas

The ideas central to this chapter are:

2.1 Partnerships between nongovernmental organizations and governmental entities are a key component of the antitrafficking movement in the United States.

2.2 The fair trade movement represents efforts by businesses in retail and agriculture to reduce or end forced labor and exploitation in their supply chains.

2.3 Collective impact initiatives use structured processes and infrastructure to develop cross-sector collaborations in response to complex social problems.

2.4 Opportunities exist for individual community members to become engaged as agents of social change in the antitrafficking movement.

3. Introduction

This chapter will focus on the interdisciplinary pursuit to address this crime in the United States. Rarely have we seen multiple layers (local, state, and federal) and multiple disciplines (social services, law enforcement, and prosecutors) work so closely and collaboratively toward a shared social justice pursuit. Still, we have seen how the issues of competing professional, ethical, and organizational missions have been a part of the antitrafficking movement. This chapter will discuss these dilemmas as controversial issues and unintended consequences. Also, this chapter will highlight gaps in services, including the identification of professionals who need to be involved in the antitrafficking efforts (schools/education systems, child welfare, etc.) but are largely absent.

In addition to the important responses to human trafficking among social service providers, law enforcement, and policy makers, antitrafficking work must also be taken up by those outside these professional realms. In this chapter, we will highlight the role of individual action and collective community approaches to address and reduce exploitation. This chapter aims to instigate exploration of the intersections of individual change and systems change. That is, what is the role of both individual and community action in tackling both the surface level of suffering produced by human trafficking and the deeper systemic, structural oppressions at its core?

4. Scientific Knowledge

4.1 Coalitions, Community Partnerships, and Collective Impact

In complementing previous focus on efforts to prevent human trafficking, prosecute traffickers, and protect human trafficking survivors, the U.S. Department of State promotes the importance of partnerships in combatting human trafficking. Referring to partnership as a fourth "p," the department encourages movement toward collaborative efforts and leveraging of resources among governmental and nongovernment entities in human rights, labor and employment, health, and law enforcement (U.S. Department of State, 2013, October 4).

Partnership between victim service organizations and law enforcement has long been a key component of the antitrafficking movement in the United States and has seen increasing reference in reauthorizations of the Trafficking Victims Protection Act (TVPA) (McSween, 2011). With influence of the Trafficking Victims Protection Act of 2000 and Violence Protection Act of 2000 [TVPA] (P.L. 106–386) and early strides in the antitrafficking movement, communities across the nation began to have difficult conversations about shared and divergent agendas in responding to and disrupting exploitation. With the support of governmental grant funding from the Department of Justice Office for Victims of Crime and the Bureau of Justice Assistance, many communities developed or expanded bisector task forces and coalitions. These initiatives focused on the identification, investigation, and prosecution of human trafficking cases, in addition to delivery of social services to survivors.

Among law enforcement entities, partners include local, state, and federal entities such as police departments, district attorneys, the Federal Bureau of Investigation (FBI), the Department of Homeland Security (including Immigration and Customs Enforcement, or ICE), the Department of Labor, and the United States Attorney's Office (U.S. Department of State, 2015).

The importance of partnership as a fourth "p" goes beyond the United States. Partnerships have also received attention at the global level and were emphasized with the creation of the United Nations Global Initiative to Fight Human Trafficking (UN GIFT) in 2008 (McSween, 2011).

The past decade's focus on partnership has not been without critique. Fukushima and Liou (2012) argue that partnerships are often focused narrowly on the prosecution of traffickers and the "rescue" and service provision to survivors. Furthermore, partnerships often include actors whose agendas and missions differ, which can create an atmosphere of confusion or distrust. These limited collaborative efforts may obscure the voices of victims and survivors, who should be at the center of collaborative efforts and partnerships (Fukushima & Liou, 2012). Indeed, there are opportunities for limited partnerships and local or regional coalitions to expand beyond traditional actors, to include greater cross-sector and multidisciplinary allies. Examples may include immigrant rights groups, child welfare organizations, rape crisis centers, and faith-based communities.

In addition to existing attention on collaborative responses to survivors, some argue for increased engagement with traffickers and particularly with industries that

Figure 8.2 *Mapping the U.S. government's anti–human trafficking initiatives.*

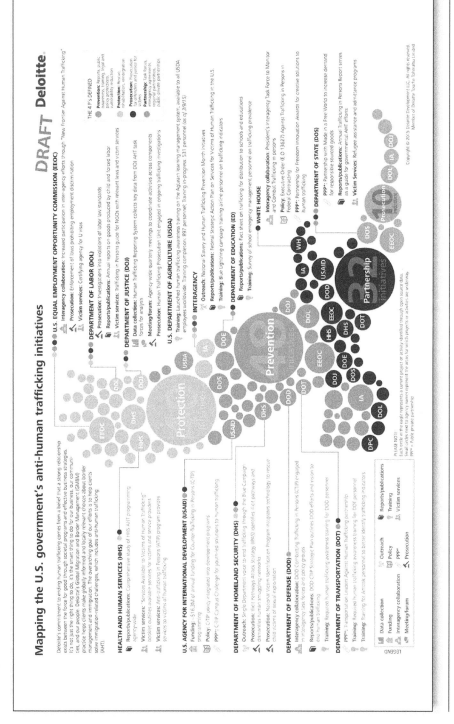

SOURCE: Reprinted from *The freedom ecosystem: How the power of partnership can help stop modern slavery* (pp. 40–41) by Sean Morris, John Cassidy, Anesa "Nes" Parker, Sahil Joshi, Aysha Malik, Danielle Melfi, and Deloitte University Press, 2015. Copyright 2015 by Deloitte Development LLC. Reprinted with permission.

use or benefit from forced and coerced labor. Instead of an abolitionist aim to end slavery outright, using an incremental or harm-reduction approach may involve working with businesses that employ exploitative practices or working directly with slaveholders (Androff, 2011). "The gradualist approach aims for incremental improvements in the lives of slaves, similar to the harm reduction model, where the undesired behavior is not the focus of the intervention, but the context and conditions associated with the behavior that cause additional harm are the subject of intervention" (Androff, 2011, p. 217). Some countries have a higher level of social acceptance of slavery practices than others and may benefit from interventions that operate within these accepted practices. Some nongovernmental organizations, for example, may work directly with slaveholders in order to provide services to those who are being exploited. Interventions may aim to improve working conditions, payments, and working hours. Androff notes that this may present ethical dilemmas for some, "as there is a danger that this line of intervention may lead to sanctioned forms of exploitation" (2011, p. 218).

Slavery No More

http://www.slaverynomore.org/
   According to their website, mission of Slavery No More is "to resource a diversity of the most effective organizations working to combat and abolish modern-day slavery and human trafficking, and to create awareness and a diversity of opportunities for meaningful personal engagement."

SOURCE: "About us" (2017). Slavery No More. Retrieved from: http://www.slaverynomore.org/about-us/.

4.2 Fair Trade and the Slave-Free Movement—Connecting Workers With Retailers

Efforts to bring about fairer and more humane working conditions have been promoted over time by the fair trade movement, which originated in the 1940s and gained momentum in the 1970s. What later became Ten Thousand Villages (www.tenthousandvillages.com) began with the Mennonite Central Committee importing embroidery work from Puerto Rico, expanding to needlework from Palestinian refugees and Haitian woodwork (Redfern & Snedker, 2002). Generally, the fair trade movement has paid close attention to equality and the rights of marginalized producers and workers. Fair Trade USA (www.fairtradeusa.org) certifies fair trade products for the U.S. marketplace, aiming to end exploitation and protect farmers.

The fair trade movement is complemented by other efforts to encourage large businesses in retail and agriculture to adopt policies and practices to reduce or end forced labor and exploitation in their supply chains. For example, the Coalition of Immokalee Workers is a worker-based human rights organization working to increase social responsibility and end exploitation in the agricultural industry (www.ciw-online.org). Their Fair Food Program began in the tomato fields of Immokalee,

Figure 8.3 *Forced labor awareness poster.*

SOURCE: U.S. Department of Homeland Security. (2014). Blue campaign force labor awareness poster [Online image]. Retrieved from https://www.dhs.gov/blue-campaign/resource-catalog.

Florida, as a worker-to-worker education program that developed new labor standards and innovative partnerships with retail buyers that include major fast-food and grocery store chains. The coalition reports that

> Immokalee has evolved from being one of the poorest, most politically powerless communities in the country to become today an important national and statewide presence with forceful, committed leadership directly from the base of our community—young, migrant workers forging a future of livable wages and modern labor relations in Florida's fields. (Coalition of Immokalee Workers, 2012, para. 1)

The coalition has also been part of large-scale efforts to uncover, investigate, and prosecute farm slavery operations in the southeastern part of the United States. Furthermore, the coalition explores the interconnections between forced labor and sexual harassment and assault in the agricultural industry, expanding its efforts to include gender-based violence. In 2015, the Coalition of Immokalee Workers was awarded the Presidential Medal for Extraordinary Efforts to Combat Human Trafficking.

More recently, the fair trade movement has included specific and targeted initiatives demanding slave-free products among retailers as well. Made in a Free World (http://madeinafreeworld.com/take_action) connects concerned citizens with businesses they frequent. The campaign encourages consumers to demand that businesses adopt a zero-tolerance policy toward slavery and make efforts toward transparency in their supply chains. See the shadow box Made in the Free World and Figure 8.5 for more about their model and mission.

4.3 Collective Impact

Collective impact represents an emerging approach that identifies social problems as complex and interrelated. This approach is based on the premise that independent action and isolated initiatives are not successful as the primary avenue toward social change. Collective impact initiatives argue for cross-sector coalitions that go beyond nonprofit and governmental initiatives. This approach draws heavily from the idea that "large-scale social change comes from better cross-sector coordination rather than from the isolated intervention of individual organizations" (Kania & Kramer, 2011, p. 38). That is, in order to best respond to complex problems, behavior change among multiple actors and systems is required.

Unlike other collaboration efforts, collective impact initiatives involve structured processes and infrastructure. Kania and Kramer (2011) describe five critical elements of collective impact initiatives:

- Common agenda—shared vision for change
- Shared measurement systems—agreement on how to measure success
- Mutually reinforcing activities—coordination of differentiated activities

- Continuous communication—regular meetings over time for trust building and development of common language
- Backbone support—supporting infrastructure and coordinator of structured process

While few have applied the principles of collective impact to the complex problem of human trafficking, new initiatives continue to emerge. The Texas non-profit organization Allies Against Slavery applies collective impact strategies through their slave-free city network model, leveraging stakeholders from multiple sectors to identify gaps in the local continuum of solutions to human trafficking (see www.alliesagainstslavery.org/mission/). Similarly, a new report developed in close collaboration by Deloitte Consulting and Free the Slaves seeks to put the antitrafficking movement within a collective impact framework (Morris et al., 2015).

Borrowing from the ecological perspective, Deloitte uses the phrase "freedom ecosystem" in defining the comprehensive array of actors, or allies, necessary for shared and sustained impact.

> The freedom ecosystem is the dynamic and diverse community of actors that is centered on slavery's victims and survivors with the shared goal of empowering these central actors to own their personal path to freedom. This ecosystem is composed of victims, survivors, and anti-slavery allies from the private, public, and nonprofit sectors converging to advance freedom in the face of the opposing slavery predators and accomplices who engage in the illicit networks that allow slavery to persist. (Morris et al., 2015, p. 5)

A collective active perspective will resist the compliancy evident in U.S. history. Kristof and WuDunn (2009) charge, "People get away with enslaving village girls for the same reason that people got away with enslaving blacks two hundred years ago: the victims are perceived as discounted humans" (p. 24). Contemporary collective action allows for collective accountability in ways that it did not previously.

Made in a Free World

Justin Dillion continued his antislavery work on the Slavery Footprint © as the CEO and founder of Made in a Free World, whose organization mission it is to assist businesses to understand their supply chain and the risk of engagement with forced labor and empower consumers to purchase products that are free from a slave-labor supply chain. The organization's website states, "we're helping businesses understand their risk of forced labor in their supply chains and giving them clear steps to support freedom for all … We are empowering companies to engage with their suppliers all the way down to raw materials. Over time, we believe that a network of aligned buyers and suppliers will systemically disrupt illicit markets that use slave labor in supply chains. Businesses have the potential to become the new leaders of a free world" (http://madeinafreeworld.com/).

Figure 8.4 *Anti-slavery allies of the freedom ecosystem.*

Allies	Functional superpower	Example organization	Example group in action
 Funder	Provides much-needed capital to support programming, research, and advocacy as well as investing in opportunities that advance a more free world	• Government agencies • Multilateral organizations • Philanthropy • Wealth managers	• Humanity United • Google Giving • Freedom Fund • US Department of Labor
 Policy maker and enforcer	Develops and implements domestic and international policies to combat slavery	• Political leaders or legislators • Government agencies • Public attorneys • Local police forces	• United Kingdom Home Office • US State Department • UN Office on Drugs and Crime • Child Protection Brigade, Haiti
 Influencer	Advocates on behalf of victims and survivors to advance the efforts of other allies	• Individual activists • NGOs • Media • Faith-based groups	• Global Freedom Network • CNN Freedom Project • Alliance Against Trafficking of Women in Nepal • The Vatican
 Convener	Assembles individuals or groups to promote collaboration within the freedom ecosystem	• Coalitions • Associations	• The White House • ATEST • National Underground Railroad Freedom Center • ASSET • United Way
 Researcher	Studies the causes and solutions of modern slavery and builds knowledge for the next generation of abolitionists	• Academia • Think tanks	• Carnegie Mellon • Carr Center for Human Rights Policy • Loyola's Modern Slavery Research Project • Human Trafficking Center at the University of Denver

Allies	Functional superpower	Example organization	Example group in action
Service provider	Works directly with at-risk populations, victims, and survivors on prevention, rescue, and reintegration	• NGOs • Victim services agencies • Medical providers • Faith-based groups	• Free the Slaves • CAST • Polaris • International Justice Mission • ECPAT • FAIR Girls • Beyond Borders
Concerned consumer	Advances fair labor practices through their purchasing power	• Public • Fair-trade organizations • Consumer-information organizations	• Harry Potter Alliance • KnowTheChain • Fair Trade International • Made in a Free World
Business	Protects workers' rights through transparent supply-chain practices or advances the fight for freedom using company-specific competencies	• Businesses • Supply chain analysts • Skills-based corporate social responsibility functions	• The Coca-Cola Company • Palantir • Salesforce • Verite • GoodWeave
Labor organizer	Organizes workers and supports them in collectively advocating for their rights	• Unions • Cooperatives	• Coalition of Immokalee Workers • Solidarity Center • National Domestic Workers Alliance

SOURCE: Reprinted from *The freedom ecosystem: How the power of partnership can help stop modern slavery* (p. 16) by Sean Morris, and Deloitte University Press, John Cassidy, Anesa "Nes" Parker, Sahil Joshi, Aysha Malik, Danielle Melfi, 2015. Copyright 2015 by Deloitte Development LLC. Reprinted with permission.

NOTE: For purposes of this report, survivors have not been identified as a separate ally and instead are considered a group that can cut across the outlined functions.

Figure 8.5 *Made in a free world supply and demand model.*

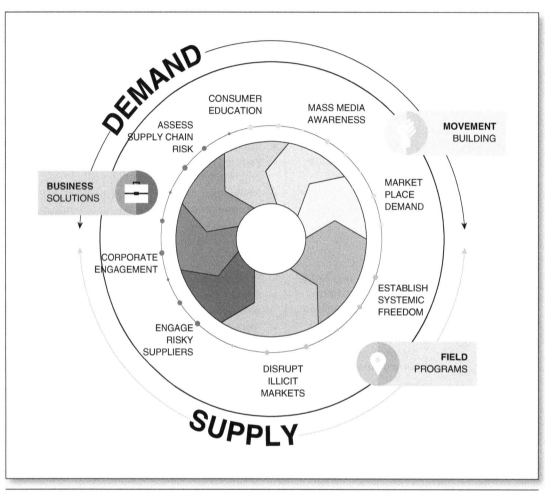

4.4 Individual Action

Included in that "freedom ecosystem" and in the move toward collective action among multiple sectors of government, business, and community, there remains power in the individual as an agent of change. In fact, during the 10th anniversary of the Universal Declaration of Human Rights in 1958, Eleanor Roosevelt remarked,

Where, after all, do universal human rights begin? In small places, close to home—so close and so small that they cannot be seen on any maps of the world. Yet they are the world of the individual person; the neighborhood he lives in; the school or college he attends; the factory, farm, or office where he works. Such are the places where every man, woman, and child seek equal justice, equal opportunity, equal dignity without discrimination. Unless these rights have meaning there, they have little meaning anywhere. Without concerned citizen action to uphold them close to home, we shall look in vain for progress in the larger world. (United Nations, 2016, para. 3)

Individual action can take many forms. While it may feel like an overwhelming or insurmountable task, becoming engaged at the individual level can involve a simple beginning and emerge over time, in accordance with your own skills and interest and the needs of your community. Community members need not be social workers, immigration attorneys, policy makers, or law enforcement officers in order to contribute to reducing the exploitation of others. In fact, our communities are strengthened when concerned citizens increase their awareness and empathy and take action. To end modern-day slavery, our communities need people in every position to take notice and action (e.g., engineers, painters, managers, teachers, bakers, banker, construction workers, and those on Wall Street).

Six practical suggestions for becoming engaged in the antitrafficking movement include:

1. Increase your understanding and awareness.

2. Purchase with information and intention.

3. Volunteer your time and skills.

4. Advocate.

5. Join others.

6. Connect the dots (U.S. Department of State, 2016).

4.4.1 Increase Your Understanding and Awareness

Given the increasing focus on human trafficking and exploitation, there are a seemingly endless number of articles, books, and films on the topic. Continue to expose yourself to content about human trafficking and use a critical eye as a consumer of this content. Be aware of campaigns that, despite good intentions, may serve to further exploit or entrench stereotypes about marginalized communities. Consider using an online alert system, such as Google Alerts or Google Scholar, to receive information about human trafficking cases, new antitrafficking initiatives, and recently published scholarly articles. Finally, learn the red flags or indicators of exploitation and use the National Human Trafficking Resource Center to report tips and learn about training and volunteer opportunities in your community.

4.4.2 Purchase With Intention and Information

Become a conscientious consumer. That is, learn about your own role in the exploitation of others and how your purchases may contribute to the exploitation of others. Consider these questions: "Who picked the cotton for the shirt on your back? Who cut the cane for the sugar in your coffee? Who fired the kiln to make the bricks in your fireplace?" (U.S. Department of Labor [DOL], 2014, p.1). The online survey www.slaveryfootprint.org poses the provocative question: How many slaves work for you? The survey is designed to empower consumers to make informed choices about the products they purchase and their potential role in exploitation. Make a commitment to learn about the supply chain of products you frequently use and limit your consumption of those items or choose slave-free products.

4.4.3 Volunteer Your Time and Skills

Consider donating your time and skills to a local organization that addresses human trafficking. While many volunteers desire direct interaction with human trafficking survivors, the impact you can make as an individual may not be in this area. Think carefully about how, why, and in what capacity you want to volunteer. Many organizations need assistance and support that does not involve working directly with survivors. For example, their efforts may be expanded with volunteer support on graphic design, web development, fundraising, research, administrative support, or gathering in-kind donations such as grocery store gift cards.

4.4.4 Advocate

Sign up for federal policy alerts from Polaris Project (www.polarisproject.org). Investigate policy advocacy efforts in your city or state. If you cannot find human trafficking–related advocacy organizations in your area, make a commitment to monitor local and state activities to address human trafficking.

4.4.5 Join Others

Broaden your individual actions to your social network. Your immediate social sphere can be an interesting starting place for conversations about human trafficking, book clubs, or a small film screening. Alternatively, join an existing coalition, student organization, or community group effort.

4.4.6 Connect the Dots

Above all, connect the dots. Do not be satisfied with simplistic or superficial descriptions of what is a complex social problem. Be courageous in going beyond the basics of human trafficking and of conscientious consumption to open up dialogues with your social sphere about some of the larger systemic issues that contribute to human trafficking (such as racism, sexism, classism, nativism, and ableism). Explore the ways in which an antitrafficking agenda may complement or overlap with other human rights movements and social justice initiatives. For example, explore connections to the decarceration movement or efforts to address income inequality, educational inequality, health disparities, disproportionality in the child welfare system, or immigrant rights. In general, taking a stand against human trafficking and being engaged in the antitrafficking movement is not limited to the work of organizations providing services to survivors. While these programs are important, there remains great work to be done on the systemic and structural issues that contribute to human trafficking.

5. Summary

Social reform is impacted by individual change and systems change. Education and awareness can positively influence individual growth and transformation as connections are made between complex social and ethical problems. Partnership building through the development of coalitions, collective impacts, and community advocacy groups allows a shared vision for sustained change. New models have also begun to take hold in the antitrafficking movement. The antitrafficking field, as with other reemerging fields, attempts to keep pace with the advancing knowledge, trends, and practices and applies strong theoretical foundations such as an ecological framework to understanding the causes and solutions for modern-day slavery.

6. Key Terms

6.1   Fourth "p"   6.3   Collective impact

6.2   Fair trade

7. Active Learning Exercises and Discussion Questions

7.1 Slavery Footprint: Then and Now

Ask students to retake the Slavery Footprint before class found at: http://www
.slaveryfootprint.org. Compare and contrast your footprint at the beginning of class
and now. What, if any, actions have you taken to reduce your slavery footprint? What
was most difficult? What was the easiest?

7.2 Address Social and Cultural Norms

Think about the social and cultural norms of your community and your upbringing
(for example as they relate to class, gender, race, immigration status). How might these
ideas perpetuate or sustain the exploitation of marginalized and oppressed groups?

8. Assignments or Homework

8.1   Hold an awareness-raising campaign or in-kind donation drive on campus. Reach out to local organizations that provide services to trafficking survivors (such as an immigrant rights organization, domestic violence shelter, or runaway/homeless youth organization). Inquire about local awareness-raising initiatives or in-kind client needs and plan the campaign according to those needs.

8.2   Explore the list of individuals the U.S. Department of State has honored over the years for their work to end human trafficking. "TIP Report Heroes" are listed at www.tipheroes.org.

8.3   Ask students to look at the www.alliesagainstslavery.org website and determine if a local organization exists. What is the history and mission of that organization? How could students become involved in a community-based organization? Is there a student-led organization on campus? Should there be such an organization? What issues should students think about when making these types of initiatives?

9. In-Class Discussion Questions

9.1   What does this list reflect about the role of the United States in the global anti-trafficking movement? In addition to recognizing the important work of those listed, what reflections or analyses can a critical lens or a feminist lens offer?

9.2   Writing Assignment: Select one individual about whom to learn more. Consider the following questions:

- How does this individual's work address the root causes of exploitation?
- Does this individual work toward micro-, mezzo-, or macro-level change? How?
- How does this individual create bridges between community organizations, the private sector, and governmental agencies?

10. Suggestions for Further Learning

10.1 **Websites**

10.1.1   Slavery Footprint—www.slaveryfootprint.org

10.1.2   U.S. Department of Labor, List of Goods Produced by Child Labor or Forced Labor—www.dol.gov/ilab/reports/child-labor/list-of-goods/

10.1.3   Fair Trade USA—www.fairtradeusa.org

10.1.4   Made in a Free World—www.madeinafreeworld.com

10.1.5   Coalition of Immokalee Workers—www.ciw-online.org

10.1.6   Allies Against Slavery—www.alliesagainstslavery.org

11. References

Androff, D. K. (2011). The problem of contemporary slavery: An international human rights challenge for social work. *International Social Work, 54*(2), 209–222. doi:10.1177/0020872810368395

Coalition of Immokalee Workers. (2012). *Immokalee today: Nothing is impossible*. Retrieved from http://www.ciw-online.org/about/

Department of Homeland Security. (2016). *Blue campaign forced labor awareness poster* [Online image]. Retrieved from https://www.dhs.gov/blue-campaign/resource-catalog https://www.dhs.gov/blue-campaign/resource-catalog

Fukushima, A., & Liou, C. C. (2012). Weaving theory and practice: Anti-trafficking partnerships and the fourth 'P' in the human trafficking paradigm. *Program on Human Rights, Center on Democracy, Development, and the Rule of Law, Freeman Spogli Institute for International Studies, Working Paper of the Program on Human Rights, 4*, 1–16.

Kania, J., & Kramer, M. (2011). Collective impact. *Stanford Social Innovation Review, 9*(1), 36–41.

Kristof, N., & WuDunn, S. (2009). *Half the sky: Turning oppression into opportunity for women worldwide*. New York, NY: Random House.

Made in a Free World. (2013). Mission statement our model. Retrieved from https://madeinafreeworld.com/mission

McSween, M. (2011). Investing in the business against human trafficking: Embracing the fourth p-partnerships. *Intercultural Human Rights Law Review, 6*, 283.

Morris, S., Cassidy, J., Parker, A., Joshi, S., Malik, A., & Melfi, D. (2015). *The freedom ecosystem: How the power of partnership can help stop modern slavery*. Retrieved from http://dupress.com/articles/freedom-ecosystem-stop-modern-slavery/?icid=hp:ft:01

Office for Victims of Crime. (2014). *Know the Faces of Human Trafficking Poster Gallery* [Online image]. Retrieved from http://ovc.ncjrs.gov/humantrafficking/Public_Awareness_Folder/images/final_poster_amy.jpg

Redfern, A., & P. Snedker (2002). *Creating market opportunities for small enterprises: Experiences of the Fair Trade movement*. Geneva, Switzerland: International Labour Office. Retrieved from: http://www.european-fair-trade-association.org/efta/Doc/2002-Market-op.pdf

Roosevelt, E. (1958). Remarks delivered at the United Nations in New York on March 27, 1958. Retrieved from http://www.un.org/en/globalissues/briefingpapers/humanrights/quotes.shtml

Trafficking Victims Protection Act of 2000, Pub. L. No. 106–386, 114 Stat. 1464 (2000).

United Nations. (2016). *Resources for speakers on global issues: Human rights for all: Quotations*. Retrieved from http://www.un.org/en/globalissues/briefingpapers/humanrights/quotes.shtml

U.S. Department of Labor (DOL). (2014). *List of goods produced by child labor or forced labor*. Retrieved from: http://www.dol.gov/ilab/reports/child-labor/list-of-goods/

U.S. Department of State. (2013, October 4). *Four "Ps": Prevention, protection, prosecution, partnerships*. Retrieved from https://ctpcsw.files.wordpress.com/2010/07/four-ps.pdf

U.S. Department of State. (2015). *Trafficking in persons report*. Retrieved from http://www.state.gov/j/tip/rls/tiprpt/2015/

U.S. Department of State. (2016). 20 Ways you can help fight human trafficking. Retrieved from http://www.state.gov/j/tip/id/help/index.htm

Appendix A

2015 NHTRC Annual Report

1-888-373-7888

NATIONAL
HUMAN TRAFFICKING
RESOURCE CENTER

NATIONAL HUMAN TRAFFICKING
RESOURCE CENTER (NHTRC) DATA BREAKDOWN

United States Report
1/1/2015 – 12/31/2015

Overview of Incoming Signals

*The following information is based on incoming signals made to the NHTRC from January 1, 2015 – December 31, 2015 about human trafficking cases and issues related to human trafficking in the United States and U.S. territories. **Signals** refer to incoming communications with the NHTRC and can take the form of **phone calls, online tip reports, or emails**. Signals regarding topics unrelated to human trafficking are not included in this report. In 2015, the NHTRC received a total of **24,757** signals nationwide.*

 21,947 Phone Calls

 1,275 Emails

 1,535 Online Tip Reports

LOCATION OF POTENTIAL TRAFFICKING CASES (WHERE KNOWN)*

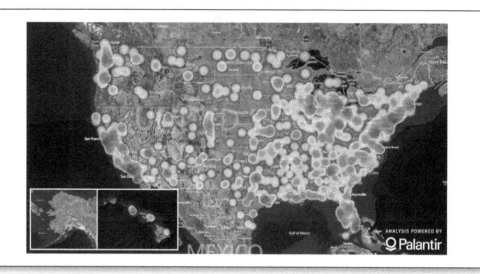

These maps only reflect cases in which the location of the potential trafficking was known. Some cases may involve more than one location and are not reflected in this map.

*****

Important Note: *The data displayed in this report was generated based on information communicated to the National Human Trafficking Resource Center hotline via phone, email, and online tip report. The NHTRC cannot verify the accuracy of the information reported. This is not a comprehensive report on the scale or scope of human trafficking within the state. These statistics may be subject to change as new information emerges.*

Appendix B

Survey to Assess Student Knowledge Regarding Human Trafficking

Survey to Assess the Perceptions, Knowledge and Attitudes of Social Work Students Regarding Human Trafficking

For the purpose of this survey, **human trafficking** is defined as "the recruitment, transportation, transfer, harboring or receipt, of persons, by means of threat or use of force or other forms of coercion, of abduction, of fraud, of deception, of abuse or power or of position of vulnerability or of the giving or receiving or payments of benefits to achieve the consent of person having control over the other person for the purpose of exploitation."[1]

Demographic Questions

Please circle your responses

1. **Gender:** Female   Male

2. **Age:**   18–22   23–27   28–32   33–37   38–42   43–47   48–over

3. **Major:**   Social Work   Non-Social Work: _____

4. **Classification:** Freshman   Sophomore   Junior   Senior   Graduate

---

[1]United Nations General Assembly. (2000). "Protocol to prevent, suppress and punish trafficking in persons, especially women and children, supplementing the United Nations convention against transnational organized crime." Retrieved from http://www.refworld.org/docid/4720706c0.html

5. **I have prior training in human trafficking.**   Yes   No

6. **I have dealt with human trafficking
    in my professional responsibilities.**   Yes   No

Please indicate your degree of agreement or disagreement with the following statements. If you are uncertain or undecided circle "neutral."

7. **Human trafficking is a problem for society at large.**

    Strongly Disagree   Disagree   Neutral   Agree   Strongly Agree

8. **Human smuggling is synonymous with human trafficking.**

    Strongly Disagree   Disagree   Neutral   Agree   Strongly Agree

9. **Prostitution is synonymous with human trafficking.**

    Strongly Disagree   Disagree   Neutral   Agree   Strongly Agree

10. **Human trafficking is a worldwide problem.**

    Strongly Disagree   Disagree   Neutral   Agree   Strongly Agree

11. **There are two categories of human trafficking—labor and sex.**

    Strongly Disagree   Disagree   Neutral   Agree   Strongly Agree

12. **Human trafficking primarily involves individuals from other countries.**

    Strongly Disagree   Disagree   Neutral   Agree   Strongly Agree

13. **Social work services should be readily available to every victim of human
    trafficking.**

    Strongly Disagree   Disagree   Neutral   Agree   Strongly Agree

14. **American citizens are not victims of human trafficking.**

    Strongly Disagree   Disagree   Neutral   Agree   Strongly Agree

15. **I am able to empathize with victims of human trafficking.**

    Strongly Disagree   Disagree   Neutral   Agree   Strongly Agree

16. **I know enough about human trafficking to serve human trafficking
    victims.**

    Strongly Disagree   Disagree   Neutral   Agree   Strongly Agree

17. **I have a working knowledge of human trafficking.**

    Strongly Disagree   Disagree   Neutral   Agree   Strongly Agree

18. **Human trafficking is a growing problem in America.**
    Strongly Disagree   Disagree   Neutral   Agree   Strongly Agree

19. **I am able to assess whether a person is a victim of human trafficking.**
    Strongly Disagree   Disagree   Neutral   Agree   Strongly Agree

20. **I know the risk factors for victims of human trafficking.**
    Strongly Disagree   Disagree   Neutral   Agree   Strongly Agree

21. **All victims of human trafficking are receptive to receiving social services.**
    Strongly Disagree   Disagree   Neutral   Agree   Strongly Agree

22. **My social work curriculum has adequately prepared me to work with victims of human trafficking.**
    Strongly Disagree   Disagree   Neutral   Agree   Strongly Agree

23. **Greater funding should be allocated to assist human trafficking victims.**
    Strongly Disagree   Disagree   Neutral   Agree   Strongly Agree

24. **I know how to provide long-term counseling for human trafficking victims.**
    Strongly Disagree   Disagree   Neutral   Agree   Strongly Agree

25. **I have a basic understanding of the different needs of human trafficking victims.**
    Strongly Disagree   Disagree   Neutral   Agree   Strongly Agree

26. **I have an understanding of the psychological effects of human trafficking that allows me to effectively work with victims.**
    Strongly Disagree   Disagree   Neutral   Agree   Strongly Agree

27. **I would be reluctant to provide social services to a victim of trafficking because of my personal beliefs.**
    Strongly Disagree   Disagree   Neutral   Agree   Strongly Agree

28. **I can appropriately advise human trafficking victims about available services and resources.**
    Strongly Disagree   Disagree   Neutral   Agree   Strongly Agree

29. **I am aware of the safety concerns of social workers when working with human trafficking victims.**

    Strongly Disagree Disagree Neutral Agree Strongly Agree

30. **Women and children are the primary victims of human trafficking.**

    Strongly Disagree Disagree Neutral Agree Strongly Agree

31. **Internationally trafficked victims use their position to gain secure legal status in the US.**

    Strongly Disagree Disagree Neutral Agree Strongly Agree

32. **All human trafficking victims voluntarily disclose their situation to professionals.**

    Strongly Disagree Disagree Neutral Agree Strongly Agree

Thank you for contributing to this survey.

Appendix C

Human Trafficking
Video Resources

Title	Reviewed by Author	Used by Author	Run Time	Producer	Access	Cost	Fiction/ Documentary/ Other
12 Years A Slave			2h 14 min	Regency Enterprises & River Road Entertainment	Purchase Only	$10.19–$39.99	feature length film, historical fiction (based on true story)
Beyond the Shadows: You Know Me				Barnardo's	Can Contact Media Team for Further Information http://www.barnardos.org.uk/ news/press_releases/media_ centre.htm		
Cargo: Innocence Lost			1h 15 min	The Journey Film Group	Purchase Only	Amazon Rent: $2.99 Amazon DVD: $199.99	
Demand			≈43 min	Shared Hope International	Watch Online https://vimeo.com/70637039 https://www.youtube.com/ playlist?list=PL141F42A9A FFEBFBC	Free	
Domestic Minor Sex Trafficking: Assessments in Ten U.S. Locations, Rapid Assessment Methodology & Field Interview Tool			≈10 min	Shared Hope International			
Domestic Minor Sex Trafficking: Assessments in Ten U.S. Locations, Identifying and Responding to America's Trafficked Youth			3 discs ≈ 10 min	Shared Hope International	Purchase Only https://sharedhope.org/ product/domestic-minor-sex-trafficking-training-guide-and-video-series/	$20.00	Training video

Title	Reviewed by Author	Used by Author	Run Time	Producer	Access	Cost	Fiction/ Documentary/ Other
Dying to Leave: The Dark Business of Human Trafficking			1h	Thirteen WNET New York	Purchase Only https://www.trainingabc .com/dying-to-leave-the-dark-business-of-human-trafficking/	$149.95	
First Response to Victims of Crime			30 min	National Sheriffs' Association, U.S. Dept of Justice	Watch Online https://www.youtube.com/ watch?v=zxavn94q6jY Guidebook Available http://ojp.gov/ovc/ publications/infores/pdftxt/ FirstResponseGuidebook.pdf	Free	
Food Chains: The Revolution in America's Fields			1h 22 min, 52 min, 30 min versions	Ro*co Films Educational	Currently on Netflix Purchase	Amazon Rent: $3.99 DVD: $9.96–$14.95	Documentary
Girl Trouble: Girls Tell Their Truth About the Juvenile Justice System			57 min PBS version 74 min theatrical version	Independent Lens, PBS	Available at UT Fine Arts Library	Free	
Half the Sky			1h 55 min	Blue Sky Films, Show of Force	Purchase Only	Amazon Rent: $3.99 DVD: $19.99	

(Continued)

(Continued)

Title	Reviewed by Author	Used by Author	Run Time	Producer	Access	Cost	Fiction/ Documentary/ Other
Human Trafficking				U.S. Dept of Homeland Security			
Look Beneath the Surface: Identifying Victims of Human Trafficking in the U.S.				U.S. Dept of Health and Human Services			Training video
Look Beneath the Surface: Identifying Victims of Human Trafficking in the U.S.			12 min	U.S. Dept of Health and Human Services	Purchase Only https://www.acf.hhs.gov/otip/ partnerships/look-beneath-the-surface	$7.99	Training video
Not My Life			1h 24 min	Worldwide Documentaries	Purchase Only	Amazon Rent: $2.99 DVD: $24.95– $37.55	
NOW: Fighting Child Prostitution			23 min	PBS	Watch Online http://www.pbs.org/now/ shows/422/video.html	Free	
Responding to Victims of Human Trafficking			20 min	Office of Victims of Crime, U.S. Dept of Justice	Watch Online https://www.youtube.com/ watch?v=9l8232BNie4	Free	Training video

Title	Reviewed by Author	Used by Author	Run Time	Producer	Access	Cost	Fiction/ Documentary/ Other
Sex + Money: A National Search for Human Worth			1h 32 min	Lot 3 Productions, photogenX	Purchase Only http://www.sexandmoneystore .com/products/121330-sex-money-a-national-search-for-human-worth	$20.00	Documentary
Slavery Out of the Shadows: Spotlight on Human Trafficking			31 min	Texas Young Lawyers Association	Watch Online http://www.tyla.org/tyla/index .cfm/projects/slavery-out-of-the-shadows-spotlight-on-human-trafficking/	Free	
Stefanie Fix: Survival			≈51 min	Hand-to-Mouth Recordings	Available on Spotify Purchase on iTunes	$9.99	
The Crime of Human Trafficking: A Law Enforcement Guide to Identification and Investigation				Office for Violence Against Women, International Association of Chiefs of Police			
The Price of Youth			9 min	WITNESS, Andrew Levine	Watch Online https://www.youtube.com/ watch?v=Hc8o_DzI-xg Purchase	Free Amazon: $2.99– $12.95	
Tricked			1h 20min	Jane Wells & John Keith Wasson	Purchase	iTunes: $3.99	

(Continued)

(Continued)

Title	Reviewed by Author	Used by Author	Run Time	Producer	Access	Cost	Fiction/ Documentary/ Other
The True Cost			1h 32min	Andrew Morgan	Purchase	Amazon & iTunes: $2.99	
Blood Diamond			2h 23min	Edward Zwick	Purchase Only	Amazon Video, YouTube, iTunes: $2.99	
Slum Dog Millionaire			2h	Danny Boyle, Loveleen Tandan	Purchase Only	Amazon Video, YouTube, iTunes: $2.99	
Trade			2h	Marco Kreuzpaintner	Purchase Only	Amazon Video, YouTube, iTunes: $2.99	
The Free State of Jones			2h 19min	Gary Ross	Purchase Only	In theaters	
Slavery: A Global Instigation			90 minutes	Brian Woods and Kate Blewett	Purchase Only	See website	Documentary

Appendix D

Syllabus for Undergraduate Modern-Day Slavery Course

The University of Texas at Austin School of Social Work
Undergraduate Studies Signature Course Program
Modern-Day Slavery: Trafficking in Persons

Semester:	Spring 2016	Instructors:	Noël Busch-Armendariz, PhD, LMSW, MPA
			University Presidential Professor, Associate Vice President for Research
Course Number:	UGS303	Unique Numbers	62050, 62055, 62060
Class Meeting Location:	School of Social Work SSW 1.214	Seminar Meeting Location:	BEN 1.106
Class Meeting Time:	Tuesday Lectures 2:00 - 4:00 pm *All students*	Required Seminar Meetings	62050: Fridays 1:00 – 2:00 pm 62055: Fridays 2:00 – 3:00 pm 62060: Fridays 3:00 – 4:00 pm Each student is assigned to a weekly seminar. Attendance required.

(Continued)

(Continued)

Contact Information:	nbusch@ austin.utexas .edu	Office Hours:	Dr. Noël Busch-Armendariz Tuesdays 11:00 am–12:00 pm & by appointment, School of Social Work 3.208G
			Graduate Teaching Assistant Tuesdays 12:00 – 2:00pm & by appointment, School of Social Work
			Institute of Domestic Violence and Sexual Assault (IDVSA) 3.212E

Course Information

I. Course Description

This course will explore trafficking in persons within the context of social justice, human rights, and feminist perspectives. The course will engage students in discourse around historical and contemporary dialog, theoretical debates, data and research findings, issues related to direct service delivery, and local, national, and global policy responses. Specific attention will be given to an analysis of traffickers and the impact of this crime on the global economy. The scope of the problem (nationally and internationally), medical, psycho-social needs of human trafficking victims, legal and criminal justice issues, vulnerabilities of victims, types of trafficking, typologies of traffickers, and community and policy responses are also included.

Students may encounter human trafficking—or modern-day slavery—in a variety of settings. This course provides an overview of contemporary issues designed to empower students with the conceptual frameworks and knowledge base necessary for effective responses.

II. Course Objectives

Upon completion of this course, student will be able to

- Use a variety of theoretical human rights perspectives to understand human trafficking and its relationship to other forms of violence against women, vulnerable adults, and children
- Understand the psychological, social, physical, legal, and financial consequences of human trafficking on victims, the community, and society as a whole.
- Identify relevant social policies and their intended and unintended consequences for human trafficking victims and those working on their behalf.
- Assess and identify appropriate individual, group, family, agency, community and societal responses.
- Identify the complex social service delivery system developed around services for human trafficking victims.
- Identify ethical dilemmas faced when addressing the needs of human trafficking, in particular, the issues of social control, self-determination, and confidentiality.
- Improve writing and primary/archival research skills.
- Engage in service learning projects to enhance classroom learning.

III. Teaching Methods

Course content will be presented through a variety of teaching strategies. For example, case studies, discussions, videos, small group work, service learning projects, book groups, news articles, examinations, readings, paper assignments, and lectures will be utilized. Videos will be used as tools for addressing key concepts in the course. The goal is to stimulate critical thinking, intellectual creativity, and sharing of knowledge and skills with and through the class. Students will be responsible for material presented through all these activities. Assigned readings are for the week in which they are listed and students should complete the readings prior to class and be prepared to discuss them.

Seminars provide students with a small-group setting to further discuss what is learned during the lecture and larger class setting. Seminars are **MANDATORY**—that is, attendance is **not** optional.

IV. Required Texts

Students will be assigned a set of required readings for this course. Assigned readings may be purchased at the Co-Op or online. Other readings will be available on Canvas.

Required texts:

- Batstone, D. (2010). *Not for Sale: Return of the Global Slave Trade and How We Can Fight It*. Harper-Collins: New York, NY.
- Kristof, N. and WuDunn, S. (2010). *Half the Sky*. Knopf Doubleday Publishing Group: New York, NY.
- Ken, P., & Hunter, K. (2008). *Pimpology: The 48 Laws of the Game*. Simon Spotlight Entertainment: New York, NY.
- Lloyd, R. (2011). *Girls Like Us: Fighting for a World Where Girls Are Not for Sale, An Activist Finds Her Calling and Heals Herself*. Harper Collins: New York, NY.

V. Course Outline/Agenda

Course requirements consist of graded papers, service learning, class participation, and attendance. Specific details for the written assignments will be distributed in class.

Assignment #1: Supply Product Chain Paper	20 points
Assignment #2: Primary Source Research Paper	25 points
Assignment #3: Service Learning	15 points
Final Exam Book Club & Presentation	30 points
Attendance & Participation	10 points
Total	100 points

Detailed prompts will be distributed for each graded assignment to guide the specific objectives of that course assignment. To do well, students should start early, revise drafts, follow instructions, use the university's writing and departmental writing labs, and ask questions. All papers and assignments are submitted on Canvas. Brief descriptions of the assignments are provided below:

1. **Product Supply Chain Paper** (20 points): The economics of human trafficking are straightforward: cheap labor lowers the cost of production, increases profit margins for producers, and lowers prices for consumers. Students will chose a product and trace its product roots. All paper topics need to be reviewed and approved in advance by the instructor. A detailed paper prompt will be provided.

2. **Primary Source & Comparative Analysis Research Paper** (25 points): Students will write a comparative paper on modern day slavery and historical slavery by utilizing a primary or archival source material along with the course readings and other research conducted. This paper builds on the product supply paper. The primary source needs to be reviewed and approved by the instructor. A detailed paper prompt will be provided.

3. **Public Awareness & Education for Service Learning** (15 points): As a required part of this course, students will engage a service learning activity. The activity will provide a learning opportunity for students in addition to serving as a benefit or contribution to our local community about trafficking & anti-trafficking. Activities may include community awareness, fundraising, and/or resource-building activities. More information about this activity will be provided.

4. **Final Exam Book Club & Class Presentation** (30 points): Students will work with their seminar groups to take a deep dive into one of the four assigned books. During the seminar and on their own time students will organize a book discussion and make a class presentation. More information about the format will be provided.

5. **Participation** (10 points): Students are expected to actively contribute to the class discussions and learning in and outside the classrooms and will be evaluated according the criteria listed below.

   a. **Preparation** – Are you prepared for class and seminar by reading the assignments? What have you learned outside of class that enhances our learning together?
   b. **Quality of Participation** – To what extent is your contribution to course discussions and small group activities meaningful? Does your participation in course discussions advance the depth of course learning? This includes your participation in the seminars sessions. Are you engaged even if you are not talking? Are you texting, reading non-class related materials?
   c. **Attendance & Engagement** – Have you attended class regularly? Are you on time to class? Do you leave early? If you need to miss class do you communicate with the instructor and TA? Do you get missed materials from colleagues or TA?

Course Calendar Overview

See Canvas for course calendar including the assigned readings.

VI. Grading Policy

94. 0 and Above	A	74.0 to 76.999	C
90.0 to 93.999	A–	70.0 to 73.999	C–
87.0 to 89.999	B+	67.0 to 69.999	D+
84.0 to 86.999	B	64.0 to 66.999	D
80.0 to 83.999	B–	60.0 to 63.999	D–
77.0 to 79.999	C+	Below 60.0	F

Class Policies

Attendance & Participation

1. Students are expected to attend all class meetings, to read all the assigned readings, and to participate in class discussions. Students are expected to be on time for class. There are no "excused" absences. See university policy on missing class for a religious holiday.

2. Students missing three or more class sessions may receive a 10% reduction in their overall course grades. Students missing more than five class sessions may receive an "F" for the course. The instructor may use her discretion.

3. If a student is going to miss class, the instructor expects that the student will e-mail her and the TA as soon as they know they are going to miss class.

Submitting Assignments & Receiving Credit

1. Students are expected to submit all assignments electronically before 2 pm on the due date to the TA.

2. All assignments need to be submitted through Canvas.

3. Assignments are to be submitted according to the schedule. All late assignments will receive a five (5) percent penalty per day (weekend days will be included).

4. Assignments turned in after the beginning of class will be considered late.

5. Students must earn a 'C-' or above to be given credit for this course. If you receive anything below, you will need to retake a UGS course of your choosing.

Writing Assignments

1. *The Publication Manual of the American Psychological Association* (APA) is the style manual to be used for all assignments. Incorrect APA style will result a deduction of points on assignments.

2. Appropriate referencing is required. Failure to use quotation marks for direct quotes or citation for indirect quotations or others ideas may result in a "0" for the paper and/or an "F" for the course.

3. All papers are to be word-processed, double-spaced, 12-point font, and normal margins.

Amendments to Syllabus

Any modifications, amendments, or changes to the syllabus and/or assignments are the discretion of the instructors. Changes will be announced in class and posted in Canvas. It is the responsibility of the student to inquire about any changes that might have been made in his/her absence.

Concerns for Safety, Confidentiality, Scholastic Dishonesty

1. Issue of Safety: As part of this course, students will have assignments working with and for agencies and/or in the community. As such, these assignments may present some minimal risks. Sound choices and caution may lower risks. It is the student's responsibility to be aware of and adhere to policies and practices related high ethical principles. Students should also notify instructor and TA about any safety concerns.

2. Issue of Confidentiality and Personal Disclosure: Personal disclosure is not an expectation or a requirement of this course. However, it might be appropriate for students to talk about personal information during class only as it relates to our learning about a particular topic. Students are expected to adhere to strict standards of confidentiality during the semester.

3. According to university policy, when a student discloses sexual assault and sexual harassment to the instructor or TA a report to university authorities will be made.

4. Scholastic dishonesty may result in a report to the Graduate Program Director, the Dean of the respective school, and/or the Dean of the Undergraduate or Graduate School. Students may receive an "F" for the course and other sanctions in accordance with university policies.

University Policies

1. **Religious holy days:** A student who misses classes or other required activities, including examinations, for the observance of a religious holy day should inform the instructor as far in advance of the absence as possible, so that arrangements can be made to complete an assignment within a reasonable time after the absence.

2. **Students with Disabilities:** You will need to provide documentation to the Dean of Student's Office so the most appropriate accommodations can be determined. Specialized services are available on campus through Services for Students with Disabilities (SSB 4.104, 471-6259). Any student who requires special accommodations must obtain a letter that documents the disability from the Services for Students with Disabilities area of the Division of Diversity and Community Engagement (471-6259 voice or 471-4641 TTY for

users who are deaf or hard of hearing). Present the letter to the professor at the beginning of the semester so that needed accommodations can be discussed. The student should remind the professor of any testing accommodations no later than five business days before an exam. For more information, visit http://www.utexas.edu/diversity/ddce/ssd/.

3. **Policy on Scholastic Dishonesty:** Students who violate University rules on scholastic dishonesty are subject to disciplinary penalties, including the possibility of failure in the course and/or dismissal from the University. Since such dishonesty harms the individual, all students and the integrity of the University, policies on scholastic dishonesty will be strictly enforced. For further information, please visit the Student Judicial Services web site at http://deanofstudents.utexas.edu/sjs/.

4. **Use of E-mail for Official Correspondence to Students:** All students should be familiar with the University's official e-mail student notification policy. It is the student's responsibility to keep the University informed as to changes in his or her e-mail address. Students are expected to check e-mail on a frequent and regular basis in order to stay current with University-related communications, recognizing that certain communications may be time-critical. The complete text of this policy and instructions for updating your e-mail address are available at http://www.utexas.edu/its/policies/emailnotify.html.

5. **University of Texas Core Values and Honor Code:** The core values of the University of Texas at Austin are learning, discovery, freedom, leadership, individual opportunity, and responsibility. Each member of the university is expected to uphold these values through integrity, honesty, trust, fairness, and respect toward peers and community. As a student of the University of Texas at Austin, I shall abide by the core values of the University and uphold academic integrity.

Signature Course Mission & Course Essentials

The Signature Courses at The University of Texas at Austin will connect students with distinguished faculty members in unique learning environments. By way of this rigorous intellectual experience, students will develop college-level skills in research, writing, speaking and discussion through an approach that is interdisciplinary, collaborative, experiential and contemporary.

This course will address the Signature Course essentials in the following ways:

1. Information Literacy is achieved throughout the course but particularly in our instruction by the university librarian and the assigned papers.

2. University Gem: We will visit the LBJ Presidential Library for a lecture on the use of primary source data that connects with the second paper assignment.

3. Writing: This course has several writing components, including two graded papers.

4. Oral Communication: Students will engage in a dynamic final exam group project in which students will present the contents of one of the assigned books.

5. University Lecture Series Events: Students are invited to the March.

Ethics and Leadership Flag

This course carries the Ethics and Leadership Flag. Ethics and Leadership courses are designed to equip students with skills to make ethical decisions in their professional roles. Therefore it is expected that a substantial portion of the course discussion and evaluation involves ethical issues and the application of ethical reasoning to real-life situations.

Human Rights and Social Justice BDP Certificate

This course qualifies for the requirements of the Human Rights and Social Justice section of the Bridging Disciplines Program (BDP). The BDP introduces students to the interdisciplinary study and practice of human rights at home and around the world. Students in this BDP will learn about the forms of oppression, marginalization, and violence that concern human rights researchers and practitioners. Through coursework drawn from the humanities, social sciences, law, fine arts, and public policy, students will develop their knowledge of the issues and debates that dominate human rights and social justice scholarship today, including an understanding of the regional contexts within which contemporary human rights violations take place. At the same time, students in this BDP will learn about the historical, theoretical, and institutional underpinnings of international human rights advocacy and social justice movements, from the legacies of colonialism and imperialism to the international institutions that were formed in the wake of World War II. Finally, through the connecting experience component of the program, students will have the opportunity to complement their coursework with hands-on experience in an organization working on human rights and social justice concerns. Students will work with their BDP advisor and the faculty panel to design an interdisciplinary strand that allows them to pursue their interests, and at the same time exposes them to multiple areas of concern for human rights researchers and practitioners.

The Human Rights and Social Justice BDP is offered in collaboration with the Bernard and Audre Rapoport Center for Human Rights and Justice at UT Austin. An interdisciplinary faculty panel guides students in selecting courses and participating in connecting research and internship experiences, which students are encouraged to pursue through study abroad opportunities.

Additional References

Akpan, U. (2008). *Say you're one of them*. Chicago: Little, Brown & Company.

Bales, K., & Soodalter, R., (2009). *The slave next door: Human trafficking and slavery in America today*. University of California.

Goldfine, A. A., Hoerrner, L. K., Batstone, D. (2008). *Not for sale: The return of the global slave trade—and how we can fight it*. New York, NY: Kennesaw State University & the University of San Francisco.

Hughes, M. D., (2000). The "Natasha" trade: The transnational shadow market of trafficking in women. *Journal of International Affairs*. (53)2, 625–651.

Kara, S., (2008). *Sex trafficking: Inside the business of modern slavery*. Columbia University Press.

Kristof, N. & WuDunn, S. (2010). *Half the sky*. New York, NY: Knopf Doubleday Publishing Group.

Lloyd, R. (2011). *Girls Like Us: Fighting for a World Where Girls Are Not for Sale, An Activist Finds Her Calling and Heals Herself.* New York, NY: Harper Collins.

Pearce, L., Q., (2007). *Young heros, Given Kachepa.* KidHaven.

U.S. Department of State. (2011). *Trafficking in persons report* (11th ed.). Washington, DC: U.S. Government Printing Office.

U.S. Department of Labor's Bureau of International Labor Affairs Office of Child Labor, Forced Labor, and Human Trafficking. (2010). *List of goods produced by child labor or forced labor.* Washington, DC.

Wheaton, M. E., Schauer, J. E., Galli, V. T. (2010). Economics of human trafficking. *Journal of International Migration. 48*(4), 114–141.

Zheng, T., T. (2010). *Sex trafficking, human rights, and social justice (Routledge research in human rights).* New York, NY: Routledge.

Index

migration and, 86–87, 87 (figure)
pimps, 103–104, 180, 184
population estimates, 122
routes in Southeastern Asia, 19 (figure)
venues for, 157
See also Domestic minor sex trafficking (DMST);
 johns' Demand typology; Pornography;
 Prostitution
Sexually exploited children (CSEC), 18
Sex workers. *See* Prostitution
Shared Hope International, 29–30, 94, 163
Shattering the American Dream typology, 28, 29,
 177–178
Shelley, L., 20, 21, 29, 34, 101
Shelter services, 222
Shively, M., 28, 224
Sigmon, J. N., 170
Signal International, 125–127
Signals, 287–288
Silverman, B. W., 134, 135
Single-point-of-contact model, 26, 172–173
Situational coercion, 103
Situational indicators, 163
Slave-free movement, 274–276, 278–279 (figure)
Slavery Footprint, 34, 36, 279, 283
Slavery No More, 24, 274
Slaves/slavery
 boundary between liberty and, 124–125
 current statistics, 3
 definitions, 61
 early accounts, 43
 false contracts and, 22
 Irish, 47–48
 modern-day comparison to, 60–61
 population, 54 (figure)
 routes for trade, 51 (figure)
 ships for, 46 (figure)
 trade after American Revolution, 57–60
 See also African slavery; American slavery
Sloan, L., 260
Small, K., 88
Smallwood, A., 45
Smith, L., 159, 162, 174, 185
Smuggled persons
 debt payments of, 183
 forced labor case, 179
 trafficking comparison, 30–31
 victimization of, 102, 162
Snow, M., 159
Social issues, 104

Social justice definitions, 12
Social networks, 282
Social service goals, 156
Social service screenings. *See* Posters
Social values, 98
Social welfare policies, 100
Sociopolitical issues, 23, 226–227
Soldiers (children as), 92, 93 (figure)
Source countries, 21
South Carolina Negro Act, 49, 62
Southern African NGO Network (SANGONet), 56
Southern Horrors (Well), 59
Spain's history of enslavement, 44–45
Spiller, M. W., 134
Spiritual strategy, 214
The State of Homelessness in America report, 159
Stiglitz, Joseph, 129
Stockholm syndrome, 161, 161 (table)
Stoesz, D., 98–99
Story indicators, 163
*Strengthening Protections Against Trafficking in
 Persons in Federal and Corporate Supply Chains*
 (Verité), 89
Strengths-based approaches, 142–144, 143 (figure)
Student survey, 289–292
Substance Abuse and Mental Health Services
 Administrartion (SAMHSA), 144
Successive mobility, 198–200
Supply and demand model, 280 (figure)
Supply chain, 127–129
Support system. *See* Professionals in
 antitrafficking field
Survey tools for assessing student knowledge, 163,
 289–292
Survival sex, 95, 159
Survivor-centered approach to services, 171–172
Survivor Network Services, 202–209
Survivors *vs.* victims, 23–24, 98
 See also Victims/survivors
Swedish model of criminalization, 257
Swepton, L., 84, 88
Syllabus for modern-day slavery course, 299–306

TABC (Texas Alcoholic Beverage Commission),
 257, 259 (figure)
Taylor, C., 46
Terrorism, 101
Testimony of survivors, 177
Texas Alcoholic Beverage Commission (TABC),
 257, 259 (figure)

Lightning Source UK Ltd.
Milton Keynes UK
UKHW031814270123
416084UK00008B/559

9 781506 305721